THE PROJECTION OF BRITAIN

A HISTORY OF THE GPO FILM UNIT

Edited by Scott Anthony and James G. Mansell

BFI

palgrave
macmillan

A BFI book published by Palgrave Macmillan

For Pat Jackson (1916–2011) and the people of the Post Office

The publisher gratefully acknowledges the support of
BT Heritage (www.bt.com/heritage) and the BPMA (www.postal-heritage.org.uk) in the publication of this book.

Our history through the post

First published in 2011 by
PALGRAVE MACMILLAN

on behalf of the

BRITISH FILM INSTITUTE
21 Stephen Street, London W1T 1LN
www.bfi.org.uk

There's more to discover about film and television through the BFI. Our world-renowned archive, cinemas, festivals, films, publications and learning resources are here to inspire you.

Palgrave Macmillan in the UK is an imprint of Macmillan Publishers Limited, registered in England, company number 785998, of Houndmills, Basingstoke, Hampshire RG21 6XS. Palgrave Macmillan in the US is a division of St Martin's Press LLC, 175 Fifth Avenue, New York, NY 10010. Palgrave Macmillan is the global academic imprint of the above companies and has companies and representatives throughout the world. Palgrave® and Macmillan® are registered trademarks in the United States, the United Kingdom, Europe and other countries.

Cover design: Mark Swan
Designed by couch
Set by Cambrian Typesetters, Camberley, Surrey
Printed in China

This book is printed on paper suitable for recycling and made from fully managed and sustained forest sources. Logging, pulping and manufacturing processes are expected to conform to the environmental regulations of the country of origin.

British Library Cataloguing-in-Publication Data
A catalogue record for this book is available from the British Library
A catalog record for this book is available from the Library of Congress
10 9 8 7 6 5 4 3 2 1
20 19 18 17 16 15 14 13 12 11

ISBN 978–1–84457–374–5 (pbk)
ISBN 978–1–84457–375–2 (hbk)

CONTENTS

ACKNOWLEDGMENTS

Our ambitions for *The Projection of Britain* were immodestly large. The idea of the book began at a screening at The Cornerhouse cinema, Manchester. Love Letters and Live Wires, the BFI's touring programme of GPO Films, had just played to a packed house. Watching the films that day we were struck by how fresh they seemed; they were funny, perceptive and heart-felt. From debates about the ethics and purpose of documentary (and indeed the operation of 'the media') to how telecommunications have altered the ways in which we interact with each other, from Britain's changing place in the world to the challenges presented by rolling out new technology in a global slump, the films lit up issues of enduring interest, relevance and profundity. And all this without even starting to unravel the ideas, influence and intellectual impact of the roll call of talent that passed through the unit: W. H. Auden, Benjamin Britten, Alberto Cavalcanti, Lotte Reiniger, Maholy-Nagy, Humphrey Jennings and on and extraordinarily on.

But the realisation that we carried away from the screening was that the resurgence of lay enthusiasm for the films was at variance with the narrower critical terms in which they were discussed. Now that the films are so much more readily available, mainly thanks to the BFI's DVD releases, the quality of contextual information around them seems even more disappointingly scant. This was our rationale for the book. We would include primary sources that would help historically and intellectually root the work of the GPO Film Unit, along with essays that attempted to address the manifold gaps in our knowledge. This effort has led us to commission, among others, a geographer, a sports historian, a musicologist, a design historian, an archivist, a collector, a writer and a post-man. *The Projection of Britain* is thus designed to consolidate, deepen and indeed trans-form the terms of reference in which the Film Unit and its work is discussed. It was also a book put together, we like to think, in the same imaginative, enthusiastic and demo-cratic spirit in which (when it was at its best) the GPO Film Unit operated.

Our ambition for this book was big, but realising it proved to be a substantially bigger challenge than we first appreciated. *The Projection of Britain* simply would not have been completed without the support of publisher Rebecca Barden, Sophia Contento, Joy Tucker and the enthusiasm, know how and support of the expert staff at the BFI, BT Heritage and the British Postal Museum and Archive. We would especially like to thank

Sean Delaney, Brian Robinson, Patrick Russell, Upekha Bandaranayake, David Hay, Sian Wynn-Jones, Adrian Steel, Laura Dixon, Siobhan O'Leary, Barry Attoe and Penny McMahon. Particular thanks to BT Heritage for their support in providing access to BT's substantial archive collection and in the production of this book.

An important staging post in the book's development was a conference called The Projection of Britain held in Manchester back in 2009. As well as those that have contributed to this volume, we would like to thank Melanie Horton, Marc Matera, Aaron Windel, Philip Logan, Charlotte Wildman, David Forrest, Penny Summerfield, Emma Sandon, Maiken Umbach, Sian Nicholas and Helen McCarthy for their input and enthusiasm beyond the call of duty. Additional thanks to the generosity, efficiency and helpfulness of the staff of the John Rylands Library, especially Stella Halkyard.

Scott Anthony would also like to thank the Leverhulme Trust for their generous support, without which his research would not have been possible, and Wolfgang Suschitzky for permission to reproduce his photographs – not only a legend of British cinema and television but an extremely nice man to boot.

James Mansell would like to thank the Leverhulme Trust-funded research network 'Relating Identities: Locality, Region, Nation and Empire' based at the University of Manchester whose support allowed him to begin this book project.

Both editors would like to direct plaudits to the transnational army of people who have contributed ideas and improvements to the book. We offer our heads on metaphorical pikes for any errors that remain.

FOREWORD

Sir Christopher Frayling

In the early 1970s, I helped – in a junior capacity – to put together a series of lectures for postgraduate art students on 'The British Documentary Movement' and in particular on the work of the GPO Film Unit/Crown Film Unit. At that stage, very little – or very little that was serious – had been written about the Unit. There was the reprinted anthology *Grierson on Documentary*, which emphasised the social and educational purposes of the documentary film in general and extolled the movie camera's ability to record the appearance of everyday life (or 'actuality'). There were Paul Rotha's essays dating from the late 1930s, also reprinted, which drew hard and fast distinctions between 'commercial advertising' and the promotion of a government department the GPO, between 'studio-made fiction' and 'the realist film', and which concluded that the *spirit* of the documentary movement was of much more long-term significance than any of the individual films which emerged from it. And there was Raymond Durgnat's then recently published *A Mirror for England* (1970), which criticised the movement for being hamstrung by state sponsorship, bedazzled by Arts and Crafts attitudes towards the dignity of labour – obscuring the grim realities of Depression Britain – and, generally, for having the point of view, and accent, of 'a Greek scholar-cum-brigadier sitting on his shooting stick and squinting through a viewfinder ... occasionally peeping at his loyal lads through the wrong end of his opera-glasses': this was jaundiced, but it was also very stimulating. Alan Lovell and Jim Hillier's *Studies in Documentary*, with Lovell's essay on John Grierson, gloomily conclude that the GPO films and others 'are unfashionable, dismissed as of little interest by younger film-makers and critics'; Grierson's conception of cinema actually *holding back* the work of contemporary documentarians – was first published while the lecture series was in progress.

So, instead of commentators, we decided to invite the surviving film-makers them-selves, then in their mid-sixties and, as it transpired, eager to talk – sometimes candidly – about the films they worked on in the 1930s and 40s: Basil Wright, Harry Watt and Edgar Anstey. Also Humphrey Spender, who was invited to talk about his photographs of 'Worktown' at Bolton, which he took for Mass Observation in 1937–40. It turned out to be an excellent decision. Harry Watt's 'irreverent memoir' *Don't Look at the Camera* (1974) was completed and published as a direct result of the lectures he gave in the series.

The moments I can best remember include the bespectacled, cautious Basil Wright (who seemed the most comfortable giving lectures) reminiscing about his struggles with the ending of the lyrical *The Song of Ceylon* (1934), which he recut following a spirited exchange with Grierson; the more rough-edged, flamboyant Harry Watt asking his audience how on earth they thought he'd managed to light and film the interior of a moving mail-van – while the letters were being sorted – in *Night Mail* (1936), and then informing them with a guffaw that the sequence was actually filmed in a cramped studio, with various helpers rhythmically jiggling the set by hand; and the tall, donnish Edgar Anstey recalling how when he screened *Housing Problems* (1935) for the slum-dwelling interviewees from the film, in Stepney Town Hall, they didn't at first recognise themselves because they'd never been photographed before. Edgar Anstey also told the story of Grierson's arrival at the Empire Marketing Board in 1927, and discovery that, as part of the Board's background publicity, a bizarre and expensive hour-long film pageant called *One Family* was irreversibly in development – about how the exotic and jolly colonies contributed the fruits of empire to King George V's Christmas pudding. The film apparently included some elegantly draped society ladies dressed up as Britannia who gratefully received these ingredients from a small boy. I haven't seen it. Harry Watt characteristically called it 'vomit-making'. *One Family*, said Anstey, came as something of a shock to Grierson, fresh from America with his newly formulated mission to educate the mass electorate.

In the discussions which followed the screenings, the issues raised by the students were mainly about realism and 'the creative interpretation of actuality' – Alberto Cavalcanti's contribution, from within the French avant-garde, especially intrigued them after a screening of the comedy *Pett and Pott* (1934), during which Basil Wright announced to them that he played the part of the vicar; the constraints and compromises of sponsorship deals (or not); the relationship between the 1930s GPO films and 1960s cinéma vérité, investigative journalism and the instant material put out on television; the surrealists and the beauty of out-of-scale found objects (we'd screened Arthur Elton's *Aero-Engine* [1934]); Grierson's often-repeated views on 'aesthetes and literary types' expressed at a time when the GPO Film Unit seemed closely linked with London 'art film' circles; the connection between the documentaries and the feature films of the period such as *Millions Like Us*, *The Way Ahead* and *In Which We Serve*. And there were animated debates about the kazoo band sequence in *Spare Time* (1939) – we screened most of Humphrey Jennings's films up to *A Diary for Timothy* (1945) – and whether the sequence was patronising or not. Also about why the British didn't feel comfortable with 'hate films' during World War II, and why the original documentary movement collapsed so relatively soon afterwards. Or did it? A wrap-up question was: did the movement deserve a major chapter to itself in the histories of British cinema, up there with Charlie Chaplin, Alfred Hitchcock, Alexander Korda, Michael Powell; Ealing Studios, Kitchen Sink and Hammer? And was it really a movement (as Grierson liked to think) at all? The jury was still out on that one. Harry Watt wound himself up all over again when he reminisced aloud about his credit as co-producer (rather than director) of *Night Mail*. And it was clear on the occasions when Basil Wright and Harry Watt were together in the same lecture theatre that the image of the Unit as one big happy family, united by a common cause, must have been just that – an image. There were clearly all sorts of creative disagreements, although the film-makers were united in their admiration for Grierson's fund-raising abilities, his organisational flair and, above all, for the risks he took in employing talented youngsters in their early twenties who knew very little about the craft of film. 'More of a design manager than a designer,' suggested one of the students. Yes, and one who could get you to work twenty-five hours a day for a very modest salary. Harry Watt admitted over a stiff drink or two in the Hoop and Toy that a) the word 'documentary' had become in his humble opinion a thought-preventer and b) where Humphrey Jennings was concerned, there were moments when 'the class war broke out between us' – in his recollection Edinburgh versus Cambridge, man-of-the-people versus arty intellectual. If only we had recorded all these sessions for posterity … But it was before the video era.

Dissolve to the second decade of the twenty-first century and the questions from the floor would be very different indeed. Better informed maybe: we know so much more about the British documentary movement and its place in cinema history – thanks to oral histories, biographies, monographs, surveys, film seasons, creative reinterpretations, careful preservation of the films themselves and the availability of most of them on video and DVD, thanks in large part to the BFI. Interestingly, the video versions were packaged as part of the history of the avant-garde. The concerns of the students would be different too: about national characteristics and the politics of identity; about gender and cultural difference; about the double-edged lessons of modernism in design – now seen as more of a style than a final solution; about the interconnections between film technology and directional 'style'; about the key importance of sound (difficult to judge on battered old prints); about how Grierson saw documentary-making as 'separate' from the mainstream – yet feature-length documentaries are now being distributed commercially in cinemas, some of them with great success; about the teamwork of the Unit and what that says about the 'auteur' theory; and about the fashionably blurred lines between 'fact' and 'fiction', drama and drama-documentary at a time when form follows fiction rather than any longer following function. Maybe it always did. Discuss. None of these concerns was even mentioned during that lecture series of the early 1970s. The ideas simply weren't in the ether yet.

Nor were the other connections between the Post Office and film history, which have since entered the cultural bloodstream. There was the series of portrait stamps issued in British Film Year, 1985, showing Charlie Chaplin, Alfred Hitchcock, Vivien Leigh, David Niven and Peter Sellers – stamps which inspired critic Philip French's immortal line, 'I don't know much about philately, but I know what I lick.' There was also the stamp which the Royal Mail claimed was the first 'intelligent stamp' – issued in September 2010 – which, when shown to a smart phone, revealed a film of Bernard Cribbins reciting W. H. Auden's poem 'Night Mail', originally commissioned as part of the voiceover to Harry Watt and Basil Wright's film of 1936.

This welcome and timely book, *The Projection of Britain: A History of the GPO Film Unit*, provides an opportunity to revisit the GPO Film Unit/Crown Film Unit, to reinterpret its work through the perspectives of today, at the movement's own self-estimation – securely to locate it within the history of British film, at a time when telecommunications have again moved centre stage. And to reconsider which of the key films deserve to be in the pantheon on their own terms, three-quarters of a century later.

The book has been written by leading specialists in film and film history, in curating and conservation, in cultural geography and literature, in the history of design, plus the head of BT's heritage division and a postal worker. Grierson's boys and girls would never have admitted it publicly, not in a month of Sundays, but I'm sure they would be pleasantly surprised.

PART ONE

Arguments, Ideas, Issues

1 / JOHN GRIERSON AND THE LOST WORLD OF THE GPO FILM UNIT

Jeffrey Richards

When Forsyth Hardy wrote, in 1947, 'There is no novelty today in the claim that documentary is *the* distinctively British contribution to cinema,' he was stating a universally acknowledged truth.[1] This state of affairs was in large part due to the fact that the historians and theorists of film in Britain were almost entirely drawn from the ranks of the documentarists, men like Paul Rotha, Basil Wright and the founding father of the British documentary movement himself, John Grierson.[2]

As a consequence, the mainstream of 1930s British cinema was effectively written off. The view articulated by Paul Rotha in his seminal 1930 volume *The Film Till Now*, together with its 1949 sequel *The Film Since Then*, that there had never been a true British film, and that the main aim of British cinema was imitation of other countries, went effectively unchallenged for decades. According to Rotha, by 1930 the British cinema had produced only one film of note, John Grierson's *Drifters* (1929).[3]

Grierson was the founding father of the British documentary movement and the man credited with coining the term 'documentary', by which he meant 'the creative treatment of actuality'. But the hour-long *Drifters* was the only major film to be directed by Grierson, although there were two subsequent shorts (*Granton Trawler* [1934] and *On the Fishing Banks of Skye* [1935]). Grierson functioned chiefly as producer, organiser, facilitator, recruiter and propagandist for the documentary movement, which he effectively founded and which was successively embodied in the Empire Marketing Board Film Unit, the GPO Film Unit, the Crown Film Unit and associated bodies such as Strand and the Realist Film Unit.

Grierson contrived to merge the liberal idealism of his father and the radical socialism of his mother, to emerge as a reformist social democrat, coming to believe in social reconstruction by the agency of the state rather than full-blown socialist transformation. He believed, as Ian Aitken

John Grierson, the founding father of the documentary movement

has put it, that society consisted of 'a matrix of interdependent relations'. His ideas amounted to a corporatist conception of society, in which individual and social phenomena were perceived as being integrated, at different levels, within the social totality. He rejected the idea that there were fundamental and irreducible divisions in society, and believed that it was an ignorance of the underlying 'continuing reality' of evolving interdependence which led to such perceptions.[4] As applied to film, these ideas led him to vigorously advocate a socially purposive cinema which would bestow recognition and dignity on the working man, neglected by mainstream cinema, and would at the same time inform and educate the newly enfranchised mass electorate to function in a participatory democracy which would achieve the organic inter-relatedness which was his ideal. 'I look on cinema as a pulpit and use it as a propagandist,' he said in 1933.[5]

The long-held ideas that the British documentary movement embodied a purer, more truthful, more authentic view of Britain and was the only repository of realism and radicalism in a commercialised industry that was essentially false, shallow and superficial, came under serious and sustained challenge from the 1970s onwards. For some critics, among them Bert Hogenkamp, Brian Winston and Don MacPherson, and the contributors to the latter's edited volume *Traditions of Independence* (BFI, 1980), the Griersonian movement was not left wing enough. They were concerned to recover and reinstate the films of such bodies as the Workers' Film and Photo League, Kino and the Progressive Film Institute. This was a worthy enough exercise but the films involved were generally primitive compared to those of the Griersonians. They played to tiny audiences of the already converted and achieved neither the aesthetic nor social success of the mainstream documentary movement.[6]

The second criticism was the one deftly encapsulated by Raymond Durgnat in his pioneering 1970 volume *A Mirror for England*, a book as influential in its way as *The Film Till Now*, and which began the move away from documentary and towards the commercial feature film as the true definer of the national identity in cinema. Durgnat wrote of the documentaries: 'Far from progressive, these films are, in spirit, just what they were intended to be: literally speaking commercials for the EMB or the GPO or any part of the Establishment, and therefore for the *status quo* of – of all periods – the thirties.'[7] This view has been tackled head on by Ian Aitken. Conceding that Grierson's view of cinema and society was 'corporatist and consensual' he argues that Grierson believed that the establishment in the 1930s, rather than working for the benefit of the nation as a whole, was encouraging the process of unregulated capitalism which threatened social stability and that, therefore, it was permissible for documentary film-makers to make radical critical films advocating social reform.[8] The filmic evidence to refute Durgnat can be found in the films sponsored by the British Commercial Gas Association, aimed at selling gas cookers and gas heating to local councils, but highlighting real social problems and suggesting solutions – films such as *Housing Problems* (slum clearance, 1935), *Enough to Eat* (nutrition, 1936), *The Smoke Menace* (pollution, 1937) and *Children at School* (overcrowded and decaying schools, 1937). The importance of *Housing Problems* was, according to Grierson, that it touched the conscience of the audience and this was the key to social reform and the avoidance of revolution and class war.[9] As he put it in an article in 1942, 'Without *Housing Problems* and the whole movement of social understanding such films helped to articulate, I think history would have found another and bloodier solution.'[10] The most significant impact of such films seems to have been on planners and opinion-formers rather than on the mass audience.

The third attack came from those like Andrew Tudor and Bill Nichols who argued that Grierson subordinated aesthetics to propaganda, neglecting the idea of film as film. But it is only necessary to read his many essays to see Grierson's concern with film as a visual art and to recognise the importance of his two most important acknowledged cinematic influences, Eisenstein's *Battleship Potemkin* (1925) and Robert Flaherty's *Nanook of the North* (1922), which taught him the importance of shooting on location, employing montage in editing and heroising the working man, all of which techniques he applied to his own principal venture into direction, *Drifters*.[11]

Fourth, the documentary suffered from another fundamental critical shift as recently summarised by John Mundy. Referring back to Alan Lovell's influential 1969 BFI seminar paper, 'British Cinema: the Unknown Cinema', Mundy wrote:

> Since the 1960s, British cinema has become much more 'known' through a process of critical recuperation that is focussed not just on notions of national cinema and national identity, but on the distinctive aesthetics of a British cinema, which is seen to be … rich, diverse and interesting. Though acknowledging the importance of the realist tradition in British cinema, much recent critical work on British cinema is at pains to celebrate its non-realist and anti-realist tradition, articulated through genres such as comedy, horror, melodrama or costume drama.[12]

This development has seen the eclipse of critical interest in the documentary and the rise of interest in Hammer horror films, 'Carry On' comedies and Gainsborough melodramas, and the canonisation of Michael Powell and Emeric Pressburger as Britain's greatest film-makers.

Fifth, the documentary movement has earned the ire of feminists. In a 1996 essay Kathryn and Philip Dodd, who begin with the bald statement: 'No-one now shares Paul Rotha's judgement … that the documentary film movement is "this country's most important contribution to cinema as a whole",' go on to criticise the 1930s documentarists' 'obsession with working-class masculinity' which was 'seen at its simplest in the countless close-ups of the male body at work'. The corollary is that 'Working-class women are simply read out of the picture or "left" at home.' They interpret this as part of a deliberate bid to create 'a new, masculine, post-imperial national identity' in opposition to the perceived feminisation of the national identity between the wars, an argument advanced by Alison Light in *Forever England* (1991), to which the Dodds subscribe, but which is actually a deeply flawed argument.[13] In the light of these critical assaults, it is time to look again at the British documentary movement.

It *was* a movement, but we should not forget the splits, feuds and disagreements within that movement. Paul Rotha famously distanced himself from Grierson. It was partly a personality clash, but Rotha also complained that his films could not express a socially progressive point of view because they were made using government money.

> I mean, take *Night Mail*. It has no social purpose whatsoever. It's a wonderful film. It's beautifully made … but what does it do in the end? It merely tells you how the postal special gets from King's Cross to Edinburgh. It cannot possibly tell you about the conditions of postal workers or anything of that sort.[14]

But Rotha is missing the point here. It fulfilled exactly Grierson's objective – to show ordinary men at work and to demonstrate the integrative role of the GPO and the railways linking England and Scotland, North and South, and bringing, in Auden's memorable verse, 'letters to the rich, letters to the poor, the shop on the corner and the girl next door'.

There are several reasons why a truly national cinema did not emerge in Britain until World War II. The first was censorship. The British film industry was strictly controlled by the British Board of Film Censors, set up in 1912. The basic rule of the censors was 'no controversy'. The avoidance of all social, political and religious controversy meant the maintenance of the status quo, which throughout the 1930s was the predominantly Conservative National Government.[15] The second problem was the internationalist outlook of the two big movie moguls, Alexander Korda and Michael Balcon, who sought to pursue a production policy that was 'less and less parochial and more international in appeal'.[16] The third problem was the audience and what they wanted. As a jaundiced Victor Small wrote in the *Left Review* in 1938:

> No-one is less interested in the fate of what might well be a social asset than the 18 millions of British citizens who pour their odd cash into cinema box offices each week. There was never any demand for British films and as yet no demand has been created ... it would seem that our film companies will never touch subjects of social significance.[17]

If there was one thing that critical opinion was agreed about in the 1930s, it was the almost total absence of the reality of contemporary British life from mainstream British cinema. The rectification of this situation became a veritable crusade in that a succession of intellectual film magazines appeared around which the documentarists grouped themselves – *Close Up*, *Cinema Quarterly* and *World Film News* – to the extent that Forsyth Hardy could talk in 1932 about 'the movement to bring Britain to the screen'.[18] But the call for a truly British cinema was not confined to small-circulation magazines and rarefied circles of left-wing intellectuals, it was made right across the critical spectrum, left wing and right wing, highbrow and lowbrow alike.

But while it is true that British film-makers seemed content on the whole with a diet of musicals, comedies and detective stories, the commercial cinema did not ignore industrial problems. The way it tackled them is typified by the films of Gracie Fields, the top British box-office star of the 1930s, and a much-loved British institution. Her films deliberately projected her as an advocate of consensus and class harmony. The central problem of unemployment was tackled in *Sing As We Go* (1934) and *Shipyard Sally* (1939). In these films unemployment in the cotton industry and in shipbuilding was met *not* by industrial unrest, strikes or sit-ins, but by appeals to reason, cheerful discussions with government and industrialists, and the eventual reopening of cotton mills and shipyards amid displays of patriotic fervour.

The films of Gracie Fields and fellow box-office chart-topper George Formby were commercially produced and released and drew in the mass audience. The British documentaries were state or company sponsored and released non-theatrically. Apart from a small fleet of mobile cinema vans which toured the productions to non-commercial venues, the films were mainly distributed free of charge as loans from the Empire Film Library. In 1934 it was estimated that 54 per cent of the loans went to schools, 13 per cent to juvenile organisations and only 33 per cent to adult groups. The number of adult viewers of the estimated 4 million a year that Grierson claimed in 1935 must have been less than half.[19] This was at a time when the average *weekly* admission figure for commercial cinemas was estimated at around 20 million.[20] The periodic attempts at commercial cinematic release of the documentaries such as 'The Imperial Six' or the 'Post Haste' group of films were failures. As Mr W. R. Fuller, General Secretary of the Cinematograph Exhibitors' Association (CEA), reporting to the Moyne Committee in 1936 on the failure of exhibitors to interest the public in documentaries, said acidly: 'No documentary has ever set the Thames afire.' Mr T. H. Fligelstone, President of the CEA, told the Committee that the public would not accept documentaries: 'The public comes to the cinema to be amused not educated.'[21] But many of the documentaries were, in fact, precisely meeting the demands of the critics if not the public for authentic pictures of British people and British life.

But what image of Britain did they present? The GPO Film Unit experimented with many different forms – comedy, fantasy, musical, animation – but historically the most significant of their products were actuality film. Of these, the ones most frequently cited are those involving real people. Pat Jackson said that 'the thrill of documentary' was 'putting the people of Britain on the screen, recorded for all time'.[22] He is right about that.

It is commonplace now for everyone to be famous for fifteen minutes. Reality television makes previously anonymous people household names and ordinary people seem for the most part quite comfortable when asked to face a camera. It was not always so. It is impossible now to overestimate the importance of the group of documentaries which featured the faces and, even more importantly, the voices of the working people of Britain.

The stress on working-class men and women was deliberate. Harry Watt recalled of the documentarists 'We were left wing to a man.'[23] But that was a spectrum that ranged from social democrat through socialist to communist. What they agreed on was the need to remedy the absence from the cinema screen of the working class in anything other than comic roles. He said:

> We, with *Coal Face* and … *Housing Problems* … and *Night Mail* started to give the working man, the real man who contributed to the country, a dignity. And *Drifters* – every credit to Grierson – was the first time … Every film we made had this in it, that we were trying to give an image of the working man, away from the Edwardian, Victorian, capitalist attitudes.[24]

On the rare occasions that the suburban middle classes appeared, they were treated comically (*John Atkins Saves Up* [1934]) or satirically (*Pett and Pott* [1934]).

The early heroes of the documentary movement were coal miners and fishermen, treated in the manner of Soviet Socialist Realism as uncomplicatedly heroic figures pitted in an eternal struggle against nature. Thus were depicted the miners of *Industrial Britain* (1931) and *Coal Face* (1935) and the fishermen of *Drifters* and *Granton Trawler*. But when they were allowed to speak for themselves they became more three dimensional and more realistic. These were real slices of life: the postmen describing how they got the mail through to a flooded village in *The Horsey Mail* (1938), the training of the post office messenger in *A Job in a Million* (1937), the men and women describing living conditions in the slums in *Housing Problems*, the unemployed miners building a social

BBC – The Voice of Britain exemplified the Griersonian's consensus film-making

centre in *Today We Live* (1937) and setting up an agricultural cooperative in *Eastern Valley* (1937). In *Shipyard* (1935) Paul Rotha celebrated the technical achievement of the shipbuilders of Barrow-in-Furness in constructing the *Orion*, but he was careful to stress the importance of the job to the economic and social wellbeing of the town. An eloquent final shot had the workers watching in silence as the ship sails away and then themselves gradually dispersing with nothing now to do.

Equally important in the output of the movement, however, were those films which stressed social integration and interdependence, Britain being linked ever closer and more cohesively by modern technology. *Calendar of the Year* (1936) and *What's On Today* (1938) featured the role of telephone, telegraph and wireless in enabling the British to share experiences of sport, holidays, harvest and Christmas shopping. The opening of *What's On Today* had a montage of everyone listening to the BBC reporting Len Hutton's latest cricketing triumph at Lords. Films like these were going with the grain of the culture of 1930s Britain, which throughout the decade elected and re-elected an all-party National Government.

Perhaps the finest example of this consensus film-making and the film described at the time as the most important product of the documentary movement is the fifty-six-minute feature *BBC – The Voice of Britain* (1935), a record of one day in the life of Broadcasting House. It involved, in varying degrees, the talents of John Grierson, Stuart Legg, Alberto Cavalcanti, Evelyn Spice, Humphrey Jennings, Edgar Anstey and Basil Wright, the stalwarts of the documentary movement, and exemplifies the message, method and approach of the Griersonians. It gave equal weight to high culture (a production of *Macbeth*, the BBC Symphony Orchestra) and popular culture (comedians Clapham and Dwyer, the BBC Dance Orchestra). It stressed the unifying and integrative nature of the institution with sequences featuring the Empire Service, Children's Hour and an outside broadcast relay from Scotland. A recurrent trope was voices from the radio heard over shots of people of all ages, classes and genders about their daily business. Prominence was given to the broadcasting of talks and lectures by prominent politicians and opinion-formers, precisely the kind of education for a democratic citizenry that was a shared objective of John Grierson and John Reith, the director-general of the BBC. A public corporation, based on 'the brute force of monopoly' and able to combine entertainment and education, was Grierson's ideal and, while it worked for the BBC, which initially had no competition, it could not work for the documentary movement, faced by the competition of the commercial film industry.

It is a commonplace of film history that World War II resulted in the twin processes of documentarisation and democratisation, the application of the ideas of realism and an authentic depiction of ordinary people. These had been the hallmarks of the pre-war documentary movement and the war saw the movement come into its own. The GPO Film Unit, taken over by the Ministry of Information and renamed the Crown Film Unit, became the official voice of the government, its work supplemented by other pre-war companies such as Paul Rotha's Strand.

The critics were united in calling for documentary authenticity, the government required the promotion of 'the people's war' and audiences were now drawn to the reality of documentaries in a way they had not been in the 1930s. Directors who had previously been almost exclusively directors of commercial feature films turned effortlessly to the documentary film; men like Carol Reed, David Macdonald, Roy Boulting and Thorold

Dickinson, and stalwarts of the documentary movement, notably Harry Watt, Pat Jackson and Alberto Cavalcanti, moved into feature films. What facilitated the move of the documentarists into features was a crucial decision arrived at by key documentary personnel in the late 1930s. Harry Watt recalled it:

> Around the middle of the '30s there was an amicable split in the documentary movement. Grierson became convinced that the enormous non-cinema going audience was the one to go after, and that a non-theatrical circuit with an assured public was better than our sporadic and fleeting showings in news-reel cinemas. Cavalcanti and I, together with Humphrey Jennings, Pat Jackson, Jack Lee and some others, disagreed. We felt we had to make the cinemas. That the non-theatrical showings were either converting the already converted, or had no lasting impact, because people never value what they get for free. Our solution was the story documentary taking actual true events, using real people, but also using 'dramatic license' to heighten the tensions in the storyline ... The war proved both our theories correct.[25]

The adoption of narrative structure and the storytelling impulse resulted in a series of feature-length documentaries which, when shown in cinemas, were both critical and popular successes: among them *Target for Tonight* (1941), *Coastal Command* (1942), *Close Quarters* (1943), *Fires Were Started* (1943), *Desert Victory* (1943) and *Western Approaches* (1944).

Grierson missed all this, spending the war in North America as head of the National Film Board of Canada. After brief and largely unhappy spells as Film Controller of the Central Office of Information (1948–50) and joint managing director of the government-subsidised production company Group Three (1951–4), he finally found a platform for the continued promotion of the documentary idea. By now television was beginning to take over from cinema as the vehicle for documentarists. Grierson moved into television, a craggy, magisterial presence, presenting 350 documentary programmes on Scottish Television in a series called *This Wonderful World* which ran from 1957 to 1967. He was preaching his gospel of documentary to the end.

The recent discovery of the short actuality films of Mitchell and Kenyon, the pioneer Blackburn film-makers, demonstrated the power and immediacy of film to capture everyday life in Edwardian Britain, the camera reanimating lives lived a century ago. It was a lost world of people, their lives and work and their familiar scenes. We should now perhaps view the documentaries of the 1930s and 40s in the same way. When we hear a narrator telling us that coal is Britain's biggest industry or that the GPO is Britain's biggest employer, we become immediately aware that we are dealing with a world as lost and gone as that of Mitchell and Kenyon. Similarly, when we see the response of a nation to a world war, something that none of us have experienced for over half a century, we need every time to give thanks to the documentarists who, whatever their constraints and their agendas, have preserved for us a living past.

Notes

1. Michael Balcon, Ernest Lindgren, Forsyth Hardy and Roger Manvell, *Twenty Years of British Film 1925–1945* (London: Falcon Press, 1947), p. 45.

2. Paul Rotha and Richard Griffith, *The Film Till Now* (Feltham: Spring Books, 1967), p. 556.

3. Ibid., pp. 313–22.

4. Ian Aitken, *Film and Reform: John Grierson and the Documentary Film Movement* (London: Routledge, 1990), p. 189.

5. D. L. Le Mahieu, *A Culture for Democracy: Mass Communication and the Cultivated Mind in Britain Between the Wars* (Oxford: Clarendon Press, 1988), p. 217.

6. Bert Hogenkamp, *Deadly Parallels: Film and the Left in Britain 1919–1939* (London: Lawrence and Wishart, 1986); Brian Winston, *Claiming the Real: The Griersonian Documentary and its Legitimations* (London: BFI, 1995); Don MacPherson (ed.), *Traditions of Independence* (London: BFI, 1980).

7. Raymond Durgnat, *A Mirror for England* (London: Faber & Faber, 1970), p. 119.

8. Aitken, *Film and Reform*, pp. 184–95

9. Forsyth Hardy (ed.), *Grierson on Documentary* (London: Faber & Faber, 1966), p. 216.

10. Ibid., p. 251.

11. Andrew Tudor, *Theories of Film* (London: Secker & Warburg, 1974), pp. 59–76; Bill Nichols 'Documentary Theory and Practice', *Screen* vol 17 (1976–7), p. 35.

12. John Mundy, *The British Musical Film* (Manchester: Manchester University Press, 2007), pp. 3–4.

13. Kathryn Dodd and Philip Dodd, 'Engendering the Nation: British Documentary Film 1930–39', in Andrew Higson (ed.), *Dissolving Views* (London: Cassell, 1996), pp. 38–45.

14. Elizabeth Sussex, *The Rise and Fall of British Documentary* (Berkeley, CA: University of California Press, 1975), p. 80.

15. Jeffrey Richards, *The Age of the Dream Palace* (London: I.B.Tauris, 2010), pp. 89–152.

16. Ibid., p. 251.

17. Ibid., p. 4.

18. *Cinema Quarterly* vol. I no. 2 (Winter 1932), p. 114.

19. Paul Swann, *The British Documentary Film Movement 1926–1946* (Cambridge: Cambridge University Press, 1989), pp. 74–5.

20. Richards, *The Age of the Dream Palace*, p. 11.

21. Ibid., p. 65.

22. Pat Jackson, *A Retake Please! from* Night Mail *to* Western Approaches (Liverpool: Liverpool University Press, 1999), p. 25.

23. Sussex, *The Rise and Fall of British Documentary*, p. 77.

24. Ibid., pp. 76–7.

25. Harry Watt, NFT Programme Note, in *The GPO Film Unit Collection vol. 2 – We Live in Two Worlds* (London: BFI, 2009), pp. 32–3.

2 / THE GPO FILM UNIT AND 'BRITISHNESS' IN THE 1930S

Scott Anthony

Over the past two decades writing about the GPO Film Unit has arguably become a way of addressing what British film (especially documentary) is now and what it could be, rather than what the Film Unit actually was. That a pioneering organisation like the GPO Film Unit has become a tradition to be taken for granted or endlessly quibbled over is perhaps not that surprising, but the serious consequence is that writing about the GPO Film Unit often deals in neat categories when the reality was far more idiosyncratic. While it is widely acknowledged that the GPO Film Unit was the first self-consciously British cinema, less attention has been paid to the material structure of this 'Britishness' (at the time 'Britishness' was invariably used interchangeably with 'Englishness') than its intellectual construction. What follows is an attempt to examine the what, why, how and who of the Film Unit's 'Britishness'.

The GPO: a British institution

When the GPO Film Unit was established the Post Office employed nearly a quarter of a million people, making it one of the largest employers in Britain. Without being too grandiose there is an argument that simply by recording the workings of the inter-war Post Office the Film Unit produced a far-reaching portrait of the nation in the same way that, for example, embedding a number of documentarists into every facet of the NHS would enable us to take the temperature of Britain in 2011. But as well as sheer weight of numbers, the GPO's importance can be couched more specifically. The inter-war years saw a revolutionary expansion of the mass media. At a time of unprecedented technological transformation, the GPO employed more scientists than anyone else. It pioneered airmail and microwave technology as well as overseeing the development of telex, teleprinting and picture telephony. The Post Master General also held powers of oversight over the BBC. Thus, the GPO's role in the provision of mail, radio and telephonic communications assigned it an important structural role in the production, distribution and consumption of media information. To an extent that it is difficult to fully appreciate today, the GPO shaped the emergence of a national media culture.

Added to the GPO's size and strategic importance is its contingent significance. Post Office reform provided a symbolic test case for the National Government's mission to guide Britain out of depression. At the level of policy, this entailed Sir Kingsley Wood, the Post Master General, dealing with accusations that the Post Office was retarding progress. Both roll-out and take-up of the telephone, for instance, were shown to be lagging behind both Germany and the United States. Conservatives favoured part-privatisation, the Liberals demanded a programme of public works, while Labour looked to the quasi-corporatist examples of the BBC, ICI and the Central Electricity Board.

Kingsley Wood's appointment as Post Master General in 1931 thus began a crucial period of 'catch-up' and modernisation. As part of the newly created public relations department the GPO Film Unit would be at the heart of the attempt to appease, explain and convince a sceptical public of the GPO's ability to refashion itself for the coming era of global telecommunications. 'We need to build up, piece by piece, a picture for our own people, and also for others,' as the GPO's Controller of Public Relations put it in 1934, 'of what this country has done, is doing and seeks to do in its endeavour to equip itself, without the revolutionary changes which most of the other great nations of the world have deemed necessary to the magnitude of the task, to meet a wholly new range of modern conditions.'[1]

Although it is ultimately reductive to do so, every stage of Wood's reforms can be tracked in the GPO Unit's films. Beginning with Wood's direct address (*Rt Hon Sir Howard Kingsley Wood* [1935]) we can chart the path of the GPO's regeneration from its hi-tech laboratories (*The Coming of the Dial* [1933]), to the expansion of the national infrastructure (*Copper Web* [1937]) and the joyous use (and misuse) of new GPO services finally revealed in customer-orientated fare such as *The Fairy of the Phone* (1936).

Under Wood's direction the GPO Film Unit's other institutional role was to help repair poor industrial relations. In the wake of the General Strike the powers of the Postal Workers' Union, as with all Civil Service unions, had been curtailed. Staff wages were perceived to be under threat from both the mechanisation and feminisation of the workforce and part of the rationale of films like *Night Mail* (1936) was to explain the collective organisational importance of even the most menial Post Office tasks and reassert the GPO's economic, social and imaginative role at the heart of national life.[2] What helps make the portrait of Britain and Britishness in the GPO Film Unit's work vital is this attempt to articulate the specific changes occurring at the Post Office against the broader political, economic and cultural renegotiations taking place at every level of society during the 1930s.

The very British idea of 'projection'

Sir Stephen Tallents had been appointed to the newly created role of Controller of Public Relations at the GPO in 1933.[3] Tallents had made his reputation as a propagandist for the new idea of Commonwealth at the Empire Marketing Board. His appointment at the GPO followed the publication of a much-cited pamphlet, *The Projection of England*, in which Tallents argued that a new type of national personality was emerging as the geography of the globe was reshaped by developments in transport and media communications. As the title suggests, he was particularly concerned with the impact of film (he

THE PROJECTION OF ENGLAND

BY S. G. TALLENTS

Tallents' pamphlet operated as a kind of manifesto for the documentarists

We Live in Two Worlds looked forward to a world without frontiers

described how 'Americans have turned every cinema in the world into the equivalent of an American consulate'[4]), though he also stressed the importance of modern design and marketing, which reflected the pamphlet's roots in Tallents' visit to the Barcelona Exhibition of 1929.

In the new world described by *The Projection of England*, a nation's image was made up of many component parts. For instance, Tallents began by listing important elements of Britain's media brand, such as Big Ben, *Punch*, the London Underground and the FA Cup Final. Tallents applied these insights to his work at the Post Office by overseeing the development of Giles Gilbert Scott's Jubilee Telephone Kiosk, relaunching Valentine's Day as a popular media phenomenon and introducing iconic services such as the Speaking Clock. The films of the GPO Film Unit were part of Tallents' wider attempt to create a kind of cultural short-hand able to embody the organisation's values in popular forms.

At a more elevated level, *The Projection of England* was also concerned with the development of mass democracy. The shape of history, according to Tallents, suggested that the scientist would gradually surpass the statesman in importance, and if Britain was to retain its greatness, it needed to foster transnational networks of collaboration across the Commonwealth and with Europe in preparation for 'the world economic unit of the future'. The distortions of the aggressive and nationalistic commercial media needed to be tempered, he believed, by the creation of an information infrastructure able to productively link like-minded professionals pursuing common tasks.

We Live in Two Worlds (1937), 'a film lecture' starring J. B. Priestley, provides a perfect illustration of the expansiveness of Tallents' liberal technocratic idealism. Beginning with two maps that illustrate 'the old world of frontiers and national difference' and the new world of 'universal trade, transport and communications', Priestley sets up a series of polarities between nationalism and internationalism, nation-states and 'ordinary sensible people', the quarrelsome world represented in newspapers and the more sophisticated understanding of the contemporary scene expressed by documentary cinema. It was perhaps not the most obvious way to sell the Anglo-Swiss telephone service.

Although *We Live in Two Worlds* is atypical in its directness, many GPO films go out of their way to encourage the viewer to see the specific work of a provincial Post Office employee as having a cumulative effect of international significance. For example, *Weather Forecast* (1934) illustrates how the safety of British ships relies on a network of international meteorological stations, while *Air Post* (1934) plots how civil aviation has reshaped the geography of the modern world. Indeed, a standard public relations technique espoused by Tallents was the mass production of maps for school children detailing how new technologies were altering established spatial and temporal relationships and by doing so were changing the path of national politics. 'Now I do not know to what extent Sir Stephen Tallents accepts Mr Wells' hatred of nationalism or to what extent he supports the continued section of the world by empires, armies, flags, tariffs, and so on,' wrote Ivor Brown in an astute review of *The Projection of England*, 'but the possibility of a cosmopolitan cohesion is still so remote that even the best internationalist may conscientiously apply himself to improving nationalism, and that, in fact, is what "national projection" is intended to do.'[5]

During the inter-war period 'projection', as promoted and practised by Tallents at the GPO, was enshrined as the British elite's ethical response to foreign propaganda. It was an intervention that sated the need for positive state action but took care to operate within strictly defined limits. It conferred greatness on communities rather than personalities and cleverly celebrated civic institutions and public events. As a Liberal confidant of Beveridge, whose grandest ambitions were curtailed by inter-war austerity, there is even a case for seeing Tallents' conception of projection as a kind of cultural Keynesianism, as well as a precursor to contemporary notions of 'soft power'.[6]

Britain's outstanding contribution to film: the documentary tradition

In 1947, *The Factual Film* report pronounced 'documentary' as 'Britain's outstanding contribution to the film'.[7] It was a judgment chiselled with all the finality of an epitaph.[8] But, although the scale of the British documentary movement's achievement continues to be vehemently debated, nobody interested in British film has been able to ignore the school of thought effectively founded by John Grierson, as a traineeship in the documentary movement became a well-worn path into both feature films and television. The personnel, political and aesthetic lineage of the GPO Film Unit reaches into the present day.

The documentary film movement's achievement, in Grierson's judgment, was to reorientate the documentary genre. While the work of pioneers such as Robert Flaherty remained tinged by Victorian anthropological curiosity (Flaherty's *Nanook of the North* [1922] turned an Eskimo living in the stark environs of Baffin Island into a global media phenomenon), Grierson claimed to have wrestled the form's focus on to contemporary social concerns.

The GPO Film Unit's attempt to define a contemporary British sensibility was especially important. Eschewing Flaherty's exceptionalism and Hollywood melodrama, GPO films instead went in search of the 'real' Britain. Thus GPO films such as *Air Post*, *The Coming of the Dial* and *Roadways* (1937) focus on how complex contemporary problems (nearly always organisational rather than political) filter into everyday life. Through the other end of the telescope productions like *The Horsey Mail* (1938), *Night Mail* and *North Sea* (1938) show how everyday feats are underpinned by a social and technological infrastructure that is seemingly all pervasive while at the same time being almost imperceptible.

However, although the content of the films was rarely overtly 'political', the thinking underpinning the project absolutely was. 'We take postmen for granted, like the milkmen, the engine driver, the coal miner, the lot of them,' as Grierson put it, 'we take them all for granted, yet we are all dependent on them, just as we are all interdependent one to another. The simple fact is that we are all in each other's debt. This is what we must get over. This is what this documentary is all about.'[9] Grierson had dismissed Flaherty's method (but not his films) for their neo-Rousseauism, escapism and sentimentalism. By contrast the GPO Film Unit's approach was impatient, optimistic and forward-looking.

As well as being British in the simple sense that they were socially rooted films, the GPO Film Unit's films were also marketed as 'British'. Struggling for a foothold in a global industry, the GPO Film Unit branded itself as a product of a certain strain of native intellectual thought. In 1933, Paul Nash wrote a celebrated essay on both the necessity and contradictions of 'being British' and 'going modern'.[10] What Nash was to do in the fine arts with the Unit One collective, the GPO Film Unit attempted to do for celluloid. It was an ambition that reflected the influence of the London Film Society. This private circle of influential intellectuals and artists (that included John Maynard Keynes, Julian Huxley and H. G. Wells) screened international films too obtuse or politically unacceptable to be freely distributed commercially. Grierson offered the GPO Film Unit as a solution to London Film Society complaints that there were no British films to set beside *Greed* (1924), *Berlin: Symphony of a City* (1948) or *Potemkin* (1925). It was a promise Grierson made good on when Basil Wright's *The Song of Ceylon* (1934, completed at the GPO) became Britain's first arthouse success when it won the Prix du Gouvernement Belge in 1935.

Lastly, no account of the GPO Film Unit's 'Britishness' would be complete without a brief discussion of how it interacted with its audience. Distributed via cooperative networks of schools, colleges, YMCAs, churches, men's clubs, women's organisations and educational associations (as well as commercial chains) GPO films drew legitimacy from their basis in associational and voluntary culture. GPO Films, to take an example at random, formed an integral part of the YWCA's activities in World Fellowship Week of 1935.[11] Thus, not only were the GPO Film Unit's films created in opposition to mainstream Hollywood, but they also aimed to stimulate a more active type of engagement with the audience. Rather than presenting spectacle to a docile mass, as the stereotype had it, non-commercial GPO film screenings endeavoured to become a conduit for a variety of non-political links. Representations of social and technological interconnectedness were to be screened in conditions that would imbue a moral and emotional sense of togetherness. If the glamour of commercial cinema came from standing apart from its audience, the British documentarists strove to become a closer part of theirs. Retrospectively, it is no surprise that the British documentary movement's greatest popular triumphs came during World War II when the GPO Film Unit metamorphosed into the Crown Film Unit and focused its efforts on servicing national morale.

The GPO Film Unit and international perspectives of 'Britishness'

So far this chapter has attempted to gain some purchase on the institutional Britishness of the GPO Film Unit, the Britishness of the ideas that animated it and the preferred mode that this Britishness took. This final section looks at who was responsible for realising the GPO's vision and how they helped shape the 'Britishness' of the films.

Tallents considered it good diplomacy to recruit expertise from the widest pool available. Accordingly, as well as the Scottish core at the heart of Grierson's inner circle, there was a large contingent of film-makers drawn from the Commonwealth (such as Len Lye and Evelyn Spice), as well as Europeans like László Moholy-Nagy and Lotte Reiniger. Moholy-Nagy's example is a particularly instructive case. As a professor at the Bauhaus school he had espoused a socially purposeful philosophy of design. In Britain he recast his ambitions on a more human scale – his engagement with various strands of documentary led him to venerate the artistic quality of 'ordinary' workmanship, for instance the skill of Lobster fishermen in Littlehampton.[12] Moholy-Nagy's involvement with the GPO, as well as his shop window displays, museum exhibitions and Imperial Airways leaflets, were not only material testament to a personal intellectual reconfiguration but they also point to a wider truth about the Film Unit's 'Britishness'.

Moholy-Nagy's enthusiasms encompassed the penguin enclosure at London Zoo, Leather Lane market, British letter-writing, the De La Warr pavilion and Eton Mess. Contemporary art historians tend to see Moholy-Nagy's work in Britain as a kind of parochial modernism, a period when his astringent talents were diverted into photographing Oxford University.[13] Yet Moholy-Nagy's work in this period could just as plausibly be evidence of an unguarded and unapologetic examination of what struck him most forcibly as 'British'. 'He hadn't come to England to judge the English,' as his wife put it, 'he had come to demonstrate a new vision.'[14] Commercial artists such as Moholy-Nagy would be crucial to articulating a soft modernist vision of the 'new Britain' that had domestic appeal yet was sophisticated enough to impress at international exhibitions like the New York World's Fair of 1939.

That the influence of occasional GPO collaborators like Moholy-Nagy was further filtered through the guiding influence of Brazilian producer Alberto Cavalcanti is also crucial. The films of the South American avant-gardist and those of his protégés are tinged with a tangible foreignness.[15] The portrait of a mildly perverse new suburbia in *Pett and Pott* (1934), the upright but amused understanding of the BBC apparent in *BBC – The Voice of Britain* (1935), and the attentiveness of Humphrey Jennings's *Spare Time* (1939) all evidence an outsider's engagement with otherwise stereotypical pillars of national life. Equally, when the Unit ventured overseas in films like *The Song of Ceylon*, images of bowler-hatted officials ('I am, Sir, your obedient servant') are intercut with footage of tribal rituals in such a way as to suggest that British manners are every bit as quixotic as Sinhalese boys dancing in Ves costume. The international perspective of the GPO Film Unit enabled it to approach the most telling characteristics of British life with a both a sense of humour and an anthropological sharpness. At its best, this influence saw the Unit's films constructively mediate notions of national difference so that they expressed a grounded universalist understanding of humanity.

Undeniably, the international influence evident in the Film Unit's unorthodox treatments of national life often coexisted with something more cloying. Here it is important to understand that the Unit's work was informed by a wider sense of veneration. This 'orgy of anatomizing, congratulating and self-congratulating upon the English national character', as Peter Mandler characterises the inter-war period, was energetically bolstered by émigré writers, artists and intellectuals in transit from fascist Europe.[16] Indeed, by the end of the era, self-consciously patriotic British artists were purposely putting such sentiments in to the mouths of foreign characters. 'If England were to be conquered, were suddenly to lose nearly all its wealth and power,' as Priestley's fictitious Czech Professor Ernst Kronak surmised in 1939, 'I think the English would soon be famous throughout the world as a race of poets, painters and actors, and life on this strange misty island, which is essentially romantic in its atmosphere, would seem to the Americans, Russians, Chinese, who by that time would do the world's manufacturing, to be a fairy tale of arts and dreams.'[17]

The ethnologist Ellen Dissanayake has argued that the traditional function of art in civilisation is to build a sense of community, reinforcing the group's cohesion and thereby helping to assure its survival.[18] This seems a fruitful way of thinking about the many-layered 'Britishness' that lies at the core of the GPO Film Unit. Like the BBC and Mass Observation, the GPO Film Unit's 'Britishness' was underpinned by a yearning for new forms of social solidarity.[19] 'Documentary cinema was an essentially British development,' as Grierson later reflected, 'its characteristic was this idea of social use. It permitted the national talent for emotional understatement to operate in a medium not given to understatement. It allowed an adventure in arts to assume the respectability of a public service.'[20] By presenting itself as 'British' the GPO Film Unit was also able to secure the widest base of supporters possible and fend off hostility from both the commercial media and the Treasury, thereby exerting a real and radical influence at a moment when the template for the nation's media personality was being etched out by its nascent mass media industries.

Notes

1. S. Tallents, *Post Office Publicity* (London: Post Office, 1934), p. 6.
2. As Grierson later reflected, 'When it came to making industry not ugly for people, but a matter of beauty, so that people would accept their industrial selves, so that they would not revolt against their industrial selves, as they did in the late nineteenth century, who initiated the finding of beauty in industry? The British government as a matter of policy.' Grierson papers, Interview in *Take One*, January–February (1970).
3. See S. Anthony, *Public Relations and the Making of Modern Britain: Stephen Tallents and the Birth of a Progressive Media Profession* (Manchester: Manchester University Press, 2011).
4. S. Tallents, *The Projection of England* (London: Faber, 1932), p. 29.
5. Tallents papers, File 19, Press cuttings, I. Brown, 'Telling the World', *The Manchester Guardian*, 16 April 1932.
6. The idea popularised by Joseph Nye in books such as *Bound to Lead: The Changing Nature of American Power* (New York: Basic, 1990), *The Paradox of American Power: Why the World's Only Super Power Can't Go it Alone* (New York: Oxford University Press, 2002) and *Soft Power: The Means to Success in World Politics* (New York: PublicAffairs, US, 2004).
7. *The Factual Film : A Survey Sponsored by the Dartington Hall Trustees* (Oxford: Oxford University Press, 1947), p. 11.
8. And hence much debated. See, for example, A. Higson, '"Britain's Outstanding Contribution to the Film": The Documentary-realist Tradition', in Charles Barr (ed.), *All Our Yesterdays: 90 Years of British Cinema* (London: BFI, 1986), pp. 72–97.

9. This is a slightly truncated form of the quote. Quoted in P. Jackson, *A Retake Please! From Night Mail to Western Approaches* (Liverpool: Liverpool University Press, 1999), p. 24.

10. P. Nash, 'Going Modern and Being British', *The Weekend Review*, 12 March 1933, pp. 322–3.

11. 'Why Not a Film Show?', *Our Own Gazette* vol. 53, 10 October 1935, p. 156; E. Colpus, 'The Geography of the Matter: Transnationalism and Interwar British Women's Philanthropy', a presentation to the IHR's Voluntary Action History seminar, London, 25 October 2010.

12. Stephanie Bolton, '"A Chronicle of Doing" – László Moholy-Nagy's Lobster Film and the Community of Littlehampton', presentation to the Perspectives on Mid-century Modernism workshop, Kellogg College, Oxford, 12 November 2010.

13. See J. Betjeman, *An Oxford University Chest* (Oxford: Oxford University Press, 1938).

14. S. Moholy-Nagy, *Moholy-Nagy: Experiment in Totality* (New York: MIT Press, 1950), p. 126.

15. An argument advanced in I. Aitken, *Alberto Cavalcanti: Realism, Surrealism and National Cinemas* (Bradford: Flicks, 2000).

16. P. Mandler, *The English National Character: The History of an Idea from Edmund Burke to Tony Blair* (New Haven and London: Yale University Press, 2006), p. 151.

17. Quoted in J. Baxendale, *Priestley's England: J. B. Priestley and English Culture* (Manchester: Manchester University Press, 2007), p. 97.

18. See E. Dissanayake, *What is Art For?* (Washington: University of Washington Press, 1988); J. Carey, *What Good are the Arts?* (London: Faber & Faber, 2005).

19. For a broader survey of this strain of democratically minded cultural intervention see D. Le Mahieu, *A Culture for Democracy: Mass Communication and the Cultivated Mind in Britain Between the Wars* (Oxford: Clarendon Press, 1988).

20. John Grierson, 'The Story of the Documentary Film', reprinted from *Fortnightly Review*, London, Grierson Archive, G3:14:5, p. 5.

3 / GPO FILMS AND MODERN DESIGN

Yasuko Suga

It was in the inter-war period that the General Post Office first began to exploit visual publicity in a serious way. Realising the dangers of appearing aloof in a time of political and economic difficulties, the GPO decided on a redesign. As a unique governmental department with its own products – such as stamps and telegrams – to sell, the GPO's new keyword had to be commercialisation. Commercial advertisements were displayed at post offices from 1921. A 'Campaign for Improving Appearance', aiming to beautify and standardise the visual impression of post office interiors, was inaugurated from the late 1920s. The *Punch* cartoon below humorously reflects these developments. The GPO's Public Relations Department (PRD), the first independent publicity function in Whitehall, was established in 1933 under Sir Kingsley Wood, the Post Master General. He invited Sir Stephen Tallents, 'a civil servant with an imagination', who was knighted for his work at the Empire Marketing Board, to be its new Public Relations Officer.[1]

The PRD consisted of a Sales Section for market research and a Publicity Section for the preparation of publicity media, including posters, exhibitions and films. The latter was made up of two professional groups: the GPO Film Unit and the Poster Advisory Group. The GPO Film Unit, a projection mechanism 'designed to give popular appeal to everyday material', was the successor of the EMB Film Unit.[2] The Poster Advisory Group (PAG) established the paradigm of the GPO's artistic standards by incorporating leading figures from both art and commerce, such as Kenneth Clark (the Director of the National Gallery), Clive Bell (the Bloomsbury Group art critic) and Jack Beddington (the publicity manager of Shell-Mex popularly known as the 'New Medici'[3]).

Although the two groups dealt with different media, they were mutually associated and influenced each other's work. The Film Officer, John Grierson, for example, who

'Brighter Post Offices', cartoon from *Punch*, 30 October 1929

was interested in avant-garde art, took a large part in poster production. At PAG meetings he came up with many ideas concerning subject matter for posters.[4] Thanks to these two professional visual media groups, the GPO played a significant role as a promoter of modernist style and of cutting-edge techniques in film and design in the 1930s.

A new corporate identity

One of the PRD's earliest jobs was to design a corporate identity, or 'house style' as it was then known, for the organisation. The GPO Film Unit contributed to this in two ways. First, it created a sense of unity among GPO staff. Showing films to staff played an important role in internal publicity and promoted unity within the organisation, as *The Post Office Magazine,* a penny monthly house journal with plenty of visual effects (above), revealed in the reception of *Banking for Millions* (1934): 'In truth, many of them saw for the first time just what their own job was. They had known it only as manipulation and sometimes rather dull routine. In the film they saw that it had something to do with the real world. In the film they saw this for the first time and they cheered.'[5]

Second, by carrying the new GPO logo throughout the world, the Film Unit promoted the recognition of the 'modern' GPO by others. GPO films were, for instance, an important vehicle for the dissemination of the new GPO logo, officially inaugurated in 1934. The new logo was designed by MacDonald Gill, the renowned designer of the EMB world map poster. The letters were Gill Sans, designed by MacDonald's brother, the typographer and sculptor Eric Gill. Gill Sans was considered at the time to be the 'most satisfying' modern typography in England.[6] This highly design-conscious logo thoroughly visualised a turning point in the administrative history of the GPO as a self-contained, forward-looking and modernist business organisation, with its own collective identity.

Domestically, the GPO films with the new logo were shown nationwide at schools, lecture societies, exhibitions, gatherings of Post Office staff, and also at commercial cinema theatres, reaching as wide a public as possible. Compared with commercial productions, they had a small distribution, but were extraordinarily successful in comparison with the way that other government departments communicated with the public at the time. Grierson went to great lengths in promoting direct contact with the general public.[7] The GPO's potential and the British

Advert in *The Post Office Magazine* reflecting the GPO's vision of modernity, © Royal Mail Group Ltd 2011. Courtesy of The British Postal Museum & Archive

GPO Logo, 1934

Night Mail poster designed by Pat Keely. © Royal Mail Group Ltd 2011. Courtesy of The British Postal Museum & Archive

documentary movement met happily here: Grierson considered non-theatrical film distribution to be poorly organised in Britain, and endeavoured to firm the ground for it. The GPO Film Unit's studio in Soho Square, where new films went on display every Friday, also provided a good platform for the avant-garde in visual culture. The Bauhaus artist-photographer László Moholy-Nagy and the composer Paul Hindemith came and watched films here.

The new GPO logo travelled widely abroad thanks to the international success of the GPO Film Unit. In December 1935, at the International Film Festival in Brussels, the GPO won the first prize in the Documentary Group for *The Song of Ceylon* (1934); a Medaille d'Honneur was awarded to *BBC – The Voice of Britain* (1935), *Coal Face* (1935) and *A Colour Box* (1935). Some films were also shown at the Venice Festival in 1938. *Night Mail* (1936) was sold to America and other European countries, and at the New York World Fair, fifteen GPO films, including *Men in Danger* (1939) and *Spare Time* (1939), were selected for screening. *The King's Stamp* (1935) went to the International Congress of Philatelists in Boston, where it caused an international sensation. *North Sea* (1938) was shown in Germany, America, France, Scandinavia, Russia and India.

GPO Films and modern graphics

Night Mail prestige booklet, with W. H. Auden's verse, designed by Pat Keely

Along with the modern typography of the new GPO logo, the graphic language of poster design was a strong buttress for the modernity the GPO aspired to. The list of commissioned designers – Graham Sutherland, John Armstrong, Edward McKnight Kauffer, Hans Schleger, Austin Cooper and many more – itself made a representation of British modern graphics in the inter-war period. The GPO Film Unit also provided many good subjects for contemporary graphics, giving designers new material, perspectives and scope for experimental design. It also materially contributed with its photograph library, which was responsible for the photographic 'stills' from the films used in posters, magazines and for exhibition purposes. These stills could be drawn upon by GPO staff as and when required.[8]

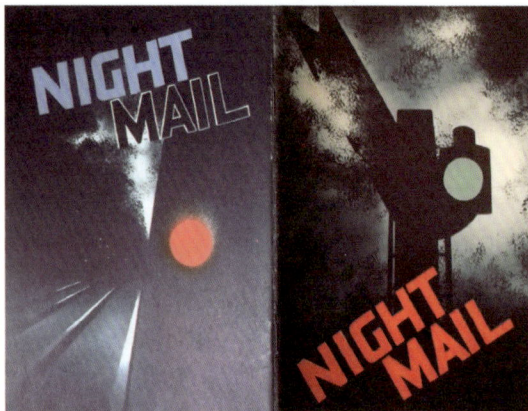

Patrick C. Keely, who designed posters for London Transport, the EMB and railway companies, and who was the first professional designer commissioned by the GPO for telephone publicity in 1931, made an important contribution to the Film Unit with his poster for *Night Mail*. The design, with striking blue background, heavily influenced by the French graphic designer A. M. Cassandre, was highly abstract compared with other cinema posters of the time. The coordinating booklet by Keely was also an important luxury product, which showed that the GPO could 'afford' to be experimental and avant-garde. Keely also designed a poster inviting the public to a GPO film display in 1935, with a projector alongside the GPO logo (opposite) – an image that symbolised the holistic nature of GPO publicity.

Cutting-edge graphic languages of the period, such as the combination of photographic elements with painted elements, pioneered in Britain by Edward McKnight Kauffer, were quickly introduced into GPO publicity. The first GPO poster incorporating a photograph was for the Film Unit. It was designed by the young talents Eckersley-Lombers. Their poster, which integrated a film still from *The Saving of Bill Blewitt* (1936) and an abstract human figure, came out in 1938. The layout, showing a screen watched by the audience watched by the viewer of the poster, perfectly captured the system of multilayered mass media in the modern age.

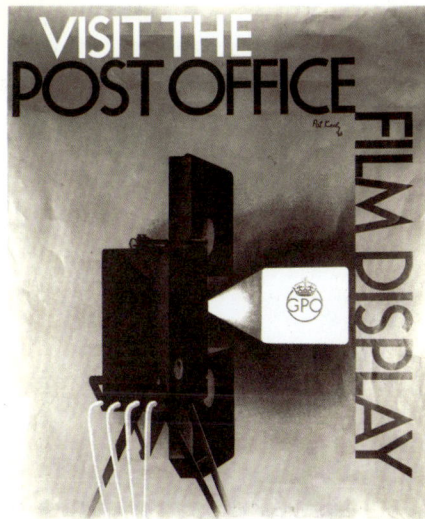

Films and exhibitions

GPO exhibitions, which often incorporated cinema halls, were also a self-conscious embodiment of modernity. The exhibitions were held thematically, concentrating on savings, telephone, telegram and 'Post Early' campaigns. They constantly adopted and even pioneered the features of modernist architecture: flat or curved white walls, the use of semi-circular space, and minimal ornamentation, and the use of enlarged photographs or photomontage images. This was attained thanks to collaboration with leading artists such as the surrealist photographer Francis Bruguiere, the leading German modernist organisation Reimann Studio and McKnight Kauffer. The sites were furnished with abundant visual publicity – posters, pamphlets and telephone models – and the GPO staff dealt with enquiries from the public.

The design of the GPO exhibitions was a talking point in 1930s Britain. *The Post Office Magazine* proudly reported that 'Post Office exhibition shops are all the talk nowadays.'[9] They were certainly popular: over 450,000 people visited an exhibition in the winter of 1933–4 in thirteen weeks, and shops operating in Nottingham, Plymouth, Scarborough and Ipswich in 1933 were visited by 148,600, 108,710, 109,108 and 50,709 people, respectively.[10] In 1936, twelve GPO exhibitions attracted a total of over 1,500,000 people. The Octagon in Bath, in which the GPO fitted a cinema hall, gathered a total of 120,000 visitors in twenty-three days; the population of Bath was 70,000 at the

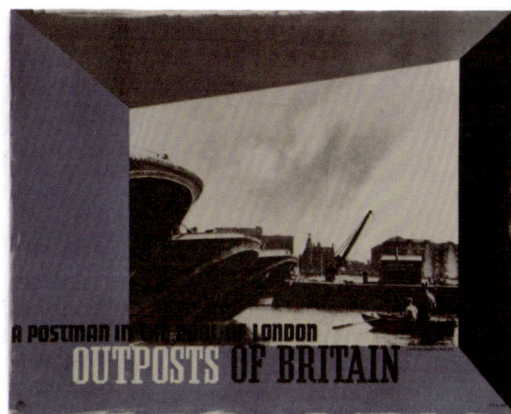

VISIT THE POST OFFICE FILM DISPLAY

FREE

Visit the Post Office Film Display, poster designed by Eckersley-Lombers, © Royal Mail Group Ltd 2011. Courtesy of The British Postal Museum & Archive

Exhibition design by G. O. Pratt and McKnight Kauffer at the British Industries Fair, 1934

time.[11] The culmination of the GPO's exhibition activities came in 1938 at the Glasgow British Empire Exhibition, noted for its full articulation of modernism in design. The GPO did not lag behind. About 27,000 people visited the Post Office pavilion.[12] We must not forget that the films of the GPO Film Unit were at the heart of these events. At the ten-day-long Olympia Radio Exhibition in 1936, for example, 62,186 people attended GPO film screenings. Numbers were similarly high at the 1936 Glasgow Radio Exhibition, at which 20,000 people attended film screenings in just one week, and at the three-month-long GPO exhibition in Manchester in 1936, at which 14,465 people saw GPO films.[13]

Division and reorganisation

The modernity the GPO projected had to be 'fun' and easily accessible, especially because many new technologies and services, such as the colour telephone, motorbike postmen and greeting telegrams, were introduced in the 1930s. That was why 'telephone chess' and other entertaining services were invented to persuade people that telecommunication was something one could live with. The 'fun' aspect in publicity was particularly emphasised after 1936. This was when Stephen Tallents left the GPO for the BBC, and a new public relations officer, E. T. Crutchley, was appointed. Unlike Tallents, who was sympathetic to modern art, Crutchley, a self-made man who established his career through the civil service, considered designs chosen by the PAG unusable because they were 'quite unsuitable for general exhibition in provincial Post Offices' and for schools with 'several millions of impressionable young minds' due to their strong avant-garde tendencies.[14] He maintained that '[I]n experimenting in design ... advanced technique ... should not be allowed to outweigh popular appeal.'[15] In November 1937, the liquidation of the PAG was officially announced.

At exactly the same time, the Film Unit faced a parallel problem of commercialism or public appeal versus what might be considered as a 'fine art' attitude. Grierson was opposed from the beginning to introducing entertainment, stating that, 'Documentary was developed on the thought that it was not there necessarily for entertainment.'[16] However, Cavalcanti was open to introducing fables, comedy and other entertaining elements into his films. The first comedy film depicting suburban life, *Pett and Pott* (1934), subtitled *A Fairy Story of the Suburbs*, was made after Cavalcanti came to the GPO and was remembered by John Taylor as 'the beginning of the division' between Grierson and Cavalcanti.[17] When Harry Watt experimented with 'the first story documentary, a breakaway', *The Saving of Bill Blewitt*, it was not Grierson but Cavalcanti who helped him as producer.[18] It originally included a love scene which was later cut out by Grierson.

This disagreement resulted in a final split within the GPO Film Unit in 1937. Grierson left the GPO with John Taylor, Arthur Elton, Stuart Legg and Basil Wright, forming film organisations elsewhere.[19] The GPO Film Unit was reorganised and the role of Film Officer was abolished, and in place of Grierson, Cavalcanti and Watt became the lead producers and directors on a non-established basis.[20] The split in the Film Unit was a significant incident not only in the context of the documentary film movement, but also in the GPO's publicity strategy. Cavalcanti remained with Watt and Jennings, not only because their entertaining approach was at odds with Grierson's theory of documentary, but also because the GPO provided suitable conditions for their visual experiment in entertainment. Grierson and others, like Clark and Bell, left or had to leave because they were in discord with the GPO's new publicity strategy under Crutchley.

The split, however, did not affect the Film Unit's activities as a publicity function of the GPO. Watt recalled that 'After the split, Cavalcanti and I immediately set out to prove our part by finding a subject which came under the umbrella of the Post Office – and would be a box-office film to go into the cinema and be paid for.'[21] This was the feature film *North Sea*, the reconstruction of a real story, depicting a radio station in Aberdeen and a ship in difficulty. The Film Unit's efforts were now more squarely focused on the leisure of the British people, rather than their work patterns, combining more romantic and comical elements, as seen in *N or NW* (1937) about a boy and girl quarrelling. *N or NW* frequently used the technique of overlapping images, and even included some Hollywood-like sensuality. The public appreciated this new approach. The *Daily Express*, for example, wrote about *N or NW* as 'one of the most imaginative documentaries I've seen'; and about Cavalcanti, 'It wouldn't be a bad thing if he were to make one or two big box-office films too.'[22] Next came the completely 'leisure'-centred *Spare Time*. The film was also well received by the public, and Cavalcanti called it 'the best job done at the GPO', though the Grierson school severely criticised it.[23] At any rate, the GPO's publicity strategy under Crutchley met with the Film Unit's new direction.

Likewise, in the field of graphic design, a new generation of poster designers – those trained to be 'designers' such as Tom Eckersley, Abram Games, F. H. K. Henrion, Hans

UNDER THE SURFACE · ON THE GROUND · IN THE AIR

POST OFFICE EXHIBITION
CHARING CROSS UNDERGROUND STATION
GPO MAY 25TH to JUNE 13TH

Post Office Exhibition, poster designed by G. R. Morris, © Royal Mail Group Ltd 2011. Courtesy of The British Postal Museum & Archive

GPO Pavilion for the
British Empire
Exhibition, Glasgow,
1938

Schleger and Austin Cooper, who formed a new criteria for
'commercial art' – were commissioned after the liquidation
of the PAG and subsequently produced many designs for the
GPO. Their styles matched what Crutchley called the 'Post
Office atmosphere and requirements'. The general image
promoted by the GPO after 1937 depicted a fantasy world of
'dream-come-true', realisable by modern communications – a
positive image of a future society built upon GPO services.
While other contemporary governmental advertisements
tended to be formal, realistic and simply didactic, the publicity arrangements of the GPO at this time were lively, humorous and 'fantastic'. The telegraph service and 'Post Early'
campaigns were notable examples of such publicity.

Opposed to the more austere forms of propaganda
favoured by Grierson, the GPO's films after 1937 illustrated, 'in the guise of entertainment', the manifold activities of the GPO – as contemporary film critic R. Howard
Cricks significantly described it: 'they represent the sugar
with which the pill of more direct advertising is coated'.[24]
This analysis could indeed be applied to all the GPO visual
publicity of this period.

N or NW

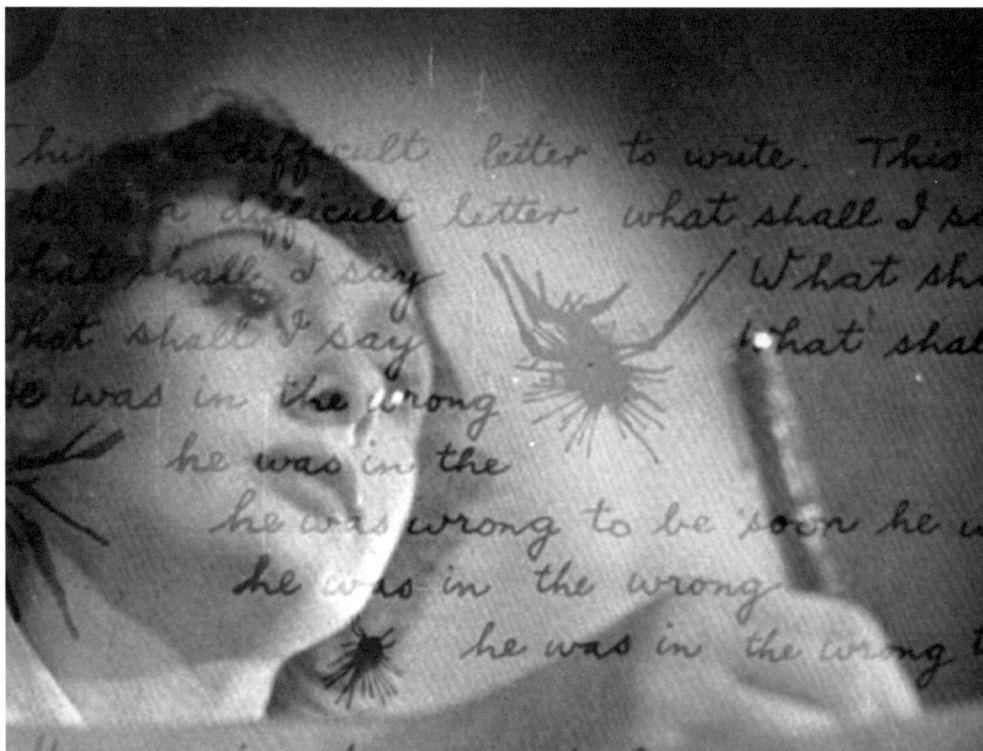

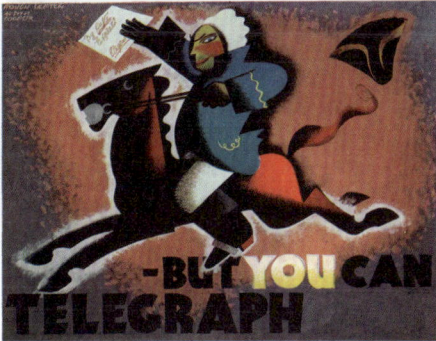

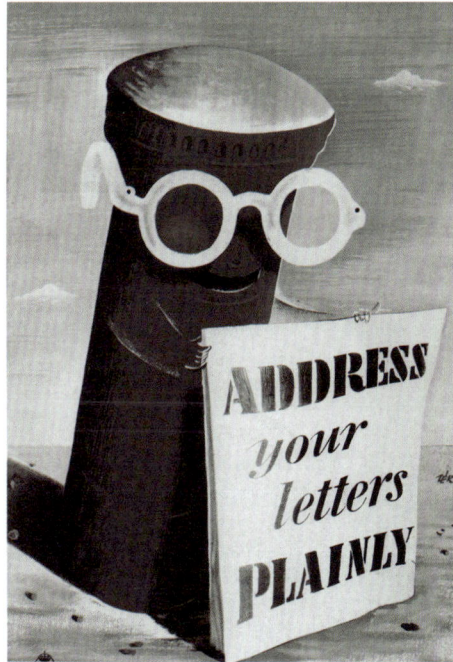

GPO posters advertising telecommunication designed by Austin Cooper

Address your letters plainly, poster designed by Hans Schleger, © Royal Mail Group Ltd 2011. Courtesy of The British Postal Museum & Archive

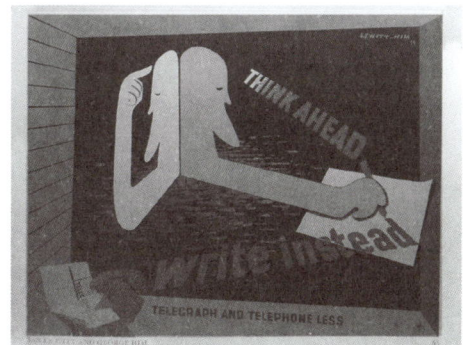

World War II and after

The Observer wrote in 1938 that 'the praise of the Post Office is nowadays in every-body's mouth; its efficiency, its courtesy and humanity'.[25] In 1939, *The Penrose Annual* acknowledged that, 'generally speaking, the public regards the Post Office as a friend'.[26] There is no doubt that visual and entertaining elements in visual publicity played a decisive role in changing public opinion. Moreover, the GPO's inter-war publicity impacted on the artistic standard of governmental publicity in general, and provided a foundation for further governmental patronage of the arts.

The success of visual publicity by the government during World War II is good evidence of this. The GPO Film Unit (which became the Crown Film Unit in 1940) continued to make a valuable contribution to government using the nationwide distribution network established in the 1930s. The inter-war pursuit of watching documen-tary films as a 'leisure' activity continued to flourish in spite of the drastically changed circumstances. The war propaganda poster was also built upon the GPO publicity function: in fact, the use of poster art had been discussed from the earliest stage of the establishment of the Ministry of Information, and this was thanks to the two GPO Public Relations Officers, Stephen Tallents and E. T. Crutchley. The dominant approach drew on the GPO's promotion of humour, fun and fantasy in its pre-war

Think ahead, write instead, poster designed by Lewitt-Him, © Royal Mail Group Ltd 2011. Courtesy of The British Postal Museum & Archive

Your talk may kill your comrades, poster designed by Abram Games, courtesy of the Imperial War Museum (IWM PST 2869)

publicity. Many well-known poster designers were used in wartime, including Pat Keely, F. H. K. Henrion, Abram Games and Ashley Havinden, all of whom had worked for the GPO.

Conclusion

GPO films played a vital part in the GPO's visual publicity campaign of the 1930s by carrying the symbolic GPO logo, functioning as major attractions at GPO exhibitions, and being advertised through poster designs. They reflected and shaped contemporary British society's imagination of modernity. The films were contextualised within the GPO's image politics to establish its corporate identity among other graphic publicity media. The 'entertaining' nature of the GPO's visual publicity developed during the late 1930s reflected the need, in Crutchley's words, to ensure the 'popular appeal' of the technology and services offered by the GPO. For good or for bad, the trials and errors of GPO publicity were reflected in, and associated with, the course of the development of British documentary film movement.

Notes

1. G. Huxley, *Both Hands: An Autobiography* (London: Chatto & Windus, 1970), p. 129; Huxley was the secretary of the EMB Publicity Committee.
2. Post Office, *Post Office 1934* (London: Post Office, 1934), p. 111.
3. C. Connolly, 'The New Medici', *Architectural Review*, July 1934. Another Medici cited was Frank Pick of the London Transport. Both Pick and Beddington worked for the Empire Marketing Board.
4. For Grierson's interests in the arts other than films, see Ian Aitken, *Film and Reform: John Grierson and the Documentary Film Movement* (London: Routledge, 1990).
5. T. Baird, 'The Cinema and the Information Service', quoted in P. Swann, *The British Documentary Film Movement, 1926–1946* (Cambridge: Cambridge University Press, 1989), p. 67.
6. *The Penrose Annual*, 1934, p. 60.
7. Royal Mail Archives, POST33/3576:12.
8. The Film Unit actually appointed one photographer for £3.10 per week. National Archives, T162/408/E1612/2.
9. *The Post Office Magazine* vol. 1, 1934, p. 306.
10. S. Tallents, 'Post Office Publicity', *Post Office Green Papers*, no. 8, 1934.
11. *The Post Office Magazine* vol. 2, 1935, p. 298.
12. *The Post Office Magazine* vol. 5, 1938, pp. 294–9.

13. Royal Mail Archives, POST33/5089.

14. Royal Mail Archives, POST33/5415:1; POST33/5699:7.

15. E. T. Crutchley, Report of Provincial Publicity Committee, 1936, POST33/5253. On the PAG see Yasuko Suga, 'State Patronage of Design? The Eliticism/Commercialism Battle in the General Post Office's Graphic Production', *Journal of Design History* vol. 13 (2000), pp. 23–37.

16. Elizabeth Sussex, *The Rise and Fall of British Documentary* (Berkeley, CA: University of California Press, 1975), p. 60; Grierson, 'Films of Fact', *The Times*, 23 November 1935 in POST33/5415:28.

17. Quoted in K. MacDonald and M. Cousins, *Imaging Reality: The Faber Book of Documentary* (London: Faber & Faber, 1996), p. 116.

18. Sussex, *The Rise and Fall of British Documentary*, p. 86.

19. These were the Strand Film Unit, founded by Grierson and Wright, and the Realist Film Unit, set up by Wright. Anstey left to work for the Shell Film Unit.

20. On the reorganisation of the Film Unit in 1937, see POST33/5199.

21. Sussex, *The Rise and Fall of British Documentary*, p. 106.

22. *Daily Express*, 18 January 1938.

23. Sussex, *The Rise and Fall of British Documentary*, p. 110.

24. R. Howard Cricks, 'Striking Propaganda Work of the GPO Film Unit', *The Commercial Film* vol. 2 (1936), pp. 4–5.

25. *The Observer*, 5 December 1938.

26. *The Penrose Annual*, 1939, p. 24.

4 / OLD INDUSTRY, NEW SCIENCE? THE GPO FILM UNIT BETWEEN PALAEOTECHNOLOGY AND NEOTECHNOLOGY

Timothy Boon

Until recently, the historiography of British documentary films in general and GPO films in particular has tended to be dominated by two confused tendencies. The first of these may be termed the 'genealogical' account, which stresses the person of John Grierson and the individuals and organisations with which he was associated. According to this, if you belonged to his social group, you made documentaries. By contrast, the formalist definition of documentary stresses the film-making qualities of documentaries; the look, structure and formal distinctiveness of documentaries, a product of their engagement with the Russian style of Pudovkin and Eisenstein. But if 'the creative treatment of actuality' is taken to allude to the higher level of cinematic literacy that documentarists were supposed to have in comparison with their competitors, then many films made under the genealogical definition simply do not count; they are simply not that different from contemporary instructional and commercial films. Both the genealogical and the formalist definitions divert attention from what we may call an iconographic approach to the subject, one that privileges the ways that documentary film-makers represented the world to audiences. This is the approach used here. One result of this shift of focus is to move away from considering the task of the historian to be to write *the* history of *the* documentary film *movement*. Instead, it implies that documentaries should be components of many histories and these should focus not on 'the movement' but on the world that the documentarists inhabited and represented.

From the point of view of the historian of science and technology, the major deficiency of the existing historiography is insufficient analysis and discussion of the fact that British documentaries consistently represented machines, the relationships of people to machines, science, rationality and rationalising responses to health issues. Particular technologies were widely considered to be emblematic of modernity in this period: the telegraph and telephone, railway and car, photograph and cinema, heavy electrical technology, broadcasting, ocean liners and steel-framed buildings. Most of these technologies were featured as the subjects of documentaries: for example, aviation in *Contact* (1933) and *Airport* (1935), broadcasting in *BBC – The Voice of Britain* (1935), railways in *Night Mail* (1936) and transport of all kinds, as well as hydroelectric technology, in *The Face of Britain* (1935). Pre-eminently, of course, among technology films, the emphasis in the GPO Film Unit films was on telephones and telegraphs. So much was argued in my book *Films of Fact*, but here I will draw a finer distinction.[1] This chapter identifies two strands in the 1930s GPO films that represented science and technology, one broadly concerned with established industries, and the other with the applied science of new high technologies. By comparing this with the works of Patrick Geddes and Karl Mannheim – who were responding as much as the documentarists to the physical and cultural impact of industrialisation – and by considering changing linguistic usage, we can see how the iconography of these films reveals a commonality with major strands in contemporary culture.

Old industries

In the films, industries tend to be represented generically as Britain's historical path to modernity. This can be seen particularly in the GPO film *Health of the Nation* made by John Monck in 1938/9.[2]

> COMMENTATOR: Two hundred years ago a nation of farmers and craftsmen. Then over the face of England there came a change. There was coal in Wales, coal in the Midlands, coal in Lancashire, Yorkshire and Durham. Coal, by the development of science, became the source of power. Coal for smelting, for iron and steel. Coal for steam and power, the power behind the Industrial Revolution. Coal and iron and steel for the needs of industry ... transport ... Coal and iron and steel for industry, coal for power.
>
> ANNOUNCER: Iron and coal and steel for the textiles of the North, cotton and wool, silk and fabrics ... Liverpool, Manchester, Oldham and Rochdale, Congleton, Macclesfield, Huddersfield, Halifax, Bradford and Leeds.
>
> COMMENTATOR: The industrial North, transformed by the machine into a land of factories and furnaces, of mines and workshops. Speed and mass production.
>
> ANNOUNCER: Steel, iron and coal: Sheffield and Swindon, Derby and Stafford, Middlesbrough, Doncaster, Coventry, Birmingham, Wolverhampton and Crewe ... Railways and shipbuilding, bridges, tools, machinery, armaments.

This sequence stresses not just industrialisation in general, but also the particularity of place and the regional diversity of Britain underpinned by specific industries – steel in Sheffield, textiles in the North West. This trope features not just in *Health of the Nation*, but also in *Night Mail*; for example, after the stop at Crewe, the train speeds on northwards, with the commentary stating:

> North! With a hundred tons of new letters to sort! The Postal Special picks up and distributes the mails of Industrial England; the mines of Wigan; the steel works of Warrington; and the machine shops of Preston.

This notion of a diverse Britain, each of whose regions is defined by its particular industry partakes of a widely shared historicist contemporary view of the nation that can be found in many other cultural forms of the era. It is present particularly strongly in the work of the Scottish polymath Patrick Geddes, for example. He believed that, in each

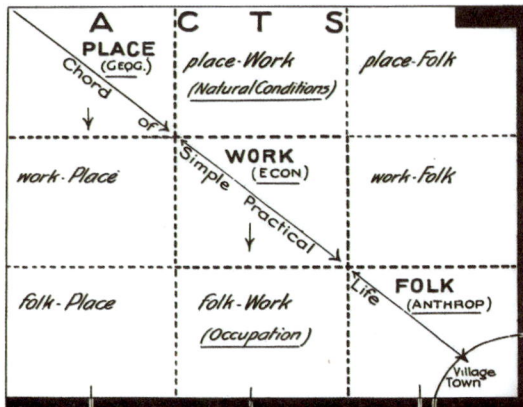

Patrick Geddes'
'idea midden'
extrapolating
Le Play's
place–work–folk
triad

Patrick Geddes'
Outlook tower
(from his *Cities in Evolution*, 1915)

historical period, each geographical area had its characteristic power sources, industries and products. He returned repeatedly to ways of classifying the world, as he sought a synthesis between the different aspects of his work in biology, sociology and town planning. He would often draw diagrams in public lectures, building up the detail as he explained his vision. He quickly expanded the place–work–folk triad invented by the French sociologist Frédéric Le Play to make nine categories from the intersections of the basic three.

For example, 'folk–places', the intersection of folk and place, denoted where different kinds of people lived, and ranged 'from farm-house or cottage in the country to homes or slums in the modern manufacturing towns'.[3] The particularity of place encountered in the GPO films quoted is found in Geddes' 'place–work'. He explained: 'place–work is a name for the "natural advantages" which determine work of each kind at the right place for it'.[4] Mining was one of the key examples of how the characteristics of place influenced location of industry.[5]

One of Geddes' main sites for exposition of his geographical thinking was the Outlook Tower in Edinburgh, which placed the character of the city in the context of broader and broader circles of space, starting at the top with a camera obscura that revealed the cityscape to the visitor and by its displays, which progressively placed the city in its regional, national and international perspectives.[6]

Geddes' geographical sense was completed by a particular style of historicisation. He wrote in his *Cities in Evolution* (1915) that:

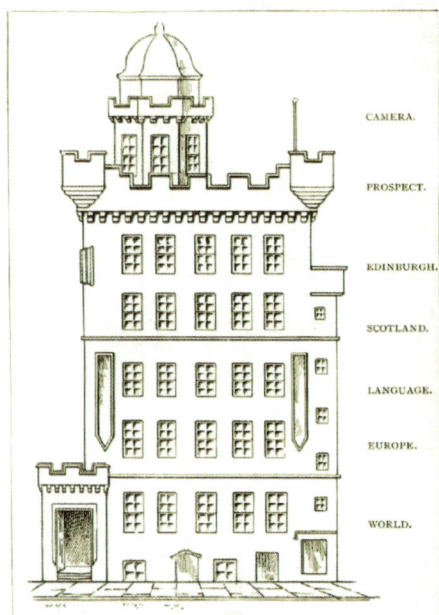

FIG. 50.—Outlook Tower in diagrammatic elevation, with indications of uses of its storeys—as Observatory, Summer School, etc., of Regional and Civic Surveys ; with their widening relations, and with corresponding practical initiatives.

Although our economists have been and are in the habit of speaking of our present civilisation, since the advent of steam and its associated machinery, with all its technic strivings and masteries, as the 'Industrial Age', we press for the analysis of this into two broadly and clearly distinguishable types and phases: ... of older and newer, ruder and finer type, needing also a constructive nomenclature accordingly.[7]

He extended this with a metaphor from archaeology, on the model of Palaeolithic and Neolithic time classification introduced in 1865:[8]

Simply substituting *-technic* for *-lithic* here, we may distinguish the earlier and ruder elements of the Industrial Age as Paleotechnic, the newer and still often incipient elements disengaging themselves from these as Neotechnic ... To the former order belong the collieries ... together with the steam engine, and most of our staple manufactures; so do the railways and the markets, and above all the crowded and monotonous industrial towns to which all these have given rise.[9]

Geddes also introduced the idea that 'a new economic order – a Second Industrial Revolution – is once more arising' and his summary of his chapter on these ages, states that 'a new industrial age is opening' and lists 'significance of oil fuel, electric industries, etc.'.[10] Furthermore, in stressing this new age, he drew a comparison between the hydro-electrically powered Swiss, French and Italian mountain districts and the 'relative backwardness and danger of this and other coal-using countries in realising this advent of a new industrial age, a Second Industrial Revolution'.[11]

New science-based Industries

It might be argued that the GPO Unit's films were only incidentally concerned with representing the palaeotechnological industries; their core concern was much more with new, science-based technologies, especially the communications technologies of telegraphy and telephony. For example, Stuart Legg's film *The Coming of the Dial* (1933), which promotes the introduction of automated telephone exchanges, starts its commentary with footage of Bauhaus refugee László Moholy-Nagy's light display machine:

> Research: the creative power behind the modern world. Building the future in the laboratory. The industrial chemist determining a carbon percentage for safety steel. The physicist analysing coloured light rays for signal lenses. The plant-breeder pollinating selected grasses for mountain pastures. These men are applying the laws of science to everyday problems. And research into the behaviour of electromagnets has revolutionised the telephone system and introduced the dial.

Here we see a radically different model of industry. This is not the palaeotechnology of coal and steel, but the applied science of neotechnology; not the technology that has created change in the past, but the science-rooted technology that was transforming the world in 1933 and into the future. Geddes, a social evolutionist, believed that social and technical change had a forward direction. He saw the world passing from the era of the first Industrial Revolution, founded on coal and iron, to one founded on electrical power and new industries. But, just as films like *The Coming of the Dial* align with Geddes' neotechnics, so they also fight against the local and particular character of regions that we saw with traditional industries. The world of applied science presented in *The Coming of the Dial* suggests an annihilation of regional particularity. Science and rationality more generally are presented as forces for overcoming regional and national difference and the ushering-in of an internationalised world enabled by science. This is also, very explicitly, seen in Alberto Cavalcanti's 1937 film *We Live in Two Worlds*, which hymns the transformative power of international telecommunications. In the words of J. B. Priestley, who wrote and appears in the film, describing the line to a remote Alpine hut:

> You see that telephone line has taken us from the first world to the second. From nationalism to internationalism. From this map – all angry frontiers – to this, showing all the lines of transport and communications: roads, railways, air services and telephone lines.

The film builds on this paean to telecommunications with extended sequences on hydro-electric power; all in all a clear statement of neotechnology.

The changing language of industry, machinery and technology

The transition from established heavy industry to science-based light industry in this period also occasioned a change in language usage. The American historian Leo Marx has undertaken a historical etymology of the term 'technology' and shown how, like one of Raymond Williams' keywords, from its older usage denoting the *study* of mechanical arts, 'technology' came to be used to refer to 'society's entire stock of technical knowledge and equipment'.[12] This 'entire stock' related not to individual machines, such as steam engines, or even to individual factories, but to large sociotechnical systems run by public corporations rather than by small family concerns. In these complex systems there was a 'blurring of the boundaries between ... the artifactual equipment (the machinery and hardware) and all the rest: the reservoir of technical – scientific – knowledge; the specially trained workforce; the financial apparatus; and the means of acquiring raw materials'.[13] This change he dates in America to the last quarter of the nineteenth century with the rise of those prototypical neotechnical concerns of the second Industrial Revolution, the electrical and chemical industries (although it is interesting to note that the word 'technology' nowhere appears in Geddes' *Cities in Evolution*). These *technological* industries, unlike the older heavy industries, came to rely on university-trained – and therefore 'professional' – scientific staff.[14] Marx shows how a metaphorical language of 'high' and 'low' inhered in the terminological genealogy of 'technology' in a way that reproduced the distinction between the useful and the fine arts; 'between things and ideas, the physical and the mental, the mundane and the ideal, body and soul, making and thinking, the work of slaves and of free people'.[15] Eric Schatzberg shows in more detail how the new meaning of 'technology' was introduced into America via the writer Thorsten Veblen in a deliberate and subtle recasting of the German term 'technik'. Losing much of the subtlety, the historian Charles Beard not only adopted the new usage, but in the 1920s endowed it with agency and connected it with progress. Beard wrote in the *American Political Science Review*:

> Technology marches in seven-league boots from one ruthless, revolutionary conquest to another, tearing down old factories and industries, flinging up new processes with terrifying rapidity, and offering for the first time in history the possibility of realising the idea of progress.[16]

Here we see not only the contrast between the old and the new, but also the sense of neotechnology itself being an agent of transformation which brings to mind *The Coming of the Dial*'s phrase 'research ... building the future in the laboratory'.

In GPO films, we never see the contrast between old industry and new technology explicitly drawn in a single film. *We Live in Two Worlds* draws a comparison between the pre-industrial eotechnic rural world of Switzerland and the world of new telecommunications.[17] *Health of the Nation* also contrasts the health catastrophe of the industrial period with the rationality of subsequent state intervention in public health. But we have to look beyond the GPO oeuvre to Rotha's *Face of Britain* (1935) to see the palaeotechnic explicitly contrasted with the neotechnic within a single film. All this, however, indicates that the makers of GPO films, not themselves scholars of technology, were all the same partakers in a culture that was experiencing a transition between these worlds, and therefore represented this across their work.

Conservative and natural law styles of thought

There are also correspondences between Geddes' account and that of the sociologist Karl Mannheim. Working within more conventional academic settings than the people discussed earlier in this chapter, Mannheim drew on traditions in German philosophy and sociology as he developed his sociology of knowledge. Early in his career, he was influenced by the sociologist Ferdinand Tönnies, who shared with Geddes and his sources a sense of the catastrophic effect of industrialisation, which he saw as replacing small close-knit communities (*Gemeinschaften*) with cold, de-personalised industrial societies (*Gesellschaften*).[18] In developing his approach to sociology, as a reaction against modernity, Mannheim distinguished between the methods of the natural sciences, which he aligned with the dehumanising impact of industrialisation, and methods proper to the human sciences that sought to recapture the 'authentic experience' that arose within specific worldviews and contexts.[19] As David Kaiser argues, 'this feature of Mannheim's sociology thus shared in the early twentieth century traditions of historicism: historical actors' specific thoughts and actions were considered inseparable from their historical contexts and settings'.[20] Mannheim's response to industrialisation clearly has an affinity with Geddes' historicist and concrete ideas on the particularity of place. For the sake of our argument, Mannheim's 1925 essay on conservatism can be seen as a summation of these previous strands. Here he proposed that the 'conservative' style of thought had been a reaction in Germany against the rationalism of Enlightenment or 'natural-law' thought. He argued that whereas conservative thought is holistic, organic, concrete and historicist, natural-law thought is reductionist and abstract, with an emphasis on universal principles of reason.[21] This resonates with the abstraction and universalism of new applied sciences, based on the reasoning of physical science, and hell-bent on expunging the local and particular with the international and universal. But Mannheim saw no distinction between old and new science and technology, as he wrote in 1934:

> In his scientific and technological knowledge man has, indeed, made miraculous strides forward in the span of time that takes us from the days when the carriage came into use; but is human rationality, in other than the technical field, to-day so very different from what it was in the distant past of which the wheelbarrow is a symbol?[22]

For Mannheim, arriving in London in 1933 as a refugee from Nazism, the modern, technological world represented a 'disproportionate development of human faculties'. Unlike Geddes and the film-makers of the GPO Unit, Mannheim would not be looking to neotechnologies to heal the wounds caused by reductionist science and industrialisation. By contrast, the methods of the historicist cultural sciences would be necessary to comprehend the world the natural sciences had wrought. Earlier, drawing on distinctions made by Wilhelm Dilthey, Mannheim made a strong differentiation between the methods of the natural and cultural sciences. His essay on historicism published in 1924 had drawn a comparison between scientific and historical understanding: 'Historians indeed may grasp through "understanding" (*Verstehen*) as an intuitive faculty of the historian which enables him to penetrate his subject-matter, into the concrete valuations of the epochs in question, to a degree which is denied us when we are dealing with nature.'[23] We may presume therefore that precisely this mode of historical understanding should be applied to grasping the nature and impact of industrial change in the past and new technological change in the present.

What we gain from looking at this small aspect of Mannheim's oeuvre is the sense not merely of an evolution (as in Geddes), but of a dialectic between the two styles of thought. In Mannheim, the conservative view is a reaction to Enlightenment rationality. But in the films and Geddes' thought, the neotechnic (or natural law/Enlightenment) is a reaction to the palaeotechnic (or organic/conservative); the response is the other way round.

Conclusions

The iconography of old and new technologies across the oeuvre of GPO films is not so much in tension, or even in dialectic, as coexisting. But that coexistence points to the dilemma of the inter-war generation, simultaneously living in the shadow of the Industrial Revolution while modernistically promoting the new technologies in an era of economic depression. In sum, we see the documentary film-makers as typical members of the society of the first half of the twentieth century, coming to terms with the modernity that industrialisation had brought. If their view of the specificity of industrial Britain and the transformative potential of new science-based industries has something in common with the writings of Geddes and Mannheim, that is because industry and science were at the core of both society and culture in that period.

Notes

1. Timothy Boon, *Films of Fact: A History of Science in Documentary Films and Television* (London: Wallflower, 2008).
2. See Timothy Boon (2004), 'Industrialisation and Catastrophe: The Victorian Economy in British Film Documentary, 1930–1950', in M. Taylor and M. Wolff (eds), *The Victorians Since 1901: Histories, Representations and Revisions* (Manchester: Manchester University Press, 2004), pp. 107–20.
3. A 1927 opinion quoted in Philip Boardman, *The Worlds of Patrick Geddes: Biologist, Town Planner, Re-Educator, Peace-Warrior* (London: Routledge, 1978), p. 470.
4. Ibid.
5. For an outline of Geddes 'thinking machines', see Helen Meller, *Patrick Geddes: Social Evolutionist and City Planner* (London: Routledge, 1990), pp. 45–52. For a more expanded exposition, see Boardman, *The Worlds of Patrick Geddes*, pp. 465–84.
6. Meller, *Patrick Geddes*, pp. 102–26.
7. Patrick Geddes, *Cities in Evolution: An Introduction to the Town Planning Movement and to the Study of Civics* (London: Williams & Norgate, 1915), p. 63.
8. Based on the nomenclature of John Lubbock in his *Pre-historic Times, as Illustrated by Ancient Remains, and the Manners and customs of Modern Savages* (London: Williams & Norgate, 1865).
9. Geddes, *Cities in Evolution*, p. 64.
10. Ibid., p. 59.
11. Ibid., p. 46.

12. Leo Marx, 'Technology: The Emergence of a Hazardous Concept', *Technology and Culture* vol. 51 no. 3, July 2010, pp. 561–77, 575.
13. Ibid., p. 568.
14. See ibid., pp. 569, 571.
15. Ibid., p. 573.
16. Eric Schatzberg, '*Technik* comes to America: Changing Meanings of *Technology* before 1930', *Technology and Culture* vol. 47, 2006, pp. 486–512, quotation at p. 509.
17. 'Eotechnic' was Lewis Mumford's extension of Geddes scheme, used to describe the era before the palaeotechnic. See Lewis Mumford, *Technics and Civilization* (New York: Routledge, 1934).
18. David Kaiser, 'A Mannheim for All Seasons: Bloor, Merton, and the Roots of the Sociology of Scientific Knowledge', *Science in Context* vol. 11 no. 1 (2008), pp. 51–87, 55.
19. Ibid., pp. 59–60, 62.
20. Ibid., pp. 62–3.
21. David Smith, and Malcolm Nicolson, 'The "Glasgow School" of Paton, Findlay and Cathcart: Conservative Thought in Chemical Physiology, Nutrition and Public Health', *Social Studies of Science* vol. 19 (1989), pp. 195–238, 197.
22. Quoted in Kaiser, 'A Mannheim for All Seasons', p. 66.
23. Quoted in ibid., p. 59.

5 / AN ARCHIVIST'S PERSPECTIVE ON THE WORK OF THE GPO FILM UNIT

Steve Foxon

Outside of the archive community, written accounts of film preservation work are few and far between. Coverage of the work that goes on behind the scenes is often neglected or overlooked in favour of the end result. But while it is the finished film people (rightly) want to see, it is worth remembering that without the protection of the original and its subsequent remastering or restoration there can be no film reviews, criticism or history.

In 2007, I was employed by the British Film Institute (BFI) on a project funded by the BFI, BT Heritage and the British Postal Museum and Archive with Royal Mail, to carry out a research and development investigation into the films produced by the GPO Film Unit held within the BFI National Archive. This in-depth assessment of the GPO Film Unit's output was undertaken in collaboration with both curators and technical archivists to produce a definitive report of exactly what was in the national collection and, possibly more importantly, what was missing. The goal of the project was to understand the condition of existing materials, the collection's stability and its future preservation requirements.

The collection

Using the BFI National Archive's filmographic and technical databases, alongside previously published documents, it was possible to trace the existence of 129 titles produced under the banner of the GPO Film Unit. A particularly delightful aspect of archive research is the recurring sentiment that, just when you think you have uncovered everything, something new turns up. This is, of course, a great way of disguising the fact that, while we think they are all accounted for, we would all be delighted to learn of a yet undiscovered 130th!

At first, 129 titles might seem an extremely large number of productions for a unit only in existence for seven years (an average of eighteen titles per year). However, contained within this total are a number of films that exist in several versions, each with a different title. These are quite common among film units and are usually born out of a production change when a film has been slightly modified or updated for a specific purpose or target audience. In the case of the GPO Film Unit, this occurred for three reasons. Theatrical sound films were recut and shortened for the silent non-theatrical market (operated under the GPO Film Library), films were updated some years after their original production (perhaps to reflect a price increase or change of service) and, lastly, some films were tailored into two versions (perhaps for home and overseas markets).

Of the 129 titles known to have been produced, elements relating to 128 titles can be found within the BFI National Archive's vaults. This is extremely unusual among documentary film collections and the completeness can largely be attributed to the excellent relationships, recent or long-standing, between the BFI, the Royal Mail and the National Archives. The 1958 Public Records Act made provision for officially sponsored films to be designated Public Records by the Public Record Office (PRO); from then on, the PRO contracted the BFI to preserve the designated films on its behalf. The retrospective designation and acquisition of pre-war GPO titles was among the first film priorities set by the two bodies following the passing of the Act, prints of some of them having been collected previously. Coincidentally, the BFI's own history had started at the same time as the GPO Film Unit's back in 1933. The 'missing title' is known to be *Distress Call* (1937), a shortened version of Harry Watt's 1937 classic *North Sea* (for which elements are held).

The condition of existing materials

In common with other national film archives, the BFI has always operated on the basis of careful control of access to master elements. However, due to the prominent place in film history the GPO Film Unit commands, the collection had already received a significant amount of access attention even before its arrival at the BFI, while the demand for booking of prints from the BFI has continued ever since. This has resulted in a cycle of use and reuse, whereby popular titles have been run and rerun until new prints have been required, then those newer elements have become worn out and the originals have again been called upon to provide new prints. Several key elements are in fragile condition and masters for some classic titles in a very tired and work-worn state. The project partners recognised that significant investment was required to reinvigorate the collection.

Viewing copies (positive prints on safety film stock used for exhibition) exist for nearly all titles. However, due to the popularity of the collection, nearly all these prints are very scratched, some with titles or sections missing and many with badly remade joins. Amazingly, some safety viewing copies actually date back to the year the film was produced! None of these prints would be considered acceptable for screening in any theatre of prestige and they remain available from the BFI archive largely as research copies for students wishing to view them internally on film viewing machines.

As noted, storage of the collection while in the hands of the BFI has been maintained within the strict guidelines of archive practice, but, alas, older elements were found to be

An archivist checks GPO film prints for mould. Image: Steve Foxon

suffering from natural shrinkage and showing some signs of age. Some negatives have also been found to have significant levels of mould growth on them – a good example being the oldest-known elements relating to *Night Mail* (1936). This can be cleaned and treated to buy time and allow successful duplication, but the ultimate deterioration of the originals is sadly irreversible. These are common challenges for archivists and, thankfully, the elements inspected proved to be free from both of the two familiar worst-case problems; decomposition of nitrate elements, and vinegar syndrome affecting acetates. The 2007 work on *Night Mail* allowed us to secure the print's longevity and remedy the problems facing this title by making new duplicate negatives on polyester film stock. It is the practice of the archive to ensure that for as long as the original masters are extant then we should always have the option of returning to them if the need arises. Thus, in the making of new material the original fine-grain elements were cleaned and returned to store.

It was always acknowledged that a duplication programme aiming to provide prints of every title was going to be extremely expensive. It was also suggested, therefore, that a tele-cine duplication programme should be considered as a low-cost alternative that was convenient for researchers, television, DVD, web-based media and small exhibition requirements. The laudable aim was to relieve the pressure of high demand on the original negatives. However, it must be remembered that only when a title is copied onto modern safety film stock can it be considered to be truly preserved.

New discoveries

A number of exciting discoveries were made during the research and development of the collection analysis, including the discovery of a new title, *Six Penny Telegram* (c. 1935), and the unearthing of master material for the Dufaycolor sections of *The King's Stamp* (1935) previously thought to no longer exist.

Six Penny Telegram is an animated advert with a catchy chorus tune and the slogan 'Send a Wire', promoting the nine words for sixpence telegram service. Though there are few credits on this film, it is probably safe to assume that the actual production was a collaborative exercise. And exercise does seem to be the right word, as the film uses models, stop-motion animation and optical and kaleidoscopic effects. The Unit's facilities in this period were poor and the budgets low but this only helped to bring out the ingenuity of Grierson's team – *Six Penny Telegram* is in many ways a trial of techniques that would be used to greater impact in later GPO films. As a piece of advertising, the film is certainly successful in communicating its sales message, as well as providing basic instructions on how the service works. *Six Penny Telegram* had remarkably never been catalogued under any publication or database available at the time and it was a chance enquiry from the Britten-Pears Foundation to one of the curators at the archive that set us searching for anything that had a similar title, or a variant of it, and led us to discover it. In a box of miscellaneous donations, an ex-release cinema print in extremely fragile condition was found simply labelled 'telegram'.

The King's Stamp examines the design and production of a postage stamp for the Silver Jubilee celebrations of King George V. Originally released with three 'Dufaycolor' sections, it has been rather overlooked critically because its availability was limited to black-and-white only viewing prints. Colour films and sections are significantly more expensive to produce and so in those rather cash-tight times, the library material was only ever released in black and white for researchers to view. A major investigation into 'Dufaycolor' films by the archive some years earlier had located the Dufay masters for these sections but as it was part of a different project, these sections were not known to be or identified as GPO elements. They had been donated by a film laboratory (it was normal for film units to lodge masters with laboratories and not back at the unit's own premises) and not clearly identified as part of a production. Nonetheless, the archive had cleaned, remastered and made new the colour sections which made it easy, once reunited, to reveal the original production in all its glory.

Another exciting find worthy of mention was the rediscovery of the title *On the Fishing Banks of Skye* (c. 1935) which, due to an anomaly in the records when presented to the archive, had been hidden within the spare material for *Granton Trawler* (1934). This film features a unique unscripted free-running commentary by John Grierson himself. As a student and follower of Grierson and his team it proved to be an exciting viewing session for both myself and the archive's Senior Curator of Non-Fiction Film, Patrick Russell, as we became perhaps the first people to see it in seventy years.

Ethics and the concept of restoration

Today's technology allows us to achieve a great deal more in the restoration of a motion picture. New digital techniques combined with traditional photo-chemical practices give us a wide spectrum of fine and coarse adjustments that can be altered and tweaked at the push of a button, both in the field of sound reproduction and picture stability and clarity. The danger, of course, is that it is now possible and all too easy to over-restore a film, to make it cleaner, more stable and brighter than it ever was originally. It is important, therefore, that a great deal of care and consideration be put in to what exactly one is trying to achieve when embarking upon a restoration.

Technical archivists are rightly cautious of the term 'restoration' as there are implications attached to the noun suggesting the return of something to its former, original, normal, or unimpaired condition. The concept of returning a black-and-white film to its original unimpaired condition is, of course, the ultimate aim for any film archivist, and one relishes the opportunity to do so. The key, of course, is to refrain from overstepping beyond the original condition and technical limitations of the film's day.

There is less cause for concern with a straightforward black-and-white film. The technology used then is still compatible with today's photo-chemical techniques and 35mm black-and-white motion picture film stock is still being manufactured. When dealing with restorations of colour film stocks, however, it is important, first, to identify what it is you are trying to achieve. It may be to extol the hidden beauty in the creators' original negative or master; it may be to recreate the audiences' viewing experience of the day, or perhaps simply to get the film out on the screen again with as close a representation to the creators' original as is technically possible. Whatever the reason, budget and technical capability will play a large part.

In the case of the GPO films, we had three colour formats to contend with. There is Dufaycolor, Gasparcolor and Technicolor. Each of the above presents its own unique challenges to the archivist, whose primary concern is the preservation of the unique elements of any given film.

Technicolor, at the time of the GPO's existence, was a three-colour, three-strip dye-transfer colour system needing three black-and-white matrix elements to make up one colour print. Len Lye used the system for his 1935 film *Trade Tattoo*, without having the need for a camera. Instead, he replicated the three matrix elements with black-and-white off-cuts from other GPO productions and then applied the Technicolor process, thus giving three juxtaposed black-and-white images appearing in yellow, cyan and magenta colours.

The problem for an archivist comes when you try to reproduce this today. The Technicolor dye transfer process was later abandoned by Technicolor themselves and the technology and equipment was subsequently sold to the Far East. There is even a debate today as to whether this capability still exists in the Far East. Thus, even the most recognised of our three formats can present a challenge if one is to faithfully reproduce the original. A duplicate negative can be struck on a modern colour negative film stock to preserve a representation of the image. However, in doing this the colour negative stock will introduce its own characteristic to the mix. If you take a digital copy then this will give a good representation of the original, but what of its long-term existence? With digital technology, a copy of a film can be taken straight from the original negative, or even a projection print, relatively quickly, avoiding the intermediates necessary in traditional photo-chemical work. But a digital copy can replicate an original faithfully for only as long as the format is supported by the hardware, and even then it is frequently argued that the way digital images are viewed adds its own characteristic to the viewing experience too.

Len Lye's next venture into colour was with *Rainbow Dance* (1936) and for this he made use of the Gasparcolor system. Gasparcolor was a system of three separate layers of colour-sensitive emulsion that worked by fixing one layer to the opposite side of the base to the other two. Gasparcolor films infuriated projectionists of the day because the bigger they projected the image the darker it became and the more difficult to focus correctly; it is indeed almost impossible to achieve a sharp focus on all three colours at the same time. This gives an almost 3D characteristic to the original. Making a copy of this onto new negative film stock introduces an additional characteristic to the end result and again when it is printed onto safety positive stock.

It is Lye's first film for the GPO, *A Colour Box* (1935), that presented the greatest challenge to us as archivists. *A Colour Box* was released by the GPO on Dufaycolor stock and, along with *The King's Stamp*, *The Heavenly Post Office* (1938), *Love on the Wing* (1938) and *How the Teleprinter Works* (1940), severely challenged the limits of 'restoration'. The technical make-up of Dufaycolor is discussed elsewhere in this book, but from the archivist's point of view the most important consideration is deciding what the restoration should achieve. The viewing experience of watching a Dufaycolor picture reveals a patterned réseau embedded within the picture which allows what is actually a black-and-white image to appear in colour. The challenge is that these obsolete colour formats are unavailable to the technicians of today. Dufaycolor and Gasparcolor are no longer manufactured and have been out of production for years. Technicolor can, to some extent, be recreated in appearance, but I think every archivist in the world would admit that 'You can't beat an original dye transfer print!' Gasparcolor and Dufaycolor can be copied onto duplicate colour negative stock, but this introduces a new set of characteristics (or look) to the colours. However, because this process copies across the imperfections and réseau pattern inherent in the obsolete format, the archivist prefers the term 'remastered' for this kind of 'restoration'. By duplicating master material which can be used to make further prints, we have secured the longevity of a title. It is at this point that I find myself falling on the age-old statement that, by retaining the original master for as long as is possible and creating a duplicate negative while the master is still good, we have kept all possible elements until a time when a faithful reproduction can be made with a known and stable life-span. Guaranteeing future existence of the GPO Films was, of course, the purpose of the project.

The work on Lye's *A Colour Box* is unique in that the BFI archive actually had access to the original Lye hand-painted master. In 1935, revealing the true glory or vibrancy of Lye's original was, in fact, somewhat hampered by the Dufaycolor process as Dufay required significantly more projected light to make a bright picture. The BFI archive's work on this title negated the need to use a Dufay element and the new master colour negative was taken directly off Lye's hand-painted work. In the past, such 'remastering' has received criticism because it denies today's audiences a true 'Dufay' experience. Sadly, there is no way around this problem and the archive knows all too well the dangers of branding it a 'restoration'. Dufay, as we know, is no longer available, nor is the nitrate-based stock which gave a certain look to a film when projected onscreen. Nor, for that matter, are carbon arc lamphouses which projected the light on to the screen and gave black-and-white films their distinct look. All the ingredients that added to the mix of a 1930s viewing experience have been surpassed by technical 'progress'. It is ethically contentious ground for film archivists, but what other option is there while we wait for technology to catch us up? Finance and the very nature of the National Archive's work necessitates that these films should be available to all. It is because of these releases that viewers, students and researchers are able to cast an opinion on the GPO Film Unit in the first place.

Original prints of *Night Mail* were worn by the film's success. Image: Steve Foxon

The 2-reel feature that set the Critics and all London Talking

"NIGHT MAIL"

2202 Feet "U" Certificate

Produced by BASIL WRIGHT & HARRY WATT
Supervised by JOHN GRIERSON

DISTRIBUTION
ASSOCIATED BRITISH FILM DISTRIBUTORS LTD.
Head Office—
A.T.P. HOUSE, 169-171 Oxford Street, LONDON, W.1
Telephone—Gerrard 2644 (5 lines)

Scottish Area—114 Union Street, Glasgow   Central 1436
Midland Area—88 John Bright Street, Birmingham   Midland 0451
North Western Area—11 Commutation Row, Liverpool   North 366
Free State Area—70 Middle Abbey Street, Dublin   Dublin 43450
North Eastern Area—87 Westgate Road, Newcastle   Newcastle 23920
Yorkshire Area—58 Wellington Street, Leeds   Leeds 20364
Lancashire Area—Ormes Buildings, 14 The Parsonage, Manchester   Blackfriars 0911
South Western Area—Dominions Arcade, Queen Street, Cardiff   Cardiff 7696

The restoration of *Night Mail*

Night Mail remains one of the most popular and instantly recognised films in British film history and was one of the most critically acclaimed films to be produced within the British documentary film movement. It was with this in mind that the BFI and Royal Mail set about planning a full restoration to ensure its existence for generations to come. *Night Mail* is an account of the operation of the overnight travelling post office train. It shows the various stages and procedures of that operation, through mail collection to sorting. The third sequence to the film, in which W. H. Auden's spoken verse and Benjamin Britten's music are combined over a montage of racing railway scenes, is an iconic sequence.

As with many high-demand titles, the film's popularity and commercial success has come at a price. The original masters have suffered much wear and tear and the original negatives have been lost. Most likely they were worn out and disposed of during the 1940s. The oldest elements held in the BFI archive were a set of fine-grain duplicating positives that had been struck form the original negative in 1940. It never fails to surprise people that ever-popular titles such as *Night Mail* do not actually have an original negative. The practice in the day was to use the original negative to strike as many prints as required. No expectation ever existed that sixty or even seventy years after the original production people would be still interested in them.

The new BFI restoration was a true team collaboration in a similar vein to the original production. Using many of the archive's skilled staff, it was carried out using traditional photo-chemical practices and also incorporated modern digital techniques too. The 1940 fine-grain positives were suffering with mould. However, they were free of the stickiness often associated with nitrate picture decomposition. When mould is cleaned off film-stock (it can usually be removed quite easily) there are stubborn marks left which refuse to come off. A cycle of passes through an ultrasonic film cleaning machine removed 95 per cent of the marks and, in most cases, this is usually considered acceptable. Wet-gate printing can then help to mask the remaining stubborn marks when producing new negatives. The mould will, of course, re-form on the original film stock and this, unfortunately, cannot be cured entirely. New negatives were then struck on modern polyester safety stock to take advantage of the original quality before the mould begins to return. This negative then allowed new screening prints to be made and also formed the basis of digital work.

The digital release version was made using the new polyester duplicate master negative struck from the fine-grain element. Each frame was painstakingly graded to capture the full values of the film, with strict attention paid to contrast, detail and consistency. The film underwent full digital picture restoration to remove the last 5 per cent of mould marks that were unremoved in the photo-chemical cleaning, as well as to improve torn and missing frames and address stability problems. The audio was transferred from the best possible source materials available and underwent further restoration to clean the bumps, pops, clicks, buzz and sound dips that are synonymous with early Visatone-Marconi recordings.

Our efforts to restore *Night Mail* were presented with many challenges, not least of which was having to be disciplined enough to not over-restore the film beyond the abilities and techniques that were available to film-makers in 1936. This is something we had very strong opinions about

Restoring Harry Watt and Basil Wright's masterpiece proved an arduous process. Image: Steve Foxon

and we hope that it is not perceived that we overstepped the mark. Much of *Night Mail* was filmed in daylight and amended in the laboratory to give the impression of night-time. This day-for-night photography can be completely reversed electronically and, while it is tempting to reveal the incredible detail of the daylight in 1936, we have remained faithful to the original production and graded accordingly. There are even a couple of reversed shots in the original where the LMS symbol on the driver's hat is mirrored; again, we have left these exactly as intended.

Night Mail had not been well served on DVD or video release until now. The previous releases had been taken from third-, fourth- and sometimes even fifth-generation material, giving the presentation a rather grey and flat appearance, with muddy details and poor sound. With the 2007 release, we worked hard to correct these problems and present the film in the highest quality possible. *Night Mail* now looks and sounds better than it has for many years, and the BFI release is currently without doubt the definitive version of this historic film.

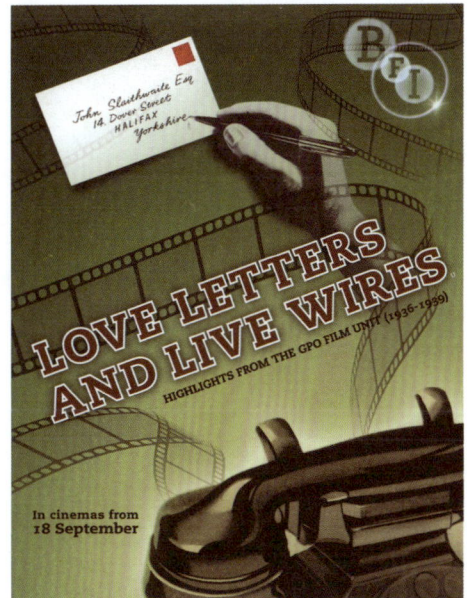

The Love Letters theatrical tour marked the culmination of the BFI's restoration project

The library

The legacy left in the care of the BFI archive is a truly remarkable one. It says something of the interest and enthusiasm the collection has provoked that, seventy-five years after the Unit's establishment, the GPO films are still in high demand. Their popularity in the early days ensured that there were substantial numbers of prints manufactured, both for theatrical distribution and the non-theatrical 16mm library. Grierson's stubborn belief in the non-theatrical market may not have generated much income for the General Post Office, but it did ensure that a significant amount of duplicate material would last into the generations of today. There is now a viewing copy in stock for practically every title in the BFI archive, be that on 35mm, 16mm, VHS or DVD formats. With the BFI's three-volume DVD set also available and a prestige touring cinema programme on offer, demand for the collection is not only as high now as it was back in the 1930s, but the archive is in a position to cater for that demand in a way that Grierson himself would have been proud of. For me, as a researcher of the British documentary movement, the collection assessment, the restorations and the subsequent DVD productions were a career highlight. I only hope when we reach the hundredth anniversary of the GPO Film Unit, the BFI and Royal Mail will consider letting me do it all again!

PART TWO

Film-makers

6 / ALBERTO CAVALCANTI

Lessons in Fusion at the GPO Film Unit

Charles Drazin

In assessing his own contribution to the GPO Film Unit, which he joined in 1934, Alberto Cavalcanti stressed the importance of his previous experience as a film-maker in Paris. That experience can be divided into two distinct phases: from 1924 he participated in the French avant-garde movement; and from 1930, as that movement began to disintegrate with the end of the silent era, he embarked on what he called the 'hard learning of sound', making eight full-length 'talkies' in France before his arrival at the GPO.[1] That move was determined by Cavalcanti's perception that the state of the film industry in early 1930s France hindered the kind of experimentation with the film medium that he had pursued over the previous ten years. In this sense, his arrival at the GPO Film Unit should be regarded less as a career break than as a decision to continue working in avant-garde, pioneering cinema. Recalling the background of his move to London, Cavalcanti commented, 'Grierson knew exactly my situation in Paris, and Grierson had agreed with my judgement on it. That's to say I was sick and tired of making talkies, and I told him. "I think sound means something else."'[2] Cavalcanti was expected to give the young film-makers of the Unit a training in film technique, but the understanding was that he would at the same time be able to pursue his goal of developing the potential of sound in the cinema.

The role of Cavalcanti as a teacher of technique and a pioneer in film style has not been disputed, but the extent to which he partook in the social aims of the GPO Film Unit has been a cause of considerable controversy. '[I]t was a great mistake to have Cavalcanti, really, because he didn't understand what documentary was supposed to be doing,' commented member of the Unit, John Taylor. 'Documentary was supposed to be for the service of the people.'[3] Paul Rotha suggested that Cavalcanti 'saw his hiring by the GPO Film unit as a stepping-stone into the

Alberto Cavalcanti

British feature industry'. He criticised the GPO films made under Cavalcanti's influence for their lack of obvious purpose: 'They each started with some universal conception and then led nowhere. It was due, perhaps, to Cavalcanti's insistence on good technique at all costs.'[4] Grierson's own pronouncements encouraged this view of Cavalcanti as the cuckoo in the documentary nest. 'The basic force behind [documentary] was social and not aesthetic. It was a desire to make a drama out of the ordinary, to set against the prevailing drama of the extraordinary.'[5] But the contradictory nature of this statement suggests the highly inconsistent attitude Grierson took to the issue. How could the 'drama' of the ordinary or 'the creative interpretation of reality' – to use another of Grierson's celebrated slogans – not be aesthetic? And just as the aesthetic clearly mattered to Grierson, in spite of his occasional denials of its importance, so too the social mattered to Cavalcanti.

While the acolytes of Grierson set documentary against the commercial features industry, Cavalcanti believed that they should be engaged in the same enterprise. The creative interpretation of reality was not the exclusive preserve of one or the other camp; it should belong to both. Cavalcanti's papers, which include his unpublished memoirs, give us some insight into his own understanding of the difference in approach.[6] Accompanying a draft chapter called 'First Work in England' is a copy of the following paragraph from Richard Barsam's book, *The Non-Fiction Film* (1973):

> Perhaps the most important difference is Cavalcanti's emphasis on the inter-relationship among the three fundamental elements of documentary film: the social, the poetic and the technical. Grierson would probably insist that the social was more important, and Flaherty that the poetic was more important; it is the measure of Cavalcanti's place in the development of non-fiction film that he emphasizes all three elements being important.[7]

The social dimension was indeed an integral part of Cavalcanti's approach to film. When he joined the GPO Film Unit, he recognised that there was a social goal to be achieved that was as much a priority as any aesthetic or technical experiment. 'The problem was visible from the outside quite clearly,' he observed. 'I knew that English cinema never showed, like the English stage since Shakespeare, any work that was dignified ... There were never dignified human beings, and that was one of the important things to achieve with documentary, and from documentary to fictional pictures.'[8]

If Cavalcanti had good reason to resent comments concerning his supposed disregard of the social, it was because he had been a pioneer of social purpose in the cinema well before Grierson had even coined the word 'documentary' – a term that Cavalcanti disliked for its narrowness. Before Cavalcanti had made *Rien que les heures* in 1926, the focus of the documentary/reality film was on far-away places – the frozen north of *Nanook* (1922) or the South Sea Islands of *Moana* (1926). But *Rien que les heures*, with its portrait of twenty-four hours in the life of Paris, was new in that it looked at the urban reality of the people who would go to see the film. It explicitly announced its mission to turn away from the glamorous figures who had previously dominated the cinema screen to look instead at ordinary and marginal lives. 'This film is not about the sophisticated and fashionable world,' an early title declares. 'It's about the everyday existence of the lowly and dispossessed.' But the real impact of the film lay in the virtuosity with which it distilled the words into moving pictures. A group of well-dressed society women gather on the steps of an elegant residence. The image freezes into a still photograph, which a hand then violently rips out of an album, tossing the scrunched-up ball on to a pile of similar rejected images.

The imaginative brilliance of *Rien que les heures* played a significant part in announcing the enormous possibilities of the cinema as a social and political tool. Shown at the London Film Society in 1928, the film introduced Cavalcanti to the future members of the British documentary movement, who enthusiastically greeted, in the words of Paul Rotha, 'the first attempt to express creatively the life of a city on the screen'.[9] Rotha singled Cavalcanti out as the only figure to emerge from the continental avant-garde of 'real documentary interest', but a significant feature of the film was the manner in which it counterpointed a factual view of the city with dramatisations of the daily lives of individual characters.[10]

In seeking to have fiction and reality work in harmony, Cavalcanti was influenced by the early films of the Soviet cinema, which the Paris ciné-clubs screened in spite of the then routine censorship of such films. He recalled the 'large fight' that greeted *Battleship Potemkin* (1925) when it was shown at the Cinéma l'Artistic on 12 November 1926. 'The noise in the cinema was deafening; the lights were switched on three times to allow the police to intervene.'[11] Cavalcanti followed the social agenda of the Soviet film-makers in taking ordinary people as his subject-matter, but also emulated them in feeling free to move between a fictional and a documentary approach. This was a point that he repeatedly stressed in interviews as well as in his own writings. At the GPO, building on the tradition of the Soviet cinema, he sought to encourage a creative flexibility that saw no fundamental distinction between the two. 'The first Soviet films that we saw in Paris – the ones that made such a lasting impression on us – were not, strictly speaking, documentary films. *But we saw them as documents.*'[12] In Britain this inter-relationship could be traced back to the founding moment of the documentary movement, when Grierson launched *Drifters* (1929) at the Film Society on the same occasion as the first British showing of *Battleship Potemkin*. The fact that Eisenstein's film was fictional – albeit inspired by a real event – did not deter Grierson from claiming it as an inspiration.

Cavalcanti regarded a fusion of forms as an inherent and felicitous aspect of film-making practice:

> I will never see the value of clear distinctions between one kind of film (documentary) and another (fictional). When we made *North Sea*, about a trawler off the coast of Scotland, we did not hesitate to *reconstruct* all the happenings we wished to show in our film – and I do not believe that this made it less real or less documentary. There are truths about the world that must be communicated in films, and we should employ – and willingly mix – *all* forms to say these truths. When we saw Dovzhenko's *Earth*, this was a completely new experience for us; maybe these were actors, but Dovzhenko was saying something to us through them (and his cameraman!) that was very true – about his country, his people and his beliefs. Most of the Soviet films that made an impression on me were similar fusions of reality and fiction.[13]

Soon after *Rien que les heures*, Cavalcanti offered another striking example of fusion with the short film *La P'tite Lilie* (1927), which featured Jean Renoir and his wife Catherine Hessling as players. It was a tragic-comic tale that – in the way of nursery rhymes turning grim history into gaiety – dramatised the words of an old French song about a sixteen-year-old girl who is pushed into prostitution and murdered by her pimp. A considerable success, it enjoyed a six-month run at the Studio des Ursulines cinema, although Cavalcanti recalled that one of the few people to object to its ironic blend of styles was Jean Cocteau, who 'alleged that a sad popular song should not be treated in a farcical sense'.[14] But *The New York Times* review of the film offered an index of the extent to which Cavalcanti had successfully challenged the established categories:

> The cinema does not rightly belong on an art page. But why should anything really beautiful be called an intrusion? Perhaps the fact that Renoir's son and daughter-in-law are actors in the *Petite Lilie* adds a reason for granting M. A. Cavalcanti's film a place in this column. Or perhaps the texture of the coarse canvas the film has borrowed from painting – to give the play, paradoxically enough, less and therefore greater reality – makes it legitimate.[15]

An important motivation for Cavalcanti's participation in the French avant-garde had been the desire to push forward the potential of the film medium. It was the same attitude that had led him in 1930 to join Paramount's new sound studio at Joinville, Paris, which had begun to produce multi-language versions of Paramount's early American talkies. Although many of his friends in the avant-garde dismissed the talkies as a threat to a pure cinema, Cavalcanti regarded them as an opportunity to develop the intrinsic properties of the cinema yet further. But it required questioning the prevailing practice. Recalling the Paramount days in his memoirs, he observed: 'The sound engineers were already difficult and tried at once to impose their value on the other crews and made themselves somehow a bit of a nuisance. Only when we used young trainees at the General Post Office in London, four years later, I realised how phoney was their attitude and treated them as they deserved ... I used bluntly to stop their fiddling by declaring: "Do it any way. If it is no good we can post-synch, can't we?"'[16] This tendency always to challenge preconceptions and received wisdom was at the heart of Cavalcanti's contribution to the GPO Film Unit. He encouraged an atmosphere of continual experimentation. The approach was that of 'Let's see ...', 'Let's give it a go ...'. In his recollections of the period, it is notable how often he uses the phrase 'study' or 'demonstration' of his work. The result was the fusion of different styles that he had so admired in the Soviet films.

Cavalcanti's first great exercise in fusion at the GPO Film Unit was that of the 'three distinct elements' which make up the sound picture, 'all of them having the same importance: words, music and noises'.[17] This sense of fusion helps to explain why he found the coming of sound exciting when so many of his avant-garde friends were dismissing it as a deadweight, reducing the possibilities of what they regarded as a primarily visual medium. The early sound films, it is true, had become static in their efforts to capture dialogue. But for Cavalcanti the great new adventure was to fuse sound and picture – neither of which had a logical priority over the other – to work in an effective harmony. When he listened to dialogue in the new talking pictures, for all their crudity, he heard not only words but also a voice. '[T]o me it was quite a wonder to listen, not only to the new voices, but also to hear the voices on the faces I knew well. That perhaps explains why my most vivid recollections of this time concerns the [actors] ... That also explains, who knows, my later experiments with voices in *Coal Face* and *Nightmail* [sic].'[18]

Sensitive to the texture of the voice, Cavalcanti was keen to explore the possibilities of variation and change. *Coal Face* (1935), which he regarded as a 'study for myself' in preparation for *Night Mail*, was notable for the range of modulation in the voices, as he sought to integrate verse, choral music and narration.[19] It was not simply a question of style; the experimentation also involved an exercise in social liberation, as he switched the perspective from the superior, Oxford accent of the objective commentator – the 'voice of God', as Grierson put it – to that of a miner relating his subjective experience.[20] In *Night Mail*, three voices share the duty of narration, Pat Jackson explaining how the letters are sorted aboard the train, Stewart Legg reciting the first half of the famous Auden poem, and then John Grierson the second, as the train passes into Scotland. Each switch represents a step up in emotional register, the final voice of Grierson himself – a Scotsman on a homeward journey – completing the transition from the objective to the subjective.

Cavalcanti was alive to how the three distinct elements of sound could blur into one another. Words were not only 'words', but also 'noises' *and* 'music' – just as 'noises' could turn into words. In *Pett and Pott: A Fairy Story of the Suburbs* (1934), which Cavalcanti regarded as another important 'sound lesson', the panting of the train carrying the commuters home becomes a rhythm that lulls them all asleep, which in turn metamorphoses into words expressing the common unspoken desire: 'The 6.15 to Sunny

Pett and Pott: A Fairy Story of the Suburbs

Green,/At home to you and seeming still,/*The Evening News* and *Standard* too,/Beside the fire, the crackling fire,/To read my *Times*.' Even the Potts' chimneypot is depicted as capable of expression. As it belches smoke, it groans at Mrs Pott's vanity in wanting a maid: 'Maid! She wants a maid!' Filmed in the summer of 1934, *Pett and Pott* was the first major sound experiment at the GPO Film Unit. Although it pre-dated the arrival of Auden and Britten, it offered important clues as to how Cavalcanti would harness them.

John Grierson's biographer Forsyth Hardy dismissed *Pett and Pott* as a 'grotesque comedy'.[21] But his comment that 'to Cavalcanti *Pett and Pott* was a bit of fun' overlooks the serious purpose and real achievement of the film. The spirit of experimentation in *Pett and Pott*, for all its crudity, was the key to advancing the medium. Critical to understanding Cavalcanti's importance is the realisation that perfection in itself was not an aim for him. Years later, he drew up a list of fourteen principles for young film-makers. The last was as follows: 'Don't lose the opportunity to experiment; the prestige of documentary film has been acquired solely by experimentation. Without experimentation, the documentary loses its value; without experimentation, the documentary ceases to exist.'[22]

It is questionable whether *Pett and Pott* can really be considered a documentary at all. It is, on one level, an experiment in the use of sound, on another a promotional film (to sell the telephone) that has the framework of a fictional story. In this respect, it anticipates another significant example of Cavalcanti-style fusion, the story documentary, which took a significant step forward in 1936 when, with Cavalcanti as his producer, Harry Watt made a short film about the Post Office Savings Bank. Instead of the usual expositional film describing a real situation with a commentary, Watt made up a fictional story about a fisherman who needs a new boat and gets the money by saving up. Much to the director's amusement, *The Saving of Bill Blewitt* (1936) came to be regarded as a landmark in the history of the British cinema. 'Such a corny story wouldn't get past the third assistant scenario editor in provincial television,' Watt wrote, 'and it is astonishing to find it described in Paul Rotha's *The Film Till Now* as "a film that was to influence others in the movement and give a line of development towards the use of story and actors."'[23]

But this 'line of development' took its most significant turn after Grierson's departure from the Unit in June 1937. The policy of the GPO Film Unit's paymasters was to support the fictional approach that Grierson had resisted.[24] After a brief interregnum, Cavalcanti became the new head of production at the Unit, which meant that the now officially sanctioned fusion of fiction and reality could express itself with a notable variety and freedom of form. There was the conventional narrative reconstruction of a trawler's rescue in Harry Watt's *North Sea* (1938), but also the modernist brilliance of Len Lye's *N or NW* (1938) and then *Spare Time* (1939), the first film to reveal Humphrey Jennings's huge individual talent, benefiting from Cavalcanti's lessons in the ease with which it was able to move between different modes of engagement.

An important feature of the fusion was its potential to appeal to audiences in the way that the more 'pure' documentary of Grierson's followers had not. Marvelling at the 'total of 1126 column-inches in the British press devoted to reviews of *North Sea*', an internal Post Office memorandum declared it to be 'the most successful documentary film produced to date'.[25] The film was only thirty minutes long, but, in Harry Watt's words, 'it was sold and people paid to see it. This was our final triumph, that people were happy to pay to see it. It wasn't forced down their necks like some handout.'[26] *The Times* was one of the newspapers of the period that helped to swell those column inches on *North Sea*. Under the headline 'Films of Fact' – a choice of words which was perhaps determined by Cavalcanti's own dislike of the term 'documentary' – it ran a feature on 'the human element' in the GPO Film Unit's output.[27] Neatly summarising the change in agenda under the new dispensation, the piece praised the progress that *North Sea* represented for the Unit in humanising its subject. 'Whereas three years ago it would have been a film primarily about a storm, today it is a film primarily about human beings and their reactions in a moment of emergency.'[28]

To the extent that an infinitely greater emergency would soon follow in September 1939, perhaps Cavalcanti's single most important contribution at the GPO Film Unit was to fashion the factual film into a tool of communication that could engage, entertain and rally the mass mainstream audience of a people at war. One of the very last documentaries on which he worked before his departure from the Unit in the spring of 1940 was *Men of the Lightship*. Using the style of dramatised reconstruction that Harry Watt had pioneered, the film chronicled an early wartime atrocity: the bombing and sinking of the *East Dudgeon* lightship on 29 January 1940. A feature of Watt's films had been the practice of having non-professional actors play the roles they might have had in real life, but the director of *Men of the Lightship* was David Macdonald, whose previous experience had been in the commercial features industry. Cavalcanti was so upset by the performance of the professional actors Macdonald had engaged for the production that he personally went down to Harwich, where the film was being made, to dismiss them all. Writing about the episode a few years later in a letter to a journalist, he recalled that it was the occasion for a comical incident: 'After a certain amount of argument on the part of the actors, the matter was taken to Parliament where a question was put and a statement made as to how two foreign gentlemen – Mr Caval and Mr Canti – came and interfered with Mr Macdonald's work.'[29] It is pleasing to be able to find in the story a personification of the quality of fusion that Cavalcanti brought to the unit. Together Mr Caval and Mr Canti were far greater than they were apart.

Notes

1. From a hand-written draft of a chapter called 'The Joinville Studios', Cavalcanti Papers, BFI Library Special Collections.
2. Unpublished interview with Barry Levine, June 1973, Cavalcanti Papers, BFI Special Collections, p. 5.
3. Elizabeth Sussex, *The Rise and Fall of British Documentary* (Berkeley, CA: University of California Press), p. 51.
4. Paul Rotha, *Documentary Diary: An Informal History of the Documentary Film 1928–1939* (Secker & Warburg, 1973), p. 130.
5. Quoted in Forsyth Hardy (ed.), *Grierson on Documentary* (London: Faber & Faber, rev. edn, 1966), p. 18.
6. Donated to the Special Collections of the British Film Institute Library in 2007.
7. Richard Barsam, *The Non-Fiction Film* (New York: E. P. Dutton & Co., 1973), p. 63.
8. Unpublished interview with Barry Levine, p. 6.

9. Paul Rotha, *Documentary Film* (London: Faber & Faber, 1939), p. 88.

10. Ibid., p. 87.

11. Draft chapter, 'The So-Called Avant-Garde', unpublished memoir, Cavalcanti Papers, BFI Library Special Collections, p. 17.

12. Notes for a talk, dated 27 April 1967, that Cavalcanti gave on the occasion of the retrospective, 'Fifty Years of Soviet Documentary Films', at the Leizig International Documentary Festival, Cavalcanti Papers, BFI Library Special Collections, emphasis in original.

13. Talk for the Leipzig International Documentary Festival, Cavalcanti Papers, BFI Library Special Collections, emphasis in original.

14. Draft chapter, 'The So-Called Avant-Garde', p. 23.

15. *The New York Times*, 4 December 1927.

16. Hand-written draft of a chapter called 'The Joinville Studios'.

17. Ibid.

18. Ibid.

19. Unpublished interview with Barry Levine, p. 11.

20. John Grierson, *Sight & Sound*, October 1934.

21. Forsyth Hardy, *John Grierson: A Documentary Biography* (London: Faber & Faber, 1979), p. 74.

22. Quoted in Barsam, *The Non-Fiction Film*, p. 63.

23. Harry Watt, *Don't Look at the Camera* (London: Elek, 1974), p. 102.

24. See Paul Swann, *The British Documentary Movement 1926–1946* (Cambridge, 1989), pp. 85–8.

25. Quoted in ibid., p. 87.

26. Sussex, *The Rise and Fall of British Documentary*, p. 109.

27. *The Times*, 28 June 1938.

28. Ibid.

29. Letter from Cavalcanti to H. A. V. Bulleid, 5 June 1944, Cavalcanti Papers, BFI Library Special Collections.

7 / HARRY WATT

On Land, at Sea and in the Air

Amy Sargeant

Harry Watt served his apprenticeship in film at the Empire Marketing Board and GPO Film Units, variously working as general dogsbody, lab assistant, editor, cameraman and writer/director, advancing, he said, more by 'luck than talent'. In turn, he oversaw the progress of junior members of John Grierson's crew. Watt provided a commentary on the activities of the Unit, delivered contemporaneously (in journal articles) and retrospectively (in his 1974 autobiography). Watt was happy to portray himself as the man 'who put the sweaty sock into documentaries' and a major proponent of 'story documentary'. But as a publicist for an enterprise dedicated towards publicity, Watt's claims (however self-deprecatingly put) deserve to be handled with caution.

Watt was the second child of a Scottish father (a lawyer who became a Liberal MP of the Asquith tendency) and an Irish mother. From his father, Harry inherited his enthusiasm for sport. At school, he became a socialist and developed his instinct for journalism, subsequently enrolling for a BA in Commerce at Edinburgh University (because he thought that the qualification would afford him the opportunity to travel). He wrote for the student magazine and invited the communist sympathiser, Paul Robeson, to address a student gathering. For *World Film News* (edited by Marion Grierson, John Grierson's sister), Watt later covered Robeson's role as the docker and tribe leader Tom Zinga in *Song of Freedom* (1936).[1] However, Watt claimed that he was no intellectual match for his contemporaries in the GPO Film Unit – citing, especially, the painter-poet Humphrey Jennings. He also remained sceptical that such figures could ever properly understand what poverty meant to those who had no choice but to endure it.

After university, Watt went to work on boats, in pursuit of a girlfriend who had gone to Canada. There he shifted about, picking up jobs at a funfair and as a waiter.

Harry Watt

Returning to London, he was hired by 'Green, the Fishmonger General' (father of the child star and adult television presenter Hughie Green) as junior partner in his various entrepreneurial schemes. Many of these proved a failure. Watt was down but not quite out when a mutual friend introduced him to John Grierson. Grierson warmed to Watt's maritime interests and offered him a place in the newly formed EMB Film Unit. Here, the 'brash, overbearing, cheeky and opinionated' youngster learned his trade, on his own admission by trial and error, from the experienced cameramen who worked on a free-lance basis for EMB, and from Alberto Cavalcanti, who came to the unit from *documentaires* and features in France. Grierson, not known for his warmth, was not a film enthusiast himself, thought Watt, but was able to inspire enthusiasm in others.

Watt's own experience of the sea prompted the invitation to assist Robert Flaherty on *Man of Aran* (1934). He spent six months working on the film commonly known as 'Balcon's Folly', increasingly frustrated by lack of progress ('I was lucky if I could carry a lens case') and by Flaherty's distortion of the lives of his subjects. Justifiably, Watt concluded that Flaherty was a romantic – in denial of a changing world – rather than a true documentarist. Flaherty rejected Watt's suggestions, refusing to concede that the islands were serviced by a steamer:

> I found out that on one of the islands ... there occurred once a year an interesting and, to me, exciting and pictorial event. All the cattle to be sold that year were herded down onto the only beach, and then pulled out one by one through the surf to a waiting steamer. The cattle sensed the danger, and went mad, so the scene became a sort of Irish rodeo. But there was also the underlying drama that the cattle represented to the islanders their total capital for that year, the proceeds of which bought the rising necessities in a changing world. A broken leg, a sudden panic in the water, and the annual ham, the oil for the lamps, the new boots for the children, would have to be gone without. And when the swell was high, there was constant danger to the men – none of whom could swim, of course – launching and relaunching their flimsy canoes, each with a battling bullock tied to the stern.[2]

Watt was then recalled, to assist Edgar Anstey (whom he replaced as director when Anstey moved to Shell) on the film *Six Thirty Collection* (1934), commissioned by the Post Office to portray the sorting and despatch of mail at the West London depot. On this two-reeler, Watt also gained his first credit as editor, thereby learning how to shoot – in future – for cutting (or, at least, how better to direct cameramen with this in mind). He never rated his own ability as a cameraman highly, being too readily distracted. With the move of the Unit to the GPO, Watt's first commission as director was a film for another institution, *BBC – Droitwich* (1935). He was also temporarily lent out to work on the canonical series, the *March of Time* (1935–51), more akin to film journalism than 'documentary' as it was understood by the Unit's intellectuals.

Night Mail (1936) is probably the best-known film produced by the Unit and probably the most loved. It also appears to exemplify the work of the Unit as a collaborative venture, with the poet W. H. Auden and the composer Benjamin Britten (who had both worked on Cavalcanti's 1935 *Coal Face*) joining forces with Watt and Basil Wright. Watt's cameramen were Jonah Jones and Chick Fowle, both former GPO messenger boys. The film's 'compellingly zesty' commentary was voiced by Stuart Legg and Grierson himself.[3] The film depicts the journey of a train from London to Scotland by

way of a litany of railway junctions, cataloguing changing accents (not entirely consistently) and landscapes, interspersed with precisely timed and coordinated operations (a bag of waiting mail is snatched from a railside gibbet without any slowing of the train's relentless passing onwards and upwards). The efficiency of the system is coupled with the sort of human detail and personal interest favoured by Watt: a farmer turning instantly to the sports page in his newly delivered newspaper and 'old Fred's coupon night', friendly banter and exchanged knowing glances between the postal workers. As it draws into Beattock at dawn, sheep-dogs race the train and rabbits scurry for cover. A mock-up of the railway carriage in which the mail is sorted was built on a cradle in the Unit's Blackheath studio (a practice employed by Cavalcanti elsewhere) and a model train was used to produce the 'clickety-clack' for the soundtrack, matched to the repetitive, rhythmic punctuation of Auden's verses, which, again, underline the personal appeal of the GPO's service:

Letter of thanks, letters from banks,
Letters of joy from a girl and a boy,
Receipted bills and invitations
To inspect new stock or to visit relations,
And applications for situations,
And timid lovers' declarations,
And gossip, gossip from all the nations,
News circumstantial, news financial,

Letters with holiday snaps to enlarge in,
Letters with faces scrawled on the margin,
Letters from uncles, cousins and aunts,
Letters to Scotland from the South of France,
Letters of condolence to Highlands and Lowlands, Written on paper of every hue,
The pink, the violet, the white and the blue,
The chatty, the catty, the boring, the adoring,
The cold and official and the heart's outpouring,
Clever, stupid, short and long,
The typed and the printed and the spelt all wrong.

Britten's scoring was augmented with the percussive sounds of chains, blocks of wood, lumps of coal shuted down drainpipes and additional whistles. The use of industrial and ambient noise (sometimes amplified) *as* music was a practice familiar to Film Society aficionados from the work of Dziga Vertov (in Russia) and Hanns Eisler (in Russia and Germany), *World Film News* carrying an interview with Eisler in May 1936. The musicologist, Kurt London, deemed the previous work of Walter Leigh and Benjamin Britten exemplary,

Night Mail

In forming the musical elements of a film into universal representations of sound. Their film music transcends the score of musical notes and absorbs within itself the sound of real life (in a stylised form), whether it be of single voices, of choruses, or of natural noises, by turning it to music and giving it rhythm.[4]

Night Mail, on release, received warm reviews from critics, including Graham Greene, at *The Spectator*, and C. A. Lejeune, at *The Observer*.[5] Somewhat perversely, but typically dourly, Paul Rotha praised it as 'a direct exposition of the spirit of an inanimate organisation'.[6] It also proved popular with audiences, with *World Film News* reporting, in June 1936, that it was booking widely and had already completed a six-week run at the Carlton: 'a record for a documentary in the West End'.[7] *Night Mail* was also successfully distributed on the non-theatrical circuit. Its subsequent reputation was guaranteed as one of the first acquisitions made by Iris Barry, as film curator at the Museum of Modern Art (MoMA), New York.

Watt praised the exemplary patronage and broad-mindedness of the Post Office as an employer of film and film-makers in the 1930s (a generosity, thought Auden, not matched by its treatment of its own employees). However, Watt also betrayed some sense of personal frustration and ambitions competing beneath the surface of the Unit's collaborative

and harmonious camaraderie. His autobiography provides a vigorous account of the practicalities involved in making *Night Mail* (including the facts that location footage was being edited while Watt continued shooting and that Watt's mother housed the crew in Glasgow when funds ran out). It also expresses resentment that Wright, whose reputation had been established with EMB's 1934 *The Song of Ceylon*, was unduly credited as Watt's co-director.

Watt found himself in familiar territory – the shore and the sea – for *The Saving of Bill Blewitt* (1936), the script of which he wrote and directed. Watt first encountered 'Bill', the Mousehole postmaster, in the local pub. In addition to essential story material (Bill queuing with children in the post office to place the 5 shillings with which he opens a National Savings account in order to save for a second-hand boat) there are shots of the community at work: laundering; wool-winding; minding the shop; quarrying; trawling; auctioning fish. Winds howl, seagulls screech and boat hulls clunk against rocks. Two upper-class visitors offer to put down a deposit of £50 on the boat when Bill can still manage only £24 14s 9d. He joins forces with his friend Joe Jago and, agreeing to a share of the catch, together they secure purchase of the *Faithful*: they would 'rather see her fishing than yachting'. Pat Jackson, serving as apprentice to the by now relatively masterful Watt, was encouraged and praised for initiative on *Bill Blewitt* – Jackson going on to direct the Royal Navy film *Western Approaches* in 1944 (similarly acclaimed by Watt). Jackson returned the compliment by praising Watt's handling of people and his use, for publicity purposes, of the story-led documentary, one advantage of which was its circumventing the need for a *March of Time*-style 'voice of God' commentary – let alone the voice of Grierson. But this was nothing new. Silent cinema exhibitors, in the 1920s, had expressed a preference for narrative films to advertise commercial interests (the 'powder in the jam' method), while Ivor Montagu had noted audience resistance in Britain to overt propaganda in favour of its incorporation into a recognisable, familiar, plot structure.

North Sea (1938), again written by Watt and produced by Cavalcanti, found Watt back in Scotland. There are lingering shots of Aberdeen's docks, houses and churchyard, the crew of the *John Gillman*, and of the wives and girlfriends the men have left behind. Interiors were, again, reconstructed in a London studio. A mixed congregation sings 'Eternal Father, Strong to Save', underscoring the action. Accents, chatter and idiom are amply recorded (a Wick Radio operator complains of 'too much blathering') and a skipper onshore immediately overcomes the superstition warning against a Friday departure when he reads the telegram reporting the *John Gilman*'s distress call: 'All around our island coast, the Post Office Radio protects our ships.' As a consequence of the success of *North Sea* in cinemas (a film which itself makes reference to cinemagoing as a popular leisure activity), Watt's introduction to features came with his appointment as second unit director on Alfred Hitchcock's Cornish smuggler saga, *Jamaica Inn* (1939), reconstructing a storm in Elstree Studio's tanks. On *Bill Blewitt* and *North Sea*, Watt cast non-actors in acting roles. In the 1970s, Watt wrote appreciatively of the use made by Bill Douglas and Ken Loach of non-actors in shorts and features.

Watt, with other GPO personnel, joined the Crown Film Unit during the war, working with Cavalcanti, Jennings and Jackson on *The First Days* (1939) and with Jennings, Jones and Fowle on *London Can Take It!* (1940). Despite evidence that the Ministry of Information (MoI) was already organising wartime film operations, Watt's memoir privileges Cavalcanti's spontaneous seizure of initiative:

> [It was] then that ... magnificent old Cav, the alien, whom some Blimps always suspected, took the law into his own hands and sent us all into the streets to film anything we saw that was new and different. Cavalcanti realised that history was being made all around us and a tremendous opportunity to record it for posterity was being lost, so six small units went out with all our film stock and filmed the extraordinary scenes of a nation amateurishly preparing its capital for a new kind of war. We filmed the frantic sandbag filling, new balloons rising up in the oddest places, endless drilling in parks, new auxilliary policemen – I remember I got a chap in plus-fours and a monocle directing traffic at Piccadilly Circus – anything that was different from the normal peacetime way of life.[8]

The First Days was bought from the GPO and distributed by Pathé, in anticipation of audience interest. People go to church on the first Sunday in September, or take to the countryside on bikes. The declaration of war is heard on the radio in a café, at home, in church or over a loudspeaker in the street. Barrage balloons are sent up, sirens go off and, good-humouredly, Londoners descend to the shelters, with the streets swamped by an almost absolute darkness: for the first time since Cromwell, theatre lights are dimmed in the West End, while in the East End, nothing can stifle the cockney voice. Pets are labelled and evacuated and the National Gallery's paintings are safely despatched to slate

North Sea

mines in Wales. The sound of London – 'London Calling' – is transmitted around the world. Reminiscent of Watt's *March of Time* experience, *London Can Take It!* is introduced and narrated by Quentin Reynolds, the London correspondent for the journal *Collier's Weekly*. The blackness of night is only briefly interrupted by flashes of searchlight and smoke. The Queen is shown surveying the damage to the streets (a cat is saved from the rubble) and the film ends with a shot of the shattered gothic tracery of the Houses of Parliament. However, its central theme is the heroism and indomitable spirit of ordinary people, who 'like great fighters, get up from the floor when they are knocked down', 'repudiating Goebbels' claim that British morale is diminished'. *Documentary Newsletter* praised the production values of *London Can Take It!*, published the Reynolds commentary and added to the film's sense of urgency, promoting American support and enlisting engagement in hostilities. Its commentary, it was remarked:

> Is in the highest tradition of good journalism while its sentiment stresses the absolute and final authority of the people of London as the front-line soldiers of the war ... the first real message from British people to American people.[9]

Following smaller collaborations with the RAF (*Squadron 992* and *Dover – Front Line*), in 1941, Watt directed the MoI drama documentary, *Target for Tonight*. Jones was re-enlisted on camera. Location material was shot at and from Mildenhall Aerodrome, with the addition of studio-shot interiors. The script was built by Watt from a cull of pilot's raid reports, attendance at pilot briefings and informal chats with everyone: 'It developed into gin with the officers, beer with the sergeants, and mammoth mugs of tea with the maintenance crews in the dispersal huts.'[10]

In 1942, following Cavalcanti, Watt re-joined Balcon at Ealing Studios, thereafter directing a succession of commercial features. Plans to dramatise the Australian contribution to the war effort did not come to fruition until 1946, with *The Overlanders*, to which Watt applied his customary documentarist's research and eye in the film's reconstruction of events drawn from the war with Japan. *Where No Vultures Fly* (1951) and *West of Zanzibar* (1953) were shot in Africa, with *The Seige of Pinchgut* (1959) marking Watt's return to Australia. Expansive locations now seemed to answer Watt's yearning for adventure, fulfilled in his youth by the sea.

Amid much high-minded theoretical wrangling and posturing over definitions of documentary during and since the 1930s, two aspects of the debate remain consistently and distinctly articulated, regardless of their combination and compromise in practice: adherence to certain final formal arrangements (here exemplified by Wright and Jennings) and adherence to certain generative procedures (here exemplified by Watt). Watt evidently held no qualms regarding studio reconstruction, where it proved a practical solution – it did not compromise the integrity of any film as documentary. In the 1930s, theoreticians of documentary took for granted the virtue of their object of study, generally sharing with its practitioners an interest in effecting social change – presumed to be for the better. However, in retrospect, I think it worth examining, coolly, the closeness of much documentary product to its less meritorious, even meretricious affiliates – advertising and propaganda. To date, commentators such as Ian Aitken, Paul Swann, Nicholas Pronay and Brian Winston have mainly debated the extent to which corporate and state sponsorship compromised the range and scope of the documentary movement. This debate reflects something of both the broader cultural anxieties and the GPO films' relative insulation from popular tastes. In the future, it may be that the GPO documentarists' dependence on patronage and the goodwill of the civic groups through which their films in their various forms were disseminated will come to be seen as portents of the problematic and blurred relationships between paymasters, producers and audiences that characterise current practices and procedures.

Notes

1. Harry Watt, 'Robeson finds Human Story of Negro Freedom in Slave Legend', *World Film News*, 1 (1936), p. 7.
2. Harry Watt, *Don't Look at the Camera* (London: Elek, 1974), pp. 57–8; for more regarding 'Balcon's Folly', see also Amy Sargeant, *British Cinema: A Critical History* (London: BFI, 2005), pp. 137–40.
3. Scott Anthony, *Night Mail* (London: BFI, 2007), p. 64.
4. Kurt London, *Film Music* (London: Faber & Faber, 1936), p. 221. Here, and in *The Seven Soviet Arts* (1937), London provides detailed analyses of German and Russian exemplars.
5. *The Spectator*, 20 March 1936; *The Observer*, 8 March 1936.
6. Paul Rotha, *The Film Till Now* (London: Vision, 1951), p. 320.
7. *World Film News* vol. 1 (1936), p. 25.
8. Watt, *Don't Look at the Camera*, p. 128. Clive Coultass suggests that Watt exaggerated the significance of their intervention: 'The Ministry of Information and Documentary Film, 1939–45', *IWM Review*, 1989, pp. 103–11.
9. *Documentary Newsletter*, 1 (1940), p. 14.
10. Watt, *Don't Look at the Camera*, p. 146.

8 / HUMPHREY JENNINGS

The Customs of the Country

Michael McCluskey

Humphrey Jennings is best known for the films he made at the Crown Film Unit during World War II. When the nation faced the threat of invasion, he projected the people's response. In the face of fascism, he hurled images of ordinary, sometimes quirky, individuals going about their day. Yet Jennings was 'more than a maker of films'.[1] When he joined the GPO Film Unit in 1934, he was already an established set designer for theatre and planned on a career as a painter. He was one of several artists brought into the GPO to help visualise the contemporary issues the Film Unit wanted to explore. He became known not for his interrogation of specific social problems, but for his evocation of British life and its many symbolic rituals. In addition to film, he pursued this evocation through other media, including poetry, painting and non-fiction writing.

Jennings's GPO and Crown Film Unit films move through urban, rural and industrial landscapes of Britain and reveal the particular challenges faced by each during the inter-war period and during the war on the home front. Throughout his career, Jennings studied the effects of industrialisation on the British landscape and people, and his films explored themes to which he returned again and again in his writing and painting: the interplay between industrialisation and identity, between technology and tradition, and between town and countryside.

Breaking down partitions

Jennings was born in 1907 in the coastal village of Walberswick, Suffolk. His architect father designed Arts-and-Crafts-style houses, and his artist mother painted and sold pottery. As a student at Cambridge University he mixed with an artistic and intellectual crowd that included William Empson, Julian Trevelyan, Michael Redgrave and Henri Cartier-Bresson. His friends and colleagues described him as a great talker whose frequent monologues were a mixed commentary on politics, art and literature. He urged his fellow artists to be modern, which, to Jennings, meant to look outward and to find new ways to capture the spirit and idiosyncrasies of the contemporary public.

Jennings saw cinema as the most direct way to tell the public about itself. He believed that documentary film should reveal the extraordinary in the everyday (in both war and peace) and show the audience that they were part of and, indeed, could shape, the extraordinary events through which they were living. Jennings acknowledged that the film-maker must craft his material in such a way as to capture the audience's attention and to make the topic relevant to their lives. In particular, he believed that the documentarist should reveal the motivations of the people onscreen, suggest the ramifications of their actions and capture what he considered to be the romance of living and working in contemporary society.

Many of his colleagues at the GPO Film Unit thought that Jennings was more interested in creating art than in creating a better society.[2] Yet Jennings saw fragmentation, juxtaposition and the experimental use of sound as a means of capturing the many facets of public life. Cinema, Jennings thought, should reveal the multiple systems and different layers of meaning operating in society. In order to affect change, the public needed to understand the embedded and intertwined assumptions about people and their physical environments. Documentary film offered a way to make visible the hidden networks that were shaping contemporary socio-economic conditions and public responses to them. Jennings's consideration of these conditions included chance encounters, common rituals and what he saw as the collective symbols of British life.

Jennings's personal, poetic style was influenced, in part, by his conception of surrealism. Jennings did not make surrealist films; however, his films share a sensibility with many of the poets and painters associated with the surrealist movement in both Paris and London. After graduation from Cambridge the newly married Jennings moved to Paris, where he met surrealist artists and tried to make a living as a painter. He returned to England and found work at the GPO with the help of his Cambridge colleagues, Stuart Legg and Basil Wright. Jennings maintained his contacts and his interest in surrealism and helped to organise the 1936 International Surrealist Exhibition in London. He eventually fell out with members of the Surrealist Group in England, who expelled him in 1946 when he accepted an OBE for his wartime films.

Jennings was particularly interested in the surrealist use of collage. Through the juxtaposition of objects not usually placed together in everyday life, surrealist collage challenges viewer assumptions and encourages the viewer to make such connections in everyday life. By encouraging viewers to see such connections in the everyday world, surrealist collage could help viewers to break visual habits and to see possibilities in everyday life that they might not have otherwise noticed. Jennings also shared the surrealist preoccupation with finding the marvellous in the everyday. Jennings looked for (and, at times, re-created) moments in public life in which objects, people or sounds seemed out of place and wove them into his films: a children's kazoo band in a murky Lancashire field, empty frames in the National Gallery, a horse bolting from a burning London building.

Such moments suggest the contingencies of everyday life, the sometimes surprising situations that must be negotiated into the individual's frame of experience. These sequences invite the film viewer to interpret the narrative and symbolic function of such ambiguous images, images that opened up Jennings to criticism from his GPO Film Unit colleagues. Basil Wright, for example, thought that the kazoo band sequence in *Spare Time* (1939) evidenced Jennings's sneering condescension towards his working-class

subjects. Jennings's intent, however, was to reveal the different actions and attitudes that constitute everyday life in Britain and to challenge assumptions about specific landscapes and populations. Jennings believed that documentary film could confront prejudices regarding different populations and break down barriers between Britain's classes and communities.

Jennings also explored the breaking down of prejudices and partitions in his work with Mass Observation, the social anthropology project that he co-founded with Charles Madge and Tom Harrisson in early 1937. His formal work with the group lasted less than a year, but the experience developed Jennings's interest in using multiple observers to document contemporary life. Mass Observation trained observers (including Jennings) to record their activities and observations in monthly reports. As Jennings and Madge explained, 'Mass-Observation is giving working-class and middle-class people a chance to speak for themselves, about themselves.'[3]

Jennings and Madge edited together observations of Coronation Day 1937 into the publication *May the Twelfth*, which juxtaposed observer reports with each other and with newspaper accounts of the day. The juxtaposition of these reports brought together different points of view, different ideas of national identity and different layers of meaning. The perspective continually shifts to reveal multiple landscapes and multiple interpretations of the meaning of monarchy, ceremony and tradition in contemporary Britain.

While Jennings's films emphasise the many identities of the British landscape and people, they also suggest the common rituals, symbols and sacrifices shared by the nation. Jennings drew on an inventory of sounds and images familiar to his contemporary audience to link the diverse sequences in his films and to suggest the commonalities of British identity. His strategy to bring together different British audiences includes references to the shared literature and history of the British people. Jennings's films refer to past military battles and struggles in the process of industrialisation, and they acknowledge the artistic responses to these events. His analysis of contemporary struggles built on the work of William Wordsworth, William Cobbett and other commentators on the effects of industrialisation on individual, regional and national identity. Jennings gathered the words of many of these commentators into *Pandaemonium*, his fragmented history of British industrialisation. *Pandaemonium* became a life-long project for Jennings that started in 1937 and remained unpublished at his death in 1950.[4] Its general theme, the effects of industrialisation on the land and people of Britain, courses throughout Jennings's films.

British landscapes

Jennings's apprenticeship period at the GPO Film Unit was guided by Alberto Cavalcanti, who remained a friend and supporter throughout his career. Jennings was eager to work with Cavalcanti, whose French films he knew through the Film Society screening of *Rien que les heures* (1926). Jennings designed the sets for the Cavalcanti-directed film *Pett and Pott: A Fairy Story of the Suburbs* (1934). Working on *Pett and Pott* instructed Jennings in Cavalcanti's avant-garde methodology for the documentary soundtrack. In one scene, the image of a woman about to scream is paired with the sound of a piercing train whistle. The sound of the machine replaces the woman's voice and signals the end to a surrealist-tinged dream sequence. *Pett and Pott* plays with the idea of the inter-war suburb as a breeding ground for uniformity, yet also suggests that deviant behaviour lurks behind the similar façades of semi-detached houses. This playfulness was typical of Jennings's later film work.

    Jennings's films use the different landscapes of Britain not as backdrops but as a means of charting the changes brought by war and industrialisation. Jennings visited the National Gallery continually throughout his life and drew inspiration from the history of art. But his set designs, paintings and films also reference the landscapes he studied on his long walks around Cambridge and the Essex countryside that surrounded his father's farmhouse. Jennings's films explore both the physi-

Penny Journey

cal and metaphorical meanings of landscape, in particular, the English countryside, the industrial north of England and the city of London. *Penny Journey* (1938), for example, tells the story of a postcard's journey from Manchester to the Sussex village of Graffham. Although the journey is brief, Jennings manages to highlight the differences between the industrial north and the rural south. The postman's round takes in the sites of the village and the surrounding landscape in static images that seem pulled from the paeans to the countryside that proliferated throughout the 1930s.

Spring Offensive

London Can Take It!

Jennings made *English Harvest* (1938) for the Dufay-Chromex production company to exhibit the results of the Dufaycolor process. Jennings chose to film labourers and their families harvesting hay on an English farm. The film luxuriates in images of the countryside. The camera captures the rhythmic movements of the farm labourers and choreographs them to Beethoven's 'Pastoral Symphony' to suggest man's harmony with the land. Both films present a nostalgic view of the rural landscape and suggest that traditional ways of life were slowly disappearing as a result of modernisation.

Spare Time (1939) documents the different leisure activities of working-class residents in the industrial cities of Sheffield, Manchester, Bolton and Pontypridd. The film marks the emergence of the mature poetic style of Jennings's best-known films. *Spare Time* uses a limited commentary by Laurie Lee to introduce three industrial regions of Britain: steel, cotton and coal. Jennings allows the sounds and images of these regions to speak for themselves. The residents do not address the camera; rather, Jennings weaves together sequences of individual and group activities into a montage of images that evoke the different interpretations of leisure time. The film does not just document workers at play. It also acknowledges the constraints placed on leisure time through the demanding work schedules and the limited public space available to these residents. The juxtaposition of the kazoo band's rendition of 'Rule, Britannia' with the image of a caged lion gestures to the cage created by this workforce's social, economic and geographic conditions. However, the film emphasises what people can create within these constraints, and it contrasts the buoyant community spirit with their dismal industrial landscapes.

Jennings communicated the changes brought to the countryside and to the city with the outbreak of war in *Spring Offensive* (1940) and *London Can Take It!* (1940, co-directed by Harry Watt). In *Spring Offensive* (above) Jennings conflated mobilisation of the land with the mobilisation of the British people. The film pairs the story of the regeneration of abandoned farmland with an evacuated boy's adaptation to the countryside. Over the course of a few weeks both the farmland and the boy become more productive under the guidance of the country people and the government land policy they follow. The film uses the erosion of city attitudes to the country (and vice-versa) to foster the communal spirit necessary for Britain's success in total war. At the end of the film the city boy is described as 'at least 90 per cent country'.

London Can Take It! depicts the damaged urban fabric but imagines the people's ability to rebuild and remain vigilant. 'London raises her head, shakes the debris of the night from her hair and takes stock of the damage done,' the commentator and American news reporter Quentin Reynolds tells us as we watch citizens adjust to the changes in their city. The human disaster is visualised through the personal items piled on the pavement outside destroyed houses. However, the city is still recognisably and determinedly London, the film shows us, despite the extensive damage done to it. The dome of St Paul's, an image of continuity in the face of change in many of Jennings's films, suggests a sense of normality amid the abnormal conditions.

Getting back to people

As Jennings described, the filming of *Listen to Britain* (1942, co-directed and co-edited by Stewart McAllister) was about getting away from landscapes and getting back to people. The film began as a record of the music of a people at war but widened its scope to include multiple sounds. Jennings and Stewart McAllister, the editor of many of Jennings's films, weaved together the everyday sounds of the British war on the home front: tanks, planes, sing-songs, dances and the wireless programmes of the BBC. Many of the sounds tell people where to go and what to do, but Jennings emphasised individual actions within the group effort to win the war: the factory girl singing as she works, the woman looking at photograph of a soldier, the man negotiating bomb damage on a walk through London.

Jennings did not approach his films with a strict list of what people to include and what those people should say and do. Because he allowed the people he encountered while shooting to help shape the film's content, he often frustrated his superiors at the GPO and the Crown Film Unit. Instead of heading out with a detailed shooting script, Jennings wandered locations, talked with people and gradually filled out his rough sketch for a film. He did not edit out imperfections; shadows, extraneous noises and unexpected movements all made it into the final cut as moments that express the randomness of life. Jennings was exacting, however, when it came to shooting sequences and capturing sounds he definitely wanted to include. He was a demanding director, but he saw film-making as a group process that involved a set of skilled workers who together crafted the final work of art.

Listen to Britain

Jennings used re-enactment in film to recreate the particular reactions to extreme moments of danger and heroism, moments that moved beyond the everyday dangers of the war on the home front. In *Fires Were Started* (1943), for example, Jennings brought together a group of firemen to document the work of the National Fire Service in defending London. The film uses re-enactment to present the real-life dangers faced by the service and to highlight

Fires Were Started

the camaraderie of the volunteers despite their different class backgrounds. *Fires Were Started* foregrounds the sacrifice of the heroic individual for the survival of the nation. From the opening title sequence, the film includes an evocative, and eerie, use of sound. A musical number staged to demonstrate class harmony ends with the wail of an air-raid siren. The silence of the men that ensues contrasts their communal song and dance; they take inventory of each other to consider who might not make it back from this call of duty (top left). The film also recognises the contribution of women to the National Fire Service. The women sit at a bank of telephones and answer calls that report on the status of fires burning throughout the city (bottom left). The importance of this communication is captured by the word 'control', which the women repeat as they answer phone calls throughout the film. The fires are under control as long as this layer of infrastructure and the front lines maintain communication.

The Silent Village (1943) is a re-enactment of the obliteration by the Nazis of the Czech village of Lidice. Jennings set the tragedy in the Welsh village of Cwmgiedd and worked with the residents to create scenes that evoke the horrors of military occupation and mass murder. In preparation for *The Silent Village*, Jennings lived in Cwmgiedd and discussed with villagers their reactions to Lidice and their likely response to German occupation. Jennings did not want to create a film that speculated on the events at Lidice. Nor did he want a film that merely acted out whatever details of the massacre were known. *The Silent Village* used the attitudes and experiences of the Welsh villagers to craft a British response to a particular historic event and to the threat of fascism in general. The film does not focus on the shock and horror of the tragedy of Lidice. It emphasises the dignity of the residents over the brutality of their invaders.

A Diary for Timothy (1946) looks ahead to the challenges of post-war renewal through the stories of a British miner, railwayman, farmer and RAF pilot. The film's commentary, written by E. M. Forster and delivered by Michael Redgrave, is directed at Timothy Jenkins, born on the fifth anniversary of the outbreak of the war. Jennings followed the lives of the four men to reveal the particular problems Britons needed to address in order to improve conditions for the next generation. Forster bristled at the choice of the middle-class Jenkins family to anchor the narrative, yet the film addresses the concerns of different classes and different regions. *A Diary for Timothy* is an account of the multiple experiences of total war and the expectations of the post-war nation in terms of health care, employment and agricultural policy. The heavy-handed message is enlivened by some surrealist sequences: a shop window filled with mannequin heads, a group of schoolboys walking through mounds of rubble, wounded soldiers performing a ballet routine.

British genius

Jennings's films gave voice to the British writers and artists he compiled in *Pandaemonium* and analysed in his literary criticism. In crafting his image of contemporary Britain, he continually drew on the tradition of British art and literature and positioned documentary film within that tradition. *Words for Battle* (1941) juxtaposed selections from British and American prose and poetry with contemporary images of the war. The words of Milton, Blake, Browning and others, read by Laurence Olivier, marked the progress made by modern Britain. Milton's *Areopagitica* is recontextualised to describe the might of the Spitfire. The excerpt from William Camden's *Britannia* is paired with an aerial shot of British land that would have taken Camden days to traverse and describe. Jennings shows the adaptability of these writers' words; descriptions written for another age are just as relevant to the wartime audience. Jennings selected the contemporary images of war from other documentary films and from archival footage. Thus, he also showed the mutability of the cinematic image and showcased the craftsmanship of artisanal film-making.

During the production of *The Dim Little Island* (1948) Jennings had one of those unexpected encounters that he often included in his films: the sight of a ship named *British Genius*. The camera's pan over the ship's name gestures to the different shades of British genius Jennings explored in this film and in *Family Portrait* (1950), his final completed film. The films, made for Ian Dalrymple's Wessex Film Productions, recognised the changes to regional and national identity fomented by international networks

Words for Battle   Family Portrait

of trade. They foreground creativity as a national resource that must be tapped in order
to fuel Britain's post-war renewal. *Family Portrait*, although formally not one of his best,
is one of Jennings's most personal films. Its commentary links contemporary Britain
with its history of invention and innovation. The portrait attempts to heal the rifts
between art, science and everyday life that Jennings saw as one of the major impacts of
industrialisation.

Conclusion

In his essay 'Only Connect', the director Lindsay Anderson described Jennings as 'the
only real poet the British cinema has yet produced'.[5] Through cinema, Jennings
attempted to connect different classes, regions and a range of personalities of a nation
he deeply loved. Like George Orwell, he did not see intellectualism as incompatible with
patriotism. His films drew on his intellectual passions and on his patriotic love of the
English countryside, the dome of St Paul's, the local pub and the British people themselves. Jennings died in an accident in 1950 while scouting for a film location in Greece.
In his pocket was a copy of *Recollections of the Last Days of Byron and Shelley*.

Notes

1. Anthony W. Hodgkinson and Rodney E. Sheratsky, *Humphrey Jennings: More Than a Maker of Films* (Hanover, NH: University Press of New England, 1982).
2. Pat Jackson, Arthur Elton, Paul Rotha and Stuart Legg, quoted in Elizabeth Sussex, *The Rise and Fall of British Documentary* (Berkeley, CA: University of California Press, 1975), pp. 158–9.
3. Charles Madge and Humphrey Jennings, 'They Speak for Themselves: Mass Observation and Social Narrative', *Life and Letters To-day* vol. 17 no. 9 (Autumn 1937), pp. 37–42, p. 37.
4. Kevin Jackson, *Humphrey Jackson* (London: Picador 2004), p. 205.
5. Lindsay Anderson, 'Only Connect: Some Aspects of the work of Humphrey Jennings', *Sight & Sound* (April/June 1954) reprinted in *Film Quarterly*, Special Humphrey Jennings Issue, vol. 15 no. 2 (Winter 1961–2), pp. 5–12.

9 / PORTRAIT OF AN INVISIBLE MAN

The Working Life of Stewart McAllister, Film Editor[1]

Dai Vaughan

The tributes to his talent – belated, sporadic – sealed Stewart McAllister's fate as the invisible man of British documentary cinema.

> Without McAllister, there would have been no Humphrey Jennings.
>
> > Ian Dalrymple

> His contribution to *Listen to Britain* was at least 50%. I mean, certainly, without Mac, it wouldn't have been the film it was. It's probably a trite thing to say that he made more contribution than Humphrey, but in a way he did.
>
> > Ken Cameron

> I don't think I knew myself just how much Stewart had given to Humphrey until he joined the Unit [i.e., the British Transport Film Unit]. Then I began to realise that what I was dealing with was – well, the spirit of Jennings, if you like.
>
> > Edgar Anstey

Does it matter?

It may be argued – and the argument has a respectable pedigree – that our understanding of works of art owes, and/or should owe, nothing to any independent knowledge we may possess of the manner of their making or of their makers' personalities. If this is the case – if, that is to say, the significance of a work is not exhausted by, and is therefore neither diminished nor enhanced by, appeal to extraneous knowledge of its author – then it is perhaps no more than a matter of verbal convenience that we choose to say, 'Here Jennings cuts from ...' and, 'Here Jennings dissolves to ...'. By 'Jennings' we mean only a sort of presumptive persona: the creative talent/talents responsible, by inference, for this film. Some of those who espouse the auteur principle might endorse this formulation. But there is surely something disingenuous about it as a justification of traditional critical practices: for, if all that concerns us is to group texts according to common signature, then why not pick on the camera-operator, the electrician, the grader? In selecting directors as auteurs, critics are acknowledging – quite rightly – that the director makes a special contribution to the films which bear his or her credit. But it is one thing to make a special contribution – even the greatest contribution – and quite another to be the sole author.

Stewart McAllister joined the GPO on 30 August 1937 in the grade of 'stills assistant', as a replacement for a cartoonist, R. Y. Ferguson, who had been employed for two months on short contract. He was paid £2 10s per week. Grierson had left the Unit at the end of June and most people seem convinced that it was Cavalcanti who gave him the job. So far as the histories go, McAllister's first work as an editor was on *Men of the Lightship*, on which he can be assumed to have begun in early March 1940. But this was a major piece of dramatic reconstruction for which a very tight schedule had been planned. It seems inconceivable that such a film should have been entrusted to someone whose capabilities had not already been demonstrated. But on what?

When it comes to documentation, technicians leave little trace. Even for films on which McAllister is known to have worked, his passage may be recorded in a bulky folder only where the request of some VIP to see the rough cut on a given date bears the laconic addendum, 'Mac says OK'. The surviving files on pre-war productions – which are few – do in some cases contain completion sheets with a space for the name of the editor; but as none of these mentions McAllister, the information they provide is purely negative. The only explicit reference to him is in a schedule of overtime worked by various people on the ARP film with the working title 'The Warning' (probably the Civil Defence film eventually released as *If War Should Come* – a title hurriedly changed, when war did come, to *Do It Now* [1939]). But this was clearly a case of all hands to the pumps.

It would be interesting to know whether McAllister had any part in the editing of *Spare Time* (1939), which is generally regarded as Humphrey Jennings's first important film. The balance of people's recollections is that he did not. There does exist a score of Handel's 'Largo' – sung by the choir in the Welsh sequence – which has pencilled on it, in addition to Jennings's jottings for which shots should go where, some more formal notes – 'End of Scene 6', etc. – in McAllister's hand. But this may simply mean that he was in charge of the ordering-up of optical – as he is said to have been on *The First Days* (1939). At all events, this film did not see the beginning of close association between McAllister and Jennings. Geoff Foot was to cut *Spring Offensive* (1940, alternative title, *Unrecorded Victory*) and Jack Lee *Welfare of the Workers* (1940).

Maurice Harvey says that McAllister made no contribution to the editing of *The Islanders* (1939), which he cut himself, and doubts whether he did any serious editing until at least the middle of 1939. One informant – whose memory has proved on the whole trustworthy – supplied a neat solution to the problem: McNaughton had fallen ill before the completion of Harry Watt's *Squadron 992* (1940), McAllister had taken over and finished it, and Cavalcanti – who had not previously considered McAllister a potential film editor – was so impressed with his work that he gave him *Men of the Lightship* to do. But McNaughton does not remember this, Cavalcanti denied it, and the records make it look very much as if the cutting schedules of the two films would have overlapped. Perhaps it happened on some other production. Or perhaps, after all, *Men of the Lightship* really did mark an unheralded and dazzling debut for McAllister.

The bombing of the *East Dudgeon* lightship happened on 29 January 1940. A letter to the Admiralty of 12 February indicates that a script for a film of the incident is being prepared by Hugh Gray; and an Admiralty reply of 13 February recommends that emphasis should be placed on the fact that lightships constitute a service to neutrals, not just to British shipping. The film was directed for the GPO by David Macdonald, who had worked with Cecil B. DeMille in the early 1930s and was responsible for such British productions as *Dead Men Tell No Tales* (1938) and *The Midas Touch* (1940). According to Watt, he just walked in and asked for a job. It would be interesting to know how McAllister, who was apparently in the habit of referring to features people as 'lice', took to this. *Men of the Lightship* 'was directed in a very straight, featurey way', remembers Joe Mendoza (formerly an assistant with the GPO/Crown Film Unit).

> Mac played hell with the editing of it to give it a bit of vim. And David MacDonald argued with him and fought with him about it; but Cavalcanti – well, I just think he's the greatest film-maker there ever has been – he stood by Mac, you know; and Mac shot a lot of extra shots and inserts and cuts and stuff after David was off the picture; and Charles Hasse, who was the director [i.e., second unit director] was kept on, and did a lot of cut ins: so that the film was very much made in the cutting room by Mac: it's got that kind of stringency, that acerbity – not from David MacDonald, but from Mac's editing.

The manner in which *Men of the Lightship* was modified in the editing may be illustrated by the sequence where the lightship is threatened by a drifting mine. What happens in the script is as follows. A few shots of people carrying out maintenance on the lantern and the engine lead into a major dialogue scene, below decks, which opens with a close shot of a concertina played by Lofty (one of the crew) and ends with his being sent up to empty the slop-pail. Then:

> On deck. Lofty throws the slops into the wind, and they blow back into his face.
> CS Lofty wipes eyes and sees (off-screen) mine. He calls, 'Fetch Skipper!'
> CS George shouts down the hatch for Skipper.
> INT. Skipper writing in book. He goes up.
> MS George and Skipper hurrying from hatch.
> CS Skipper and Men. 'Where is it?'
> and only then do we
> CUT to LS Small black object floating in sea.

In the film, however, what we get is:

> Some chat between two men as they service the lantern ('Coming round the King William tonight?' 'If we get back in time.')
> LS Mine (to which we cut as if it were in some way cued by the dialogue – and the more unexpected for that).
> LS Lightship, seen from a low, 'bobbing' position – i.e. from the mine's 'point of view'.
> CS Skipper writing in logbook.
> CU 'Crew ready for relief by Argos ...'
> Closer LS Mine
> Closer LS Lightship
> Below: Man oiling engine – slowly, meticulously.
> MS Mine ...

There is nothing extraordinary about this. Few directors insist upon the letter of the script; and to create anticipatory tension by intercutting is a familiar enough device. The pay-off comes with the next cut: from the closest shot of the mine, with its detonator studs clearly visible, to Lofty's fingers pressing the studs of his concertina. It is to this end that the premonition of the mine has been introduced: a truly alarming juxtaposition which owes its force to our recognition of a purely visual, formal metaphor.

There is another point to be made about this intercutting. Whereas in the script our 'sighting' of the mine is coincident with the men's, in accordance with the principles of psychological realism, the film as cut, by anticipating the sighting and by adopting the 'viewpoint' of an inanimate object, is placing itself in the distanced position of the teller of tales. And when Lofty does react to the offscreen object, what we first cut to is not the mine but a squabble of gulls: so that, at precisely the moment the man is accorded recognition of the mine, we are denied it.

Target for Tonight (1941) offers plentiful evidence of this tendency in McAllister's editing. Like *Men of the Lightship*, *Target for Tonight* faces the problem of what to do about material which, while

Men of the Lightship provides a vivid illustration of McAllister's editing skills

necessary to the telling of the story, might seem to entail the assumption of an impossible (i.e., enemy) viewpoint. Here, even more than in the earlier film, McAllister's solution has been to go for abstraction. This, again, draws attention to the status of the images as being – while obviously keeping their own referential relationship to a prior world – a part of the telling, not a part of the told. There is no possibility of our constructing – or believing that we are being required to construct – a common reality encompassing the re-enacted British and the German actuality material in *Target for Tonight*.

The climax of the bombing raid in this film provides an even sharper insight into McAllister's handling of documentary material for the construction of narrative. On the approach to the target, as the bomb-aimer is saying, 'Steady – steady ...', there is a very strange cut on the pilot from a low-angle close shot to a level close-up: a cut which, in most contexts and especially at the time, would be considered unacceptable. In itself, this might be seen simply as adding an edge of discomfort to the dramatic situation; but it is matched shortly afterwards by an almost equally peculiar cut, from profile close shot to frontal close-up, on the helmeted silhouette of a German A-A officer: and we notice that, while the cut-in on the pilot has immediately preceded the release of the bombs on to the target, the cut-in on the German immediately precedes the gun-burst which will damage the *Wellington*.

However, this use of a self-conscious editing device to state a parallelism in the action does more than underline the mutuality of war; and it does more, too, than block any suggestion of shared linguistic status between the newsreel and non-newsreel elements, the German becoming thereby purely emblematic of opposition. It performs a function which goes to the heart of the relation between documentary and narrative. Had it been a feature film, F for Freddie would at the very least have had to beat off an attack by German fighters as she limped home on a defective engine. The fact that this does not happen maintains the documentary response whereby we grant the events a different level of credence from that of fiction. But aesthetic satisfaction cannot be won by purely negative means – by the repudiation of those internally generated (or generically conditioned) expectations which form the structuring drives of drama as we know it. Something must replace them. In *Target for Tonight* they are replaced by a formal symmetry between the first half – briefing, take-off, journey out, bomb on target – and the second half – *Wellington* damaged, journey back, landing, debriefing. And the parallel between the close-up cuts on the pilot and the A-A gunner, emphasising the mirroring of attack and reprisal, serves to signal this structural symmetry: serves, that is, to provide us with the option of alternative satisfaction (the formal) to those (of dramatic escalation) which we will be denied.

For want of a better word, I have spoken of 'symbolism' in discussing how McAllister, in the very act of insisting upon the documentary status of his images – upon our reading them as the footprints of elusive beasts – is able to bend them to the purposes of simile, of punctuation, of differentiation between levels of discourse, of markers of the architecture of form, and so forth: functions which, in mainstream film-making, might soon overburden the easy trade it assumes between narration and narrative. McAllister seems to recognise in his editing practice, regardless of whether or not he ever formulated it outside of that practice, the essential antipathy between documentary and realism. Jennings's practice – particularly as revealed in such a film as *Words for Battle* (1941) – tends towards a form of symbolic usage; but whereas the 'symbolism' of McAllister was, on the whole, transient and generated from within the text, that of Jennings consisted more in the importation of associative, connotative meanings from the wider sphere of culture and history. The two were to prove compatible. Indeed, it may well be that in this tendency towards symbolic working we see the common ground – the aesthetic and procedural as opposed to the ideological/personal common ground – for the Jennings/McAllister partnership.

By the time we come to the central films of the oeuvre, the partnership is such that we sense no distance between the contributions of the two men. If we wish to explore further the ground – filmic as opposed to personal – on which Jennings and McAllister met, let us look again at the opening of *Listen to Britain* (1942): at the cut from a Spitfire to the dipping wheat. In one sense, this might be considered simply a cut for 'action continuity'; but at the same time, it would seem an evasive and somewhat arch way of stating the idea of low flight in a fiction film, where the option of actually shooting a plane depressing the wheat could be assumed to have been available. Much of the unfailing effect of this cut lies, in typical McAllister fashion, precisely in the reverberations which are set up between the simple referentiality of the shots and the signification implied in their use: so that the juxtaposition of Spitfires and wheat becomes not only an ideogram of low flight but, in a retrograde movement from this to its component images, a statement about the relation between our air defences and the earth's bounty which – for example – may lead us to understand this idyllic landscape as representing also the nation's food supplies.

Here and there, in *Fires Were Started* (1943), there are passages whose success we may be inclined to attribute to one or the other partner. When Heavy Unit I sets out for the fire, and we are given a succession of close-ups in which only Jacko – the one marked out for death – is seen against a background of flames, this is surely Jennings at work. Or it could be Pennington-Richards, the camerman. On the other hand, between the discovery of Jacko's helmet and the dispirited scene where the men lie exhausted on their bunks is a brief sequence of shots consisting of the ammunition crates which have been saved from detonation, the sign 14Y at the station entrance (as seen by Barrett when he arrived), the gateway of the station with dust blowing past it and, finally, a blossom-laden tree. These shots – which gain much of their force from the fact that they are totally detached from the implied perceptions of our protagonists – look like another example of McAllister making poetry out of trims and offcuts. But it could easily have been Jennings's idea. Again, the transition from the expository 'training' sequence back to the action at 14Y is marked by a mix from a low-angle shot of two extension ladders, reaching towards each other in chevron, to the clock in the mess-room with its hands registering 'one': virtually a compositional inversion. Here there is no question of the ladders symbolising a clock or the clock hands symbolising ladders. Nevertheless, it is more than a piece of geometrical jokery. The suggestion is present that it is only a matter of time before the men will be climbing such ladders in earnest. In addition – and here we are reminded of the twin jump-cut in *Target for Tonight* or of the paraffin lamp and radio valve in *Listen to Britain* – the juxtaposition serves a structural purpose: by drawing attention to itself, it punctuates the return from the expository to the narrative emphasis in what might otherwise have seemed an uncomfortable slurring. We almost hear the new sequence 'click into place'.

> They fought like cats. 'Cause they were both completely different – yet very similar. I think they both wanted the same thing – just went a different way round to get it. When a film was being cut, Humphrey and Mac were always in the cutting room together. I think that's why this curious amalgam of the two personalities came through. I mean, Humphrey didn't script the following day's work and leave Mac to cut it. They worked together all the time.
>
> Ken Cameron

> Mac was always hammering on about how he wanted it to be, and how the structure should be. They were a very good partnership, because they had great respect for each other; but they disagreed a very great deal. Their way of making progress was arguing *against* each other; and if they could beat the other one in argument, they thought they'd won.
>
> Sir Denis Forman (Chief Production Office, Central Office of Information, 1947–8)

> I realised how intensely serious he was about his editorial work. I am sure he felt that he was carrying the full weight of every production, and I once heard one of his seniors giving him a vehement telling-off for imagining that he was the only person who mattered in the Crown Film Unit.
>
> William J. MacLean

The non-representability of the technician's experience reaches beyond the literary genres. Time after time, when people were talking to me about McAllister, they would tail off and gaze into the distance with a slight frown, as if looking for something they knew was there but had unaccountably mislaid. It was a look I came to recognise. Had McAllister been a director, people would have brought to mind things he had said and done which could be construed as illuminating his preoccupations, style or methods. But for an editor the model of the demented artist was not found proper. His unremitting application was therefore perceived – or rather, one might say, had been entered into the brain's index – as eccentricity; and what was recalled about him were the stories – good pub anecdotes – which had accreted around this. Of course, everyone knew there was really more to it. That was what they were seeking when the look crossed their faces. But the 'more' seemed no longer to be there.

One might almost say that McAllister is not remembered at all. What is remembered is a scattering of incidents in which he figured. Moreover, I had somehow imagined, at the beginning, that with sufficient perseverance I would at least discover the 'facts' of his life. Only gradually did I realise that a process of irreversible information-decay had already been at work, and that many of these facts no longer existed in any form, physical or mental. This was brought home to me by Ken Cameron saying, of *Listen to Britain*: 'Of course, everything you see now of it comes from a dupe. It's a good dupe, but nevertheless it's a dupe. The original neg was lost. It was sent to America during the war, and I think it was sunk, or something happened to it.'

But it is not only onlookers, close or distant, who cannot avail themselves of the unifying 'artist' model for McAllister. It was not available to him, either. And this absence of a socially sanctioned model – this 'ideological blur', as I have elsewhere called it – may explain the constant tendency of his behaviour towards forms of excess. Many administrators have untidy desks; but few have pyramids reaching to the ceiling. John Legard tells, with wry retrospective affection, how Mac once grabbed him by the lapels and shook him, furious because he had inadvertently borrowed a couple of shots from his rushes. Joe Marks describes a gloomy man – 'never called me by my first name, just "Marks"' – making life a misery for all around him with a pettiness well beyond the demands of budgetary sense. Ian Dalrymple has a story of McAllister, having set out at 3 a.m. to investigate some local branch line on foot, being discovered in his garden at 8 o'clock photographing tulips. These excesses represent a curious disengagedness from the expectations governing normal conduct, and an inability to handle them. Jenny Stein mentioned an occasion when, some years after her marriage, while her children were still young, McAllister paid her a visit. 'He'd brought a big sack of oranges for the children. It was really a rather extravagant present; and I didn't quite know how to receive it. I didn't know how to receive it because he didn't know how to give it.' His isolation from social norms had trapped him into a cruel paradox whereby – and I have encountered many examples – his attempts to reach out to other people were seen only as 'symptoms' of his loneliness.

Perhaps one thing can be guessed with confidence. In view of his failure with women – a failure which seems to have shown some promise of reversal only in his last few years – we may reasonably assume that the most important relationship of McAllister's life was his working partnership with Jennings. (It was a partnership which he had every reason to think would continue. Anstey says that 'Humphrey Jennings was going to do a picture on the history of the railways, which – contrary to many reports of the time – he was very excited about … He and I talked about it two or three times; and immediately prior to the trip he went off on, when he got killed, we'd had a session … So I was pretty certainly seeing Mac also at that time.') If it is true that, as Dalrymple observed, 'without McAllister there would have been no Humphrey Jennings', it is certainly also true that without Jennings there would have been no Stewart McAllister. It is not easy to find the ideal complementary talent to one's own; and for an editor, the 'secondary' character of his or her role makes it more essential than for a director. Several accounts mention McAllister's reluctance to talk about this partnership. Yet what could he have said? To the extent that he was himself a part of what his questioners meant by 'Jennings', he could scarcely go along with the mythologised reality: Jennings as a personage, *fons et origio*, back-formed from their own experiences of the films. Yet at the same time he could not disassemble the myth without being, within what he knew to be his questioners' terms, disloyal to Jennings's memory. As this point, I suspect, McAllister must have begun to seem invisible to himself.

Note

1. Selections from Dai Vaughan, *Portrait of an Invisible Man: The Working Life of Stewart McAllister, Film Editor* (London: BFI, 1983), prepared by the editors.

10 / JOB IN A MILLION
Evelyn Spice at the GPO

Barbara Evans

In a review of new documentaries released in 1934, film-maker, historian and critic Paul Rotha enthused:

> It is in the last film of the group, *Weather Forecast*, that we find sound entering into an imagistic sphere. Directed by Evelyn Spice, the second woman director to emerge from Grierson's banner,[1] it tells the story of the collection and dissemination through Post Office channels of information relating to weather conditions ... Spice's shooting is worth careful watching. She is bringing something to her handling of documentary material, particularly human material, which [until now] we have been unable to get.[2]

These comments highlight two of the qualities Evelyn Spice brought to the British documentary group at the GPO – her singular ability to portray the daily life and work of ordinary men and women on film and her enthusiastic dedication to the developing art of film sound.

As the sole Canadian and one of the few women in the group, Evelyn Spice's journey from her roots in the Canadian West to an integral position in the Grierson coterie at the GPO at first glance seems an unlikely one, but in fact those very roots were to prepare her well for her future documentary career. Born in 1904 to a farm family in Yorkton, Saskatchewan, in the heart of the wheat-growing prairies, she completed her studies at the University of Manitoba before beginning her working life as a teacher in a one-room rural schoolhouse, an experience that would find visual expression in a later film, *Prairie Winter*.[3] But Evelyn's dreams and ambitions lay well beyond the country schoolroom and in 1929 she graduated from the acclaimed School of Journalism at the University of Missouri, one of the first of its kind, where she had found herself a pioneering woman among the men in the programme, no doubt good preparation for the predominantly male working environments she was later to encounter in the world of documentary film production.

Her first full-time reporting job was at the Regina *Leader-Post*, in Saskatchewan's capital city. As jobs for women were scarce, she accepted, though reluctantly, a position as social reporter. But covering social events was not how Evelyn Spice intended to spend her working life. Luckily, fate soon intervened in the guise of a young English journalist who was visiting Regina at the time. The young woman was Marion Grierson, the younger sister of John Grierson, the British documentary movement's founder. With Marion's encouragement, Evelyn decided to take the adventurous step of travelling to England and, in 1931, as she later recalled, acting on 'impulse, inspiration of unknown source' she embarked for London 'on a trip of discovery'.[4] The two women were to remain close friends over the years, co-directing the 1937 *Around the Village Green*, a documentary that took a prescient look at rural depopulation.[5]

Soon after Evelyn's arrival in London, Marion introduced her to John Grierson. He invited her to the film unit, his interest piqued in part because of her experience with the new 'American' approach to journalism. Walter Williams, the influential founder and first dean of her alma mater, the Missouri School of Journalism, had authored *The Journalist's Creed*, which included the following principle:

> I believe that the public journal is a public trust; that all connected with it are, to the full measure of their responsibility, trustees for the public; that acceptance of a lesser service than the public service is a betrayal of this trust.[6]

Williams believed in 'a greater, finer and more useful journalism,' and his statement of journalistic ethics was to influence Evelyn profoundly throughout her film-making career. With this background, she joined the group of documentary film-makers surrounding John Grierson, as one of the earliest members of the group.[7]

From the very start, she found the intellectual and creative milieu she encountered in London inspirational and exhilarating, filled with the kind of progressive ideas and spirited debate on which she thrived. The young members of the British documentary movement felt themselves on the brink of a new and exciting world filled with boundless creative possibilities. As well as such documentary film-makers as Basil Wright, Edgar Anstey, Harry Watt, Marion and, of course, John Grierson, her circle included thinkers and artists like Benjamin Britten, who was to compose the music for her later film *Calendar of the Year* (1936), W. H. Auden and Aldous and Julian Huxley. Carl Dreyer might stop by, or Moholy-Nagy, or the composer Paul Hindemith. Subsequently, Alberto Cavalcanti and the New Zealander Len Lye joined, as well as the brilliant animators, Lotte Reiniger and Norman McLaren, the latter of whom subsequently rose to fame with the National Film Board of Canada and who worked as Evelyn's assistant on the film *A Job in a Million*, which she directed for the GPO in 1937. Friday night film screenings were arranged, followed by lively discussions in the local pub. From correspondence we know Evelyn immersed herself in the political and artistic culture of the day, avidly reading Marx and Lenin and enthused by the Soviet film screenings she attended. Later, Evelyn described the excitement and sense of community and camaraderie she felt there as akin to what must have been experienced by the Bloomsbury Group or members of the Algonquin Round Table.

As well as intellectual inspiration, other attractions were at work. Marion Grierson married Donald Taylor, another member of the Grierson group. Evelyn was to marry fellow Canadian cameraman, Lawrence Cherry, and John Grierson himself had married Margaret Taylor, Donald's sister, although he disapproved of couples working together and kept his own marriage to Margaret, who worked with the group, a secret for eighteen months.

Although Spice's best-known work was done with the GPO, her development as a film-maker, as with most of the members of the group, can be traced back to its origins with its predecessor, the Empire Marketing Board. The line of distinction between production at the EMB and the GPO was often blurred as the people involved were largely one and the same and production overlapped. *The Song of Ceylon* (1934), which is credited as a GPO film, had actually begun with the EMB as its sponsor but was completed at the GPO, where its soundtrack was created. Even Evelyn, when recalling her work in the two units, sometimes confused the two, recalling the first film she had directed, *Fenns* (1932), as a product of the GPO when in fact it had been produced under the auspices of the EMB. As Rotha says, most of them could not have cared less about Empire butter or Empire lumber, but were enthused by the possibility of making films with a social purpose.

At first, Evelyn acted in a secretarial capacity for Grierson, answering the telephone, performing typing and filing duties and, as she later recalled, just being useful. This may seem surprising for a woman with a degree in journalism, but her recollections appear to be without rancour as, in fact, Grierson put many of the people he hired into menial caretaking jobs before rising to loftier positions. And, as an added bonus, working with the Grierson group in whatever capacity gave Evelyn the opportunity to immerse herself in the world of film-making, editing 35mm footage from the EMB's *One Family* (1930) into silent films for distribution to schools since, as she noted, there was little original film being shot at the time.[8]

Among the earliest films Evelyn directed was the delightful *Spring on the Farm*, made in 1933, part of a series produced for children on agriculture in Great Britain. The film included many of the signature touches found in her later work at the GPO. The film critic of the *Manchester Guardian* praised it for conveying 'a strong sense of the business of preparing to live' including it in a number of films 'that show that powerful drama is to be found in everyday work'.[9] According to the programme notes, *Spring on the Farm* would be 'a revelation to many to see how numerous and varied are the activities of farm life'.[10] This no doubt reflected Evelyn's early farm experience in Canada.

The EMB and its film unit were laid to rest in 1933 as a result of government cuts. Evelyn attributed its demise in part to Canada's decision to no longer support it with funds. 'So goodbye EMB,' she later wrote. 'What now?' She recalled the apprehension experienced by members of the group over their uncertain future. 'There were some anxious times,' remembered Evelyn, 'until it was finally settled. The unit was to go over to the GPO.'[11] Sir Stephen Tallents, the director of the EMB, had made it a condition of his appointment to the Post Office that he bring his film-makers with him.

With the change, the group moved not only to bigger premises but also into sound in an expanded way. Evelyn described the new premises on Tottenham Court Road as two floors of offices, 'some of them, and even corridors, turned into cutting and writing rooms'. The group also had studio space in South London at the old Blackheath Art Club building, founded in 1885 as a residential arts club with studios and a gallery. And, with the GPO, there was more money which, although they were all still working for minimal wages, Evelyn felt provided them with more leeway to experiment with sound. It was around this time, too, that Alberto Cavalcanti arrived at the GPO, bringing his interest and experience in sound and the avant-garde to the group.

An article entitled 'Successful Women: Evelyn Spice' in the 26 November 1936 issue of *The Lady* provides a profile of Evelyn and, at the same time, a glance into the working environment at the GPO:

An image of Spice which accompanied the article about her in *The Lady*

'Spice', as they call her, in the college manner, at the Unit (the whole atmosphere there is of an austere and enthusiastic laboratory in one of our older universities), is a Canadian, and something of a surprise. One imagines a woman film director (if one has ever imagined such a being) as something crisp-voiced and hectoring, in trousers. But Evelyn Spice is a gentle-looking young woman, with soft fair hair and a soft Canadian accent; no one could be shy or frightened of her. This partly explains her success in making country folk and workers act without self-consciousness, and in conciliating people who began by declaring that they wouldn't have films messing up *their* office or factory or kitchen or farm.[12]

Evelyn Spice always maintained that she never found being a woman in a male-dominated environment a problem. According to her son, Bill Cherry, 'She felt that the group was working together towards something new, a common goal, that they were in a process of discovery ... There was no time for back-stabbing or gender politics. They were ahead of their time.'[13]

The film for which Evelyn Spice is perhaps best remembered today is *Weather Forecast*, one of the first of the group's films, she noted, to have 'interesting work on the sound track'. Completed in 1934, *Weather Forecast* exemplifies the qualities she brought to bear on all her films: a keen observational eye, a careful attention to sound and its creative potential and a regard for the commonplace activities of everyday life. With typical modesty she claimed that though she was named as director, she always felt that the film owed its existence to a teacher in the north country who had suggested the idea.[14]

Once again she was paired with George Noble, the veteran cameraman she had worked with previously on *Fenns*. Intriguingly, Evelyn's description of how she came to direct *Fenns* gives a glimpse of the almost casual way Grierson could hand out assignments. She had been running the switchboard 'very badly' she recalled, 'until one day chance sent me out into the Fenn country (no one else available, I expect)', with Noble. Her outsider's eye, she considered, gave her a fresh perspective on her subject matter. 'It was lovely footage,' she said, '– as I remember Grierson saw a film in it. It was due, I am sure, to the fact that I saw the lowland country with the eyes of a stranger – the windmills, the old grist mill, the wind in the willows and stirring the waters of the canals.'[15]

An amusing portrait of George Noble, one of the camera stalwarts of the GPO, was later given by Harry Watt, who described him as 'a bit of a rogue who always wore the same dirty shirt. And had great success with women, which infuriated the male members of the group,' perhaps indicating the existence of a certain amount of male rivalry in the Unit. Noble's favourite utterances were, according to Watt: '"All right, what've we got today? None of this arty-farty nonsense. You know George's motto 'Dead on and pin sharp'. None of these bloody low angles and high angles. I've got a hangover." But having said that, he'd go out and work like hell to get the stuff.'[16]

Describing the warm working relationship she had with John Grierson, Evelyn later wrote:

> As a producer, he cut through to the essence of the matter ... immediately, decisively. It was a pleasure to run footage with him, for he put you right ... often with one short sentence. You could see, immediately, what the film needed; and take heart, and go and do.[17]

She recalled the financial crises faced by the group. 'Grierson had to convince people in government that this unit was a good thing. He needed films to show. At this time there was a desperate need for *Weather Forecast*. Apparently it did its job,' she noted, referring to the film's successful reception.[18] Documentaries like *Weather Forecast* could play in theatres throughout Britain, including the commercial cinemas of London's West End.

Up until then, documentary sound in Britain had been used for mainly descriptive, expository purposes. The arrival of Alberto Cavalcanti heralded a new interest in exploring the potential of sound for the British documentary film-makers and Spice paid special tribute to his contribution towards the success of *Weather Forecast*, 'teaching and inspiring us to use sound imaginatively'.[19] Although the original use of sound is the element of *Weather Forecast* that is most frequently cited, the visual and narrative aspects of the film should not be overlooked. Rotha praises the film, among a group of documentary films he especially singles out, for its skill in photography and experiments with filters, artificial lighting and cameras.[20] '*Weather Forecast* is just as thrilling as a gangster film' said one critic.[21] 'A grand film ... it has a natural drama of its own which has been handled with great skill and no fatuous emphasis on "the perils of the deep" and all that stuff,' wrote another.[22]

Spice worked in a straightforward and unembellished, low-key style, eschewing the romanticisation and dramatisation of much of the work of the British documentary movement. In the spirit of George Noble, the camera is positioned most frequently at eye level, avoiding dramatic angles. *Weather Forecast* demonstrates Spice's concern with process, close-ups of isobars and teleprinters are intercut with shots of the commonplace activities of ordinary people, whether women workers in the telegraph office, the fisher-man bringing in his nets or the farm woman whose washing is buffeted by the storm, a far cry from the pickaxe-wielding miner of *Coal Face* (1935), the noble worker of *Industrial Britain* (1931), or the dramatically photographed herring fisherman of *Drifters* (1929). John Grierson himself lauded Evelyn as the woman who 'brought into focus for the first time in the simplest way, the simple proposition not just that the working-class were fit to put on the screen, but there was a drama on the doorstep ... that there was drama in the ordinary ... poetry in the ordinary'.[23] He noted that in embarking on the film, she had asked herself, 'Who depends on storm signals to guide them in the every-day tasks of making a living or maintaining a home? What are these people like? Where do they live? What do they do? Armed with this information,' he continued, 'she set out with a cameraman, photographed people in their natural haunts ... and built up a film that was hailed for its human quality.'[24]

Evelyn recalled the collaborative nature of her fellow film-makers in the rush to finish the film:

> Everyone helped in its final hours. The negative cutters worked through the night – and Arthur Elton helped to find a substitute shot, when the chosen one could not be located in the negative! It was hand-joining, with paper clips holding the film down on blotting paper.[25]

The film's release was greeted enthusiastically. An article in the *Yorkshire Post* compared Spice's work positively to the romanticism of Robert Flaherty, calling *Weather Forecast* 'quite the best documentary' the critic had seen, commenting effusively on the film's soundtrack:

> Miss Spice has recognized that a talking film is composed of a sound sequence and an image sequence, but that these two sequences are not necessarily bound together in a purely literal relationship. Images can be shown unaccompanied by their natural sounds, and sounds can be heard unaccompanied by their natural images. This divorce is easier to manage in a documentary than in a dramatic picture, but in it, I feel sure, lie the seeds of nearly all real progress in talkie technique. It represents, roughly, a progress equivalent to the progress in music from unison to harmony.[26]

Telegram from John Grierson to Evelyn Spice informing her of the success of *Weather Forecast*

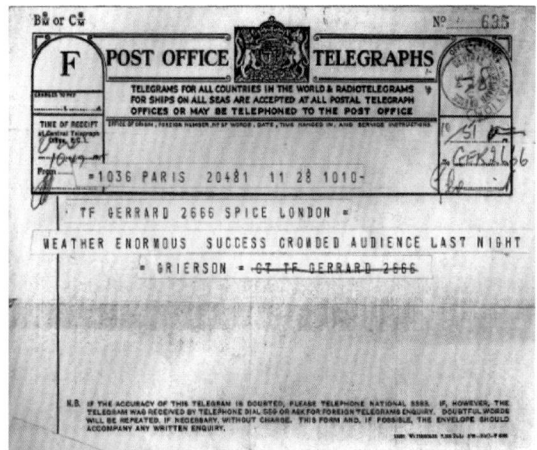

Although the ground-breaking nature of *Weather Forecast* may not be immediately apparent to the contemporary eye, at the time its 'expressive' and 'experimental' use of sound was widely admired.[27] Echoing the glowing responses of other critics, Rotha, writing in *Sight & Sound*, praised the film, calling it 'an entry into a new and immensely exciting world where anything might happen':

> Sound used thus in documentary opens up a new vista for experiment and theory, making illustrative music and the old-fashioned narrative commentary as obsolete as a pre-war movie ... As in the growth of silent documentary, so in sound has the Grierson unit, collectively and individually, shown the opening to new and intensely interesting developments, which are likely to be received with enthusiasm in every quarter where cinema is intelligently understood.[28]

John Grierson extolled the film, saying 'there is more exciting discourse on sound in Cavalcanti's new film *Pett and Pott* and in Evelyn Spice's *Weather Forecast* than anything I could possibly define'.[29] Rather amusingly, though, the inherent danger of voiceover narration that could be perceived as stating the obvious, even while attempting to be poetic, was all too apparent at one screening. The first words of the film, 'The weather is always with us', evidently provoked outbursts of laughter, accompanied by cries of 'You don't say, mate!' and 'No, really?' from the audience.

It should be emphasised, though, that Evelyn's interest in the creative use of sound was not simply a result of Cavalcanti's influence, but had been forged in her earlier film, *Spring on the Farm*, which features many innovative touches on its soundtrack, working in playful counterpoint with the images to project a sense of youthful spontaneity and joyous exuberance, its feeling of freshness and newness underscored by its 'novel use of sound from spinet, harp, a boys' choir and laughing children'.[30] The commentary is spoken with the delightfully unaffected voice of a child – a far cry from the standard, frequently authoritarian, male voice that was to feature in so many of the group's films over the years.

Discussing Evelyn's background in journalism in relation to her particular film-making abilities, Paul Rotha observed:

> In the British school it is curious to note how the women directors have been more successful than the men in handling people. Evelyn Spice, in 'Weather Forecast' and her farm films, and Marion Grierson have both, I suggest, handled their characters with greater sympathy than is found in other documentaries ... Spice shoots her material almost carelessly, with little or no attention to fancy tricks or camera set-up. But what she loses in style she more than gains in human values. More probably, the success of these two directors is explained by the fact that they came to documentary from journalism. Interviewing and reporting were familiar jobs and they carried this valuable experience into the cinema.[31]

The journalistic experience she had gained in small-town Saskatchewan was to benefit her work at the GPO. During her holidays from the 'Old Mizz' School of Journalism, Evelyn had worked as a reporter in the small town of Yorkton and she gave credit to the human drama she encountered there as influencing her later film-making practice:

> She had to cover everything that could bear the light of print: fires, police courts, fairs, calf shows, political meetings, ladies' teas, weddings, funerals. After numerous associations with such

a wide assortment of topics and people her perspective on life increased tenfold, giving her a sure foundation for her future work.[32]

Certainly this real-life experience would have provided her with a unique slant on the world that neither Grierson nor any of her other film-making colleagues at the GPO could rival.

In the following years, Evelyn continued to make films for the GPO, including *Calendar of the Year*, which traces the effects of Post Office telecommunications on people's daily lives over the space of a year, and the dramatised documentary *A Job in a Million*, the story of a young lad's training to become a Post Office messenger boy. And, like other members of the British documentary movement, she also made films outside the GPO, working with Strand Films, headed by Paul Rotha and, later, Stuart Legg, and the Travel and Industrial Development Association, where she made *Around the Village Green* with Marion Grierson in 1937. All of her future films were to bear the hallmark concerns with the drama of everyday life and the expressive use of sound which had marked her career at the GPO.

Evelyn continued working in London until 1939 when she and her husband, Lawrence Cherry, made the difficult decision to return to Canada, 'as war became more and more imminent, and the populace was being fitted for gas masks', she wrote, observing that 'vital changes were taking place in the film industry as a whole'.[33] She was in all likelihood referring to her fear that more overtly propagandistic films would become the norm, a prospect she viewed with abhorrence.

On her return to Canada, Evelyn lamented the loss of the worldly environment she had left behind in London and often longed for the intellectual and creative excitement she had found there. But her early experiences with the EMB and the GPO, where she had been 'schooled in the techniques and philosophy of the documentary film ... embodying all the arts, and bearing a considerable responsibility to society' were to remain an influence through all of her future film-making activities.[34] She continued making films under the name Evelyn Cherry, having been advised, to her chagrin, that for the sake of her career, it would be expedient to go by her husband's name. Her work was to take her, along with Lawrence, to the newly formed National Film Board of Canada in Ottawa, established by John Grierson in 1939, and later to their own production company in Saskatchewan, Cherry Films, where she worked until her retirement in 1985.

Notes

1. The other, and first, woman director to whom Rotha refers was Marion Grierson, who worked with the British documentary movement but whose films were produced outside the GPO.
2. Paul Rotha, 'Documentary – Some New GPO Sound Films', *Sight & Sound*, Autumn 1934, p. 118
3. *Prairie Winter* was made in 1935 with Scottish film-maker Jenny Brown, independently of the GPO but contemporaneously.
4. Evelyn (Spice) Cherry, *Biographical Material, 1970–1980* (Ottawa: National Archives of Canada), 21 February 1974, p. 2.

5. Evelyn Spice and Marion Grierson were to co-direct a later film, *Around the Village Green* (1937), for the Travel and Industrial Development Association (TIDA), which worked closely with film-makers from the EMB and the GPO.
6. Ronald T. Farrar, *A Creed For My Profession: Walter Williams, Journalist to the World* (Columbia: University of Missouri Press, 1998), p. 203.
7. Ibid., p. 3.
8. Cherry, *Biographical Material*, p. 1.
9. '"Weather Forecast", John Grierson's New Films', *Manchester Guardian*, 26 October 1934.
10. Programme notes '"Weather Forecast" Series of Six Short Super Films' (London: New Era), no date.
11. National Archives of Canada, Evelyn Cherry Fonds, vol. 32, File 32-2.
12. 'Successful Women: Evelyn Spice', *The Lady*, 26 November 1936.
13. Conversation with Evelyn Spice's son, Bill Cherry, 5 May 2010.
14. Cherry, *Biographical Material*, 11 October 1968, p. 2.
15. Ibid.
16. Elizabeth Sussex, *The Rise and Fall of British Documentary* (Berkeley, CA: University of California Press, 1975).
17. Letter from Evelyn Cherry to James Beveridge in response to a request from Beveridge for her recollections of her time with the British Documentary Movement (Ottawa: National Archives of Canada, 29 November 1974), p. 3.
18. Cherry, *Biographical Material*, 11 October 1968, p. 2.
19. Ottawa, National Archives of Canada, Evelyn Cherry Fonds, vol. 32, File 32-2.
20. Paul Rotha, *Documentary Film* (London: Faber & Faber, 1952), p. 157.
21. *Evening Standard*, 20 October 1934.
22. Programme notes for '"Weather Forecast" Series of Six Short Super Films'.
23. Text of speech given by John Grierson in Regina, Saskatchewan (University of Stirling, Grierson Archives, no date, pp. 5–6).
24. John Grierson quoted in an article entitled 'Human Quality', probably from the *Winnipeg Free Press* (newspaper cutting from Evelyn Spice's personal papers, no date).
25. Cherry, *Biographical Material*, 11 October 1968, p. 2.
26. *Yorkshire Post* (30 October 1934, newspaper cutting from Evelyn Spice's personal papers).
27. 'Unusual Films – Edinburgh Guild's Season Opens', newspaper cutting from Evelyn Spice's personal papers, no date.
28. Rotha, 'Documentary'.
29. John Grierson, 'Introduction to a New Art', *Sight & Sound*, no date, p. 104.
30. Programme notes to a screening of a series of 'Six Short Super Films'.
31. Rotha, *Documentary Film*, p. 150.
32. 'Prairie Winter is background for an enterprising young Saskatchewan woman who is engaged in "shooting life"' (Philip A. Novikoff, *The Country Guide*, no date).
33. Cherry, *Biographical Material*, 21 February 1974, p. 2.
34. Ibid., 1 September 1977, p. 2.

11 / THE JOY OF DROOLING

In Praise of Len Lye

Kevin Jackson

Leonard Charles Huia Lye: born Christchurch, New Zealand, 5 July 1901; died New York, 15 May 1980. Painter, film-maker, sculptor. And many other things: ferocious autodidact, traveller, amateur ethnologist, print-maker, prose-poet, book designer, psychological and biological theorist, bohemian, breath of fresh air. In the eyes of some admirers, a modern shaman.[1] During the first mature stage of his artistic career, he was a pioneer of 'direct cinema' – the art of creating films without the use of a camera. In later years, he was a major presence in the world of kinetic art, and of sound sculpture.

For good or ill, he has been credited as the progenitor of the modern-day music video – one reason why it was MTV which sponsored a retrospective of his work at the Pompidou Centre in 2000. There is a case to be made that he was also – via a degree of influence on the American film-maker and occultist Harry Smith – a force behind the psychedelic light shows of the late 1960s.[2] And, for those who care about such things, Len Lye has long been regarded as an antipodean jewel in the crown of the GPO Film Unit.

Yet Lye has never enjoyed much more than a coterie species of fame outside his native land. Only a few of his films were commercially available, and to grasp the bulk of his output you usually had to rummage in film archives, haunt art galleries, or pirate VHS tapes. It was a glum fate for the work of such a generous and genial talent. But all that has changed, changed wonderfully. Lye's early films have started to be made available in gloriously restored versions on DVD – notably in the admirable GPO Film Unit collection *We Live in Two Worlds*, which includes *Rainbow Dance* (1936), *Trade Tattoo* (1937) and *N or NW* (1937), as well as essays by Lye's biographer and most important critic, Roger Horrocks.

Still more encouraging are developments in cyberspace. Thanks to YouTube, anyone with access to the internet is now no more than fingertip away from just about everything that Lye directed. Questions of lost royalties aside, this development would surely have delighted Lye, a democratic spirit who always sought the largest possible audience for his works.

In the 1930s, he was certainly – like Cavalcanti and Jennings and William Coldstream – one of the vivid talents who helped confound the received idea that John Grierson's band of boys and girls were dour souls. Only four of Lye's films were directly sponsored by the Unit: *A Colour Box* (1935, 4 minutes), *Rainbow Dance* (5 minutes), *Trade Tattoo* (5 minutes) and *N or NW* (7 minutes). It seems, though, that the Unit and its allies also helped Lye find other sponsors throughout this lively period: the Imperial Tobacco Company for *Kaleidoscope* (1935, 4 minutes), Shell-Mex and BP for his stylish collaboration with Humphrey Jennings, *Birth of the Robot* (1936, 7 minutes), and Imperial Airways for *Colour Flight* (1938, 4 minutes).

This is, to be sure, a modest sum, even when augmented by the two non-commercial films Lye made in these years (in 1934, the 3-minute *Peanut Vendor*, aka *Experimental Animation*, which showed a monkey puppet dancing to that jazz tune, and in 1937 *Full Fathom Five*, with a young John Gielgud reading three passages from Shakespeare). But it is work of enduring value, and without Grierson as patron it seems most unlikely that Lye could have managed it. His filmography tells the tale: Lye spent the better part of five years fruitlessly trying to find backing for his films after completing *Tusalava* in 1929. Grierson was the right Maecenas at the right moment.

Lye made his major public debut with a screening of *Tusalava* at the London Film Society on 1 December 1929. It was not a wild success, though it affected some viewers powerfully. One of them was Lye's future wife Ann, who reported that it gave her goose bumps. Another was the influential Bloomsbury art critic Roger Fry, who was moved to write Lye a letter:

> I thought you had seen the essential thing as no one had hitherto – I mean you really thought not of forms in themselves, but of them as movements in time. I suspect it will need a new kind of imagination to seize this idea fully but you are the first as far as I know to make a start.[3]

A lot of viewers, however, were left baffled and disconcerted. The Lord Chamberlain's office placed a temporary ban on screenings, suspecting that it must in some elusive manner be indecent, and all about sex (which, in a very broad sense, may be true. *Some* kind of reproduction is at work ...). Though *Tusalava* had a few more screenings over the next couple of years, it became pretty much a lost film until 1967, when Lye introduced it to an enthusiastic audience in Canada.

It is no wonder that early audiences found the work baffling. *Tusalava* draws heavily on a body of images that few viewers of the time would either have recognised or relished: on the one hand, what would then have been termed the 'primitive' forms of Maori, Australian Aboriginal and Samoan art; on the other, 'primitive'-flavoured European modernism *à la* Gaudier-Brzeska. In Lye's words: 'To get the spirit of the imagery I ... imagined that I was myself an Australian Aboriginal who was making this animated tribal dance film.'[4]

Lye had laboured on the work for two years with a concentration that bordered on the heroic. Between 1927 and 1929 he sketched some 8,000 basic drawings for the nine-minute film. His ambition, he explained, was to make a film about the 'beginnings of organic life'. And the title? '*Tusalava* is a circumspect Polynesian word [in fact, a Samoan word, or words: *tusa lava*] inferring that eventually everything is just the same.' Lye continued:

> *Tusalava* opens with dots rising in a black panel, left, as the script writers say, while a cog-chain affair rises straight up in a black strip, right. In the white space centre, two grubs arise and assume a fertility pose (whatever that is) whereupon the dots in the panel become trapped in a cocoon which extrudes a huge grub … The grub divides. One half absorbs the other, and then becomes metamorphosed into a cross between a huge spider and an octopus with blood circulating through its arms. Finally, this anxiety thing attracts an embryo token figure that has developed in the cocoon and the scene ends with dots and welling circles. Life's gone full circle. The End.[5]

'Grub' is an exact term, here: part of this *Tusalava* imagery was derived from an article about the Australian Aboriginal deity the Witchety Grub, which he had seen in *National Geographic* magazine.

Half a lifetime later, in the late 1960s, Lye met a scientific documentary-maker called Sen, who was at work on a film about microphages. Sen pointed out to Lye how similar his creatures were to viruses as viewed through electron microscopes. And soon after this, an article in *Life* magazine showed Lye the similarity between his beings and antibodies. Lye was enchanted by these resemblances. For him, it confirmed that putting oneself in touch with what he termed 'the Old Brain' was a mode of authentic revelation. Lye's 'Old Brain', his custom-built version of the 'Unconscious', is a repository of wisdom to which everyday consciousness has no means of access, but may be reached in trance states. As far as one can judge, his belief in Old Brain wisdom was quite real, not just a fancy way of talking about artistic inspiration. Hence the temptation some have felt to speak of Lye's art in the same breath as shamanic rituals.[6]

His background, though, was more suburban than tribal. The Christchurch in which he spent his childhood was, in the words of Katherine Mansfield – who soon fled it – 'a little land with no history', a land that knew nothing of 'ghosts and unseen presences'.[7] Or much, come to that, of the arts. Lye's childhood was financially impoverished, too. His father had died of tuberculosis when he was only three, leaving his mother Rose Ann to do what she could to support herself and two young boys. There was one notable year of respite, from 1908 to 1909, when the family moved to Cape Campbell lighthouse; the boy Leonard was enthralled by the sunlight, the sea, and the life to be found in rock-pools – all images which vivify his later paintings.

With almost no hints, cues or encouragement from those around him, he had determined by the age of thirteen to be an artist, and sought out tuition. He was lucky in finding a sympathetic teacher, a Mr H. Linley Richardson, who, as Lye recalled, 'gave me the great revelation … by telling me that a person who had his own theory of art, right or wrong, was better than he who was sweating it out with someone else's theory'.[8] (Compare William Blake: 'I must create a system, or be enslaved by another man's': *Jerusalem*.) Hunting around for scraps from which a Lye Theory might be cobbled together, he hit on the idea that it might be possible to 'compose' motion as one composed music – this being the art of the choreographer, of course, as well as that of the film-maker and the kinetic artist. And he noted that the body tends to respond to exterior motions with motions of its own – a kind of physical empathy. This was enough to start with, and he launched a hunt for the books that might help him develop these nascent theories.

Two titles stood out. One was Ezra Pound's study of the Vorticist sculptor and draughtsman Henri Gaudier-Brzeska; another was Freud's *Totem and Taboo*, which he read in the mistaken belief that it would have something to say about dance. But the most important encounter of his teenage years was with the art of the South Pacific, which was easily available in New Zealand's museums. He also managed to see an Australian documentary film, *Pearls and Savages* (1921), which included some ritual dance sequences from Papua New Guinea. It was this screening which fired him with the ambition to explore the effects of motion in film.

In 1922, he travelled to Australia, where he soon landed a humble job in a Sydney firm that specialised in making commercials. In his freer moments, he could watch animators at work; and in the evenings, he sometimes stayed on in the offices, making scratches on to black leader and projecting the results to see how they looked. Promising, but not satisfying, was the answer. Restless, he resolved to travel on to Samoa and experience Polynesian indigenous cultures at first hand. This he did so enthusiastically that it aroused the anger of the local administrator Major-General Richardson, who considered Lye a troublemaker and resolved to be rid of him. By this time, Lye had been reading about the activities of the Meyerhold theatre in Moscow, and was attracted by the prospect of working with the company. The artist and the government man negotiated, and in the end Lye was given a free pass back to Australia. There, he spent a year working at manual jobs and saving enough money to devote several months in 1926 to drawing and sculpting. His ambition, he recalled, was to have done with European artistic traditions entirely, so as to concentrate, as he put it, on 'black art'.

In September that year, he met a drunken ship's stoker in a bar, bought the man's papers for five pounds, and worked his passage – not to Russia, after all, but to London – carrying with him little more than a few drawings and a few pounds. But his head was teeming with visions and inspirations: Meyerhold and Vorticism, Samoan and Hawaiian *tapa* patterns, cave art and ritual dance, the mysteries of motion. It was time to pass from apprenticeship to creation.

When Lye arrived in London, he made an immediate and powerful impression – colourfully dressed, 'zany', often laughing. As the painter Julian Trevelyan recalled: 'He was like a man from Mars, who saw everything from a different viewpoint, and it was this that made him original.'[9] He fell in with a group of artists and intellectuals living in Hammersmith and Chiswick, including the poet Robert Graves and Graves' lover Laura Riding, and he threw himself into a frenzy of painting pictures, designing book covers, working in batik, assembling 'constructions' of earth and stone ... and drawing *Tusalava*.

He had hoped that the nine-minute film he created would be the first panel of a cinematic triptych, but the lack of popular response sent him back to his other projects. He designed books for the Seizen Press, run by Graves and Riding, and wrote a book himself: *No Trouble*. And he began to slap paint straight on to celluloid – an activity so enjoyable, he said, that it made him 'drool with pleasure'.

A Colour Box was his first film to be seen by a mass audience – a direct film, of abstract images painted directly onto film stock, set dancing to the music of 'La Belle Creole' by Don Barreto and his Cuban Orchestra, and transferred to Dufaycolor for exhibition prints. The purity of the exercise – as with all his other GPO productions – is mildly, but only mildly, compromised by the inclusion of a plug for postal services; otherwise, it was unadulterated Lye. And, for many viewers, wildly impressive. One reviewer said that 'You've never seen a colour film until you've seen a Len Lye effort.'

Not everyone was enraptured: 'After watching the waves, stripes, blobs of violent tints, suggesting tartan, bandanna, boarding-house wallpaper, fruit salad, chromatic spaghetti and an explosion in a cocktail bar, I half expected to find myself coming to in a dentist's chair.'[10] But this was a minority view. As Roger Horrocks and others have pointed out, most previous animators had tried and rejected the technique of direct cinema, finding the instability and roughness that inevitably came of hand-painting wholly unsuited to their aesthetic of smooth surfaces and geometrical perfection. It took Lye to appreciate that the jitter and flicker of this method had a merit of its own – a merit akin to the expressive coarseness of jazz instrumentation. It might be said that Lye's work is the among the best of all visual evocations of jazz – at least, of jazz in its upbeat, witty, life-affirming dimension – and it found a comparably broad public. The critic David Curtis once noted that *A Colour Box* was seen by a larger audience than any experimental film before it, and most since.[11]

Lye's next GPO film was even more impressive: a miniature ballet, performed by just one dancer – Rupert Doone – against a constantly changing backdrop, and to the sounds

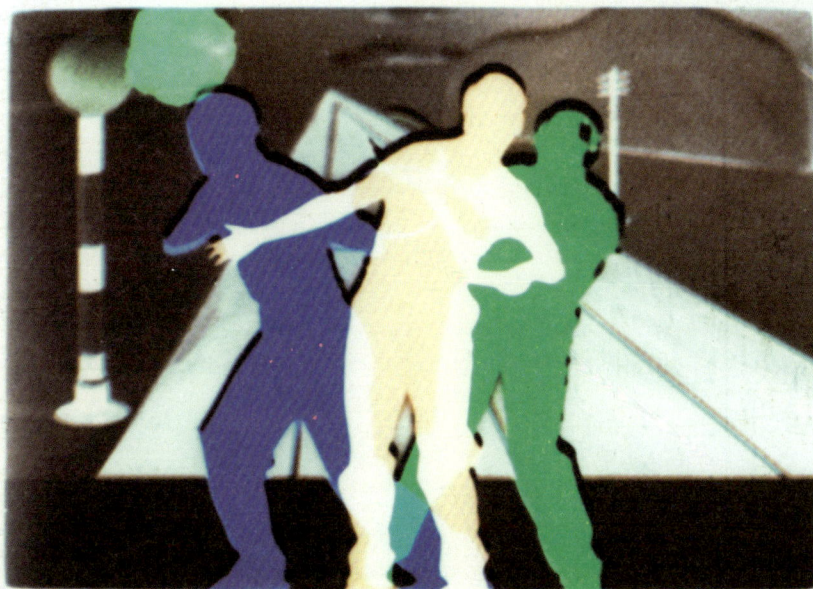

Rupert Doone, formerly of the Ballets Russes, performed the cinematic ballet that is *Rainbow Dance*

of 'Tony's Wife' by Rico's Creole Band: *Rainbow Dance*. The brilliance of the colours here, and the unflagging invention of their patterning can still astonish. Lye shot Doone's movements in black and white, and then used the three matrices of the Dufaycolor process both to fill in Doone's silhouette and to provide a contrasting set of colours and other images for the backgrounds. Doone's actions are simple enough: he is seen doffing his raincoat and umbrella after a storm, taking off for a country hike, fooling around with a tennis racket – but the complexity of the whole is quite dazzling. The only moment of bathos comes at the very end, where a announcer's voice delivers in received pronunciation the commercial sting: Post Office savings can provide everyone with a pot of gold at the end of their rainbow.

Trade Tattoo follows much the same technique, though in this instance Lye did not shoot any original footage, but used various offcuts from GPO productions – about furnace work, the docks, the railways and the postal services; he also floats in animated words, some of them simply free-floating verbal tokens from the world of business correspondence – 'inst.', 'ult.' and so on. The moral is that one must post mail on time in order that the nation's producers can maintain their vital rhythms; again, it is Lye's alchemical transformation of everyday sights that stays in the memory.

Lye's swan-song for the Unit – *N or NW* – was a departure from the earlier work in several ways: it was shot in black and white; it used actors and dialogue; and it told a whimsical little story – of a lover's tiff that threatens to grow into a full-blown separa-tion. Cupid, in the form of an attentive GPO employee, saves the day. It is deliberately daft, and the lead performances, by non-professionals, are probably even more comic than they are intended to be. Otherwise, it is a remarkable little work, and one that seems to have been strongly influenced by Lye's recent association with the British surrealists.

Most of *N or NW* is resolutely non-realist; shot from 'impossible' angles, multilayered with superimposed hand-writing, or mounted in dream-like images where mysterious fragments of faces appear from behind giant sheets of writing paper. The heroine's first attempt at a reproving letter to her beau is filmed from beneath a glass screen – an anticipation of Clouzot's *Mystere Picasso* (1956). The passage of a letter across London is conveyed by a shot of a post-box, dancing in mid-air as it whizzes through the streets. Only at the end, as the lovers are reconciled for an idyllic sunny day of swimming, does the style become orthodox. Unless, that is, one is tempted to read the otherwise innocent image of the family of swans as being somehow – in a way that would cheat the Lord Chamberlain – 'about sex'.

N or NW was far from being the end of Lye's film career. Over the next few years he made *Colour Flight* (1939), *Swinging the Lambeth Walk* (1940) and *Musical Poster # 1* (1940) before joining forces with Realist Films to make shorts for the Ministry of Information and others: *When the Pie was Opened* (1941), *Newspaper Train* (1942), *Work Party* (1943), *Kill or Be Killed* (1943) and *Cameramen at War* (1944). In 1944 he moved to New York, where he made many episodes for the famous *March of Time* series until 1951, at the same time as working with the literary critic I. A. Richards on some educational films about the world language system of Basic English that Richards had developed with C. K. Ogden, William Empson and others.

N or NW brought out the uncanny in badly addressed envelopes

In later years, he was able to return to his pre-war vein of direct film and experimentation: in the 1950s, he made *Color Cry* (1952), *Rhythm* (1957), *Free Radicals* (1958) – probably the most famous of his later films, and made by scratching shapes onto black leader – and *Peace* (1959), a commission for the United Nations. His other arts took priority for the next two decades, and he only came back to cinema at the very end of his life, with a revised version of *Free Radicals* (1979), *Particles in Space* (1979) and *Tal Farlow* (1980) – left incomplete at the time of his death, and taken over by his assistant Steven Jones and his widow.

Late in life, musing in prose about the 'meaning' of *A Colour Box*, Lye suggested that what was really important about it was 'the joy of drooling over colour. Maybe that's it – the joy of drooling?'[12] As far as the higher modes of criticism are concerned, the emotion of joy has long been an unfashionable one, particularly in the context of abstract art forms, which are usually encountered and praised in terms of spirituality (Kandinsky), existential heroism (Pollock) or existential-heroic spirituality (Rothko). But for those who can still tolerate the notion that simple pleasure is a wholly legitimate end of art, Lye's work needs no special pleadings. Thanks to new technologies of distribution, his work is nowadays beginning to find an ideal audience – a large and creative one that not only enjoys Lye's verve and invention, but is taking cues from his methods and producing all manner of responses, tributes and reworkings. Most of us still need to know a lot more about him; but otherwise, the future for Lye's reputation, like *Rainbow Dance*, looks refreshingly bright.

Notes

1. See Barbara Rose, 'Len Lye: Shaman, Artist, Prophet', in Jean-Michel Bouhours and Roger Horrocks (eds), *Len Lye* (Paris: Editions du Centre Pompidou, 2000), pp. 216–22.
2. See Rani Singh (ed.), *Think of the Self Speaking: Harry Smith, Selected Interviews* (Seattle: Elbow/Cityful Press, 1999), p. 44, and William Moritz, 'Len Lye's Films in the Context of International Abstract Cinema', in Bouhors and Horrocks, *Len Lye*, p. 195.
3. From a letter dated 3 November 1929 cited by Roger Horrocks, 'Len Lye: Origins of his Art', in Bouhours and Horrocks, *Len Lye*, p. 178.
4. Cited in Jonathan Dennis, 'Tusalava', in Bouhours and Horrocks, *Len Lye*, p. 184.
5. Len Lye, 'The Tusalava Model or How I Learnt the Genetic Language of Art', unpublished essay, 1972, cited in Dennis, 'Tusalava', p. 184.
6. A speculation: Lye may well have discussed some of these notions with his close friend Robert Graves, the poet, who from the early 1920s onwards was trying to articulate a theory of poetry which proposed that the 'inspired' poet was in a state of mind identical to that of the entranced shaman – though Graves used the term 'witch doctor'. Graves was prompted to write in these ways after many discussions with the great anthropologist and healer Dr W. H. R. Rivers, whose own working term for the Unconscious was 'the Unwitting'. See Martin Seymour-Smith, *Robert Graves: His Life and Work* (London: Paladin, 1987), pp. 96–9. Graves, incidentally, also introduced Lye to T. E. Lawrence – Lawrence of Arabia – who admired the New Zealander greatly.
7. Cited in Wystan Curnow and Roger Horrocks (eds), *Figures of Motion: Len Lye, Selected Writings* (Aukland: Auckland University Press, 1984), p. x.

8. Cited in ibid., p. xi.
9. Cited by Horrocks, 'Len Lye – Origins of his Art', p. 178.
10. Cited by Jonathan Dennis, 'A Colour Box', in Bouhours and Horrocks, Len Lye, p. 192.
11. Ibid.
12. Cited by ibid., p. 193.

PART THREE

Key Documents from the History

of the GPO Film Unit

KEY DOCUMENTS FROM THE HISTORY OF THE GPO FILM UNIT

As well as their cinematic work GPO film-makers were also active, often prolifically, as writers and theorists of film. The following pages collect a selection of these writings alongside the kind of ephemeral documents (letters, memos and promotional material) which allow us a unique insight into what it was like, and what it meant, to work on documentary films in early twentieth-century Britain. The selection includes previously unpublished memoires by sound technician Ken Cameron and a history of the Unit by film critic Forsyth Hardy, alongside articles from the film magazines – *Cinema Quarterly*, *World Film News* and *Documentary News Letter* – which the GPO film-makers were associated with as editors or as regular contributors.

GPO

A DISPLAY OF POST OFFICE SOUND FILMS
will be given in
KING GEORGE V HALL,
Central Telegraph Office Building,
St. Martin's-le-Grand,

between the hours of 12 noon and 3 p.m. from September 30th to October 11th (excluding Saturdays and Sundays)

YOU ARE CORDIALLY INVITED TO ATTEND

ADMISSION FREE

T H E G. P. O. FILM UNIT 1933–1940, Forsyth Hardy

Film critic Forsyth Hardy was an early supporter of the GPO Film Unit's work. In 1990, drawing upon a lifetime's insight, he wrote this short history of the Unit

© Royal Mail Group Ltd 2011. Courtesy of The British Postal Museum & Archive

In 1933 when the Empire Marketing Board was disbanded its fledgling Film Unit had taken its first hesitant steps towards what was to become the British Documentary Film Movement. As one of the very junior departments of the Board it had been created "to bring the Empire alive" -- to bring the day-to-day activities of the Empire at work into the common imagination: a heady purpose when initially the Unit consisted of two film-makers, Walter Creighton and John Grierson. Creighton made the long-forgotten theatrical film, <u>One Family</u>. Grierson made a film of the Scottish herring fleets, <u>Drifters</u>, and documentary was launched.

Grierson recognised from the beginning that it would not be enough to repeat the relative success of <u>Drifters</u> which went into the cinemas as soon as it was completed. If he was to create a "movement" which had been in his mind ever since he returned from his three years' study of mass communication in the United States he would need to find young people of like mind. One had already sought him out: Basil Wright who had seen and been inspired by <u>Drifters</u>. He was joined by Arthur Elton who had had some experience in the scenario department at Gainsborough.

Gradually the unit of like-minded people grew: J. D. Davidson, the cameraman; John Taylor whose sister Margaret had helped Grierson to edit <u>Drifters</u> (she later became his wife); Paul Rotha who made some experimental poster films during the few months he was a member of the unit and who was to record documentary achievement over many years; Evelyn Spice the Canadian, recruited by Grierson's youngest sister, Marion, who continued to work in films when she returned to Canada; Donald Taylor who married Marion and later worked independently; J. N. G. Davidson from Ireland; Edgar Anstey who preferred film-making to employment as a scientific assistant at the Department of Scientific and Industrial Research; Stuart Legg and Harry Watt.

Grierson had the backing of Stephen Tallents, secretary of the E.M.B., who had first engaged him and who, in Grierson's words, "marked out the habitation and the place for our new teaching of citizenship and gave it a chance to expand". Tallents was a civil servant and a diplomat of long experience who could not only recognise and sympathise with Grierson's promotion of the film as a vehicle for the stimulation of democratic thinking: but also had the skills to counter some of the confrontation which Grierson's ideas provoked among politicians and in the film trade. Together they led and inspired the young film-makers who were still feeling their way and could not yet match enthusiasm with accomplishment.

While Grierson was training the young men and women he had selected their achievement in film terms could hardly be huge, although there were already indications of individual qualities. Basil Wright had given a lyrical quality to his films of country life, O'er Hill and Dale and Country Comes to Town. Arthur Elton had demonstrated his scientific emphasis in Upstream and Shadow on the Mountain. Stuart Legg had made The New Generation for the Chesterfield Education Authority. Robert Flaherty, on Grierson's invitation, had shot material in the English Midlands which formed the basis of Industrial Britain. These films went into the cinemas and were beginning to make the existence of the Unit known. There was other work in progress, including Basil Wright's films on the West Indies, Anstey's Uncharted Waters on Labrador and Elton's long film on aeroplane engines. In Grierson's words, it was the only group of its kind outside

Ruasia "devoted deliberately, continuously, and with hope, to the highest forms of documentary".

When the Unit, humbly housed and its members inadequately remunerated, was threatened with extinction, Grierson turned his formidable energy towards saving it. He had as allies the film societies throughout Britain at whose performances his films had been regularly shown and also, more importantly because of their influence with policy-makers, journalists and film critics who respected his aims and who welcomed his films as an antidote to commercial cinema. Grierson himself wrote and lectured tirelessly about the documentary idea and had the help of members of the Unit who were almost as eloquent and certainly as determined. They had many supporters in journalism and politics and all were made to realise that the end of the film unit fostered by the Empire Marketing Board would be a national tragedy.

I was one of those caught up in this promotional protective barrage. Before meeting Grierson I had seen Drifters and had written enthusiastically about it, welcoming it for its content and technique and not forgetting that it was the work of a Scottish director. I was writing about films for The Scotsman and also collaborating with Norman Wilson in editing and publishing Cinema Quarterly, the first journal in Britain to take the film seriously as an art form and to which Grierson and his colleagues regularly contributed. But I was only one of the many writers who voiced concern about the threat to documentary. Among others were Caroline Lejeune of The Observer, W. A. J. Lawrence of The Times, Ernest Dyer in Newcastle, Cyril Ray in Manchester, Cedric Belfrage in London and Aubrey Flanagan who, in the film trade paper, Today's Cinema, always tried to off-set the trade's opposition with constructive comment.

The decisive element in the many-sided argument was the action of Sir Stephen Tallents (knighted in 1932). When his Board was closed down he accepted an appointment as Public Relations Officer at the Post Office on the understanding that he would take with him the film unit and the Empire Library which Grierson had been steadily building up. Tallents was appointed by Sir Kingsley Wood, then Postmaster General. The association between Tallents and Grierson was important for the movement. It was to be maintained through the war and after.

And so the G.P.O. Film Unit, which was to carry the flag for British documentary and influence the use of the film in industry and by public bodies, was born -- or reborn if we take into account the fact that Grierson and his colleagues were still there. Grierson welcomed it "for the story of communications was as good as any other and in one sense it was better ... we had at least the assurance of imaginative backing. With Tallents behind it, the documentary idea prospered at the Post Office and in surroundings which at the beginning seemed singularly unpromising".

There was inevitably an overlap in the work done by the old and new units. It had been Grierson's practice to accept commissions from other departments and organisations. At the moment of transition the most important of these were Song of Ceylon for the Ceylon Tea Propaganda Board and B.B.C. -- The Voice of Britain for the B.B.C. Basil Wright's film on Ceylon was both his outstanding personal achievement and one of the two or three films everyone associates with the G.P.O. Film Unit. I recall Grierson and Wright screening it for me before it had been publicly shown. They were both a little apprehensive for a reason I did not learn until afterwards: there had been a disagreement between them about the ending of the film. At Grierson's insistence Wright had made the alterations the producer wanted. How would I react? My response apparently gave him all he wanted. Grierson merely said to him "You see?".

Song of Ceylon gained the top award at the Brussels International Film Festival in 1935. This gentle and poetic film offers as moving an experience today as when it was first shown.

B.B.C. -- The Voice of Britain was by far the longest and most expensive film made by the G.P.O. Film Unit. It cost £7,500 -- a large sum in 1934. The chronicle of a day's broadcasting in Britain both dramatised and humanised the material, so that its different compartments had vitality and the whole had unity. I wrote at the time of the virtue of the film's seeing eye which "operates everywhere, inside Broadcasting House as well as outside, ranging the panorama of a listening Britain". Several members of the unit worked on the film. To Stuart Legg, with his meticulous concern for accurate detail, probably belongs most of the credit. Not for the last time did he demonstrate his patience in researching a subject which might have produced a mere joyless jumble of mechanical explanation and self-conscious justification.

The Post Office was among the departments for which the E.M.B. Film Unit was making films. Two of them were by Stuart Legg, The New Operator (1932) and Telephone Workers (1933). The scale of production was naturally greatly expanded by the G.P.O. Film Unit. In dealing with distribution Grierson found it helpful to offer films in groups, as with the Industrial Britain group. He assembled another group which, distributed by A.B.P.D., had considerable success in the cinemas. They were all about Post Office activities. They included Evelyn Spice's Weather Forecast (1934) about the collection and dissemination of information about weather conditions; Stuart Legg's Cable Ship (1933), on the repairing of submarine telephone cables; Six Thirty Collection (1934) in which Edgar Anstey described the collection, sorting and dispatch of the early evening mail collection at a large London post office; Under the City (1934) in which Arthur Elton collaborated with Alexander Shaw in describing the maintenance of telephone cables under London's streets; and Harry Watt's Droitwich (1934) on the erection of the tallest radio mast made in Britain.

Meanwhile, the transition from E.M.B. to G.P.O. was taking other forms. Grierson's unit had initially been housed in a cutting room in Dansey Yard off lower Wardour Street. From there he moved with his first recruits to two rooms on the top floor of 179 Wardour Street. When I visited him there I thought I had never seen so many people working in so small an area. The tallest had their heads out of skylight windows! There was more space -- but not much more -- at the next location, offices on the third and fourth floors at 37-39 Oxford Street. It was not, however, until the G.P.O. Film Unit moved in 1934 to 21 Soho Square that it found an adequate home, although even here some of the members worked from desks in corridors.

About the same time the Unit acquired studios at Blackheath with access to sound equipment. Earlier films like the Industrial Britain group were essentially silent films with commentaries added at the behest of the distributors. To have control of sound in their films meant a great deal to the directors. It added a new dimension to their experimentation. It also gave them freedom from the cramping conditions which applied to the use of music. As Grierson put it, if they wanted music "we find it cheaper to have it written for us. If we want natural sound, the producer drives out and gets it. If we want to orchestrate sound we sit in the sound van and arrange the re-recording as we think best.

If we want to play with sound images, or arrange choral effects, or in any way experiment, we have no one's permission to ask and no considerable overheads to worry about, because we do most of the work ourselves".

The experimental use of sound was to become characteristic of the G.P.O. Unit's films. Six Thirty Collection was probably the first documentary to use authentic sound. The experimentation quickly became much more adventurous. It was present in Song of Ceylon where, among the orchestration of music, voices, narration and natural sounds, the long sustained tolling of a single peal of a temple bell is for me an abiding memory. By the time Coal Face was made in 1935 experimentation had become an obsession. Night Mail (1936) would never have been the film it was without the imaginative orchestration of sound, music, and verse.

All the members of the unit participated in this experimentation. They were encouraged to do so as much by Grierson himself as by Alberto Cavalcanti who, after experience in studios in Paris, joined the unit in 1934. Just as Grierson had employed Flaherty for the inspiration the members of the unit would derive from "the finest eyes in cinema" so he thought of Cavalcanti as someone who would stimulate the innovotive use of sound. The key appointments which were to bring lustre to the G.P.O. Film Unit's output were made by Grierson. When Basil Wright told him that W. H. Auden wanted to join the unit he was urged to bring him in at once. Similarly Grierson asked the Royal College of Music if they had a bright young student who could write a little incidental music for a forthcoming film "Yes", they said. "Benjamin Britten".

Often overlooked but a favourite film of Grierson's was Granton Trawler (1934). In one sense it was a throwback to his 1914-18 war-time experience in trawlers converted into mine-sweepers. He shot it during a holiday and experienced the worst storms the North Sea can produce. He claimed that he was never sea sick but when, with Edgar Anstey, I met him at Granton harbour as he stepped off the Isabella Greig he looked as if he must have missed sickness by a hair's breadth. He and the hand-held camera, still running, had been blown over in the gale. When Anstey came to edit the film -- "See what you can make of it" said Grierson -- he decided to keep the shots of heaving deck and tumultuous seas as recorded by the camera skittering about the deck. It was a modest little film which in place of commentary contained some of the unit's first experiments with sound. Grierson had a great affection for the trawler and its crew and was saddened when he learned that the vessel had been lost at sea, sunk by German bombs when fishing, unarmed and flying the British mercantile flag, in September, 1941.

Grierson's boyhood was spent in a mining community in Stirlingshire. He knew about the life of the miners from first-hand observation. His mother had run a soup kitchen for them when they were on strike. It was not until he made The Brave Don't Cry for Group 3 in 1952 that he was able to give full expression to this. The association may in part have explained why Coal Face (1935) was made. It did not appear to have any obvious link with the Post Office. Shooting for it was done over a period by several members of the unit. The material was given to Stuart Legg to assemble. Basil Wright was asked to shoot some exteriors of coal mines in Scotland. W. H. Auden wrote a madrigal for the film, sung by female voices as the miners returned to the surface:

O lurcher-loving collier, black as night,
Follow your love across the smokeless hill;

Your lamp is out and all your cages still;
Course for her heart and do not miss,
For Sunday soon is past and, Kate, fly not so fast,
For Monday comes when none may kiss:
Be marble to his soot, and to his black be white.

Earlier the film made some factual statements about the importance of the coal industry to Britain, its use in power generation, the dependence on it for rail transport and marine traffic and the use of coal in homes all over the country. These statements were delivered in a flat voice, in contrast to the emotional rendering of the madrigal. If the sound recording had not been so inadequate the film would have made a much stronger impact.

The main value of Coal Face was as preparation for Night Mail (1930, the most celebrated of all the films made by the G.P.O. Film Unit. It began humbly enough as a record of the journeys of the Postal Special between London and Scotland during which letters were collected, sorted and delivered by apparatus at points along the route. I was asked by Grierson to make the journey (as others doubtless were) and give him my impressions. The experience certainly gave me an understanding of the physical demands made on the postal workers who worked in shifts -- Scotland to Carlisle, Carlisle to Crewe and Crewe to Euston. Their sorting had a kind of rhythmic fascination as the letters found their niches in the panel in front of each sorter, the process interrupted occasionally by an indecipherable address or an obscure location. I can still recall the thump of the leather bound bags of mail hurtling into the collecting van at the front of the train.

Night Mail was a truly collaborative effort by the unit. Basil Wright and Harry Watt were told by Grierson that a film on the overnight mail train was to be made. Both made investigative journeys. Wright wrote an outline which Watt developed, although there was never a fully detailed script. Watt had a unit consisting of Chick Fowle and Jonah Jones as cameramen and Pat Jackson and W. H. Auden as assistants. Wright had R. Q. McNaughton as editor while Grierson and Cavalcanti had an oversight of all that was happening.

Gradually the film grew. Steam-driven trains have always made good film material since the days of The Great Train Robbery in 1903 and not forgetting Von Sternberg's Shanghai Express and all the others before dull diesel engines took over. Visually Night Mail gained immensely from the aerial shots as the train sped northwards through the dusk or the fleeting shots taken of its illumined windows as it thundered through silent stations. It was Grierson's decision that the northward journey should be shown. The shots of the rounded Border hills in the grey light of early morning are among the most memorable in the film. It was Grierson also, according to Basil Wright, who was conscious, when seeing a rough assembly, of a lack: "There's something missing. What we haven't got here is anything about the people who are going to get the letters. We've only the machinery of getting the letters from one point to the other".

It was then that the idea of using verse written by Auden originated -- verse which, with the music composed by Benjamin Britten, was to give the film its most (but not its only) distinctive quality. Watt was opposed to the idea and gave Auden a hard time as the poet wrote verse which Watt discarded as unusable, either because it did not fit or sometimes because the verbal images were too strong for the pictorial equivalent. At the same time Watt was struggling with the sound-track. Sound recorded on the train was unsuitable and eventually he was forced to use a Bassett-Lowke model engine on a miniature track on a table. There was collaboration all the way through, with Stuart Legg speaking the rapid passages of Auden's verse and Grierson himself giving emotion to the closing lines.

Night Mail was a success from its first public showing at the Arts Theatre, Cambridge. The success was repeated all over the world. I can give two examples from personal experience. There was a 16mm copy in Copenhagen at the outbreak of war. It was shown so often to the young Danish documentary makers (as I found when researching for a book on Scandinavian cinema) that it was scratched into unrecognis-ability. The other is from Canada where Sydney Newman told me that Grierson forbade the screening of the film as he wanted Canadian film-makers, to evolve their own style. When, disobeying this injunction, Newman copied a shot of a locomotive's wheels in motion for a film he was making, Grierson immediately recognised it.

1936 was probably the most fruitful year of the G.P.O. Film Unit's record. It was in January of that year that Grierson saw the work of Norman McLaren at the Scottish Amateur Film Festival in Glasgow. I was sitting bedide him at the time and he immedi-ately asked me brusquely to arrange a meeting. Grierson dismissed Camera Makes Whoopee, in which McLaren had exploited every device available to the new 16mm camera he had been given but was fascinated by the short film Colour Cocktail McLaren had made by painting directly on positive film rescued from newsreels with the images scraped off. He was told that when he had finished his course at the Glasgow School of Art there would be a job waiting for him at the G.P.O. It did not work out quite like that: McLaren did not finish his course and paid a visit to Moscow before reaching Soho Square in January 1937. Grierson gave him the opportunity to accompany Ivor Montagu to Spain to film what became The Defence of Madrid.

Grierson believed that every film-making unit should have an artist who could exper-iment and not be held to account for everything he did. At the C.P.O. this role was filled first by Len Lye, the New Zealander, who brought Colour Box to Grierson and Cavalcanti and who made Rainbow Dance (1936) and Trade Tattoo (1937) for them. In these two films Lye combined recognisable figures with abstract elements moving rapidly on the screen in syncopation with jazz. Produced by Grierson, Trade Tattoo had a characteristic message: "The rhythm of trade is maintained by the mails. Keep in rhythm by posting early". There were visuals from Drifters, Industrial Britain, Cargo from Jamaica and other films which strengthened the structure. Len Lye deserved credit for his imagina-tive sound-and-picture experiments and Grierson for recognising how his gifts might be harnessed to persuasive purposes.

McLaren's experiments were in the same area -- i.e., the application of paint direct to the celluloid. In Love on the Wing (1937) McLaren gave more than a hint of the visual ideas he was to develop in other films in Britain and later in Canada. There was, for example, his freedom of line by which an envelope could become a galloping horse which in turn could split into two dolphins in pursuit of each other. McLaren was to become a considerable figure in the world of film animation with a quite astonishing range, from Dots and Loops to his anti-war film, Neighbours.

Grierson had a genius for identifying exceptional talent. Perhaps the fact that the G.P.O. Film Unit was the only film school in Britain to which hopeful tyros applied by the hundred was a help; but Grierson had an uncanny gift for seeing beyond mere aspiration to real vision. (later Sir William) Coldstream put the point well when he said "Grierson, through his ideas and his organisation, attracted to himself some of the most remarkable of the younger generation of painters, writers and composers. They were all, I believe, drawn to the Unit for much the same reason as myself: the opportunity to work in a new medium which seemed technically and socially appropriate to the times".

What was life like to work for Grierson at the G.P.O. Film Unit? It was the opposite of a quiet backwater. It was always a challenge. As a producer Grierson was tough, imaginative, far-seeing, single-minded, determined to maintain the Film Unit's premier position and its high standards of craftsmanship. He could be difficult and demanding. When he barked out an instruction he expected it to be carried out at once. This applied as much to his wife, Margaret, as to any member of the unit. Yet he had a well concealed sense of humour and loved to tell stories. He had a soft side, revealed when anyone went to him in trouble. An old acqaintance called on him one day unexpectedly. He was out of work and had no money. Within minutes Grierson gave him £5 to buy food for his wife and family.

He was unpredictable and had no hesitation in cancelling an appointment at the last minute if he found he had something more important to do. On some days he would decide to go to the studios at Blackheath without advising his long-suffering secretary, Phyllis Long, so that visitors might arrive only to find he was elsewhere. This was the behaviour not of someone indifferent to the accepted tenets but of a man who was the focus of pressures from every direction, creative as well as administrative.

Much of the administrative burden was carried, at both the E.M.B. and the G.P.O., by Stanley Fletcher. On the occasions I met him he seemed to have a permanently worried expression. There was much cause for it. He was the link between the Film Unit and officialdom. He had to ensure that the annual budget covered all production and non-theatrical requirements, as well as office staff, accounting for over-spending with carefully worded minutos to A. G. Highet in the Public Relations department and the Accountant General's department. He smoothed ruffled feathers when something was said or done which upset the civil servants or when a request had been made for some facility which seemed outrageous to them. Fletcher's appointment as office manager continued until the war.

The Post Office exercised very tight control over expenditure which in film-making is all but impossible. Any request to the Accountant General's department or the Establishment Division had first to go to the Public Relations department and only if it were approved would it be forwarded. Inevitably, there were long telephone conversations with Fletcher (or, if the disputed matter were serious enough, with Grierson). The rule was rigidly applied, the only exceptions being the regular indent for stationery and furniture but even this had to be covered by the year's overall estimate of expenditure. The creative work of the Unit would never have been possible had not this trouble-shooting been done by Fletcher.

Grierson's other personal assistant was J. P. R. Golightly who had the manner and appearance of a country gentleman or perhaps a tutor to a well-to-do family. He looked after Grierson's personal affairs and tried to keep the Unit on an even keel. If a problem of personnel suddenly arose Golightly would be expected to solve it. Grierson's protective friendship was to continue until Golightly died, his last years spent with Margaret at Tog Hill, Grierson's home in Wiltshire. But that is looking far ahead.

Some of the day-to-day administrative burden was carried by Grierson's secretary, Phyllis Long, who was with him throughout the E.M.B. and G.P.O. periods. To work for Grierson did not mean a quiet, orderly life. There were ups and downs, good and bad times, crises, successes. When she first started work at the E.M.B. she was terrified of Grierson. She had to work hard at her shorthand. His accent, a Scottish foundation with an overlay of American, presented an obstacle which was overcome only with time and patience. I recall being with Grierson one day when he barked at her "Get Dand". He meant Charles Dand, a friend from his years at Glasgow University (and much later a colleague at the Central Office of Information). Instead Miss Long got Arthur Dent on the phone, apparently at a time when the B.I.P. chief was the last person to whom Grierson wished to speak. The resultant conversation, with embarrassment on both sides, was a model of diplomatic fencing. There was no reprisal. Like others who worked for Grierson, Phyllis Long valued the experience. If nothing else it added to her vocabulary.

At Soho Square the day for Grierson would often begin with the viewing of rushes, in the presence of the director responsible. When the rushes had been threaded up on the projector the director would inform Golightly who would tell him to wait in the theatre. Waiting could take a long time and apprehension would mount by the minute. Suddenly Grierson's door would open with a crash and he would be heard coming down the passageway. He would sit down and say "Right. Shoot". Afterwards he would be brutally frank. I was present at his invitation at more than one of these sessions and my sympathies were invariably with the direetor. No excuse or explanation would be tolerated. There were frequent rows, most often between Grierson and Harry Watt, but there was only one outcome. Grierson was tough and unyielding and, once he had made up his mind, never wavered.

There were, of course, moments of relaxation, most often in the Highlander after the day's work was done. An institution valued by the members of the Unit and others who shared their attitude to film-making was the Friday night screening in the theatre at Soho Square. If someone somewhere was doing something unusual in documentary it would quickly find its way into the programmes for these privileged occasions. The work of the Unit was gaining more and more recognition overseas and directors who wanted to come to the fountainhead, as it were, brought their films for appraisal and guidance to Soho Square. I attended these screenings whenever I was in London and always found them stimulating.

Grierson wrote ceaselessly at this time for a wide range of publications, from high-brow quarterlies to daily and Sunday newspapers. There were always articles for Phyllis Long to transcribe for such publications as Everyman, New Britain, Artwork, Cinema Quarterly, World Film News and, later, Sight and Sound. Only his secretary could decipher his miniscule handwriting which wriggled across the pages of a series of black bound foolscap notebooks. In time he persuaded the Post Office to give him a cylinder type dictaphone into which he would dictate in the evening and, the following morning, hand three, or four cylinders to PhIlis Long to transcribe. He never indicated that there were corrections or changes of mind and she had often to listen to an entire cylinder before starting to type. Grierson was never to write a book but he was grateful, after his fashion, for the compilation of his articles I made after the war and published under the title Grierson on Documentary.

Much of Grierson's time was devoted to trying to get theatrical distribution for the films. This effort reflected a modified recognition of the prestige such distribution gave. It also produced some revenue which helped the overall budget. It took months for him to secure the release of a group of films through Ideal Films but he never wavered in his belief that there was a market for them. He went several times to the Academy Cinema in Oxford Street to show the cutting copy of <u>Industrial Britain</u> to Elsie Cohen and get her opinion of it. She was always very helpful and he valued her comments.

A letter he wrote to me on February 4, 1936, expressed very fully his attitude to theatrical distribution. I shall reproduce it here as it is available nowhere else. He was prompted to write after reading a review I had written of a book by Paul Rotha.

"I have just read your review of Rotha's book and congratulate you as usual on knowing, as only a few critics do, what you are writing about. But I have a complaint. It is not, I think, the best tactic, whilst we are building up a movement, to emphasise its relative insignificance in the theatre world. A better line is surely to indicate what has been achieved and is increasingly being achieved, despite the youth of the movement and its lack of support except the goodwill of people like yourself. When you consider it from that point of view the progress is remarkable. Starting from scratch a very few years ago, with no regard at all in the theatres for industry, work and workmen, you have the success of Rotha's films, of our own G.B. group (<u>Industrial Britain</u> alone doing over a thousand theatres), of our <u>Weather Forecast</u> group (each one getting on to a thousand theatres) and particularly the recent circulation of <u>B.B.C.-- The Voice of Britain</u>, with documentary moving up into the feature spot itself. Add to that the influence of documentary on Andrew Buchanan, the arrival of the parallel movement from America in <u>The March of Time</u> and the increasing circulation of people like Mary Field, Roy Lockwood and the Travel Association, and you have an all-in circulation for this documentary approach which is far greater than anyone could have foretold three years ago, apart altogether from the non-theatrical and specialist circulation. The fact is the more impressive when you consider the sponsored origins of most of these films, and the overcoming of exhibitors' resistance in this respect.

"Incidentally, when you mention Rotha and Edinburgh you should remember that Edinburgh is notoriously one of the blackest spots in the country for documentary, despite your own great efforts.

"But it is not a question of making an absolute case for documentary success in the theatres. The shadows of Hollywood are large, and naturally. See documentary as a fight for just ten minutes' time in the average theatre programme. It is not by any means a prairie fire, nor was it intended to be, but the damn thing is positively ablaze for all that. It may even penetrate the deeper, because of its non-spectacular origins and relative inability to command the blazing publicity of Wardour Street. You can even positively say that it has achieved within the past two years an audience of twenty-five millions in the theatres. This is the figure for our own stuff alone.

"But as I say, it is a question of tactic. Writing to you as a partner in the process of building this new field, I am sure the emphasis of the positive side makes better material for conversion than the sad song of negatives. They only tend to justify the dumb-heads in their apathy. We get enough of that sort of thing from Lejeune, God knows!"

To this revealing letter Grierson added a postscript which he must have written after reading something I had written about the films of Jenny Brown (later Gilbertson), a

Shetland film-maker he had encouraged and who remained a close friend throughout her life:

"Reading your follow up on Jenny Brown's complaint some of the emphasis is taken out of the above but I shall send it. If you batter away like that you will do something, remembering always that Edinburgh is a cinematic slum so far as-advanced showman-ship is concerned. Don't encourage them by suggesting other places are the same. Tell them they're backward; and particularly backward of Glasgow, which they are. We rubbed that in, in connection with our Post Office shows, and Edinburgh straightaway beat the Glasgow record!"

Desirable although theatrical distribution was, it was not the only method of making the films available. At the E.M.B. Grierson had established the Imperial Institute Film Library, very largely based on material from the Canadian Motion Picture Bureau, some of it used by Basil Wright in making <u>Conquest</u> and <u>Lumber</u>. Many of the Canadian films were re-edited by the younger members of the Unit. As the G.P.O. films were completed they automatically went into what became the G.P.O. Film Library and reached a very large audience using 16mm equipment. Grierson often claimed that there were more seats available outside than inside the cinemas. As he moved around the country lectur-ing on documentary he stimulated a demand for the films.

At Soho Square a non-theatrical department was set up under Thomas Baird, a Glasgow teacher. He was asked to organise a travelling film unit scheme to show Post Office films throughout the country. By 1936 it was estimated that the scheme reached 500,000 children and 25,000 adults a year. When Baird was awarded a Fulbright Scholarship in 1937 and left for the United States, he was succeeded by Russell Ferguson, also from Glasgow. The travelling film units were adopted by the Ministry of Information and were an important outlet for propaganda films during the war.

The success of the G.P.O. Film Unit was not achieved without criticism and resist-ance. There were three main sources: the film industry, the Treasury and politicians. Sections of the film trade thought that the production of films for other departments by the G.P.O. was unfair competition. Gaumont-British had begun to show an interest in the production, distribution and exhibition of educational and instructional films and did not relish having to compete with a government department engaged in similar activities. Neville Kearney, Secretary of the Film Producers' Group of the Federation of British Industries, maintained that the Post Office was using public funds in a manner "highly prejudicial to the development of an important and growing industry". The fact that the G.P.O. Film Unit productions were judged by polular acclaim and critical appraisal to be infinitely superior to the films made by the commercial companies was an additional source of resentment.

The Treasury could not ignore a protest of this kind. It was recognised that the citi-zenry needed some light shed on the increasingly complicated processes of government and that the film was the best method of explanation available. But should one depart-ment, the Post Office, accept the responsibility for all departments? Grierson and Tallents thought there should be a unit prepared to do this for the government. Grierson in particular profoundly believed in the value of the film for mass communication. He did not see this fully realised in Britain (although it conditioned much of his thinking) but he did in war-time Canada where he had charge of information by films for all the departments.

A Select Committee on Estimates was appointed and, after six months, reported that the raising of the level of social consciousness and the interpretation of the drama of everyday life had little connection with the advertisement of rates for the parcel post and the virtues of the new telephone system. The Committee concluded that, when existing commitments had been met, the G.P.O. Film Unit should confine itself to strictly Post Office activities. Given their beliefs, Grierson and Tallents did their utmost to circumvent these restrictions but inevitably relations with the Treasury became strained. At the same time there was a much more exacting control of budgets by the Post Office and the abandonment of the device by which the distribution company, New Era, had been the nominal employers of the Unit's staff, apart from Grierson.

The third source of criticism was political. The Unit was suspected, on laughably inadequate evidence, of being a hot bed of Communism. At Glasgow University Grierson had been a leading member of the Fabian Society and the Labour Club and he made no effort to conceal his advocacy of social reform. Harry Watt was a lifelong Socialist. Other members of the Unit were Left in their sympathies. But none of this reached the screen, except in broad, unexceptionable terms. The suspicions continued and found some public expression. Inside the Unit they were not taken seriously, even after a Special Branch agent had been charged with keeping its activities under review. According to Ritchie Calder, "Grierson and I had the dubious distinction in 1936 of sharing, for different deviations, the same Special Branch 'shadow'. We materialised our 'shadow' and got on friendly terms with him".

Meanwhile the Unit got on with its job of making films. Among the senior directors Harry Watt was a rebel. He had many disputes with Grierson, especially over the credits for Night Mail. He and Basil Wright appeared jointly as producers. Harry insisted that he had directed the film and was ready to admit that Wright could have been credited, in larger type if need be, as producer. He never forgave Grierson and Watt tended to distance himself from the Chief.

When he was asked by Grierson to make a film about National Savings, he thought of it as "a ghastly assignment. Organised saving seemed like organised religion, and equally repulsive". He wrote a story about a fisherman's savings which was filmed at Mousehole in Cornwall. The leading part was played by the local postmaster, Bill Blewitt -- "the beginning of a long association and, a great friendship". They met in a pub, Watt not knowing he was the postmaster he had been asked to contact. The Saving of Bill Blewitt (1937) was the first story film made by the G.P.O. Film Unit. Watt learned a great deal from Cavalcanti -- in the handling of acting, the use of dialogue, editing, continuity, everything indeed which a fictional film requires and which came naturally to the experienced Cavalcanti. With Blewitt as his hero and Cavalcanti as his mentor the film could never have failed.

The Saving of Bill Blewitt marked a change of approach and style for, the G.P.O. Film Unit. In place of visuals backed by spoken commentary there were characters who spoke about their life and work. It was what we called the humanisation of documentary. Encouraged by Cavalcanti Watt was the leading exponent of this story style which departed so radically from the didactive nature of the films which preceded it. Watt had already had a taste of story film making with Flaherty in the Aran Islands. When he was given his next subject he was ready for it.

North Sea (1937-38) was a rewarding subject for Harry Watt. It was about the ship-to-shore radio service by which the lives of many fishermen are saved in winter storms around the coasts of Britain. He found his story in the records of the Post Office and the shipping companies. He also found the oldest trawler in the harbour at Aberdeen and selected his crew from out-of-work fishermen at the Labour Exchange. He added Bill Blewitt as a gesture of recognition for the help the Cornishman had given him and to encourage the crew members that film acting wasn't really so very difficult. They had three weeks "of smashing seas, screaming wind, cold -- always cold -- and the utter fatigue of trying to keep upright and dry, while doing a job". The result, according to Flaherty, was "one of the most significant short films that has ever been made ... real incidents such as North Sea must be happening everywhere, every day -- incidents that, if they were filmed, would, as the North Sea film does, get right under the skin of this country and its people".

North Sea was a resounding success in the cinemas and continued to be in demand for many years. Another of the Unit's somewhat more unexpected successes was The King's Stamp (1935). Grierson gave the subject to Coldstream whose first film it was. The idea was to commemorate the printing of the King George V Silver Jubilee stamp which it was considered would have an interest for stamp collectors. Just how big a world-wide interest astonished everyone. The film began with an account of the design-ing, lithographing and printing of the stamp and continued with dramatised sequences of the origin of the penny post and the reactions of the first members of the public to the purchase and use of the new "government labels". The differing styles of the sequences, including some obviously amateur performances, and the fact that they did not produce a harmonious whole, did not affect the popularity of the film. Coldstream anguished over it. Britten wrote the music.

With Basil Wright as producer and with music by Walter Leigh, Coldstream was also the director of The Fairy of the Phone (1936), a fanciful musical comedy on how to use the telephone. Distance has lent some enchantment to what was regarded at the time as rather an amateur effort. The music was tuneful and the girls of the telephone exchange might have been under-under-studies for Jessie Matthews. It has survived as a curiosity: documentaries have been duplicated throughout the world by the thousand but not The Fairy of the Phone.

The same claim for uniqueness could be made for Pett and Pott, a grotesque comedy on which Cavalcanti's influence predominated. Humphrey Jennings who had just joined the unit designed the settings. Herbert Read praised it for its asynchronous devices used to heighten the comedy. Wright said of it that "We got away with Pett and Pott because Grierson is a great salesman. He told everyone what a wonderful film it was and made sure that nobody ever saw it".

Sir Stephen Tallents left the Post Office in mid-1935 when he accepted a public rela-tions appointment at the B.B.C. He was followed as Controller of Publicity by A. G. Highet who appeared to be regarded as a kind of bogey man by the members of the Unit. He was dour and distant and made only occasional visits to Soho Square. When he was expected Phyllis Long tried to tidy the office aad ensured that Harry Watt's Daily Worker was out of sight. Grierson had many arguments with him over plans and proposals. Probably his civil service, training did not include coping with anything as unruly as a film unit.

Appointed as Public Relations Officer was Ernest Tristram Crutchley who had the Film Unit as one of his immediate responsibilities. His relationship with Grierson inevitably differed from that of Tallents although he regarded him as "a fine artist and a film producer of eminence". When there were disputes or disagreements he tended to turn to Highet for guidance. He was to play a constructive role later in the arrangement made for the transfer of the G.P.O. Film Unit to the Ministry of Information where it re-emerged as the Crown Film Unit.

When in June 1937 Grierson told his secretary that he had been to see Highet to hand in his resignation she was stunned, as also were the members of the Unit when they learned of it. Behind his decision were a number of factors. Among the negative ones was his increasing frustration at the restrictions being placed on his work by civil servants who did not share his imaginative vision of the service the film could render in public education. But Grierson as always was thinking positively. The documentary idea was spreading far beyond the Post Office. The senior directors had departed to help major industries and departments to use film for informational and promotional purposes: Shell and B.P., London Transport, Imperial Airways, the Gas industry, the Orient Shipping Line, the Scottish Office. In each case a film-maker trained by Grierson at the Post Office or inspired by his example was given responsibility for a film programme. The documentary film movement was growing apace.

This wider impact, not confined to Britain, is not part of this survey. It is important to remember, however, that it would not have taken place but for Grierson, initially at the Empire Marketing Board and, during its most significant period of growth, at the Post Office. It is a record of which any institution could be proud.

After the departure of Grierson (and of Wright, Elton, Legg and Golightly to form Film Centre), the overall direction of the G.P.O. Film Unit was in the hands of Cavalcanti and Harry Watt. In North Sea they had proved that story films could not only serve a purpose related to the work of the Post Office but also provide dramatic entertainment for audiences in cinemas. The films they initiated, when they were not story films, were not didactive in style and content. A minor example of this was News for the Navy (1937), directed by Norman McLaren. Within the simple framework of a girl's action in sending a newspaper to her fiance on a warship at sea the film succeeded in showing how packages were collected, sorted and dispatched, by using escalators and miniature underground railways in London. There was no credit on the film for an editor (Stewart McAllister perhaps?) but the film was certainly edited with remarkable skill.

Another film to which Norman McLaren contributed, Mony a Pickle (1938), made for the Scottish Post Office Savings Bank for showing initially at the 1938 Empire Exhibition in Glasgow, had some highly ingenious touches in a sequence in which a young couple indulge their dream of their perfect home -- if only they could afford it. Many years later this technique was to re-emerge in a masterly way in McLaren's Neighbours. The other sequences, not individually credited, were directed by Maurice Harvey, J. B. Holmes, Harry Watt and Richard Massingham (remembered for his comedy of a visit to the dentist, Tell Me If It Hurts). One sequence made comic play out of the mispronunciation of McLaughlin while a third embraced pathos in a shot of an old miner, rapidly going downhill according to his mates, studying his savings bank book perhaps to see if he had enough to pay for his funeral.

An example of Cavalcanti's growing influence within the unit was to be found in the films he made in Switzerland in collaboration with the Swiss Post Office. The most ambitious of these was We Live in Two Worlds (1937). It was scripted by J. B. Priestley who also wrote the commentary. He took Switzerland as an example of both nationalism and the new internationalism of transport and communications. Priestley constructed what he called a "lecture film" from material given to him. As the cameraman was John Taylor it was all of excellent quality. The music was composed by Maurice Jaubert. The experience of working with Grierson, Cavalcanti and their colleagues prompted Priestley to pay tribute later in his book Rain Upon Godehill to the "earnest and enthusiastic young men who were making our documentary films, in which branch of the art we were then leading the world. I had liked what I had seen of their realistic non-fiction films -- Drifters, Song of Ceylon, Night Mail, The Voice of Britain and the rest -- and I liked the enthusiasm of these rather solemn young men in their high-necked sweaters. Most of them worked like demons for a few pounds a week, far less than some imported film stars were spending on their hair and finger nails. They were rapidly developing a fine technique of their own, so rapidly that if you wanted to see what sound and camera really could do, you had to see some little film sponsored by the Post Office."

The two other films resulting from the Swiss collaboration were Line to Tschierva Hut and Men of the Alps, both skilfully photographed by John Taylor. Apart from their inherent merit the Swiss. films lent an exotic touch to programmes of G.P.O. productions.

On the home front (with war expectation in the air) there were still films to be made. Produced by Cavalcanti and directed by Harry Watt Big Money (1938) had as its unlikely subject the work of the Accountant General's department at the Post Office. Watt succeeded in finding a human frame for it. Roadways (1937), with direction jointly credited to Stuart Legg and William Coldstream, dealt with the growth of road traffic in the 'thirties, a subject rapidly out-dated no matter how far-seeing the treatment. The Horsey Mail (1938) was directed by Pat Jackson, a protégé of Sir Kingsley Wood who quickly showed an aptitude for film work. This was a straightforward account of how the Post Office got letters to Horsey village and outlying farms when they were cut off after the East Norfolk sea wall gave way in a storm. Much later Pat Jackson was to direct such major films as Western Approaches. The Islanders (1939) was produced by J. B. Holmes who was later briefly to supervise the Unit's output. Directed by Maurice Harvey it showed the importance of communications to the islanders in Eriskay, Guernsey and the Inner Ferns. It had music by Darius Milhaud and was beautifully photographed by Harry Rignold and Jonah Jones.

Spare Time (1939) gave Humphrey Jennings his first real opportunity as a director although he had worked as an assistant on several other films. Its aim was to show how working-class people (or lower income groups as Basil Wright called them) used their leisure hours. The examples were drawn from three industries -- coal, steel and cotton. There was a good deal of random shooting but the film lacked cohesion. There was some contemporary criticism of a condescending attitude towards the subject. Jennings, later to make memorable films, had his critics within the Unit. He was unpredictable, found it difficult to arrange a production schedule and was renowned for the excessive footage he shot. He could be relied on to throw a tantrum if he did not get his way. He was, however, always defended by Cavalcanti who thought of him as a film poet with "quite huge possibilities".

At the outbreak of war the G.P.O. Film Unit moved temporarily from Soho Square to what was thought to be a more secure building in Savile Row. It was not long, however, before they were all back in Soho Square. In the disorganised state of affairs existing then, with the Ministry of Information barely functioning and the Post Office occupied with more pressing business, there was nothing for them to do.

Cavalcanti is given the credit for deciding on his own initiative to send out small units to film what was happening in London. They shot for some days and assembled a considerable footage: sandbag filling, balloons rising, endless drilling, the evacuation of children. The result was The First Days (1940) with a commentary written by Robert Sinclair. The Ministry of Information did not know what to do with it so Cavalcanti and Watt took it to Wardour Street where eventually Pathé agreed to distribute it -- and pay for it, an arrangement of some importance to future arrangements for showing government financed films.

The Unit was approached by Air Vice-Marshall Boyd, commanding officer of the Balloon Barrage, and asked to make a film to show the value of the barrage. Most of the balloons were in the dock areas but a German raid on warships in the Firth of Forth meant a sudden change of plan. A squadron in training at Cardington in Bedfordshire was ordered to be in Scotland within twenty-four hours. Harry Watt filmed the preliminaries and accompanied the convoy. In Scotland the film-makers had some alarming misadventures including spending a night in the cells in Edinburgh after they had been arrested on suspicion of being spies. The German raid was re-constructed. Watt was proud of his inter-cutting of the aerial combat with shots of a whippet chasing a hare in a field below described to him by two eye-witnesses of the actual raid. Squadron 992 (1940) was one of the Unit's most successful films.

Watt was to make several films on the general theme of Britain standing alone in the world. The first was Dover - The Front Line (1940), filmed at the height of the Battle of Britain. After I had reviewed the film in The Scotsman Watt wrote to me suggesting that I had been too kind to it: "I didn't think it so good myself. It had a lack of punctuation which I found irritating and which inclined to leave one breathless and dissatisfied; but funnily enough it had a huge box-office success and went down very big with the public. I feel that this is not so much the merit of the film as a terrific desire on the public's part to see reality on the screen, and in the inhabitants of Dover they recognised themselves".

In his letter Watt went on to describe Britain Can Take It (1940) which he said he had just completed. Filming was done when the action was thickest in London and members of the unit, which included Jennings and Ralph Elton with Stewart McAllister editing, had many narrow escapes. One of them occurred when Wyatt and Elton were filming on the roof of the London University building in Malet Street and a land mine, which came down by parachute, exploded in Tottenham Court Road. Thousands of panes of glass crashed from the windows of the surrounding buildings. They were still shaken when they heard "whish-whish-whish" which they took to be another parachute. Instead it was the sound of hundreds of pigeons dislodged from their roosting places at the British Museum.

The commentary, written by Quentin Reynolds and edited by Watt, was recorded at Denham. Ken Cameron, who had joined the Unit and was in charge of the recording, was aghast at the volume of Reynolds' voice. It was his suggestion to place the microphone practically down his throat and to ask him to whisper. The device worked magnificently and the Reynolds whispered growl became one of the best known voices of the war. The film was made primarily for America. Harry Watt thought it "the most important film we have ever made and, if we had done nothing else, has justified our existence as a propaganda body in this war. It is going to get wide distribution from Warners in America and we are hoping to follow it up with a series of films made primarily for America".

One of the most ambitious of the early war films was Men of the Lightship (1940), a reconstruction of the bombing by two Nazi planes of the East Dudgeon lightship and the machine-gunning of the crew as they tried to escape in a small boat. Like lighthouses, lightships are supposed to be internationally sacrosanct. David MacDonald, the Scot who directed Alastair Sim in This Man is News and This Man in Paris and who later became head of the Army Film Unit, offered himself as director of the film. His attempt to use stage actors misfired badly and when Cavalcanti, producer of the film, saw the rushes, MacDonald was asked to think again and enlist men with real experience of the sea. The result was a highly dramatic and moving film although still on the theme of "taking it" rather than attacking the enemy. That did not come until Target for Tonight. Stewart McAllister edited the film, Ken Cameron recorded the sound and the music was by Muir Mathieson. It was the last film produced by Cavalcanti before he went to Ealing.

The Story of an Air Communique (1940) described how the R.A.F. arrived at their enemy casualty figures. It was made for the Ministry of Information and was one of the last to carry a credit to the G.P.O. Film Unit before it became the Crown Film Unit. The change had taken place by the time Harry Watt directed Christmas Under Fire (1941), again with a commentary by Quentin Reynolds and with carols sung by the choir of King's College Chapel, Cambridge. The opening words of the commentary were; "The Christmas trees will have to be very small this year, to fit into the air raid shelters". Watt called it a "weepie" - something to make the American public uncomfortable while they gorged themselves at Christmas.

Cavalcanti had departed for Ealing in the summer of 1940 and had been replaced by Ian Dalrymple. "He is now settling down", wrote Harry Watt to me in October, "and beginning to realise that although we do look a lot of scruffs we do sometimes show a knowledge of cinema".

A lot of scruffs? Although the Unit's headquarters had been very briefly in Savile Row, its members could not lay claim to Savile Row tailoring. Their priorities lay elsewhere. They certainly had not joined the E.M.B. and G.P.O. Film Units for financial reward. Salaries were never much more than bread-line level, especially for the young trainees who received only thirty shillings (£1.50) a week when they started. What was it that attracted them and led them to endure such working conditions?

The Film Unit was an exciting place to work in the 'thirties. Those who joined Grierson were persuaded that they were making a contribution to something worthwhile. Every member of the staff, down to Mrs Fox, the tough little cleaning woman, was made to feel that they were part of a team. There were no unionised lines of demarcation. Everyone pitched in, regarding of their job, in an emergency -- to collect rushes from the laboratory or take them down to Charing Cross station and put them on a train for Blackheath; or at a moment's notice to answer a call to go to the studio and appear in a film scene. The friendly atmosphere was infectious and was not disrupted by Grierson's forbidding manner.

On a different level the, senior directors recognised Grierson's larger purpose and were excited to be part of it. They had helped the documentary idea to grow. When they left the G.P.O. Unit they took with them Grierson's teaching and example. One or two of them, notably Stuart Legg and Norman McLaren, followed Grierson to Canada and helped to give the National Film Board its pre-eminence as a propaganda unit during the war. The G.P.O. Film Unit was Britain's only film school during the 'thirties. When war broke out there was a pool of experienced young film-makers on which to draw. Even if that WAS never the intention it was a fact and the Post Office had made it possible.

The Post Office celebrated the fiftieth anniversary of the founding of the G.P.O. Film Unit at Filmhouse in Edinburgh on October 1, 1983. The film programme consisted of <u>Colour Box</u>, <u>Coal Face</u>, <u>The Fairy of the Phone</u>, <u>Night Mail</u>, <u>Rainbow Dance</u>, <u>Mony a Pickle</u>, <u>North Sea</u> and <u>Britain Can Take It</u>. Among those present were four of the pioneers, Edgar Anstey, Stuart Legg, Harry Watt and Basil Wright; Marion Grierson, Phyllis Long and her husband Arthur Cain, Jenny Gilbertson and many others associated directly or indirectly with the documentary film movement. It was a fitting location in which to pay tribute to the Scot who founded the G.P.O. Film Unit and gave meaning to British documentary.

Edinburgh, October 1990. Copyright: The Post Office.

The G.P.O. Gets Sound, John Grierson

A prolific writer on film, John Grierson's published articles tell the story of the GPO Film Unit as it developed in the mid-1930s. In this short article he outlines his ambitions for sound film

Cinema Quarterly, 2 (1934), pp. 215–21

I SHALL not, in this, attempt a theory of sound but merely record the sudden possession of sound apparatus. The plaintive miracle of this event, the learned but sometimes too hopeful followers of cinema might note. Whatever one's theories, access to the means of production is not easy for art. The apparatus costs three thousand pounds or there-abouts; the re-recording apparatus is a luxury over and above that. This is the machine which orchestrates the different elements of sound – the natural sounds, the music, the dialogue – and, in effect, makes a considered sound strip possible. Add to these purely engineering costs the cost of your sound cameramen; add the cost of orchestras at two guineas per instrument per session of four hours; add the cost of a created music. Access to the means of production is clearly not a simple matter. That we have found an economic basis for it in government propaganda and, with it, have retained the same freedom for directors we enjoyed with the E.M.B., represents a relief and thankfulness I leave to the imagination.

We waited five years for sound at the E.M.B. We saw our first film fall in the gulf between silence and sound, and our subsequent films pile up in silence on a fading market. Our solitary access to sound last year was bound to be a disappointing one, for, selling some films to G-B., we were reduced to attendant orchestra and attendant commentator. Under such conditions responsibility passed out of our hands and experiment was plainly impossible. The result—in *Industrial Britain*, *O'er Hill and Dale*, *Up Stream* and the others—was, I suppose, competent. From any considered point of view it represented no contribution whatever to the art and practice of sound.

By access to sound, I mean an intimate relation between the producer and his instruments. I mean a relationship as direct as we have established for him in the matter of camerawork. He is his own first cameraman and the silly mystery with which professional cameramen once surrounded their very simple box of tricks, is over and done with. With us, the producer is his own sound man too, and in the same simple sense. In the studio the old camera nonsense has become attendant on the apparatus of sound. Mysterious bells are rung, and rung as for some great religious ceremony. High priests gabble in the same essential idiom as Thibetan priests over their prayer wheel, and a dozen perfectly unnecessary, or perfectly unimportant hangers-on, create atmosphere in the background. To convince so many important young men that so far as production is concerned they are only a bunch of chauffeurs who should be driving the car where you want it to go, is obviously too difficult for a mere documentary director. And it is probably not worth his trouble. Other phalanxes of experts lie beyond: knowing exactly – on one showing of your film and a couple of rehearsals – what music you want. And with studio overheads – the hangers-on nursing their overtime as religiously as their machines – and variation from the routine job is too expensive anyway.

By access to sound I mean the absolute elimination of these comic barriers between the producer and the result he wants. I mean the elimination of both economic and ideologic overheads. At the G.P.O. we have established it from the beginning. We have one sound engineer, and a good one. For the rest, if we want music – and we do not want it much – we find it cheaper to have it written for us. If we want natural sound, the producer drives out and gets it. If we want to orchestrate sound we sit in the sound van and arrange the re-recording as we think best. If we want to play with sound images, or arrange choral effects, or in any way experiment, we have no one's permission to ask and no considerable overheads to worry about, because we do most of the work ourselves. We are even free, as on one occasion recently, to make our own orchestra. The instruments and players were as follows. One rewinder (Legg), one trumpet, two typewriters (office staff), one empty beer bottle (blown for a ship's siren), one projector (by the projectionist), some conversation, two pieces of sand paper (Elton), the studio silence bell (myself), cymbals and triangle (Wright). Walter Leigh arranged and conducted. The result was our title music for *6.30 Collection*. It cost us the hire of the trumpet.

Indeed it is remarkable that our experiments have all made for cheaper sound. It costs five pounds, I believe, to have a professional commentator, but we have never thought of spending so much on so little. We do the job ourselves if we want a commentary, and save both the five pounds and the quite unendurable detachment of the professional accent. Better still, if we are showing workmen at work, we get the workmen on the job to do their own commentary, with idiom and accent complete. It makes for intimacy and authenticity, and nothing we could do would be half so good. You will see the result in both *Cable Ship* and *Under the City*. In *6.30 Collection* – a highly symphonic account of the Western District Sorting Office in London – Legg carried the connective commentary. Natural noises and some odd conversational scraps picked up by the microphone, told the rest of the story. No music was used in this film. In *Under the City*, we had music written for the beginning and the end and for a very beautiful slow motion sequence of an opening cable. In *Cable Ship* we borrowed some Mendelssohn to take a ship sentimentally to sea. The continuous undercurrent of music we have renounced. It was expensive, and none of us knew what it was there for anyway. We leave it to the less businesslike commercials.

These represent first variations and possibly not very important ones. *6.30 Collection* however, is probably the first documentary made entirely with authentic sound. It was not of course, a case of taking our sound anyhow. The noises of the sorting office were to some extent orchestrated. The racket of the interior grew with the increasing traffic. It swelled, it had lulls. It was broken by the repeated call of the bagmen coming to empty more letters on the facing tables, by the staccato machine-gun beat of the stamp-cancelling machines, by the careful introduction of oddments of conversation on allotments and this and that, by the choral effort of the dispatch men calling the destination of their bags across half the world, by a beautiful scrap of whistling. When the rush was over and the litter was swept from the deserted and now silent tables, we synchronized the swish of the brushes and crossed the sound of a starting train. And on the train and the ship and the aeroplane which followed, we crossed the chorus of destinations across half the world, repeated in its authentic monotone.

I do not pretend these are other than beginnings in the use of sound, but I feel they are right beginnings. I noticed when we showed the film at the Phoenix in London, that the natural noises and the overheard comments, orders, calls and conversations, created a new and curious relationship between the audience and the screen. The distance was broken down in a certain intimate delight – I presume – at seeing strangers so near. Eavesdropping, who knows, may yet be one of the pillars of our art. There was one superb sequence that we could not use. A dispatchman, edging unwittingly up to the microphone, loosed his more private opinion of some new and officious supervisor. The vocabulary was limited, but the variations were ingenious.

What we shall call the crossing of sound, to save the more difficult mention of asynchronism, is obviously a first consideration even in such simple experiments. There was a dilemma in the making of *Cable Ship*, for we began and ended on the same trucking shot of the International Telephone Exchange, to which our cable story related. As the first shot passed from one foreign switchboard to another, it was synchronized with telephone patter in the different languages involved. But to repeat this at the end would, we felt, be very ordinary, for the cable story had added other, less obvious, sounds to the patter of languages. Behind them were cable ships searching for faults, grappling for cables, mending them. The second time, we synchronized with the sound of a navigation order on the bridge of a ship, the order repeated, the ship's telegraph rung. Someone has just told me that he heard thirty years ago a discourse on flight, in which the lecturer maintained that the secret of bird flight lay not in the feathers, but in the air-spaces between the feathers. This I think, will serve very well for a working definition of the art of sound. The spaces between are the incidental sounds which, in a species of imagery, give perspective.

In our B.B.C. film and Savings Bank film, there will be, I hope, more mature developments. At one point in *6.30 Collection*, we thought of introducing the voices of the letters as they passed along the conveyor belt. We bought, in Woolworth's, a sixpenny book on "letter writing for all occasions," and had a mind to build up a rigmarole of excerpts from business letters, love letters, coy letters, angry letters, desperate letters, vain letters; but the trick was finally reserved. In the Savings Bank film, we shall probably put it into effect, and for better reason. The Savings Bank is probably the finest example of mechanized clerking in the country. It is a wilderness of filing systems and of machines which add up your deposits and calculate your interest. If I remember rightly, they even go to the trouble of checking up their calculations and confessing any wrong they have done you. The visuals plainly did less than justice to the reality which was there, tucked away in a myriad numbered slips: representing so many human cares and fears and hopes and responsibilites. Detaching them from the regimented mass, it is easy to see how resolutions are made every new year, are broken, are taken up again: how no description of the citizen's year can be half so true or half so intimate as the rise and fall of the millions at the Savings Banks. Something of this we shall try to tell, for over the mechanical visuals we propose to put a chorus indicating – it may be in short snatches of confession, or in plain objective record, or in *vers litres* – the human reference behind the slips of the filing cabinets.

Once, in Paris, before the coming of sound, I heard an *émigré* choir sing a background for *The Village of Sin*. They sang a harvest song for a brilliant harvest scene, and brought the audience to its feet. Walter Creighton recorded a similar chorus for his Canadian harvest scene in *One Family*, but made the mistake of associating "We Plough the Fields and Scatter" with the manipulators of the Winnipeg Wheat Pit. Chorus does not stop there. In *Three Cornered Moon*, you remember, snatches of conversation, held together, made a choral accompaniment for an unemployment sequence. People spoke in truncated desolation. In *Beast of the City* the monotonous sound of police calls on the wireless swept across the crime of a community. What development there might be if the often beautiful formulae of sound and word which occur in life were to be given dramatic value! I hold myself a house lease in eighteenth century English in which I swear by the Blessed Trinity, and an insurance contract with Lloyds is the most attractive hunk of English in commercial use to-day; a repetition of Lloyds list with its lovely ships' names and strange ports of sailing would make a splendid attendant sound on the commerce of the world.

And why not, at last, use the poet? The *vers librists* were made for cinema. The monologues of Joyce, covering as they do the subjective aspects of human action, are as important for the sound film as the dialogue of the dramatist. The masked changes in O'Neill between the word spoken and the word thought represent the simplest properties of any considered sound film. Eisenstein has possibly put the monologue too high in his account, by isolating it from chorus. It is only one species of choral effect, limited somewhat to personal story. The larger possibilities lie beyond monologue, I believe, in the poetry which, in the case of streets, say, will arrange some essential story in the mumble of windows, pub counters and passers-by. Our B.B.C. film will make some effort in the complementary direction. We try there to make our childrens' talk (a reading from Kingsley's "Heroes") cross-section an afternoon. We play Beethoven to cross-section a London night in one mood, and jazz to cross-section it in another mood. We read a psalm across starting machines, and a Shakespeare sonnet, with instructions to shipping mixed, across the coming of night.

1938–1940 G.P.O. Film Unit

For a Scot it is unfortunate that virtually the whole of the British film industry is centred in and around London. Today there are minor, and relatively insignificant, outposts of production in Scotland. In 1938 even these did not exist. So London it had to be. Once again my Aunt proved to the hilt her completely unselfish attitude to my future career. When she knew the way my mind was working she prepared to raise our tent and to emigrate to the Sassenach South. She even, although I did not know it at the time, started plans to sell her beloved Lammerlaw, and the beautiful furniture it contained. She knew that London flats would never accommodate seven foot wardrobes of inch and

Sound technician Ken Cameron joined the GPO Film Unit in 1938. In these memoirs he recalls the extraordinary lengths to which the Unit went to capture the sounds of everyday life. Unpubished memoir. Courtesy of BFI

a half Spanish mahogany, or dining room tables which varied in length from seven to fifteen feet. The decision to move was taken. But where to move? Film studios in the greater London area were widely separated from Welwyn in the North, to Pinewood and Denham in the West, to Islington in the East and even Blackheath in the South, with occasional spots like Lime Grove bang in the middle. Since I had no idea where, or if, I would get a job, we tried to settle on some locality which was more or less equidistant from them all. We ended up in Hendon. As it happened this was about as far as possible from my ultimate place of work, Blackheath. The British film industry in 1938 was going through one of its periods of doldrums in which it always has stagnated, now is stagnating, and so far as I can see always will stagnate. I wrote the usual letters. Sometimes I got a polite rejection. More often I got nothing. But I did try my luck with my old sparring boss Cavalcanti. Although I did not know it for a long time he passed my letter of application for work over to Stanley Fletcher, who was the civil servant in administrative charge of the G.P.O. Film Unit, with the scribbled footnote "I believe our sound problems may be solved". He summoned me for an interview at the Joint in Soho Square, and offered me the job of second - very junior - assistant to the Sound Department at a salary of £2:10s per week. Since very few members of the Unit actually received paper money in their weekly pay packets - as opposed to mere coins - this was quite something. Obviously my four years of academic toil at Gilmorehill had paid off. Naturally I jumped at the job.

However problems did arise. In those days sound was very much the poor relation. Sound was tolerated because it was a necessary evil. It was not a medium for artistic creativeness. The sound track was only there because audiences insisted on it. This philosophy, which existed to a greater or lesser extent in all studios, did not make for very amicable relations between the sound engineers and the other, more elite, technicians. And the G.P.O. Film Unit disposed of its sound men with a rapidity which was truly frightening. My boss saw the writing on the wall, and he made me somewhat less than welcome. Frankly I don't blame him. He had tried very hard, poor chap, to make bricks without straw. The equipment he was given must have been old-fashioned in the days of "The Singing Fool". The only place it might have been welcome was the Science Museum. This is no reflection upon the MarconiVisatone Company which built it. It is simply that certain technical advances had taken place since its creator stuck string and Seccotine together. My immediate superior, the first assistant, also realised that my appointment smelled somewhat of nepotism, and, while I do not think he ever actually sabotaged my faltering footsteps, he was, shall we say? not over helpful.

The inevitable soon happened. My boss was fired, and the middle man of our sound triumvirate shortly obtained employment elsewhere. Since they were both likeable people, and popular with the Unit, there was, at first at least, a certain coolness towards the new arrival. Even my attempts to join the technicians' trade union were thwarted, and for a while I was a pariah among men. Fortunately my good friend Cav. was loyal to me. At first he had to be. He had got the Unit into this mess and he had to get it out of it. We came to a useful mutual understanding. He agreed to fire me only every second week, which left me alternate weeks for my resignation. But somehow these dramatic departures never took place. We usually met on Friday evenings at our regular watering hole in Greek Street and settled our differences. In those days Scotch was only eight pence a nip.

It has been said many times that it is not absolutely necessary to be mad to work in the film business, but that it certainly helps. I have met many eccentrics in the last forty years. I have met men who take snuff and women who smoke pipes, men who wear thick fur coats in the summer and those who spend early frosty mornings running round the park practically naked, men who became Town Councillors for fun and those who persisted in wearing dark glasses even while looking at the screen. My particular eccentricity was wearing the kilt. I suppose it started when I was at school when it was practically compulsory. It lasted through my student days at University, possibly because many students did, and anyway it is the most thrifty and comfortable of garments. When I became properly involved in the film industry I decided that this would be my peculiarity. I am sure I was unique, and if one is different from everybody else in films one is half way there. I have heard of no other technician, even in Scotland, who sported this particular madness. It even occasionally had its uses. On more than one occasion I have heard of potential customers discussing where to record a certain music session, and they have decided to go to that studio where that lunatic always wears a kilt. The Americans loved it, although they still persist in referring to the garment in the plural. I remember once having a free day in Toronto, and deciding to visit Niagara Falls. The first two people I met there were two Scots also wearing their national garb. We spent a great day together. Once I was on holiday in Germany and ran into three youths also on holiday, not only wearing the kilt, but also, curiously enough, wearing Glasgow Academy Ties. I even turned, up at a gala premiere of a film at Graumann's Chinese Theatre in Hollywood in full highland evening dress - a most resplendent outfit. It was rather disappointing that nobody paid the slightest attention! Perhaps my most vivid recollection of my sartorial oddity was on one blisteringly hot Sunday afternoon driving down the Eltham Bypass to Glyndebourne, again in evening dress, and having a puncture and being forced to change a wheel. Passing motorists gaped at the sight with considerable surprise. Somehow one has to make oneself stand out from the run of the mill. I may not have been very good sound engineer, but at least I was different.

In those days there were two main tasks ahead of me, apart from survival, that is. I had to get help. Although I was only too happy to do everything in my power to make what I jokingly called my department a success from scrubbing the sound truck floor to sticking on stamps, there were certain operations in sound recording for which four hands were essential. It is true, although highly discouraged - that today, with modern tape recording equipment, it is possible for one man to produce an acceptable recording. But with the photographic system of recording then in force I was simply not able to be in two places at the same time. Grudgingly my superiors recognized this and I was permitted the services of a uniformed Post Office messenger boy when, and only when, this assistance was essential. I was therefore faced with the problem not only of teaching myself the intricacies of recording but of teaching this callow youth as well. Never was there a more blatant example of the blind leading the blind. I was also responsible for seeing that at all times this sixteen year old looked smart, clean, respectable, and a worthy member of His Majesty's civil service. This meant that all the really dirty jobs remained with me.

The second, and much more important job, was to try to convince my Lords in Soho Square, and through them His Majesty's Treasury, that the vanful of decrepit antiquated junk that we laughingly called our sound channel, should be replaced, if not by new and contemporary equipment, at least by something which promised that what emerged from the loudspeakers in the theatre stood a chance of bearing some relationship to what entered the microphone. Memoranda from me started to drop into Soho Square like confetti. And I secured useful help from acquaintances in R.C.A., the Company representing the Radio Corporation of America in this country. They knew - I cannot think how they found out - that there was just a chance that the only British government film unit might be considering up-dating its recording facility. And if any company was to get the contract they were going to make sure that their only real rival, Western Electric, did not. Looking back over these years I have a feeling that a little skullduggery went on. At any rate R.C.A. came up with the offer of an almost new recording channel, already installed in a streamlined van of frightening proportions. This they offered, together with such ancillary equipment as was necessary to provide us with a modest, but acceptable, re-recording theatre, for a sum which was not outrageous. Naturally I plugged for this with every effort at my disposal. And early in 1939 I won. The monstrous machine, newly painted in Post Office red, with the G VI R crest on both sides, arrived at Blackheath. Thank God it fitted into the garage.

There was of course, the minor problem of finding out how it all worked. But R.C.A. obligingly provided an engineer for a few weeks to take over, and I gladly resumed the role of second fiddle.

In the spring of 1938 the G.P.O. Unit, in conjunction with the B.B.C. decided to make an expensive prestige documentary on the history and development of television, which by now had started regular transmissions from Alexandra Palace. The intricacies of the story have long been forgotten, but I do recall that the script, for some obscure reason, called for the services of an elephant which among its other duties, was required to ascend the stairs of our little studio at the end of Bennett Park, Blackheath. Now it so happened that we had a caretaker there, a small wizened cockney by the name of Ernie Pring, who cleaned and generally officiated from a glorified cupboard down in the basement. He had a typically pawky east end sense of humour, and was universally liked. It also so happened that one day our elephant arrived at the studio. (The Post Office in those days could get hold of anything if it really set its mind to it). Since the residents of Bennett Park were sometimes apt to be a little tricky about some of our activities we impressed upon the elephant's keeper that every effort must be made to restrain his charge from, shall we say? adding to any debris on the street. Although as elephants go it was a very small one nevertheless it had great potential. The keeper knew all the tricks, and by keeping a firm grip on the beast's tail all seemed under control. Apparently this is the approved way of reducing such inclinations. Eventually all was ready and our artiste was conducted through the studio door when, momentarily, the grip on the tail was released. The poor animal had contained himself for a very long time, and now realised that it was time to pursue the course of nature. The heavens descended. The floor was soon awash and we retreated to the stairs, and the call went out for Ernie. The little wizened head peered round the corner, took one look, and said "I'm not paid to clear up elephant's piss" - and disappeared.

It was all in vain. When war broke out in a few months television transmissions had to stop for the duration. The film was abandoned and never saw the light of day. I wonder if the elephant ever forgot its moment of triumph.

Around about this time the ominous rumblings in Europe had been getting more pronounced. One day I was summoned to the Presence. It seemed that the Royal Naval School of Photography had acquired a Visa tone portable recording channel, not vastly different to the one we had recently disposed of. They needed urgently to record the sounds made by the, in those days highly secret, anti-submarine detection equipment known as ASDIC. They had nobody who knew how to work the channel, and I was a government servant, and therefore presumably trustworthy. The result of the meeting was that I was sent down to Portland, in the foul of winter, to spend many cheerless days on the bridge of a submarine chaser, recording what I can only describe as the pings and echoes of outrageous fortune. I was accommodated at night in a pub of indescribable squalor and discomfort, and I spent my days floundering through the turbulent currents of Portland Bight trying unsuccessfully to avoid vomiting over the Officer in charge. I was treated by the Officers on board as quite the lowest form of animal life, either because I was a civilian or because I worked for the Post Office - or both. When we came ashore each evening I crawled back to my slum, while the officers, without even a "Good Night", drove back to the Officers' Mess, presumably to spend the evening drinking duty free pink gins. I had to get the day's film sent back to London to be developed and printed under the watchful eye of an assistant who had to make sure that no unauthorised person got so much as a glimpse of the outside of the can. I suppose this exercise had some ultimate value in training ASDIC operators to recognise the difference in sound between a submarine and a shoal of fish. But certainly the whole thing induced in me a dislike for Royal Navy Officers that I have not lost to this day.

During the first six months or so of 1939 I was gradually accepted as a tolerable member of the Unit by the more or less senior technicians - by that I mean the men who were paid three to four pounds a week - men like the late and great Humphrey Jennings and Stewart MacAllister, Richard McNaughton, Pat Jackson and Chick Fowle, technicians who in their own way made a very great contribution to the image of the British Cinema. And with my gigantic new beauty of a sound truck I travelled the length and breadth of Britain. I was not allowed a driver. I had to drive this unwieldy pantechnicon myself, and this alone was frequently far from funny. On one occasion I was on a location for Humphrey Jennings for a picture called "Spare Time". I recall being in the Lake District one day when Humphrey indicated a narrow tortuous road leading up the side of a mountain which, to me at the wheel of my over laden and underpowered colossus seemed marginally less precipitous than the North face of Everest. "Meet us at the top", he said as he drove off in his chauffeur driven Daimler. I could not conceive what gems of sound I was expected to capture at that formidable altitude, but I knew better than to argue. My post was as yet by no means a sinecure. So, with a great deal of grinding of gears and boiling of radiator, I fought and reversed, and navigated and slithered, until we attained the rarified summit. Humphrey, puffing at a large cigar, was slightly piqued at my tardy arrival. When I pantingly enquired where he would like me to set up my microphone, he told me not to bother. He needed the presence of the sound truck merely so that he could put the camera on its roof. What dramatic effect would be obtained by this additional eight feet of altitude was never revealed because, being the Lake District, it promptly started to rain and continued to do so for the rest of the day.

I gained a useful cachet from driving this official vehicle. I was presented with a pass which enabled me to obtain petrol and oil from Post Office garages throughout the country without payment. I wish I had such a document now.

It was about this time that I was presented with a new assistant. Jack Lee, one of the Unit's directors and general factotums, had a younger brother Laurie, who in years to come achieved near immortality when he wrote his magnificent "Cider with Rosie". He had recently returned from a sojourn in Spain playing his violin throughout the Spanish civil war, a laudable if somewhat curious occupation. He had decided that he wanted to become a member of our happy band, and the only possible niche for him at that time was in assisting me. Poor chap. I never thought that loading magazines and topping up batteries were quite the right activities for one who specialised in poetry and his fiddle. He did not stay with me long, although we became good friends.

The European rumblings reached a climax at the end of August 1939, and the Unit was instructed to make a film with the utmost speed called "If War Should Come". It was to be a modest affair intended to tell the British public, in simple visual terms, what to do at once; how to dig trenches, how to put on gas masks, and generally how to behave when the now inevitable disaster happened. We made the film in, as I recall, the record time of about two days. We were all summoned to The Joint at 9.00 a.m. on Sunday September 3rd to take copies of the film to cinemas in the Greater London area for immediate screening. Unfortunately, by 11.00 a.m. war had come. This rather upset the direct message of the film. In any case all cinemas were closed. After all our hard work we thought that Hitler had invaded Poland for the sole purpose of ruining our efforts. Undismayed, we all rushed back to Blackheath, through the wailing of the sirens, to remake and re-record the film which was to be called "Do It Now". My memory escapes me as to whether it ever saw the silver screen. We all had more important things to do.

Like everybody else in my age group I registered for National Service and was duly called up. But before I had time to do up the buttons on my battledress or bash a single square I was reserved, and sent back to Blackheath. I felt at this time that my five years in the Officer's Training Corps at school had been rather wasted.

However, in the early days of the phoney war we did make some quite good films. Cavalcanti's "The First Days", David MacDonald's "Men of the Lightship", Harry Watt's "Squadron 992", Humphrey Jennings' "Spring Offensive" and many others were intended to make it abundantly clear to the British public that we were quite invincible and that the whole tiresome episode would soon be just a memory.

In 1940, after the evacuation of Dunkirk, it was all too clear to every inhabitant of the United Kingdom that we were going to be in for it in a very big way. The Prime Minister made his famous speech of "fighting on the beaches and fighting on the landing grounds". And our little Unit was told once again to make a film with all possible speed, a film of defiance and courage and determination. "Britain At Bay" was the result. It is rather strange that this film has not survived to the extent that other, some say lesser, films have, although much of the material shot for it has been used countless times in subsequent compilations. The Unit assembled all its talent, and every director and cameraman worked literally night and day. It is questionable whether much of a script ever existed. It was simply a matter of accumulating a mass of usually dramatic film, and using it to illustrate one of the fastest produced commentaries of all time. J.B. Priestly wrote and spoke it, superbly, in a matter of hours. It was recorded at Blackheath, with a laboratory standing by to give the processing top priority. When a rough cut had been assembled to fit the commentary, late one evening, the composer Richard Addinsell started to write his music. This was completed, orchestrated and copied throughout the night. Meanwhile an orchestra was booked under Muir Mathieson's direction to record at Elstree the following morning. Simultaneously the film was finally edited and titles photographed. We mixed the final sound track that afternoon and saw the first combined print that evening. The film reached the London cinemas on the following day. It was a rush job. But it did show what the Unit was capable of. It possessed exactly the atmosphere of tension and drama that was needed. Priestley's narration and Addinsell's music were quite brilliant. Even now, some fifty years later I can still recite the commentary by heart, and know practically every semi-quaver of the score. The Unit, it was still the G.P.O. Film Unit in those days, had really got the bit between its teeth. The credit for the film lies at no particular door. Cavalcanti, Jennings, Watt, everybody made their contribution. It was very well worth while.

When things warmed up and other things started going bump in the night the geography of our studio presented certain problems. A brief scrutiny of the map of Greater London will show that Blackheath lies more or less in the centre of a semicircle of dockland, and it became obvious to me amongst others that the studio - a building constructed of material which would hardly stand the impact of a damp squib - was not the safest home for what we prided ourselves was the centre of Great Britain's propaganda motion picture industry. The G.P.O. had by now handed over its sometimes intractable unit to the Ministry of Information, and officials there decided that all the members of the Unit who could easily be moved should be relocated in the peace and safety of Denham Studios, the one studio which was about as far as possible from the target of enemy activity. The sound department, however, was not so mobile. The theatre, its projection room, the sound wiring and so on had a degree of permanency, so we were left to hold the fort. I really believe the rest of the Unit forgot all about us. The Denham contingent took over what was known as the Old House, and its ancillary buildings. This was a delightful old mansion with lawns running down to the river. It used to be the headquarters of Sir Alexander Korda's staff, and the grounds had appeared in a number of Korda's pre-war London Film productions. About this time the Ministry of Information adopted the G.P.O. Film Unit completely, and we were renamed the Crown Film Unit. For the next twelve years, until it was unhappily and disastrously disbanded as a Government economy measure, the output of the Crown Film Unit became the inspiration of the world's documentary film making. The original conception of Grierson, supported for many years by the guiding hand of Cavalcanti, had created not only a first class teaching ground for technicians, but also a factory which turned out many films which are still prescribed study in film schools throughout the world.

1940–1943 Crown Film Unit

Soon after Crown was formed the Ministry of Information reorganised its hitherto incompetent Films Division. The useless old civil servant who ran it was removed, and Sidney Bernstein took overall charge. Jack Beddington, formerly of Shell, was appointed Head of the Films Division and immediately brought a new life and a sense of urgency into the University of London building in Bloomsbury, which was its headquarters. They recruited people like Montague Slater, John Betjeman, Arnot Robertson and others who knew how to get the right message over to the people. And they appointed a new Producer in Charge for Crown, a former film editor of enormous experience, Ian Dalrymple.

Dal occupied Korda's vast old office at Denham, a beautiful room over looking the river. To be summoned to the Presence involved a promenade which seemed about a hundred yards across the carpet to his desk where one stood like a small boy in the presence of his Headmaster. At the end of the interview we felt like retreating backwards, with a respectful bow at each six paces. It is not that Dal was a forbidding character. It was simply that he took a lot of knowing, and perhaps did not always approve of the somewhat undisciplined atmosphere which was by no means diminished by the Unit's new, exotic title. We also commandeered Korda's former private theatre as a review room together with a set of very presentable cutting rooms. Since the main Denham studios were still functioning, and incorporated a very efficient and well equipped sound recording assembly, I was left very much alone in the cold, dark fortress of Blackheath, with little to do when no location work offered. In 1940 Harry Watt, Humphrey Jennings, Stewart McAllister – and indeed the whole Unit - produced a film in two weeks which probably had as much influence in furthering our cause in the United States as any film ever made. It was also a tour de force for the London correspondent of the American Colliers Weekly, the vast, self-opinionated, gravel voiced Quentin Reynolds, who wrote and spoke the narration. The film was simple and brilliantly edited. The opening narration: "I am speaking from London. It is late afternoon, and the people of London are preparing for the night. It won't be a quiet night......." set the tone for as dramatic a ten minutes of movie as has ever graced the cinema. The film was called "London Can Take It". And I am happy to say that it incorporated a sound track of the London Blitzkrieg which at that time was unique. The nights I had spent at Blackheath, cowering in the basement with a microphone on the roof, had not been wasted. The film was shown hugely throughout the free world, and it boosted the reputation of Quentin Reynolds to enormous heights. It is rumoured that he showed it throughout the United States as virtually his own creation. Certainly his was the only name to appear on the screen. The Ministry officials seemed happy with our efforts and instantly called for a sequel, rarely a wise move in the cinema. Still, "Christmas Under Fire" was made shortly afterwards. This was not the enormous success of its predecessor, but it gave me the wonderful opportunity of recording the famous Festival of Nine Lessons and Carols in King's College, Cambridge. With my limited equipment this was a challenge which was almost insuperable. It was further complicated by the fact that Cambridge was practically the centre of R.A.F. fighter activity, and the constant roar of Spitfires and Hurricanes played havoc with the angelic boys' voices. Humphrey, who was in charge of the operation, put a halt on fighter activity for a couple of hours. Unfortunately the time came when we had not completed filming and almost every fighter in the district flew over to find out what was going on. Still I suppose it helped the atmosphere.

The other really major effort of the Unit in 1940 was Harry Watt's "Target for Tonight", the feature length film intended to demonstrate to the world that Britain was fighting back. Harry and his cameraman Jonah Jones, Julian Spiro, who was Harry's faithful assistant and who later on made many memorable films himself, and I, spent several weeks at Mildenhall aerodrome with an operational squadron of Wellingtons. The actors were all played by actual serving airmen, from Air Marshal to A/C plonk, and few of them saw the end of the war. It was a superbly made film and its success was inevitable. It ran in three major West End houses simultaneously, and, to the best of my knowledge, was the only feature length film ever to be shown at the same time in all three major cinema circuits in the United Kingdom. It became almost embarrassing. Few of the independent houses played it, and had full houses. You could not get away from it. There was certainly one independent cinema in Glasgow which displayed a huge canopy banner announcing "The only cinema in Glasgow not showing 'Target for Tonight'". This may not have been strictly true, but the queues lasted all day. In America too it made history. Sister Aimee Semple MacPherson converted her Angelus Temple for motion pictures, and tens of thousands of the inhabitants of Los Angeles thronged to see it. It is reported that in the continents of North and South America the film was seen by fifty million people. It is fair to say that "Target" and "London Can Take It" did a great deal to convince the people of the United States that Britain was not yet the chicken about to have its neck wrung. I was extraordinarily fortunate during the Blitz. I travelled right across London twice every day, in the Underground full of sleeping refugees from the East End, who spent the late afternoon until the early morning lying huddled together on the platforms, in safety from the bombardment but hardly in comfort. The bombs involved the cordoning off of great areas. The London transport system was magnificent. As Quentin Reynolds put it: "Londoners always got to work, one way or another". But in all these years I never suffered so much as a scratch. In our flat in Hendon we did not lose one window, although many of our neighbours were less fortunate. My most terrifying experience was one day when I was recording the London Philharmonic Orchestra under Malcolm Sargent in the old Queen's Hall in Langham Place. At the end of the afternoon we had completed all the principal recording, and sent the orchestra away, with the exception of the first trumpet. For some film we needed the trumpet call from Beethoven's Leonora. As the orchestra left the sirens sounded and the mighty cacophony began, even now on the recording one can hear the unsynchronised beat of the German bombers punctuated by the thumps from the guns in Regent's Park. When we had finished recording I was on the roof of our sound truck, about eight feet high, packing away cables. I heard something coming down which sounded definitely unfriendly and apparently in my direction. I jumped off the roof in one leap and landed in the gutter beside a policeman. The bomb landed in the Café de Paris in Piccadilly Circus - not far away as the bomb falls - killing over three hundred people. It was a most unpleasant evening. Shortly afterwards the Queen's Hall itself suffered a direct hit.

But in the intervals between the excitements of location work I was still stuck at Blackheath. It had its occasional compensations. Blackheath was also the headquarters of the Ministry's mobile projection units, and one of their tasks was to provide the equipment and staff for the Prime Minister's frequent after-dinner screenings at Chequers, his country residence in Buckinghamshire. Mr. Churchill was a keen movie fan, and when he set his mind on seeing a new American film a copy was flown over for him. One night I was working very late on some completion work for "Target for Tonight". In our little theatre were Harry Watt, Julian Spiro, Stewart McAllister and myself. I remember there was a thumping air raid in progress. When we finished our chores, around 2.30 a.m. I strolled out of the theatre to get a breath of fresh cordite and saw in the lobby a pile of fourteen brand new cans of film. The film had a title I had never heard of. It was obviously intended for an imminent screening to the Prime Minister. It was called "Citizen Kane". I mentioned this to Harry, who had read of its extraordinary reputation in American newspapers. We decided to steal a march on the P.M. and to run the film during the remaining hours of the night. We were, undoubtedly, the first people in

Europe to see one of the most remarkable films in the history of motion pictures. I cannot describe the effect this screening had on us. Orson Welles' unbelievable new techniques, the acting of the Mercury Players, the deep focus photography and the brilliant score by Bernard Herrmann, who, until his early death in 1975 became one of my very great friends - all this, in the early hours of the morning in the middle of a major air raid - was an experience I shall never forget. We left the theatre chastened and subdued, realising that we all had a great deal to learn. I have seen "Citizen Kane" many times since that night, and have learned more from every viewing, but never did Welles have a more attentive audience than on that night at Blackheath.

But the time had come to end the Blackheath/Denham situation. It was decided to concentrate the activities of the recently formed Army Film Unit and the Royal Air Force Film Unit with those of Crown in one large and efficient conglomerate at Pinewood Studios. Here we had access to four large and well equipped stages, many cutting rooms and offices, and two recording and two review theatres. Although the three units operated independently there was inevitably a cordial and valuable collaboration - particularly between the technical personnel. The Royal Air Force was in charge of security, and there may have been the occasional case of pique when a member of the unquestioned senior organisation, Crown, had to fight his way past an armed guard before he could get into his own office. But on the whole the arrangement worked well.

With the two service units and the one civilian unit all operating together on very much the same sort of work, problems occasionally arose, particularly when members of Crown were called upon to film on army or air force establishments or upon naval vessels at sea.

Pressure was raised, both from within and without the Unit to regularise members' position vis a vis service personnel. It was frequently embarrassing for technicians to visit officers' and other ranks' messes in civilian clothes. Film making is often a dirty job, and the rigours of wartime clothes rationing made the availability of presentable lounge suits at the end of a day's shooting quite a problem. Although members of the Unit had not quite sunk to the present day levels of patched jeans and dirty T-shirts which seem to be the fashion in studios today, nevertheless the sartorial appearance of a rather ragged bunch of men was not always acceptable to the commanding officer of a bomber squadron. Nor were the members of Crown always happy to cart along formal wear, with nowhere to change, before an evening meal in the mess. So the War Office officials were persuaded to kit us out in a sort of War Correspondent's uniform, with a pass permitting us to wear it when on actual duty with the Unit. I must say we had a somewhat Fred Karno appearance en masse, but most thought it was a step in the right direction. And it made a dramatic difference to our clothes rationing position. Perhaps it is not altogether fair to say that some of us used the privilege to travel on the Underground at half fare, but ticket collectors were far to busy to demand our leave passes or whatever. We wore battledress with no insignia other than a "Crown Film Unit" flash on our shoulders, and a C.F.U. crest cap badge. We wore collars and ties which, in those days, gave us the superficial appearance of officers, and we were instructed in the elements of military etiquette. At least we were taught when and how and whom to salute. This did, however, have a side effect which sometimes caused a little confusion. A few members, I can recall Humphrey Jennings, Jack Holmes, Jack Lee and myself, were members of the Pinewood detachment of the Home Guard, which involved the wearing of other ranks' uniform. We had to be very careful when in the street to remember how we were dressed. Crown's uniform of collar and tie and trench coat was quite definitely that of an officer. But my up-to-the-neck blouse, greatcoat, and my shining chevrons of a corporal in the Home Guard made me very much another rank. When approaching a real live genuine service-man - and it was impossible to move a few feet in London in those days without doing so - some rapid thought was called for to determine whether one was a saluter or a salutee. I know I had one or two embarrassing moments, and once caught a real rocket in Uxbridge High Street.

At about this time I was joined by Ken Scrivener, who from those days up until the present has been a close and valued colleague. We worked together in utmost harmony for thirty five years, and while I have now faded from the scene, our new company, which succeeded Crown on its demise, still boasts one of the most conscientious and talented re-recording engineers in the country.

A most important figure became associated with the Ministry of Information film production set up in the early forties. Muir Mathieson, unquestionably the leading light in British film music, and until his recent death one of my greatest friends, became music director to the Ministry. He taught me everything I was to know about music recording. And although a remark like this sounds pompous and egotistical, it is only too true that one could not work with Muir almost daily without some of the skill and excitement and love of his job attaching to his colleagues. Muir (of course he was a Scot) had been music director to Alexander Korda, and perhaps his most important and far-reaching contribution to the cinema was his persuasion of the great names of British music to work for this relatively new and not entirely respected art. Ralph Vaughan Williams, William Walton, Arnold Bax, Arthur Bliss, William Alwyn, Richard Addinsell, Malcolm Arnold, and countless others made their film music debut through the almost impertinent bullying of the then youthful Mathieson. When he first became associated with the official propaganda machine we got the benefit of his enormous talent. The first film Crown made at Pinewood was Jack Holmes' "Coastal Command", a film grandly conceived and executed. Muir had no doubts about the composer for its music. The grand old man of British music, Ralph Vaughan Williams, was asked - he was practically told – to write it. And he accepted. And I was privileged to be put in charge of the recording. I worked with Vaughan Williams many times in subsequent years, but I shall never forget the thrill of the sound of this magnificent score, played by the Royal Air Force Symphony Orchestra of some ninety players in the big H.M.V. studios in Abbey Road. His representation of the Sunderland flying boat take-off, on four trombones with orchestral accompaniment, was to me one of the most exciting moments in motion picture music.

We occasionally used No. 1 Theatre at Pinewood for more modest music recording sessions. By Blackheath standards it was enormous, but for our prestige films we, together with the Service units, began to look around for an auditorium where we could make use of the full strength of the R.A.F. Orchestra. This orchestra had an interesting history. Musicians were in no sense a reserved occupation and many fine players were called up, or enlisted, for the armed forces. Fortunately for British music the R.A.F. had the foresight to divert many fine players into a branch of the service where their talents could be put to good use. They did, it is true, their period of square bashing, but before long the orchestra's headquarters at Uxbridge - conveniently near to Pinewood - became the rehearsal centre of one of the finest orchestras in the country. With violinists like

Sidney Griller, pianists like Denis Mathews, and the incomparably fine horn player Dennis Brain, there was assembled an array of talent of truly impressive stature. I used to travel daily from Finchley Road tube station to Uxbridge in company with young instrumentalists whose very conversation was an inspiration. Once in Uxbridge we used to cross over to the Express Dairy for breakfast, to consume scrambled dried egg of unbelievable beastliness. I made many good friends who are my sparring partners at recording sessions today; they on their side of the microphone and I on mine.

I believe we were the first recording organisation to make experiments with Town Halls at Wembley, Watford and Hammersmith for music recording. These halls are still among the most popular for gramophone records. In those days, to prepare a hall with music stands and chairs, recording equipment, mobile projection apparatus and so on, ready for a 9.00 a.m. downbeat, meant a very early start indeed. But the results on the soundtrack were dramatically more exciting than anything we had ever been used to. The assistant to the commanding officer of the R.A.F. Orchestra was a young man, Sergeant, later Flight Lieutenant, John Hollingsworth, soon to be a great buddy of mine, who died soon after the war at a tragically early age. He became Music Director for Crown in the post war days when Muir resumed his full time activities with the feature cinema. He subsequently attained musical near-immortality when, as assistant conductor to Sir Malcolm Sargent in the post war Promenade concerts, he was forced to take over the whole concert series at a few hours' notice when Sir Malcolm was taken seriously ill. John was due to have Christmas lunch with my Aunt and myself one year, but never arrived.

He was found dead in his flat the following morning. On that day music lost a fine conductor and I lost a great companion.

One of the most exciting, to me, films of the early war period was Humphrey Jennings' "Listen to Britain", a cameo of Britain at war told entirely in sound. The climax of the picture was the filming of one of Myra Hess's National Gallery lunchtime concerts, with Myra and the R.A.F. Orchestra playing the Mozart G Major Piano Concerto. Indeed the film was originally conceived by Jennings around the concerts, because its shooting title was "National Gallery". The set-up for the recording of this was hideous in its complexity. We possessed no portable equipment and cables had to be run from the courtyard behind the Gallery to the concert hall along about a quarter of a mile of ventilation tunnels. This recording started a happy friendship with Myra, soon to become Dame Myra Hess. A brilliant player, a great teacher, and a charming and lovable personality. When Humphrey set his mind on a sequence for a picture nothing would divert it. He had no qualms about persuading Her Majesty the Queen to wait behind after the concert to secure some much needed close-ups. Later on he practically set the East End of London on fire (for the second time) to obtain a realistic reconstruction of the 1940 Blitz. Humphrey, alas, is no longer with us. He was accidentally and stupidly killed soon after the war on a Greek island, trying to secure a camera angle minutely more effective than a nearer safer one.

These were all great people to know; great and talented friends. To recall conversations over snack lunches and leisurely pints of beer, with fine technicians, great authors, actors and musicians, is to open an old diary of fascinating memories.

A most important component of the sound track of a major documentary film was the sound effects track. We had all been brought up in the tradition that everything in a true realist film should be genuine. We very rarely used professional actors because we were convinced that the actual man doing his own job gave a more convincing performance than somebody impersonating someone else. We only built sets in the studio when, for one reason or another, it was impossible to film on the actual location. The true reasons for this were not the reasons of economics, although such considerations had to come into it. It was all part of the philosophy of the documentary film. Unquestionably many of our films lacked some of the technical polish which glossed some of the alleged feature documentaries which emerged from other studios, but we like to think that what they lacked in technical expertise they gained in the genuine atmosphere of truth. We followed the same policy with our sound effects, perhaps sometimes to absurd lengths. In Jack Holmes's "Coastal Command" a great deal of the action took place in a Sunderland flying boat. It was shot in a flying boat, in the air, with the actual crew playing their operational roles. It was hardly likely that we should spoil the ship by using the incorrect engine sounds. Even if the cinema-going public could not tell the difference, a member of a Sunderland crew would. And if you cheat once you have lost the confidence of your audience. But the days of light, mobile recording equipment had not arrived. Our sound truck, as we have said, was vast. Ten enormous accumulators drove a large generator for the camera and recorder motors. Several more supplied power for the amplifiers, mixing desk, loudspeakers. Rolls of film and so on literally added tons. To make it more difficult Sunderlands were operating only off the Western Isles of Scotland. Even the Air Ministry jibbed at releasing one down to southern England simply to capture the noise of its engines. So I drove the truck up to Cumberland, embarked it on an empty tanker, sailed through stormy seas to Islay in the Hebrides, and waited until a Sunderland flew overhead. With the sound happily in the can we returned to Pinewood. For Jack Lee's "Close Quarters", the story of an operational raid by a submarine, we were forced to build a replica on the stage at Pinewood. The Royal Navy were less than willing to put an operational submarine at our disposal for several weeks. But the noise of depth charges exploding, as heard from inside the hull of a submarine, was a very characteristic one. So once again we made the journey to Scotland, to the submarine base at Rothesay in the Isle of Bute, this time with a transportable Western Electric recording channel borrowed from the Army Film Unit. This was also enormously bulky, but at least it could be separated into its component parts, and installed in an empty compartment of the submarine. We set to sea, we submerged, and we were duly depth-charged - at a discreet distance. Although the explosions sounded exactly like dustbins dropping from a height at least it was the real thing. Perhaps our philosophy was a little misguided and extravagant, but it was the philosophy of the documentary movement and our consciences were clear. They were certainly substantiated later in the war when the V1 flying bombs came over the south and east coasts. We recorded the real thing then; nor was it a funny sound. A V2 rocket was beyond us, but we even managed to capture that by accident.

We got into a little trouble once when Humphrey Jennings was making "The Silent Village", the story of the extermination by the Nazis of the Polish village of Lidice as a reprisal for the assassination of the German Marshall Heydrich. The film was really a reconstruction of what might have happened under similar circumstances had the Nazis overrun this country. The location chosen by Humphrey for the reconstruction was the village of Cwm Giedd in the Rhondda Valley of South Wales. There was a sequence of German loudspeaker cars slowly cruising through the village, broadcasting to the villagers the announcement that, unless the assassins were delivered up to the authorities for punishment, every man would be shot, every woman and every child would be taken away to labour camps, and the village would be razed to the ground. All this had happened in Poland, and the sequence was a tense and dramatic one. To record this announcement satisfactorily every experiment failed, and the only chance of getting the right effect was, literally, to broadcast the announcement – in English with a German accent - in the open air at night, when no outside interference could disturb the clarity of the track. The loudspeakers would have to be played very loud with the microphones a long way away. All this was easy enough. Unhappily we omitted to tell the residents in a half mile radius of Pinewood of our intentions. Early one morning everybody in the district was startled by a German-sounding announcement of terrifying threats to the "People of Cwn Giedd". Police telephones rang. Police cars arrived at the studio. There was a terrible hullabaloo. Humphrey shrugged the matter off with his customary sang froid, but the situation took a great deal of explaining. For some reason the Crown Film Unit had blotted its copybook amongst its neighbours, not for the first time, nor for the last.

One of the duties of the Films Division of the Ministry of Information was to act as a form of security censor for films to be shown in public cinemas. To this end, Jack Beddington, the Head of the Division, used to run a new feature movie almost every morning, quite early, in his theatre in the Ministry of Information building at the University of London. He had no objections to members of the Crown Film Unit attending if their own jobs made it possible for them to get away. I often used to turn up and share an eight o'clock coffee with Jack. One day, I believe it was late 1943, I mentioned to him how dearly I should like to pay a brief visit to Hollywood, to see for myself how things were actually done over there. To my amazement he said "Why not?". One week later I was on my way.

Those who worked for the GPO Film Unit were expected to muck in and help out with all sorts of odd jobs. Here Film Unit employee Edith Stedman tells her story

'My Day's Work at the Film Unit', Edith Stedman © Royal Mail Group Ltd 2011. Courtesy of The British Postal Museum & Archive

The Post Office Magazine, January 1939, p. 16

My Day's Work at the Film Unit

by Edith Stedman

FRIDAY the 13th. As I tear off the calendar I realise that it is going to be a real 13th.

A glance at the diary. Yes, the set downstairs has to be a furnished room, but no furniture has turned up although it was ordered days ago. I run down hatless to the village. By ten o'clock they will begin shooting for "N. or N.W." and that furniture simply must be in position.

There seem to be more shops in Blackheath that sell furniture than I knew existed, but none of them had heard of a tiger-skin rug, a divan, a sideboard and chairs for the Bennett Park Studio. Just as I am in despair and walking back I hear footsteps behind me. Someone has remembered. He has the order but cannot deliver it before noon. I fly to the railway station, engage every available porter and their barrows and arrive in triumph with the furniture on time.

I return to my day's normal work. It is varied, but however hard I work I never lose interest because, above all, film-making is exciting. There is the typing of scripts, which are often revised three or four times until I know them off by heart, but there is the thrill of seeing the whole thing on the screen in a few months' time.

Perhaps you will think that the most exciting part of my work is " acting," but to tell the truth I cannot act a bit. I am told, however, that a documentary film is of people at their own work, so I just have to do exactly what I am told by the Director. Once I was called down to the Studio to take a letter in shorthand, for the film called *Big Money*. The amusing part was that the sound engineer complained of a strange noise during the rehearsal, and it was traced to the leading man's shoes, which had a slight squeak. The shoes were removed, I stifled my inclination to laugh and the dictation continued.

The most comfortable role was that of a " wife " listening to her " husband " reading the paper in a breakfast scene and talking about the Budget. We were provided with real food—sausages, eggs, bread and butter, and tea. During the rehearsals I made a good meal and thereby saved myself the cost of lunch.

Another rush job was running round Blackheath to fix up eight Scottish trawler-men in lodgings. The Unit went up to Aberdeen to make a big picture dealing with the North Sea, and they 'phoned to say they were bringing the men down for a week. We had a huge model of the inside of a trawler in the Studio, and the crew sat up in the " rocker " which was moved up and down to the rhythm of the sea.

Then there is the Display Section. I had to mind a baby for them one day whilst they took the mother down to be " shot." The switchboard was busy, so the poor mite had to be " roped in " on a chair until mother returned.

A scene from the Unit's film "North Sea"

Bennett Hall is an old Manor House, and if ever there was a ghost I am quite sure it is now " laid." It is usual to take down a letter to the accompaniment either of " Swiss yodelling " or the noise of twenty trainees being taught to work a projector. Once I was sure there was a ghost coming up the stairs, but the rattle-rattle, clank-clank was a heavy slave chain being dragged along for a film about negroes.

If any of my readers come down here as film stars, please don't come to me while I am taking three trunk calls at once and say, " Oh, did *you* write that article ? " I'm telling you, " You have been warned " . . .

Moving Silhouettes, Lotte Reiniger

German silhouette animation film-maker Lotte Reiniger was one of several avant-garde artists who found their way to the GPO Film Unit from mainland Europe in the 1930s. Here she offers a rare insight into the behind-the-scenes method which went into making her beautiful films

'Moving Silhouettes', Lotte Reiniger, *Film Art*, 3 (1936), pp. 14–18

Film is motion. The great sensation of the early films was the fact that photographs could be seen moving on screen. It seemed to be a wonder and well I can remember my excitement being taken to a picture for the first time to notice that the people on the screen were really moving.

In those early days a *chasse* or a pursuit was always the action, and the audience loved to see jumping horses, speeding carriages and rushing trains. There was usually a small plot, very simply acted, to give a reason for the hunt. The audience only became film conscious when the chase started. Something new was born, never seen before, *the film*, an independent form of expression, borrowing neither from the novel, the theatre or painting – just pure and simple motion on screen.

A world of experimental variety was thrown open; but by exploitation of the technical resources and the artistic possibilities of this new medium, the film developed to such an extent that it now looks back ungratefully and rather with scorn on the good old days – the basis of its glory. I regard this as rather unjust.

However, such are the penalties of evolution. Artists and commercial people constantly try – sometimes working together, but more often opposing each other – to discover new means to bring fresh life and further development to this new art. In this big army which is crusading after new land for the screen, the silhouette films I happen to make only play a very modest part. But at the same time this branch also deserves a certain amount of interest, being part of the "trick-film-salvation-army" that creates motion, not by photographing natural movement and mounting it, but by artificial means.

The genius of Disney and his followers has made the audience love this kind of fake motion, and by now it has acquired a special place in the development of the cinema.

In the silhouette film, instead of the creator playing with drawings, the marionettes play before the camera. These marionettes are not moved by strings or sticks, but constructed with as many limbs as possible. They are laid flat on a glass table; thus the light from underneath does not show the joints when the camera looks down on them to take the picture, frame by frame. When the camera is at rest the figures can be touched and moved into the next position for a further shot to be taken. And so *ad infinitum*.

I have always been fascinated by the problems of artificial movement in films, and since I became mixed up in this unfortunate business – which is a long time ago now - this medium has never failed to keep me interested. Of course I like to experiment with different variations of abstract movement for background, lighting effects, etc. But the real sensation for me has always been – and will always be – the discovery of various possibilities of screen rhythm which, to my experience, is the most essential part of film art. For here rules are to be found that have nothing to do with other arts and essentially belong to the screen, and the screen alone.

All this business of discovery and experiment was much simpler in the silent days. Filming, for one, was less expensive then and the artist could go about his own ways more easily. Also the screen's genuine rhythm spoke more for itself.

In the present stage of sound film production, where one has to consider the things that are heard was well as the things that are seen, sound illustration has become a reliable guide. The musical score has increased its importance, and one can always be certain now to have the same musical value, whether performed in a small or a large film theatre. The creator of trick-film movement can be compared with the choreographer of the ballet – only he has not the space of the stage, but the more flat conditions of the screen to consider.

The ideal state for artists like us would be where we could make a film as we like, and add the musical score afterwards. This process, however, would increase the cost of the film considerably, and at the moment there is not sufficient money in these *shorts* – at least not in Europe. It is therefore wiser, from an economic point of view, to have the sound track made first, measure it carefully and only commence the film after this has been done.

The preliminary work for this is to make as many drawings as possible, to find out how many movements are needed for each bar and whether the figure can carry out these movements in that space and time. This is the most elaborate part of the preparations and often takes longer than the film itself.

To give a practical example, I have exactly illustrated how movement in a silhouette film is worked out. (See Text).

I have endeavoured to show here how musical value is transformed into screen-space-value. The movement in question comes from my Papageno Film, set to the music of Mozart's Magic Flute. It is the final duet between the lovers, happily united at the end. They dance and sing:

Welche Freude wired das sein
What a pleasure that will be

16   17

NO. I. WHAT—
They approach in rather fast motion. 6 frames for one step.

NO. 2. A—
They bend a little lower to prepare for the jump. 4 frames down.

NO. 3. PLEA—
Papagena is lifted up in 6 frames.

NO. 4.
The highest point is reached in 6 frames, arms and legs moving quickly.

NO. 5. SURE—
Moving down the figures come very close together, Papageno swinging her legs forward quickly, in 4 frames only.

NO. 6. THAT—
The figures now nearly overlap. This opportunity is taken to change the position of their bodies, so that they may continue in another direction. The movement here is very quick as to be in the next position soon, which is allowed to continue 4 frames.

NO. 7. WILL—
They have turned round. She glides more gently now to her new place. 7 frames.

NO. 8. BE.
They get into the position for the next step, separating a bit from each other.

NO. 9. INTERVAL OF EIGHT FRAMES.
The interval allows them to get into the right starting position for the next line. 8 frames.

The measure of sound allows for so many frames each syllable:

TEXT: What / a / ple / sure / that / will / be
FRAMES: 6   4   12   4   7   4   8

with an interval of 8 frames at the end.

The arrows show the direction of the movement and the probable distance from one position to the other, for just that size of figure. This means 48 frames or the equivalent of two seconds in time. And so the whole action is worked out. As I have to avoid making mistakes during the photographing, this preliminary timing is highly necessary. To me this work is one of the most pleasant parts of the whole film. It is surprising how with each different score fresh problems of interpretation arise, and although I have been engaged in this sort of work for a long time, each new film seems to me like a start again.

And this is perhaps good, for without it I certainly could not help feeling a certain amount of bitterness towards an industry that fails to appreciate the hard work put into the creation of a silhouette film, – after all an artistic achievement, – yet is always ready to squander money on things of little importance.

Grierson resigned from his position at the GPO Film Unit in 1937. This is the letter he wrote to confirm his departure

G.P.O. Film Unit,
21, Soho Square,
W.1.

4th March, 1937.

Dear Boyd,

    This is to confirm my talk with you yesterday.
I propose, with your agreement, to bring my resignation
into effect at the end of June.   This period is
perhaps good sense on all sides.   The G.P.O. Unit will
benefit from a considered and unhurried change-over
which, with the alterations in personnel we discussed,
may be a trifle complicated, and I myself want
breathing space in which I can do something to secure
my material future.   There is the further point that
we will have to give the new producer good notice.
Everyone is heavily engaged at this time of year.

    I look forward, as I told you yesterday, to
some continued association with the work we have done
here.   In any case, I am sure the Unit will continue
its effective work for the G.P.O.

                            Yours Sincerely,
                            John Grierson

Cavalcanti in England, Elizabeth Sussex

After Grierson left the GPO Film Unit it fell to Alberto Cavalcanti to steady the ship. Many years later in 1975 film writer Elizabeth Sussex encouraged him to reflect on his relationship with his fellow GPO film-makers

Elizabeth Sussex, *Sight & Sound*, Autumn 1975, pp. 205–11. Published by BFI

Alberto de Almeida Cavalcanti, a Brazilian who first made his mark in films with the French avant-garde in the 1920s, spent sixteen of his most creative years in England. He was a key figure first in John Grierson's GPO Film Unit and then in Michael Balcon's Ealing Films—the only two movements that have pioneered styles of film-making indigenous to Britain. What exactly was Cavalcanti's contribution to both these set-ups and consequently to British cinema, and has it been sufficiently recognised?

In recent years, evidence has emerged of a strong division of opinion between Grierson and Cavalcanti, but its true nature is still concealed behind what are represented as rather petty squabbles about things like credits. Was Cavalcanti's light being deliberately hidden under a bushel from the time he began to break new ground at the GPO and his name was allegedly omitted from the credit titles of his key experiment *Coal Face*? Did he make the contribution that really put British documentary on the map? Is he perhaps the most underestimated figure in British film history?

This article, which is an attempt at reassessment, is based on recent conversations with Cavalcanti in his Paris flat and with Sir Michael Balcon at his home in Sussex. It also draws on the mass of interview material with Grierson and other members of his movement collected for my book *The Rise and Fall of British Documentary* (University of California Press, 1975).

'I don't know very well how you can explain,' said Cavalcanti. (He sat surrounded by surrealist objects both sacred and profane. Above his head hung a huge portrait of his mother. The family resemblance was striking.) 'I don't want to appear a nasty old man, and I don't want to appear as a man who is taking advantage, but I am puzzled and astonished by certain events that I learned in succession from time to time including this last winter, that made me sort of wonder and find that the disagreement was much deeper than I thought — because as a matter of fact, being out of work, I wrote to Grierson in great innocence, which I wouldn't have done, to ask for a job when he was in TV in Scotland.'

It seems that Cavalcanti, who has been lecturing at the Film Study Center in Cambridge, Massachusetts, over the last few years (at seventy-nine he says he cannot afford to retire), was told 'partly by people from Chicago and mostly people in Canada that Grierson had a very strange behaviour towards me when he left the GPO. It had started in London when he was at Film Centre but I never paid any attention to it and never thought it was important. Knowing what happened when he went to Canada, I realised it was—that he had a kind of bitter attitude, for instance films I had to do with were forbidden to the Canadian Film Board boys ... All the films that I made at the GPO were forbidden, and that was very peculiar.'

It appears to be true that Grierson banned screenings of early British documentaries to his Canadian team, and although his reasons for this are hard to comprehend they may have had nothing to do with Cavalcanti. All this was a very long time ago. When I met Grierson only a few years back he was full of enthusiasm about the early days and gave no indication of animosity towards Cavalcanti.

But Cavalcanti has also been upset by things like the discovery that his name is not included in the entry on British documentary in the Bordas *L'Encyclopedie du Cinema*—"It quotes all the names of everybody of the Grierson crowd and doesn't quote mine. I could very easily go to them and say "Who is the person who gave you this information?" I think I have the right to do that, but I just did not care and said, "Oh well, to hell with it. What I did, I did ...""

The recurrent argument about credits is a very considerable puzzle.

'Everybody knows that the credits in the GPO film unit were full of fantasy, and of Grierson fantasy,' says Cavalcanti, and Grierson himself said that he was quite sure some of them were still 'totally wrong'.

'The selflessness of some of the documentary people was a very remarkable thing,' said Grierson. 'They didn't put their names on pictures. People finally had to try to discover where the credits lay, and the poor old Film Institute has never quite discovered how the credits of documentary lie even today, because we kept on putting on the names of the young people, not the names of the people who were concerned. There were years when Cavalcanti's name never went on a picture. We weren't concerned with that aspect of things, with credits. It was only latterly that credits became important to the documentary people.'

What credits in particular are wrong?

'My name is not on *Coal Face*,' says Cavalcanti. 'I cut the film completely myself, the whole conception of the sound. It was library film. Harry shot one sequence, and Jennings shot one sequence. We used some of the old Flaherty tests ... I faked— I did lots of shooting in the studios to be able to cut the Flaherty material in, and I wasn't given a credit. I didn't complain. After all, it was a small film. It was an experiment for *Night Mail*. On *Night Mail* I have the Auden and Britten title for "sound direction", which doesn't exist as a credit. Well I did much more than that because the whole cutting, the conception of the whole thing, is the result of *Coal Face*. But I didn't care about that at all. I had no credits for half of the stuff I did, so it's funny to accuse me of *wanting* credits. If I had insisted on being given what I made I would have many more, I assure you.'

'In afterthought,' wrote Paul Rotha in his recent *Documentary Diary* (where incidentally he implies that Cavalcanti had been complaining for many years that his name had been suppressed by Grierson from credit titles and publicity on GPO films), 'I think Grierson had a valid point in this one-sided argument when he recalled that Cavalcanti had asked for his name to be left off such films as *Coal Face, Granton Trawler* and *Night Mail* when they were made because he felt that association with such *avant-garde* work might jeopardise his chances of employment in British feature film production at that time.' When did Grierson have this recollection? According to Rotha's footnote, it was during an interview with him at Devizes on 17 June 1970.

The idea that he wanted his name left off for this reason infuriates Cavalcanti even more than the idea that he wanted it on: 'I wasn't named three-quarters of the time, and then they say I was trying to grab a position in the fiction industry. I stayed for seven years at a wage of misery — I had to begin with £7 a week — because I was tired of fictional films in France. I was doing them, and I was very successful with the comedies I was doing, and I didn't want to go on. I wanted to experiment in sound.'

It is certainly very easy to find evidence which suggests that Cavalcanti's primarily aesthetic contribution to British documentary has always been a little underplayed by comparison with that of the social propagandists who took their lead directly from Grierson. Yet Cavalcanti's contribution is acknowledged to have been a large one. To understand it properly, I think we have to go back to the beginning, which for Cavalcanti was earlier than it was for most of the others. In the 1930s, in fact, all the documentary people were rather differently placed in relation to each other from the way they are now. When Cavalcanti came to England to join the GPO film unit in 1934, he was thirty-seven years old and had a whole career behind him. Born in Brazil, he seems to have been a lot brainier and at least a little more argumentative than average from the beginning. He began law studies at the age of fifteen and remembers being the youngest student in the university, but-he was 'expelled because of a quarrel with an old professor.' His father sent him to Geneva on condition that he steer clear of both law and politics, and he trained as an architect. At eighteen he was working in an architect's atelier in Paris. From there he switched to interior decoration and then to the art department of the film studios. He did set designs from 1922 for Marcel L'Herbier, Louis Delluc and others, and he became a member of the *avant-garde*, which he describes as a movement of inward as well as outward dissent and strife.

'We hated ourselves ... We couldn't bear any of the others. We had one thing in common and one only—we were in disagreement with our masters' art, the art of the people we were working for. I thought L'Herbier didn't face films to try to make them speak their own language. He tried to make films speak literature, and all our masters used films as kind of novels or plays. They weren't concerned in finding a language for films. We all had that in common: we thought there was a language, and that it must be searched for, it must be found.'

In retrospect Cavalcanti sees something constructive not just in the search but in the whole atmosphere of mutual criticism: 'I don't know if that hatred among ourselves was not a good thing. I think it was. And we had a trump card in our hands. We were friendly with all the great artists of our time in Paris — all the painters, sculptors, writers. They liked us and they helped us. Now if you compare what they call the *nouvelle vague* with that, the *nouvelle vague* is totally different . . . They don't detest each other at all. They love each other. They praise each other. They push each other. All that should improve on us, on the generation before, but it doesn't because they know nobody among the painters, the people in the other arts. They are completely self-centred in films, film magazines etc. That is the true difference. When I came to England I was surprised by how much film people there were sort of tied together.'

Cavalcanti came to England after several years in which, due to the arrival of synchronised sound, no *avant-garde* work had been possible. He had even had a period of exile from the studios 'because the French like the Americans thought the silent film directors couldn't do sound pictures,' but he came back to make French and Portuguese versions of American films for Paramount. These were followed by a series of French comedies of his own which he claims were 'terrifically successful commercially' but very primitive' in their use of sound. 'I had learned sound the hard way,' he says, 'the know-how to record dialogue, but I thought dialogue was one small part of sound and not the sound film.' The moment Grierson's unit got its own recording equipment, he broke a contract to come over to England.

Grierson was happy. 'My boys don't know anything about sound,' he said, inviting him by all means to amuse himself for a while at the unit's newly acquired studio in Blackheath. Grierson's boys knew about Cavalcanti, of course. He was one of the names that had impressed them at Film Society screenings. Grierson was lucky or, perhaps more accurately, knew how to use his luck. First Flaherty, now Cavalcanti. Apart from any other considerations, the reputation of the fledgling school of British documentary was obviously much enhanced by its ability to attract international names like these.

Cavalcanti settled in contentedly: 'I was so happy I stayed seven years there, and I think the result was very good. But the atmosphere in Blackheath was wonderful, you know. . .' With the exception of Grierson, who worked mainly from the unit's offices at 21 Soho Square, Cavalcanti found himself 'the only sort of middle-aged person there.' Budding directors like Harry Watt and Basil Wright and Humphrey Jennings, then still in their twenties, naturally looked up to him as a film-maker of stature as well as someone with all the technical knowledge they still lacked.

'I was enormously grateful to him and always shall be, apart from his friendship which I managed to obtain, for all the things he did on films I was working on like *Song of Ceylon* and *Night Mail*. His ideas about the use of sound were so liberating that they would liberate in you about a thousand other ideas,' says Basil Wright. He remembers having both Grierson and Cavalcanti in the same set-up as 'absolutely magical . . . worth a million pounds to any young man to be there.' Harry Watt goes further. 'I believe fundamentally that the arrival of Cavalcanti in the GPO film unit was the turning point of British documentary,' he says. 'If I've had any success in films I put it down to my training from Cavalcanti, and I think a lot of other people should say the same thing.'

Grierson's relationship with Cavalcanti was always a little different. 'He only came to the studios to upset my work,' Cavalcanti claims now. 'He used to shift everybody all the time, which upset me a lot . . . Indeed everybody knew this well in Blackheath.' People knew it and, like Cavalcanti himself perhaps, chose mostly to make a joke of it?

'It must have been very difficult for Grierson when we technicians more and more turned to Cavalcanti with our problems,' wrote Watt in his recent autobiography, 'but he (Grierson) was honest and shrewd enough to realise how much more polished and professional our films were becoming under Cav.' In fairness it must be added that Harry Watt was never quite on Grierson's wavelength as far as work was concerned. For some people, Grierson was still the dominant influence. For instance, despite his warm appreciation of Cavalcanti, it is Grierson's artistic contribution to *Song of Ceylon* that Basil Wright has almost total recall of, and indeed describes in every detail with undiminished gratitude to this day.

In any case, arriving as he did at such a crucial moment in the GPO film unit's story, Cavalcanti's influence as a teacher and adviser really goes without saying. More than that, however, the story of Grierson's movement is one from which Cavalcanti, at least in spirit, had never been entirely absent. Himself a pioneer in the making of *avant-garde* films virtually indistinguishable from what Grierson labelled 'documentary', his example was there from the beginning, and indeed the influence on British documentarists of Cavalcanti's *Rien que les heures* (1926), which was shown in London earlier than the famous Film Society programme introducing *Drifters* along with *Battleship Potemkin*, is put on record by the movement's own historian Paul Rotha.

Rien que les heures, the first film to attempt to show the ordinary daily life of a city, is well worth a fresh look with the eye of today. A great deal about it helps to illuminate Cavalcanti's career as a whole: the dramatic approach, the social consciousness in contrasting the lives of rich and poor (not in fact the prerogative of the Grierson school), the surrealism (for as Cavalcanti points out, the French *avant-garde* 'included all the surrealist tendencies of that time'). Its reputation suffered an initial neglect because its thunder was stolen by Ruttmann's *Berlin*, completed later but shown first in Britain and America. In subsequent years, like so much to which the British documentary movement laid special claim, it acquired that aura of potential boredom which comes of being taken too seriously. According to Rotha, for instance, 'Cavalcanti may have failed, at the time, to bring a full social realisation' to his aim which, again according to Rotha, was to show 'Man against the Street, against the turmoil of the City.' The conscious aim seems to have been a little different.

'*Rien que les heures* was an accident,' says Cavalcanti, 'because my first film (*Le Train sans yeux*) was shot in the studios in Germany and the producers didn't pay the bills and the film was held up by the studios, who wouldn't release the negative for copies because they hadn't been paid. So I got a few friends together, and we said, "We must do a film at all costs, because we are going to miss this winter. My film is not coming out. People will think the worst." We made a script, and it was the cheapest film you could imagine. It cost at the time 35,000 old francs, which is nothing at all. We had no studio. We shot everything in the streets, and of course we cut it very quickly and it came out as it was. The idea was that films were always about faraway places, about the sunsets over the Pacific etc., and nobody had an idea that life in the town in which you lived was interesting. That was made clear in *Rien que les heures* ... and it immediately came to look like a social document. It is a clumsy social document, but it is a social document about the lack of work, about the lives in miserable places. It had a lot of trouble with the censors, you know,'

Rien que les heures is an odd mixture of images of a Paris not frequented by tourists. A kind of theme suggests itself in the recurrent shots of a lame and wretched woman dragging herself at a snail's pace along alleys and byways, but these shots seem to be presented quite without comment. They are bizarre, incongruous, even comical—especially in juxtaposition with the light Parisian songs that Cavalcanti himself selected to accompany a recent screening at the National Film Theatre. Perhaps it is because these shots, in their sad hopelessness, come so near to provoking laughter that they remain so strongly in the memory. Cavalcanti has been accused of a certain lack of warmth in this film, and a certain lack of feeling in general. I think it is not fully understood that his vision is surrealist rather than realist, and always therefore had the virtue of avoiding sentimentality. Apart from that, it was to be another eight years before British documentary attempted any comparable social document, in the sense of showing conditions during the Depression.

One of Cavalcanti's earliest experiments at the GPO was a fantasy called Pett and Pott which cannot be counted among his best work. According to Basil Wright the idea of recording the soundtrack first and putting on the picture afterwards was Grierson's as well as Cavalcanti's; it was a way of getting the unit accustomed to using its newly acquired sound-recording equipment. The idea of making it a grotesque comedy Wright thinks must have been Cavalcanti's, because it stemmed from the kind of films he had been making earlier in France. But Cavalcanti was more successful in the light fantastic vein with avant-garde films like, for instance, the charming La P'tite Lili (1927), which, he says, was shot in the studios in three days when a patch of grey weather prevented exterior filming on Yvette, the big production based on a Maupassant story which he was directing at the time.

'I bought the short ends of the big film. It *(La P'tite Lile)* cost 7,500 francs altogether. We didn't pay the cameraman (Jimmy Rogers) or artists or anybody. When we were looking for a story, Catherine (Hessling) sang the song, and I said "That's it!" The film lasted seven months at Les Ursulines. Two features were changed because people used to come and complain "We want to keep *La P'tite Lili* in the programme but we are bored to see the big film twice." It went into all the cinemas, was sold abroad, was made into a sound film with Milhaud's music, and I never saw a penny. The distributors took it all...'

Well, *Pett and Pott* wasn't at all like that, although it had the benefit of most of the available talent at the GPO film unit. Basil Wright and Stuart Legg were assistant directors; John Taylor photographed it; Humphrey Jennings designed the sets. Perhaps it just went to prove that, like oil and water, frivolity and British documentary don't mix. Certainly Paul Rotha has strayed far from the point when he describes it in *Documentary Diary* as showing 'Cavalcanti's influence at its most mischievous.' This attitude, however, is not unique. John Taylor, for instance, remembers *Pett and Pott* as 'the beginning of the division ... I mean, looking back on it, at was a great mistake to have Cavalcanti really, because he didn't understand what documentary was supposed to be doing.'

Was Cavalcanti in some way undermining Grierson's work? What exactly was the difference of opinion between them? 'The only fundamental difference was that I maintained that "documentary" was a silly denomination,' says Cavalcanti. 'I thought films are the same, either fictional or otherwise, and I thought that films ought to go into cinemas. Grierson little by little started creating the theory that they should be put in a different, what he called non-theatrical circuit, and I thought it was as silly as calling those films documentary. I say, if films are good, they should and could be shown anywhere. There is no reason why they should be destined only for the parsons and for the church halls etc.

'I had a very serious conversation in the early, rosy days with Grierson about this label "documentary" because I insisted that it should be called, funnily enough (it's only coincidence but it made a fortune in Italy), "neo-realism". The Grierson argument — and I remember it exceedingly well — was just to laugh and say, "You are really a very innocent charactcr. I have to deal with the Government, and the word documentary impresses them as something serious, as something ..." I said, "Yes, as something dusty and something annoying." But that was his argument, that documentary was a kind of name that pleased the Government...'

Of course this is much more than an argument about labels. Cavalcanti is attacking the whole basis on which Grierson decreed that documentary should develop. Cavalcanti's whole approach to life is so very different from Grierson's that it is possible he never realised the increasing gravity of his offence.

In 1937 Grierson left the GPO film unit and set up Film Centre in order to extend documentary into a wider field. Sir Stephen Tallents who, as secretary of the Empire Marketing Board and public relations officer at the GPO, had always given him such invaluable support, had left the GPO in 1935 to become controller of public relations in the BBC overseas services and was now an active member of the Imperial Relations Trust set up in 1937 by the Government. It was this Trust which first sent Grierson as film consultant to Canada, New Zealand and Australia.

After Grierson's departure the GPO film unit continued as creatively as ever under Cavalcanti. Humphrey Jennings made *Spare Time* and Harry Watt made *North Sea*—the former being attacked by the Grierson school when it came out, and the latter receiving slightly grudging praise. It was said that Cavalcanti lacked Grierson's ability to deal with the higher civil servants at the Post Office, and certainly there is evidence that Cavalcanti was no political operator. He could inspire creative people whom he approached on a personal basis, but he never really sought power and was never able to make the most of it when he had it. Both Grierson and Cavalcanti were dedicated to their work, but Cavalcanti was the more vulnerable in being, by comparison, politically naive.

When war broke out in 1939, Grierson had gone to Canada to set up the National Film Board—an exceedingly impressive operation that in itself demonstrates the difference between his kind of ambition and that of the unaggressive Cavalcantis of this world. There seemed to be a situation of considerable confusion at the newly created Ministry of Information, which took over the GPO film unit. According to Harry Watt, there was a longish spell when nothing at all happened because no instructions came through: 'Then Cavalcanti took it upon himself to send us out. This is where Cavalcanti was great. He said, "History is being made. We can't sit here."' All the members of the unit, which included Watt and Jennings, went out and shot everything that looked interesting, and a film was quickly put together. Called *The First Days,* it was quite a promising start to the unit's wartime activities — particularly in the area that would be cultivated by Humphrey Jennings.

Before Cavalcanti left the GPO film unit, which became the Crown film unit when it was taken over by Ian Dalrymple in 1940, Harry Watt made *Squadron* 992 and *Dover Front Line*, Jennings made *Spring Offensive*, Jack Holmes had begun *Merchant Seamen* and ideas for *London Can Take It* and *Target for Tonight* were being discussed. In fact, the unit was fairly well set on the course that it would follow throughout the war.

Why did Cavalcanti leave the GPO film unit and go to Ealing Studios? According to both Cavalcanti and Ian Dalrymple, it was basically because Cavalcanti could not be officially in charge there as a Brazilian. 'They wanted me to get naturalised,' says Cavalcanti, 'and I didn't want to get naturalised ... I don't believe I could be English just by changing my passport, and as I couldn't become French ...' And then he adds that there were people appointed to the films division of the Ministry of Information whom he did not like: 'I was unhappy ... So I was looking for a job, and Mick (Balcon) had lost lots of his technical people because they had been mobilised ... and my contract with Ealing was very pleasant because I had one film as associate producer and one film as director. So that suited me fine, and I felt that I was much better remaining a Brazilian at Mick's place.'

'We were all a bit at sixes and sevens at the outbreak of war because there were signs that the Government had in mind throwing the film industry overboard and not bothering about it very much,' says Michael Balcon. 'It was a curious position because they had founded the Ministry of Information . . . and indeed there was a films division there, but there wasn't very much direction as far as the then Post Office film unit was concerned. That was quite in the early days. I think there was an element of dissatisfaction amongst these men who felt that they were capable of making a greater contribution. Many of them, and Cavalcanti in particular, were terribly worried by the sort of bureaucratic control that was even stronger in wartime than in peacetime, and there were signs that the unit was going to break up. Happily it was restored later on, because Dalrymple was made the head of the unit and he whipped it into shape and it did magnificent work during the war. But at this particular time they wanted a breakaway, and there were opportunities at Ealing and Cavalcanti was the first to come over. We told him that if we were allowed to go on — there was some doubt at the outbreak of war — we'd he very happy to have him because, apart from anything else, apart from his great talents as a film-maker, any sort of personnel that could be retained without difficulty was something to be grateful for.'

For the second time in England, Cavalcanti found himself in an atmosphere in which he was almost completely at home. His memories of Ealing are full of affection. 'Mick was the best producer I ever had,' he says. 'He was very understanding. He had been in films for years, and he knew the public and he had a sense of box-office that was quite deep, because sometimes he said, when he saw the rushes, "I don't like this. That must be remade." If you kept on trying to ask "Why, Mick?" or "Can't you tell me what's wrong?" very often he didn't know, but he sensed it was wrong. He had an uncanny sort of instinctive sense of films.'

'He fitted into our pattern very well because, you see, I was at the crossroads myself,' says Balcon. 'By the time the war broke out, I'd been at it for twenty years and so had Cavalcanti, but Cavalcanti had devoted his life to what we now call the documentary field. I had spent the whole of my time in the normal commercial field where, I suppose, the motives that guided us were (a) to found what we thought to be a native industry without being dominated by America, and (b) of course to make films which were as good in marketing terms as the American films which then dominated the whole world. I don't think we had our minds very much upon finer issues which developed later, as to the importance of the films and what they meant in social terms. We were engaged in a commercial operation.

'I felt of course — most of us felt quite definitely at the outbreak of war — that the type of film we'd been making in the past would not do, either in war conditions or in the future, and that is why I was eager to get Cav into the studio. I felt sure, to use these ugly words, some cross-fertilisation of our respective experiences, something different, would emerge — and indeed it did. I suppose, to an extent, because he had certain influences on the Ealing output ... It's not being egocentric to say that I was in charge of the whole output there and my word went, but it was a very democratic control that I exercised and the whole thing was run on a group basis, and of all the group there — and there were some very talented people — I would say that Cavalcanti was the most important and the most talented of the people available to talk to and work with.'

What sort of influence did Cavalcanti have on Ealing films? Balcon pointed out that most of Ealing's young talents like Charles Frend, Penrose Tennyson, Charles Crichton, Robert Hamer got their first chance to direct there: 'Now, however talented they were — because take a man like Hamer, he was a minor poet, a brilliant mathematician and could have had a career anywhere — they were still short of experience in dealing with visual images on the screen. And this is what Cavalcanti could do for them. He was a vastly experienced man as to how to transfer images to the screen — a curious man, you know, in some respects, until he got going. By virtue of the fact that he didn't know English very well, he could sometimes be completely inarticulate, especially when he got excited. But somehow when he was on the floor, near the camera, talking to these people, just some little things he could do would make all the difference Men like Charles Frend, good as they were, made better films with Cavalcanti by their side. Apart from anything else, he was a man of infinite taste. He knew about settings. He knew about music. He knew about European literature. He was a highly civilised man. They all were, but he was a particularly outstanding figure All those things helped to make good films ...

'This is why, and I may be wrong, I always thought that Cavalcanti was better producer material than he was director material. Now that doesn't in any way denigrate him because, in the days that we were working, I thought the talents were equally important and probably the production talent rather more important. But everybody doesn't think that way, and most producers always want to be directors. Cavalcanti wanted to be a director, and of course he directed some films of some importance, but I still think his great work was and still could be if he were going on today, in production and the influences he brings to bear on other people. I think that must inevitably be so with films in the English language because, even if he speaks many languages, there must be some difficulties in directing English actors for anybody who hasn't complete mastery of the language. From the visual side he'd always be alright. Whether he was equally good in the direction of actors is a matter for discussion.

'One thing I want to emphasise is that he is a great film man. If I point out what appear to be certain slight weaknesses or imperfections, it is because it would be wrong if I didn't. It wouldn't be fair to a really very important man ... I know no better sequence for direction than the last incident in *Dead of Night*. If you look at it and examine it, it's still largely a terrifically visual sequence. This is Cavalcanti at his best. Another film that was well directed by Cavalcanti was *Went the Day Well?*. Oddly enough, it's never been recognised as an important British film. I think it was.'

Based on a story by Graham Greene, who seems not to have liked the film ('We added so many episodes,' says Cavalcanti, 'that perhaps he couldn't recognise it'), *Went the Day Well?* (1942) is an imaginary account of what happened during the German occupation of the English village of Bromley End over the Whitsun weekend of 1942. The Germans, disguised in British uniforms but just occasionally giving themselves away by, for instance, bashing a troublesome small boy about the head, writing their sevens in the continental way, or bringing the odd bar of 'Schokolade Wien' from home with them, have their path smoothed by British quisling Leslie Banks. All the adult villagers are rounded up in the church; the children confined in an upstairs room of Marie Lohr's manor. Nice people who try to resist are ruthlessly put down, until the tide turns in favour of the villagers. It is devastating to see the cold-blooded revenge they now wreak on the men they had initially entertained as guests in the vicarage, the manor-house and elsewhere according to their station. Sweet young English girls are seizing the guns from German corpses, vying with each other to shoot down as many of the beastly hun as possible. It's not like killing real people. It's a sort of sport. The main emphasis that Cavalcanti himself puts on the film, which he regards as his best film at Ealing, is its deeply pacifist nature: 'People of the kindest character such as the people in that small English village, as soon as war touches them, become absolutely monsters.' It says something for the British film industry and government that such a film was able to emerge at such a time, and the fact that there were some reactions against it is hardly surprising.

Went the Day Well? pulls together most of the threads that run through Cavalcanti's work: the documentary authenticity, the drama, the surrealism. A remarkable thing about him is that, despite being a Brazilian with a European background, or perhaps because of it, he could put his finger precisely on the essential Britishness of the British and make it a special point of interest. The documentary movement may have gained more than anyone was aware of from this ability of his to see and draw out what was there already. Michael Balcon describes what his arrival meant to Ealing: 'I don't think that up to that point the films I was concerned with, with certain exceptions, had a special trade mark of their own. We know the Jessie Matthews comedies were this; the Hulbert and Courtneidge comedies were that; but the outputs as a whole didn't have any particular stamp to them. He certainly helped me, probably more than anybody else, to create an image. The whole of the Ealing output had a certain stamp on it. Whether I would have done it on my own I don't know. But most certainly I acknowledge, and always have acknowledged, that of all the help I got his is the help that was the most important.'

That surrealism is part of Cavalcanti's view of life has been evident from the outset, but the British are not naturally given to understanding surrealism or the various extensions or applications of it. As far as Cavalcanti is concerned, we are likely to be much more impressed by the surrealist shock tactics of *Dead of Night* than by the grim humour of certain scenes in *Went the Day Well?* where realism has simply been carried a stage further into surrealism. This kind of effect can be achieved only by first ensuring plausibility and then demonstrating the implausibility of the plausible. The only British director who has become master of it is Lindsay Anderson, and it is interesting to realise that in this way Anderson's documentary roots are much closer to Cavalcanti (himself an ardent admirer of the work of Humphrey Jennings) than to Grierson.

Although the other features Cavalcanti directed at Ealing — *Champagne Charlie* and *Nicholas Nickleby* — are less noteworthy, he was also involved in a programme of short films which Michael Balcon describes as having been 'right up Cavalcanti's street'. Some of these he directed — propaganda films like *Yellow Caesar*, instructional films like *Watertight* which (oddly?) are not included in the main histories of British documentary. Cavalcanti is still very enthusiastic about the distribution that these documentaries got in the cinemas, because each of them went out with a big picture. Balcon finds less significance in this: 'They were propaganda films during wartime, and there were fewer films available in wartime than there were in most normal times ... As you know, short films have always been a difficult market, because only West End houses ran these supporting short feature programmes. Most of the houses in the provinces have always gone for double feature programmes. In wartime it was different ... Also I might tell you that although they liked us to make them and we could get them into the West End, I can't pretend that even in wartime the rest of the country were falling over themselves to book these films. They had to be forced wherever we could in support of features.'

The documentary story never really changes. It only seems to now and then.

At the beginning of the war Cavalcanti also completed an anthology film called *Film and Reality*, which was commissioned by the British Film Institute. A sensible and occasionally exciting collection of excerpts from realist films including newsreels, produced up to that time, it provoked some extremely angry reactions from British documentarists. According to Paul Rotha, still apparently bitter about it when writing his *Documentary Diary* of 1973, it 'did less than justice to the social aims of the British documentary group, whose work as shown, when at all, was inadequate and false. In spite of protests by the Associated Realist Film Producers, especially in a strong letter to *The Times*, the film was not withdrawn although some film libraries abroad would not distribute it. It is, I am told, still in use in some places today.'

Rotha goes on to report an argument that took place in the *New Statesman* in June 1942, as a result of film critic William Whitebait's remark that Ministry of Information films 'set a very high standard indeed; and the tradition that has produced them owes more to Cavalcanti than to any other man.' To this Rotha replied that 'one man, and one man only, John Grierson, was responsible for the birth and inspiration of the 300-odd British documentary films made between 1929 and 1939, including those of which Cavalcanti was himself director.' Harry Watt then joined in: 'It was Grierson's drive and initiative that obtained the formation and sponsoring of the EMB Film Unit, from which eventually so many offshoots have sprung. But I, as a film worker with both men, would like to say that I am convinced that it was the introduction of Cavalcanti's professional skill and incredible film sense that raised the standard and reputation of British documentary to the pitch where today it has become a considerable influence on the cinema as a whole.'

Rotha then claims: 'For my own part, as a result of my letter quoted above, I was told that references to my work were in due course removed from *Film and Reality*.' To this he appends the footnote: 'I am happy to record, however, that Cavalcanti and I have always remained the best of friends.'

Cavalcanti does not deny the friendship. The trouble, he suggests, was because the film was too long and he cut out the only Rotha excerpt along with one or two others. 'Rotha was very cross about it. He wanted to be in it.' Cavalcanti also explains: 'With my wrong sense of humour I did a bad turn to Grierson. I put Mendelssohn's *Fingal's Cave* over *Drifters*, which was putting it back into romantic sort of films, and I don't think that pleased Grierson at all … But really you must realise that Grierson at the bottom was quite a demagogue. Yes, his parents being parsons and so on, he had a kind of disposition for preaching. And preaching and that sort of thing delighted him, and he was very good at it too, I thought.'

The truth of the matter is that the only thing seriously wrong with Cavalcanti's *Film and Reality* is that it is not the selection that Grierson or Rotha would have made. On the contrary, it gives an encouraging impression of the wide variety of film material shot in a realistic vein long before British documentary was even contemplated. From Marey and the Lumière brothers, through early newsreels and interest films, clips from the *Secrets of Nature* and X-ray films used in medical diagnosis, there is no mention of British documentary except to say that Charles Urban, director of *Romance of the Railway* (1907) was grandfather of it. *Song of Ceylon* eventually comes up at the end of a section (mainly devoted to Flaherty) about 'Romantic Documentaries of Faraway Places'. *Drifters*, *Industrial Britain*, *Housing Problems* and *Night Mail* occupy part of a section (which opens with *Rien que les heures*) on 'Realistic Documentaries of Life at Home.' Here British documentary is described as a 'movement to use film for civic education'. Here too an extract from a French film made by Jean Benoît-Lévy in 1932, showing a potter making a pot, compares very well with one's memory of the similar sequence shot by Flaherty in 1931 for *Industrial Britain* and admired almost to distraction by Grierson. At the end of this section Pare Lorentz's Plow that Broke the Plains is described as owing much to the British school. The Cavalcanti moves on to 'Realism in the Story Film': Stiller, James Cruze, Eisenstein, Zecca, Dieterle, Méliès, Pabst, Renoir etc., obviously nothing more of British documentary.

I cannot help feeling that Cavalcanti had worked with the documentary movement long enough to realise that Mendelssohn's *Fingal's Cave* was not the only bad turn he would be accused of having done to Grierson in all this. In fact, he dared to give the impression that his conception of 'realist films' was wider than the idea which Grierson labelled 'documentary'. If it was his 'wrong sense of humour' that made him go so far, I do feel that he has since paid dearly for it.

How is it possible to be fair to everybody in circumstances like these? Pointless to say the arguments don't matter because they do — particularly when the spokesman for a movement famed for its liberal-mindedness can still regret some thirty-five years later that an intelligent and informative film has not been taken out of circulation. I can only say thankfully that I saw the film recently at the British Film Institute, that as long as this applies reassessments are possible, and the chance remains that time will set every-thing right.

'If there is a British cinema,' says Michael Balcon, 'I would put Cavalcanti's contribution pretty well as high as any ... because in a curious way the work he did doesn't reflect itself in credit titles.' This is the problem. Cavalcanti's reputation is to quite a large extent dependent on the word of those who worked with him, but no injustice is neces-sarily implied by this. Very often there was no way to indicate by means of credits an influence as varied and subtle as his. Like Grierson's initial feat in getting finance for documentary, the stamp that Cavalcanti subsequently put on it could only be belittled by the sort of abbreviated job descriptions that credit titles amount to. This is perhaps why it still remains unclear whether Cavalcanti really cared about having credits at the time or not. It was always a debatable kind of compliment.

Cavalcanti still speaks warmly of the atmosphere at Ealing: 'There were no petty jeal-ousies, no difficulties at all.' Yet he left Ealing in the late 1940s, basically because it seemed to him that he could earn more as a freelance than under the terms of his Ealing contract. He and Michael Balcon disagree about the fairness of the deal he was getting from Ealing at the time, but both say he left in order to earn more money.

'It was a change of mood,' says Balcon. 'All the wonderful things, the group things we did, the ideas which made us tick during the war, began to disintegrate. There wasn't the same motive, and it became a harsher and rather more cynical period. People's values began to alter, and their success began to be measured in terms of money, and if Cav were to completely examine himself over these things, he was tempted away the same as all the other people. It was Oscar Wilde who said that a man can resist everything except temptation, and this is what happened . . .

'I'm the first to admit that this group work of ours worked for twenty years, but when we gave it up none of its as individuals were as important as we were collectively ... Everybody went out and had plenty of things to do, but when you come to examine it in terms of results none of us were as good separately as we were together. I think that Cav missed it more than anybody else. I just talk of it in general terms, the support he got from being with Ealing Studios.'

Certainly Cavalcanti's career seems rarely to have been as satisfying or as successful since he left Ealing. Around 1950 he left England altogether, apparently intending to set up home in his native Brazil. When I asked him about this in an earlier interview, in 1971, he said, 'Oh, don't talk about it. It was a mistake to go to Brazil, and I lost in fact everything I had. It's quite an unhappy adventure. No, it is a mistake to send a boy of fifteen away from his country, because it's from fifteen to twenty-five you settle your entourage and choose your friends.'

In the latest interview he described a very confusing situation in which he was trying to create a film industry which would have a real local spirit in Sao Paulo, while Italian technicians were plotting to push out the other nationalities, and Americans were accusing him of being a communist and there were documents reminiscent of the Inquisition deposited in the Brazilian Foreign Office. (I hope I have interpreted his meaning here correctly.) Certainly he said he had a contract for three years, but at the end of the first year he was thrown out because they didn't understand what he was after. He made two films and was halfway through another. He had six complete scripts ready for the second year, but after he left, production was almost at a standstill for two years.

'Why did you go to Brazil?' I asked him. 'I lost my mother,' he said. (His mother was a considerable personality, known to all his friends as a great and good influence on his life.) 'And I had a big project for an independent production. I had the rights of *Sparkenbroke* by Charles Morgan. It was — I still believe it was — the best script I ever made. It's a bad novel, but it's a good film story ... I had made all the choice of locations, and I had discovered beautiful places that were quite unknown, and all of a sudden I received from that collaborator of Rank (I was working for him) a letter saying that my script was above the understanding of the public. I had lots of times in my life had it told to me, and of course I was disgusted. It was about four months work, and very expensive work. To make a long script is a big job. So I had an invitation to go to Brazil to lecture about films to the Museum of Modern Art at Sao Paulo, and I accepted and went.'

Cavalcanti's story is latterly a sad one. There can be no getting away from that, although I feel at a disadvantage in commenting on the later years because there have been a number of films in Brazil, Austria, Rumania, Italy (in the 1950s) and more recently a couple of plays (one of them by Dürrenmatt) on French television which I, like most people in Britain, have not seen. The Austrian film, *Herr Puntila und sein Knecht Matti* (1955), was based on the comedy by Berthold Brecht, and something of the charm that endeared Cavalcanti to the many British film-makers who have been indebted to him, emerges very simply from his account of his first meeting with the revered Brecht:

'I had a great, great admiration for him. I thought he was a master—even better than a playwright, he was a great poet. I liked scripting what he did very much, and the first script he refused. The second script *(Herr Puntila)* he sent me (I hadn't met him), I refused. It was the play; he hadn't changed a line. So I said at the start—he had made lawsuits against Fritz Lang, against Pabst, against all my colleagues—so I said, "I am in the basket. He's going to annoy me no end." But I had a very intelligent woman producer, who said, "Look here, this is silly. You and Brecht are made to be friends and to understand each other. You speak the same language. Come with me to Berlin." And I shall never forget—it was a summer day like this—and I came to his house. The big room had three windows towards the cemetery. He immediately took me by the arm, as if he knew me all the time. He knew I had refused his script. He knew we were going to try together to make one, and he took me to the window and said, "Do you know who is buried there?" I said, "No." He said, "Hegel."

'It's a sad thing to say,' Cav added, 'that he is buried just by Hegel now.'

Film and Reality, Basil Wright

With a boldness only equalled by that of Dr. Johnson when he set out to compile his English Dictionary, Cavalcanti has, in *Film and Reality*, attempted, all on his own, to describe the development of the realist film over the past fifty years in an opus which runs for an hour and three quarters and contains extracts from fifty-eight different films.

The result is a remarkable document, impressive for the wealth of its contents and (to myself at least) in many places controversial as regards its choice of material, and its attitude towards the social, as opposed to the academic or aesthetic development of the realist film. But whatever else it may be, it is certainly stimulating; after seeing it most people will find themselves considering the wider perspectives and the future possibilities which arise from this particular branch of film making.

Film and Reality, being as it were the only visual reference-work dealing with a special type of cinematic endeavour, deserves close and detailed attention from the critical standpoint. And if my own criticism should appear too personal, no doubt others, including I hope Cavalcanti, will hasten to correct, refute, or amplify.

After he left the Unit in 1940 Cavalcanti attempted to tell the story of 'the documentary movement' through *Film and Reality*, a film featuring excerpts from the most important documentaries to date. Here, fellow GPO stalwart Basil Wright gives his opinion on Cavalcanti's choices and outlines his hopes and fears for the future of the documentary film

'Film and Reality', Basil Wright, *Documentary News Letter*, March 1942, pp. 40–2

I. The Scope of the Film

As might be expected, *Film and Reality* is at its safest when it deals with history, or with chapters in realist development which can be regarded as more or less complete.

The First Section (which is preceded by a prologue detailing Dr. Marey's early experiments and the first film made by the Lumières), explains how a new form of dramatic entertainment quickly arose from the new invention. Extracts from *The Life of Charles Peace*, *The Great Train Robbery*, and *The Assassination of the Duke of Guise*, reveal how the essentials of the movie medium were quickly lost as producers turned more and more to the straight photography of theatrical mime. Incidentally D. W. Griffiths was probably the man who did most to rescue cinema from this blind alley, and this section might well have ended with a brief extract from *Birth of a Nation*.

The Second Section shows how newsreels and interest films have always formed a continuous thread of contact with reality, whatever deviations the rest of the cinematic world might he indulging in. Here Cavalcanti very properly points out that both the newsreel and the interest film, being forms of visual record and little else, are unlikely to vary much in attitude and content, being affected only by improvements in photographic apparatus and similar mechanical developments. There is certainly little difference between the rioting suffragettes of 1906 and the panicky crowds milling around the killer of King Alexander in 1934.

Two excerpts in this section have a special visual impact. The first is a short sequence of Chinese families burying their dead after the execution of revolutionaries in 1909; this might have been made yesterday. The second is an extract from Ponting's famous film of Scott's last expedition; which is, with Nanook, a remarkable reminder of the superb photographic quality which was obtainable with the old orthochromatic film. Incidentally, the camera which Ponting used on this expedition has been in possession of the British documentary movement since 1932 and as far as I know is still in use.

The Third Section is perhaps the most complete and most memorable of the whole opus. But I wonder if Cavalcanti is right in describing *Documentaries of the Far-Off Lands* by the epithet "romantic"? It hardly fits Poirier's *Eve Africaine*, and Allegret and Gide's Voyage au Congo, both of which confirmed for me once again my feeling that the French directors who took their cameras overseas were often more voyeurs than voyageurs. Nor, certainly, is the word "romantic" applicable to Wavrin's Pays du Scalp. This, like Buñuel's Land Without Bread (not represented in the film) is a straight ethnographic study; and the sight of natives eating live slugs, however well filmed and however interesting, is hardly romantic.

Flaherty, of course, is the big man of this section, which is indeed completely over-shadowed by the wonderful tattooing sequence from *Moana*; but here again I would even prefer to use the adjective "exotic" in its original dictionary sense, to "romantic".

The terrific realism of the crossing of the river in *Grass* is the other dominating factor in this section. *Grass*, without doubt, is one of the great realist classics, and worthy of constant revival along with *Nanook* and *Moana*. And, talking of early American films of fact what has become of Chang, with its terrific picture of man's eternal struggle with the jungle?

But it is Section Four, dealing as it does with the sociological development of the film of fact which has obviously given Cavalcanti the most trouble and which is bound to be the most controversial. For this is the point where the historical merges with the contemporaneous, and where, incidentally, Cavalcanti's pre-occupation with aesthetics is at its most dangerous. Personally I do not believe that any one man is in a position to select extracts from the huge bulk of production during the past ten years. With practically all the producers and directors of the films still at work, a personal selection is bound to be too arbitrary. Far better to have a selection committee, however heated the discussions which might result.

As it is, I think that Cavalcanti has mixed two things – firstly the real meaning of the sociological approach which was preceded and signalled by his own *Rien que les heures* and by Ruttmann's *Berlin* and which under Grierson's inspiration and leadership has formed the permanent basis of all documentary production in this country for the past twelve years. Secondly - and this is very surprising from Cavalcanti – he has, in dealing with the Grierson documentary, almost ignored the dynamic use of sound a factor to which he himself has made such a great contribution. The various early experiments in sound were important not merely from the aesthetic point of view but because they were designed to strengthen and clarify the sociological angle. Yet, barring an extract from *Housing Problems* and another from *Night Mail*, the uninitiated might well get the impression that the realist film had hardly left the stage of musical accompaniment.

One of the most important developments in documentary has been the introduction of dialogue sequences, using sometimes raw material, sometimes actors, sometimes a mixture of both. Yet, in the extract from *North Sea*, Cavalcanti gives us a sequence which might just as easily have been shot in the *Drifters* period as in 1938, whereas the great wealth of dialogue material in the film (e.g. the conference in the cabin) obviously had an absolute claim for representation.

Similarly the historical importance of Rotha's *Contact* is hardly great enough to justify its inclusion if it is to mean the omission of the same director's *Shipyard,* in which the sociological approach and also the use of sound is far more representative of both the aims and the development of the realist movement in Britain.

Other selections in this sequence are more a matter of personal choice. I myself think that Cavalcanti has done less than justice to *Rien que les heures*, *Turk-Sib*, *Drifters* and *The Spanish Earth*, but others may think otherwise.

There is one other omission, and that is the analytic film dealing with mechanical or scientific processes or with their theory and practice – a *genre* which Britain has, in its documentary movement, done pioneer work. No reference at all is made to such films as *Aero-Engine*, *Transfer of Power* or *Airscrew*.

As regards the Final Section, which is entitled "Realism in the Story Film", I confess to being entirely baffled. I agree in some respects with Cavalcanti's contention that: "To-day the theatrical film still holds a prominent place in the cinema, but has undergone no fundamental change since the days of *The Assassination of the Duke of Guise* and *The Lady of the Camellias*. Film technique has been developed mainly by seeking to represent reality. Because the film-maker's material is not make-up and scenery, but photography and sound-recording, the best work in the cinema has been done by those who have remembered what the first inventors never doubted, that the essence of cinematography lies in its power to represent reality."

But I find it difficult to reconcile the structure and choice of his last section with his thesis.

It begins beautifully with a magnificent sequence from Stiller's *The Old Manor*. Then comes the river crossing from *The Covered Wagon* (speaking personally once again, I would have chosen, from the point of view of realism, the Indian attack on the encampment – do you remember the horse galloping off the cliff?) Then – after a moment of perfunctory mix – we are treated to three comparisons. The first is between Eisenstein's mutiny sequence from Potemkin and a stagey version of the same thing made in France by Ferdinand Zecca in 1907. The second depicts the clearing of the court room during the Dreyfus investigation, as done by Dieterle in *Emile Zola* (1937) and by George Méliès (c. 1900). The third contrasts a scene from *Love from a Stranger* (Britain 1937) with Sarah Bernhardt in *The Lady of the Camellias* (France 1912).

I am no doubt very dull in the head, but I do not see how these contrasts add to the argument. Zecca's *Potemkin* is as wildly funny as you might expect; Eisenstein's mutiny scenes are still dramatic, dynamic, and the whole sequence is still an absolute classic of cutting. But if, as I take it the contrast needed is between theatricalism and realism in the story film, the argument surely can only be effective if two early contemporary works are chosen. A big sequence from a de Mille super would have been a reasonable contrast.

The scene from *Emile Zola* is apparently chosen not for its essential interest, but because it matches the scene from the Méliès' film. *Zola* was a magnificent film, but this sequence, torn from its context, means very little in terms of realism or anything else.

Finally we have *Love from a Stranger* – a sequence put in to show that films are still sometimes no more than photographed stage plays. Could we not have taken this for granted? The sequence is merely boring and forms no sort of contrast to the historically interesting excerpt from the Bernhardt film, which might well have been included in the first section.

The film is not yet over. To conclude it we are given three extracts from story films, presumably because they are notable for their realism. Of the first two of these – *Kameradschaft* and *Le Grand Illusion* – I do not think anyone could complain. But why the troopship sequence from *Farewell Again*? For myself at least it formed a depressing, lamentable, and very bewildering ending to 9,500 feet of impressive or stimulating material of all sorts.

Film and Reality is too important a work to be glibly dismissed with faint or frantic praise. And whatever I may have said about it I am certain that it does, despite the faults I have stated, form a remarkable document which will be of great use to students and to all others interested in the realistic approach to cinema. It would be interesting to make a parallel job called *Film and Reality No. II*, which would be devoted, not to aesthetic considerations, but to a study of the sociological approach combined with the new developments in technique which arose from the desire of realist film-makers (especially in Britain, due to Grierson's genius) to find more vivid means of expression. Himself a pioneer in this field, I am certain that Cavalcanti would agree, and would, this time, consult his contemporaries more freely on the selection of the relevant material.

II. Today and Tomorrow

Not the least valuable aspect of *Film and Reality* lies in the fact that it is bound to stimulate many of us to consider the present state of affairs in the development of the realist film, and to look a little way into the future.

Cavalcanti's survey very properly stops short before September, 1939...Since then we have had two and a half years of war in which needs as well as conditions of film-making have changed very considerably. All available personnel have been pressed into the urgent needs of wartime propaganda and wartime information. Output has increased enormously.

When the war began documentary was no longer in its experimental stage. Realist traditions had by then been firmly established, and the results of the experiments of the previous ten years had been crystallised into several different styles. Nevertheless that static stage, which in any movement is the prelude to complete necrosis, had in no sense been reached. On the contrary, in the years immediately preceding World War II the realist movement was beginning to concern itself firstly with larger and broader treatments of subject matter, and secondly with an increased use of dramatic incident and dialogue (cf. *The Londoners* and *North Sea*, to give but two examples).

In some senses the gulf between the documentary and the realistic film story was narrowing. Not only had the British realist movement begun to influence film-makers in other countries (most notably the U.S.A., where a vigorous documentary movement was by now established) but also there was, in the studio world, a recrudescence of that realistic approach which had flared up all over the world in the mid-twenties but which had been thoroughly smothered by the coming of sound.

The realist workers in those days were increasingly occupied with internationalism. It wasn't mere chance which found Cavalcanti in Switzerland shooting the material for *We Live in Two Worlds*, or which found Grierson and myself, in the same country, discussing with the International Labour Office plans for world production, distribution, and international exchange of all films of sociological content.

By 1939 the realist film movement was all set for a series of major developments. Where do we stand now?

I am not one of those who believe that war essentially stifles all creative impulse, although I am certain that it limits it. To this it is, I think, correct to add the rider that discipline is good for the creative worker, provided the discipline comes from the right quarters and with the right motives. The motive for making wartime documentaries will be regarded by no one as other than sensible. Indeed, the most striking thing about the last two years of realist film making has been that – if only for lack of any official lead – the documentary workers have evolved their own discipline and done all they can to impose it on themselves. There has, in other words, been no diminution of the basic documentary thesis: "We are propagandists first and film makers second."

Literally hundreds of films have been made during the past two years, and it is perhaps only too easy to forget that their widespread distribution, both in the cinemas and non-theatrically, has given the documentary film an audience coverage infinitely larger than anything it had attained in peacetime.

The urgencies of the moment make for simplicity of construction and treatment. Only in a few major efforts (e.g. *Target for Tonight*) is it possible to elaborate the script and involve oneself in the complications of a large number of interrelated incidents.

I would sum up the existing situation first by claiming that documentary has no cause to be ashamed of its wartime record. Its workers, often under extraordinarily difficult circumstances, have fully carried out the jobs that needed doing. But secondly, I feel that this is no time for complacency. I think all of us feel that much of our production is not up to that level of achievement which we have always set ourselves.

Is it enough to satisfy the demands of official sponsors, however well we do it? It is surely our job, as pioneers (and such we have always been) to be a step ahead of the rest.

Now, and for the remainder of the war, the keyword is "Urgency". Today the realist film needs to achieve greater punch. It must be active. It must without fail and without pause devote itself to the urgencies of the moment with the same dynamic emphasis which marked the revolutionary period of the Soviet film. The social experience of documentary is ideally suited to this propaganda task, which is, firstly to impel immediate and all-out action in the direct crisis of war, and secondly, to pave the way for the post-war drive; both these aims being completely interwoven.

I believe absolutely that the revolutionary technique is now the only technique. Whether you like it or not, we are undergoing a world social revolution here and now, and it is a revolution which must continue after the war, and continue with increasing strength. For that is the only thing the people of Britain are fighting for.

It is today the job of documentary to integrate the immediate war-effort with the facts and implications of radical social and economic changes which are part and parcel of it.

Only from this standpoint can we get into our films the dynamic impulse which will strengthen their propaganda value to this nation and its allies.

The realist tradition is rich in the abilities for the job. The whole trend of the 'thirties was towards this dynamic concept (we said we were trying to make peace as exciting as War), and the films which were made tended more and more to sacrifice purely aesthetic considerations to the need for pungent comment and the imaginative presentation of facts and problems.

Today the intensification of effort which is so urgently needed depends on an equal intensification of morale-propaganda; and if we don't pull our punches any longer we have a vital contribution to make.

I believe that the future of the realist film (if one can spare a moment to look ahead in such parochial terms) lies in the attitude and action which I have outlined. Our films must be the shock troops of propaganda. It is no longer policy to compromise with timidity – either among ourselves or in others. The documentary movement is part of a continuous process and a continuous progress towards a new deal in life for the peoples of the world. And the only slogan worth having today is "Speed it up!"

Stuart Legg: A Close Up, Donald Alexander

Among the less celebrated GPO film-makers is Stuart Legg, who is profiled here by his colleague Donald Alexander

'Stuart Legg: A Close-Up', Donald Alexander, *Documentary Film News*, 7 (1948), p. 68

At first sight, Stuart Legg is a sombre puritanical character, with a keen nose for detail, and paradoxially, an aptitude for wearing primrose neckties. We remember with embarrassment our muffled rage when he took over the producership of Strand in 1937 (Rotha was at that time leaving for a year's session at the Museum of Modern Art in New York) and he promptly announced his intention of descending on our snug location in South Wales 'to help with our dialogue shooting'. (It was our first dialogue film, and he was only taking wise precautions, but what we expect from the old governor we do not always take from a new broom.) Within one hour of his arrival, he had made himself more helpful than any producer we have ever known, which helpfulness continued for the next three days, without Stuart ever apparently emerging from the background or visibly opening his mouth. When he got back he told his wife Margaret that he was greatly impressed with our capabilities as a director, and she dutifully passed on the information. Thereafter we would have died for him gladly – certainly we were prepared to work ourselves to death. Now, we too, produce – but that high level of skill or that low level of cunning we dare not hope to attain.

As a servant of documentary Stuart is prehistoric. He is first found in the Cambridge reminiscences of equivalent old-timers like Basil Wright and Humphrey Jennings, busily working away on Power (production: Cambridge Film Society), and developing a majestic social conscience. (Incidentally, he once accused us of being dominated by a social conscience; that's like Stuart's puritanical nature, to attribute to others the virtues he is too austere to claim for himself.) It is true he so far deviated from the stern line of duty as to meet his wife while he was still in stain pupillari: but in fairness it must be recorded that Margaret Amos was a don's daughter.

After leaving Cambridge, Legg worked with Gaumont British Instructional from 1931-2; then he joined the Empire Marketing Board Unit and stayed on, after the GPO took over, until 1937. Next he was translated to Film Centre, and very soon afterwards to Strand, where he stayed till the summer of 1939. From then on he fits into the pattern of the development of the National Film Board of Canada, first of all in Ottawa, and latterly in New York. His chief for so long, John Grierson, gives Legg maximum credit for the 'World in Action' series, which in international short films distribution ranks second only to the older 'March of Time'. Now there are rumours that he is coming back, and that is the second most heartening piece of news we have heard in a long time.

From the beginning Stuart Legg never made the pretty films, which hit the headlines and got the swagger box office bookings. Certainly he directed BBC Voice of Britain, and (with Anstey) Under the City, but his has mostly been the hard graft of contriving something out of nothing, of personally editing ramshackle material into presentable shape; of pulling whole series of films out of limbo, of pioneering difficult projects. The cutting-room and his office-desk have been the control points at which he has always been found with his coat off and his sleeves up, pushing out more product to the minute than any other film maker since D. W. Griffith. We remember Wings Over the Empire – probably the most thoughtful and moving of all the Strand Imperial Airways films, patched together out of all the bits and pieces discarded by the directors who had shot (or had shot for them) their private material for their private epics. We remember how through Legg the evolutionary plan which Julian Huxley was struggling to communicate to us stupid film-makers suddenly began to illuminate the whole series of zoological films made at Strand, and how it reached fulfilment in Hawes' Monkey into Man and in Legg's own Fingers and Thumbs. We remember, too, how he sat down and wrote a treatment for an Economic Survey of Scotland, which country he had never visited, and how little that line was altered in the final Wealth of a Nation after we (who were indigenous anyway) had been for months on the spot reporting with a camera.

Working and living hard, harder than circumstances really require, seems always to have been Stuart and Margaret Legg's motto. But typically, some of the most memorable things about them are their contributions to the off-duty apocrypha of documentary. On a Friday night or a Saturday morning, out would come the old Rolls-Royce (yes, it was a Rolls-Royce: touring model, vintage 1924, picked up for £60), and we would trundle off from the workaway Legg domicile on Shooter's Hill to a clapboarded farm in Lamberhurst, Kent, from which Stuart fondly imagined he would some time be able to commute (poor Stuart, there was no commuting for him until he took out a season from New York to Ottawa). And very determinedly we would ride horses at Tenterden, or pace the back seat quarter deck of the Rolls down to the Elephant's Head at Hook Green, and stay watching cricket and playing darts and drinking vast quantities of beer for a long summer's evening. Once we took Legg on a ceremonial drive round Scotland, with Grierson and Wright acting as official cicerones to this country he had written up but never seen. We remember every roaring detail from the preliminary dinner at Rogano's Sea Food Restaurant to the formal visit to the Grierson ancestors in a churchyard beside Bannockburn, and Stuart's gloomy acceptance of the evolutionary plausibility of a hairy Highland Cow, contrasted with Grierson's rapturous and improbable claim never before to have encountered the species. That time we were stationed in Glasgow – at the Central Hotel – because Grierson insisted (probably rightly) that it was the only place to which important contacts could decently be invited. Stuart stuck it for one night; the next day we moved to a quiet pub in Bath Street where our joint social consciences were not offended by 'plain breakfast' (coffee and roll) at 2s. 6d., and where the beer was better. Our contacts still came to the Central; like them, we just called in.

<u>Statement of clothes totally lost or spoilt during location</u>
<u>work - 1942</u>

Note: I have been working on location on two films -
'I Was a Fireman' and 'Lidice' for nine out of
the eleven months of this year. Both these
productions were distinguished by the dirtiest
locations imaginable θ i.e. the docks during a
blitz fire and a Welsh coal-mine both below and
above ground. In both cases the dirt and smoke
and fire were part of the story and were treated in
most realistic way possible.

It would not be in anyway an exaggeration to say
that the following clothes have been totally
lost as a result of the above work.

    One pair of walking shoes (value £2.10)
    One good suit (value £6.6.)
    At least three pairs of socks (these get
        ruined particularly when wearing wellingtons -
        value approx 3.6 per pair)
    One pair of flannel trousers (value £2.2.)

Also spoilt with tar, fire etc - but now repaired
one overcoat (value £8.8)

The above would definitely not have been lost and
spoilt but for work on location

                Director. 24.11.42

NFT Programme Notes, Harry Watt

I presume that previous filmmakers writing and speaking during this series have detailed the documentary credo – that we set out to dramatise reality and give a dignity in films to the everyday person and the everyday event. But there were, of course, amongst ourselves, endless theories and discussions as to how we should carry this out. We started with the belief that we must influence films as a whole, and in our tiny beginnings this was a glorious conceit, because, of course, we couldn't start to get our films shown in the cinemas. We worked endlessly, living, eating and sleeping documentary, and the arguments went on. What form should films take to make the maximum impact?

I came very much under the influence of Alberto Cavalcanti. He had had an unfortunate flirtation with commercial films in Paris, and in despair, chucked in a lucrative contract and joined us in Soho Square. He had the enormous advantage of being an experienced, skilled filmmaker, while we were learning our job by trial and error, and he and I were certain that we must, somehow, without compromising, crash the commercial cinemas before we could make our influence felt or approximate to our original ideals.

Around the middle of the '30s there was an amicable split in the documentary movement. Grierson became convinced that the enormous non-cinema going audience was the one to go after, and that a non-theatrical circuit with an assured public was better than our sporadic and fleeting showings in news-reel cinemas. Cavalcanti and I, together with Humphrey Jennings, Pat Jackson, Jack Lee and some others, disagreed. We felt we had to make the cinemas. That the non-theatrical showings were either converting the already the converted, or had no lasting impact because people never value what they get for free.

Our solution was the story-documentary, taking actual true events, using real people, but also using 'dramatic licence' to heighten the tensions an the storyline. *The Saving of Bill Blewitt* was my first essay in this direction, although it never saw a cinema. But *North Sea*, made in Aberdeen, with the interiors done in the studio in London, did get considerable theatrical distribution, and did, I believe, make money. This was what Cavalcanti and I wanted, because 'Cav's' experience and cynicism told him that as soon as we proved there was money in documentary, then 'the trade', and therefore the public, would take notice of it.

The war proved both our theories correct. The non-theatrical makers were geared for the enormous number of instructional, training and morale-films needed, while we did more publicised feature documentaries. The tragedy was that our story-films made us interesting to commercial interests, and most of us were seduced away from documentary. Looking back, I regret this a lot. At the end of the war, the lack of old-stagers weakened documentary so much that the Crown Film Unit became an easy target for a stupid and unnecessary economy cut. The amount of money involved was infinitesimal – half an aeroplane or something like that.

While realising there is nothing more boring than looking back, I do feel that the story-documentary that Cavalcanti and I plugged so hard has largely been forgotten in present-day realist circles. The great advantage in telling a story is the infinite variety of treatment one can obtain on any subject. There is an inevitable sameness about commentary films, and every angle and twist seems to have been done before. I'd like to see the documentary movement start the argument all over again.

Looking back on the work of the GPO Film Unit, Harry Watt regretted that his contribution to the development of the 'story documentary' had not been more influential in the history of documentary film

Courtesy of BFI

PART FOUR

Aesthetics

12 / RHYTHM, MODERNITY AND THE POLITICS OF SOUND

James G. Mansell

The body of work produced by the GPO Film Unit has transcended the purpose for which it was originally intended – public information – and entered the canon of cinema history. It has done so for a variety of reasons, but among them, there can be no doubt, is the memorable use of sound effects in films such as *Night Mail* (1936) and *The Song of Ceylon* (1934). The GPO Film Unit went out of its way to record the incidental sounds of everyday life and to present these in creative combination with speech and music. Grierson's followers were indeed among the first film-makers in the world to work in this way. Their pioneering and evocative sound worlds have lent GPO films an enduring appeal in the British imagination. Yet, for this very reason, we should remain critical about what we hear. The famous soundtracks of GPO films, after all, were auditory interventions in the sound culture of their time.

E. Anna Claydon points out in her contribution to this volume that GPO soundtracks were self-conscious attempts to shape a modern British identity. They were also, I will argue here, bound up within a politics of aurality no less specific to the period. Incorporating the clanging noises of factory production, the rattle of train travel or the electro-magnetic pulses of global trade was inevitably to enter into a dialogue about noise and its effects in modern life, a topic which greatly exercised many Britons in the inter-war period.[1] It was widely agreed in the 1930s that modern technology had created a noisier world. The internal combustion engine of the motor car and the loudspeaker of the gramophone set were singled out as the worst offenders of the day. To some, noise symbolised the vibrancy and excitement of modern life. The futurist movement in the arts, for example, enthusiastically made music out of city noises. For many more people, however, noise was a painful and disturbing by-product of technological modernity. The medical profession feared that continued exposure to noise was creating irreversibly neurotic urban populations in industrial nations. Such warnings were in evidence at the Noise Abatement Exhibition held at London's Science Museum in 1935 (below). In this light, Grierson's desire to capture and represent 'the million and one sounds which ordinarily attend the working of the world' seems decidedly more political than it otherwise might.[2] So controversial was it, in fact, that members of the GPO Film Unit failed to agree about how it should be achieved.

REPRODUCTION OF EXHIBITION STAND

This exhibition stand was presented by the Anti-Noise League at the 1935 Noise Abatement Exhibition held at the Science Museum. The stand shows a thermometer and the varying danger of different kinds of noise to health. Placed either side is the logo of the national Anti-Noise League and promotional posters which read 'Help to Banish Unnecessary Noise' and 'Quiet Brings Comfort, Health and Efficiency'. This image was reproduced in *Quiet*, the magazine of the Anti-Noise League, in Autumn 1935, p. 22

Disagreements about sound were sometimes overt in the GPO Film Unit, but for the most part can only be perceived through a close reading of the diverging representational strategies at work on screen. These subtle differences – especially between the films which bear Alberto Cavalcanti's influence on the one hand, and those made by Humphrey Jennings on the other – hinge upon the representation of social rhythm and its accompanying noises. Modernity is presented as a rhythmic force in GPO films, but GPO film-makers were at odds about British workers' relationship to the global dance of industrial capitalism.

The Unit began to experiment with the incorporation of 'found sounds' in 1934 when it moved to new studios in Blackheath and acquired its first mobile sound-recording equipment: 1934 also saw the arrival of Cavalcanti from Paris. Sound technician Ken Cameron recalled that Cavalcanti 'had been building up a very fine reputation for himself in France for his novel and skilful use of sound, and Grierson got him over here to give us the lowdown'.[3] Cavalcanti had an instinctively avant-garde approach. He had previously worked, after all, with the experimental director Marcel L'Herbier and the surrealist composer Darius Milhaud. He instigated a tripartite approach to the soundtrack at the Unit, insisting upon the blending of not only dialogue and music, but also noises. Cameron explained that Cavalcanti:

> Soon taught us one of the fundamental principles of the sound track. That it should be composed of three separate entities, each of which would at times take upon itself the whole job of illustrating and emphasizing the visuals, while the others would help each other to achieve that aim. In a well-designed track they are equally important, and only when the design and execution of each is correct does the track fulfil its purpose. These three are, of course, the dialogue, the effects and the music.[4]

Cavalcanti was nonetheless particularly enthused by the experimental use of effects, especially noisy ones. 'Pictures are clear and specific, noises are vague,' he explained. 'That is why noise is so useful. It speaks directly to the emotions.'[5]

Although Grierson supported the incorporation of everyday noises in documentary films, the direction taken by Cavalcanti and his followers – the composer Walter Leigh, Ken Cameron and, to begin with, Humphrey Jennings – was not necessarily to Grierson's liking. The many divisions between Grierson and Cavalcanti's approach to documentary film have been well documented in this book and elsewhere, but rarely has the question of sound been included in this discussion. In addition to his insistence upon the use of three distinct elements in the soundtrack, Cavalcanti also encouraged the use of un-synchronised sounds. Synchronised sound includes speech produced by a character on screen, or, for example, the sound of a train passing the camera. Unsynchronised sounds are those whose source is unknown because they are produced by something outside of the visual field presented on screen. The possibility of using unsynchronised sound appealed to the avant-garde sensibilities of Cavalcanti and his followers. Cameron, for example, enthused that:

The skill in fitting effects to a picture is partly, of course, finding a sound-track which effectively matches the picture or action appearing on screen, and arranging it so that the two appear to be synchronous. But a more interesting sidelight in this process is achieving an effect by laying, not the sound represented by what is happening on the screen, but by what may be happening just round the corner – out of range of the camera.[6]

This technique is demonstrated to good effect in *Pett and Pott: A Fairy Story of the Suburbs* (1934), the first film to bear Cavalcanti's influence. In the montage sequence which tracks Mr Pett and Mr Pott's rail journey from the city to the suburbs, the sounds of the train are used alongside poetic chanting to lend emotional drama to separate scenes of a suburban robbery. In *The Fairy of the Phone* (1936), to offer another example, an unsynchronised electronic bleeping heralds the arrival of the fairy as she joins the final chorus of GPO telephonists.

It was precisely this use of sound, according to Cameron, that accounted for the artistic value of the British documentary film. He acknowledged, however, that unsynchronised sound took the documentary away from the Griersonian model of realistic film. 'Although Grierson's definition of the documentary film still holds good,' explained Cameron, 'something else has crept in, something indefinable, yet something which has raised the status of the British documentary film as such to a level unsurpassed.'[7] Grierson and Rotha were bitterly critical of *Pett and Pott*, suggesting that it subverted the primary aim of the documentary: to record the daily lives of working people.

Grierson's hostility to unsynchronised sound, we can speculate, was based on his fear that it would lead GPO films to be formally experimental at the expense of the realism he preferred. He rejected the social value of the city symphony film genre (including Walter Ruttmann's *Berlin: Symphony of a City* [1927], for example) on the same grounds.[8] An additional explanation, however, is that a strong precedent had been set in Soviet realist cinema (which strongly influenced the ideals of the British documentary movement) for the synchronous and rhythmic presentation of working noises alongside scenes of heroic and rhythmic work. Dziga Vertov's first sound film *Enthusiasm* (1934), for example, which was screened at London's Film Society, included long scenes of toil in the industrial Donbass region accompanied by synchronised but uncomfortably dissonant mechanical noises in rhythm with the work being performed.[9] The implication in *Enthusiasm* is that, however unpleasant the noises may be, the Soviet worker gladly bears the burden. It was also a typical finding of industrial health researchers, in Britain and elsewhere, that factory workers were psychologically unaffected by noisy working conditions, so long as the noises were rhythmically in time with the work they were performing.[10] This was the logic, too, of the BBC's 'music while you work'. Synchronicity, therefore, had simultaneously cinematic and social meanings in the context of sound.

Although Cavalcanti's experimentation with unsynchronised sound was clearly not intended to subvert the findings of industrial health experts, of whom he was probably unaware, it nonetheless derailed what would have been the more straightforward method of representing working-class soundscapes: the noise of working rhythms presented in time with images of rhythmic work. The working-class heroism which Grierson wanted to project in GPO films could have been achieved by following this model, and one 'suspects that Grierson would have preferred it to. But, thanks to Cavalcanti, this was not the path that was followed.

Instead, films such as *Night Mail*, arguably the pinnacle of Cavalcanti's experimentation with the soundtrack, presented noise as a creative force in modernity, a welcome side effect of industrial work which could be divorced from its original source in order to provide new material for the artist. In this sense, Cavalcanti was following in the footsteps of futurist noise artists such as Luigi Russolo.[11] Rather than tying noise to industrial work, Cavalcanti freed it to become an autonomous element in the film-makers' expressive palette. Instead of using noise to underline the heroic rhythmicity of modern work, he encouraged his followers to find the amusing, the whimsical and the charming in noise. The famous collaboration between Benjamin Britten and W. H. Auden which concludes the film's soundtrack is an example of this.

Cavalcanti's tendency towards using unsynchronised sound can also be found aplenty in *Night Mail*. The subtlety of the signal box's mechanical system of sounds, for example, is contrasted with the thunderous sound of the steam locomotive as it passes by. At a local station where a passenger train has stopped to let the 'postal special' overtake, the camera lingers on the faces of two of this train's crew as the screaming whistle of the post train is heard rapidly approaching. A classic example of asynchronous sound, it creates the space–time continuum of the scene without any recourse to the visuals except for the turning of heads as the stationary crew attempt to catch a glimpse of the passing express. The moving train is represented only by the crescendo and diminuendo of noise as it races through the station.

Cavalcanti's creative use of noise in this way was itself subversive in the 1930s. The Anti-Noise League, led by the influential physician Lord Horder, argued, in opposition to industrial health researchers, that noise was extremely damaging to the mental health of industrial workers and urban populations. The image presented by *Night Mail* is quite the opposite: here postal workers are seen operating in perfect harmony with the clanging, cracking and bleeping of the railway network. Human and machine rhythmically blend into one. Noise is the creative energy produced in the process.

The GPO film to most explicitly address the theme of working rhythm, Len Lye's *Trade Tattoo*, made in support of a 'Post Early' campaign in 1937, followed in this trajectory by presenting scenes of working life accompanied not by noise but by five dance tunes performed by the Lecuona Cuban Band. *Trade Tattoo* is typical of the work of the GPO Film Unit: it deliberately documented not only the everyday spaces reached by postal services, but also the everyday rhythms which governed their operation. Although there are no working sounds in the film, Lye presented the rhythms of national and international trade as if they were the same as the syncopated rhythms of the Cuban band accompanying the images (opposite). Modern work patterns are deliberately likened to the swinging rhythms of the band in order to distance them from the potentially de-humanising nature of industrial work. The suggestion is that the labourers of the British Empire are united by the common purpose and social solidarity to be found in their working rhythms. Work becomes a global dance routine bringing pleasure to all involved. GPO films commonly presented work in this way, in part to demonstrate the modernity of Post Office operations, but also to boost the morale of a working public during a period of intense economic uncertainty.

Many different kinds of work were represented by GPO films, but in each case, as in *Trade Tattoo*, this work was shown to be part of a system of free and global commerce compatible with liberalism and the British Empire. This was true of the earlier *The Song*

of Ceylon, which also likened the everyday rhythm of trade in the Empire to music. By doing so, it showed that Ceylonese and British rhythms, however different, were analogous. Scenes of everyday Sinhalese life, particularly its musical and dance customs, are contrasted with the equivalent 'music' of shipping horns and the telephone conversations taking place in British offices. The two are presented in a rhythmic harmony of global trade.

Such films were clearly open to the critique that they 'sugar coated' the pill of capitalism for the British people. Although he was a follower of Cavalcanti in aesthetic terms, Humphrey Jennings evidently felt this way and did not share the Brazilian's optimism about noise. The films which Jennings made independently of Cavalcanti's direct influence – *Spare Time* (1939) and *Listen to Britain* (1942), in particular – present noise, and rhythm, in an entirely different way to *Night Mail* and *Trade Tattoo*. Jennings was, in fact, the most attentive of the GPO film-makers to everyday sounds. His films contain rich soundscapes of working life and of workers' leisure time. Yet in contrast to Cavalcanti and Lye, who blurred the distinction between music and noise, Jennings was careful to maintain as sharp a distinction between the two as possible.

In *Spare Time*, for example, the noises of the coal miners' working lives are contrasted starkly with the musical pastimes which fill their leisure hours. *Spare Time* implies that steel, cotton and mine workers experience two kinds of temporality, the rigid structure of work time which is associated with noise (such as the siren, horn and clatter of the mine), and the free and expressive time which is best represented by the musical activities undertaken between working hours. Although it is clear that spare time is just as ordered and regularised as work time (for example, in the steel industry, in which spare time sometimes falls in the mornings), workers mark out spare hours with the sounds of trumpets, kazoos and pianos in order to make them their own. Freedom is music, enslavement is noise. Industrial work is not heroic in *Spare Time*. There is a clear simile made, for example, between the cage of the tiger in the zoo and the cage which takes the miners to their place of work.

The wartime *Listen to Britain* similarly contrasts the musical leisure activities of off-duty soldiers with the starkly presented noises of British industry and rail transportation. Ambulance workers rest at their station to the sounds of a woman singing and playing the piano. The climax of the film is the montage sequence which juxtaposes the exquisite delicacy of Myra Hess performing a Mozart piano concerto in front of weary military personnel at the National Gallery with the noise of a factory at work. Although Jennings suggests a similarity between factory noises and music, he is careful in his indication that noisy work must be balanced by the restorative power of music listening. In relation to World War II, Jennings argued that:

> More than ever when men are flying through the night and women are away from their homes and their children their hearts have need of music. All kinds of music – classical music, popular music, home-made music, the nostalgic music of a particular region and just plain martial music to march and work to. For music in Britain today is far from being just another escape: it probes into the emotions of the war itself – love of country, love of liberty, love of living, and the exhilaration of fighting for them. Listen ...[12]

He believed that musical temporality offered refuge from the noisy reality of modern life. This is clear in his films, but it is also underlined in his book *Pandæmonium* (published posthumously in 1985), a selection of writings from British history which traced the spread and impact of industrialisation on the British people.[13] Music is one of the themes of the book. In one extract, drawn from Hugh Miller's 1846 text *First Impressions of England and its People*, the contrast between industrial noise and leisurely music, which became typical of Jennings's GPO and Crown films, is at the fore. Jennings quoted the following passage from Miller's book:

> Almost all the larger towns of England manifest one leading taste or other. Some are peculiarly literary, some decidedly scientific; and the taste paramount in Birmingham seems to be a taste for music. In no town in the world are the mechanic arts more noisy: hammer rings incessantly on anvil; there is an unending clang of metal, an unceasing clank of engines; flame russles, water hisses, steam roars, and from time to time, hoarse and hollow over all, rises the thunder of the proofing house ... the noises of the place, grown a part of customary existence to its people, – inwrought, as it were, into the very staple of their lives, – exerts over them some such unmarked influence [causing them] to fill up the void by modulated noises, first caught up, like the song of the bird beside the cutler's wheel or coppersmith's shop, in unconscious rivalry of the clang of their hammers and engines.[14]

Miller's final argument could equally be Jennings's also: 'The people live in an atmosphere continually vibrating with clamour; and it would seem as if their amusements had caught the general tone, and become noisy like their avocations.'[15] Jennings differed, therefore, from Cavalcanti, who thought of noise as a creative and expressive force in its own right. For Jennings, noise (a machine force) should always be balanced by its opposite, music (an essentially animalistic force).

There were distinct differences, then, in GPO film-makers' approach to representing noise and everyday rhythm. Although they were undoubtedly pioneering in their use of sound effects, their varying approaches to sound were also part of a broader culture of aurality in early twentieth-century Britain in which representations of noise were, by necessity, interventions in politicised debates about industrial modernity.

Notes

1. On the inter-war cultural politics of noise, see Karin Bijsterveld, *Mechanical Sound: Technology, Culture and Public Problems of Noise in the Twentieth Century* (Cambridge, MA: MIT Press, 2008).
2. John Grierson, 'Creative Use of Sound', in Forsyth Hardy (ed.), *Grierson on Documentary* (London: Collins, 1946), p. 91.
3. Ken Cameron, *Sound in Films: A Speech Delivered at the British Film Institute's Summer School at Bangor, August 1944* (London: BFI, 1944), p. 3.
4. Ibid.
5. Alberto Cavalcanti, 'Sound in Films', in Elisabeth Weis and John Bolton (eds), *Film Sound: Theory and Practice* (New York: Columbia University Press, 1985), p. 109.
6. Ken Cameron, *Sound and the Documentary Film* (London: Sir Isaac Pitman & Sons, 1947), p. 8.
7. Ibid., p. 5.
8. John Grierson, 'Documentary (2): Symphonics', *Cinema Quarterly* vol. 1 (1933), p. 137.
9. On *Enthusiasm* see Lucy Fischer, '"Enthusiasm": From Kino-Eye to Radio-Eye', *Film Quarterly* vol. 31 (1977–8), pp. 25–34.
10. This was the conclusion, for example, in H. C. Weston and S. Adams, 'The Effect of Noise on the Performance of Weavers', in Industrial Health Research Board, *Two Studies in the Psychological Effects of Noise* (London: His Majesty's Stationery Office, 1932).
11. James G. Mansell, 'Luigi Russolo's Art of Noises', *The Senses & Society* vol. 2 (2007), pp. 391–5.
12. Humphrey Jennings, 'The Music of War', from a hand-written file entitled 'The Music of War Treatment, Crown Film Unit' relating to *Listen to Britain*. Humphrey Jennings Collection, Item 7, Special Collections, British Film Institute Library.
13. Humphrey Jennings, *Pandæmonium, 1660–1886: The Coming of the Machine as Seen by Contemporary Observers*, ed. Mary-Lou Jennings and Charles Madge (London: Deutsch, 1985).
14. Ibid., p. 232.
15. Ibid.

13 / VOICEOVER/COMMENTARY

Martin Stollery

Film historians and theorists have typically adopted one of two approaches when discussing voiceover in GPO films. Some tend to use overly generalised terms in their discussions. Ian Aitken, for example, refers in his otherwise ground-breaking book on John Grierson to the 'usual voice-of-God narration' in 1930s GPO Film Unit productions.[1] Other historians and theorists have identified a few exceptional and distinctive uses of commentary in individual GPO films. The most often-cited example is Lionel Wendt's voiceover commentary in *The Song of Ceylon* (1934), which I discuss elsewhere.[2] Neither approach is satisfactory. The former tends to conflate GPO with other types of non-fiction film commentary. The latter lacks a sufficiently detailed analysis of the stylistic norms against which to evaluate apparently exceptional and distinctive examples such as *The Song of Ceylon*.

In order to progress our understanding of this issue we need to pitch discussion somewhere between broad generalisations and individual case studies. What follows is an initial survey of some of the norms of commentary in GPO films, primarily those produced during Grierson's tenure as head of the Film Unit, compared to other non-fiction film practices within the British context in the 1930s. Further analysis, beyond the limited scope of this chapter, could assess the extent to which independent British documentary films of the 1930s adhered to the norms outlined here, and the extent to which the norms changed in the transition from the GPO to the Crown Film Unit.

'Cutting to the commentary' and the 'Voice of God'

British documentary theorists and polemicists were keen from the outset to distinguish their use of commentary from its uses in other types of non-fiction film. In 1932, Grierson, in the opening section of his manifesto, 'First Principles of Documentary', separated documentaries from 'lower categories' of non-fiction such as interest films and travelogues. For Grierson, one characteristic of these 'lower categories' was that they were 'cut to the commentary, and shots are arranged arbitrarily to point the gags or conclusions'.[3]

We should not necessarily accept the accuracy of this description of the 'lower categories', nor the value judgment implicit in Grierson's use of this term. The British documentary movement eventually dominated the field in terms of cultural prestige during the 1930s, but other British non-fiction film-makers were often just as thoughtful in their approach to commentary during this period. Mary Field and Percy Smith, for example, similarly argued in a book on their film series *Secrets of Nature* (1922–33) that non-fiction films should not be 'a lecture illustrated by moving pictures'.[4] Field and Smith outlined a sophisticated approach to commentary, albeit one that differed in certain respects from Grierson's. Specifying what is distinctive about GPO films during the 1930s should not necessarily equate to judging them superior to different uses of voiceover in other types of non-fiction film.

The most influential non-fiction film series of the period to be 'cut to the commentary' was *The March of Time* (1935–51). The series' producers developed this approach into a fine art which deserves further analysis in its own right. After *The March of Time* began in 1935, it provided a powerful model for non-fiction commentary. However, Paul Rotha in particular remained keen to emphasise differences between *The March of Time* and British documentary ideals. In his 1936 book *Documentary Film*, Rotha recommended more intimate, informal and spontaneous alternatives to 'the detached "Voice of God" which seems so dear to some producers of documentary'.[5] In the 1939 edition of his book, Rotha specifically criticised *The March of Time*'s 'familiar method of presentation ... the strident voice', and concluded that it 'has already lost its novelty'.[6]

Grierson had a different relationship to *The March of Time* and the 'Voice of God' because he was employed as a British consultant to the series from 1936 onwards. Several of his 'documentary boys' from the GPO Film Unit worked on British editions of *The March of Time*. Nonetheless, we should be wary of subsuming British documentary, or even just GPO voiceovers, under a generic 'Voice of God' category. Harry Watt recalled with some bemusement having to adjust to the distinctive *The March of Time* approach where, 'having found, or been given a subject, you wrote the commentary ... in your version of Timese ... [and then] ... went out and shot to illustrate the commentary, word for word'.[7] Edgar Anstey recalled that *The March of Time*'s producers rejected his proposals to break up the commentary in the editions he worked on. Anstey wanted less commentary and longer passages of synch dialogue between ordinary working people.[8] Both of these recollections suggest differences between British documentary commentary and *The March of Time*'s 'Voice of God'.

A crude but useful measure of these differences is the average percentage of screen time that commentary is present in different types of non-fiction film. Table 1 sets out the percentage of screen time that commentary is present in a small, random sample of GPO films.[9] Benchmarking is provided by a random sample of an equivalent number of American *The March of Time* editions from 1935 to 1939, and Gaumont-British newsreels from 1934 to 1939. The comparison shows the GPO films tend to laconicism, with an average of 38 per cent, notably lower than the other two groups at 70 per cent and 48 per cent, respectively. The range of results for the GPO films is the widest of the three groups, from 22 per cent to 56 per cent, which suggests, compared to their counterparts, the greater flexibility British documentary film-makers enjoyed in constructing their soundtracks. The highest result, 56 per cent, in the sample of GPO films, does not reach the lowest, 63 per cent, for *The March of Time*. Statistical analysis therefore provides

GPO film	Commentary %
The Coming of the Dial (1933)	55
Six Thirty Collection (1934)	27
Weather Forecast (1934)	22
Coal Face (1935)	33
Calendar of the Year (1936)	49
Night Mail (1936)	24
Big Money (1937)	53
Roadways (1937)	28
What's on Today? (1938)	35
The Islanders (1939)	56
Average	38

Table 1
Predominance of
commentary in GPO
films

some evidence that Grierson's stricture against 'cut[ting] to the commentary' was followed within GPO films, if only on the basis that they contained less commentary to which images could be cut.

Further analysis could consider whether there are characteristic patterns of correlation and divergence between commentary and visual images in GPO and other non-fiction films from the 1930s. Relevant issues would include, as Watt pointed out, the way in which editing from shot to shot in *The March of Time* is often motivated by a verbal cue in the commentary. GPO films, with their less prevalent commentary, sometimes include notable shots to which no verbal reference is made. One example would be the shots of people relaxing, camping and playing an accordion by the roadside in *Roadways* (1937). Commentary in GPO films also sometimes triggers montage sequences that amplify a point without further verbal elaboration. An example is *Big Money*, where the statement, 'the money markets of the world … they're waiting for news of the British budget', is followed by a montage of printing presses, headlines on posters and the distribution of newspapers, accompanied solely by the urgent rhythms of Brian Easdale's score.

Celebrity voices

Another way GPO film-makers sought to distinguish their commentaries from other media voices during the 1930s was by avoiding professional commentators. Grierson wrote in 1934 that:

> It costs five pounds, I believe, to have a professional commentator, but we have never thought of spending so much on so little. We do the job ourselves if we cut a commentary, and save both the five pounds and the quite unendurable detachment of the professional accent.[10]

Two years later, in his book *Documentary Film*, Rotha advised against using voices with 'broadcasting or theatrical associations'.[11] To a certain extent, as Grierson makes clear, this approach made a virtue out of low-budget necessity. Professional commentators were relatively costly. This approach was also consistent with British documentary's celebration of the supposedly ordinary and typical. Identifiable voices such as Westbrook Van Voorhis' 'Voice of Time' in *The March of Time*, or E. V. H. Emmet's commentary for Gaumont-British news, employed dramatically portentous or light-hearted styles of delivery. These vocal styles differed from the calmly moderate yet committed sobriety, occasionally extending to rhetorical flourishes or gentle whimsicality, favoured in GPO films. Van Voorhis' and Emmet's voices also connoted entertainment value and a particular type of celebrity that Grierson generally sought to avoid during the 1930s.[12] Grierson's attitude on the issue of celebrity commentators during the 1930s may also have been hardened by his irritation at the terms imposed by the theatrical distributor of *Industrial Britain* and the other 'Imperial Six' films in 1933. One of the conditions of distribution was that the commentary had to be spoken by the well-known British character actor Donald Calthrop.[13]

Accents

A more vexed question is raised by the next two sentences in Grierson's essay. He continued:

> Better still, if we are showing workmen at work, we get the workmen on the job to do their own commentary, with idiom and accent complete. It makes for intimacy and authenticity and nothing we could do would be half as good.[14]

Grierson's polemical assertion does not tally with the subsequent dominant practice in GPO film commentaries. Table 2 shows that the typical accent heard in the random sample of GPO films is unmarked received pronunciation (RP), sometimes with traces of what linguists call marked RP, or hyperlect, which connotes a very high level of social privilege. The accent of the typical GPO film commentary is broadly consistent with the style of voice heard making announcements or reading the news on BBC radio during the 1930s. *BBC – The Voice of Britain* (1935), which profiled a range of mid-1930s BBC personnel, is an aural testament to the closeness between the two.

Table 2
Commentary accent

There are two main reasons for the divergence between Grierson's statement about workmen doing their own commentary and the standard practice in GPO films. The first relates to the organisation of production within the GPO film unit. Film-makers within the Unit sometimes provided commentaries for their own and others' films to save money, to foster collaboration and as part of an ethos of gaining experience in every aspect of film-making. Grierson preferred to recruit Oxbridge graduates whose accents tended towards

GPO film	Accent
The Coming of the Dial (1933)	RP
Six Thirty Collection (1934)	RP
Weather Forecast (1934)	RP
Coal Face (1935)	Paralect
Calendar of the Year (1936)	RP
Night Mail (1936)	RP (several) Paralect (John Grierson)
Big Money (1937)	RP
Roadways (1937)	RP
What's on Today? (1938)	RP
The Islanders (1939)	RP

marked or unmarked RP. The second is that using workers to speak commentaries in documentaries met with resistance. Rotha used a Barrow shipbuilder to voice the commentary in *Shipyard* (1935), but Gaumont-British Instructional cut the film down to one reel and imposed E. V .H. Emmett's voice upon the version of the film shown in newsreel theatres.[15]

Shipyard's fate highlighted the limits of the commercial sector of the film industry's tolerance in the 1930s. Nevertheless, by the time the GPO Film Unit acquired sound technology there was some debate about the standardisation of broadcast language. The *People* newspaper, for example, ran a campaign in the early 1930s against the BBC's Advisory Committee on Spoken English and its promotion of a single standard.[16] Consequently, there was some cultural precedent for a minority of GPO films to cautiously push the boundaries in this area. *Coal Face* (1935) was produced by GPO Film Unit personnel through a production company, EMPO, that placed it at arm's length from their more mainstream productions. The commentary was written and spoken by Montagu Slater in a paralect (close to RP but retaining some traces of his Cumbrian accent). Slater's commentary is featured in a film that deals with miners, traditionally the most radical section of the British working class. Slater was also a long-serving member of the Communist Party of Great Britain. Like most GPO film commentators, he was not identified in the onscreen credits, but his voice would have added an extra resonance for anyone who recognised it and knew his personal history.

Grierson himself contributed to another experiment in this area. He spoke the unscripted commentary for the unreleased *On the Fishing Banks of Skye* (1935). The commentary seems to be describing events as they occur, from the perspective of someone on a fishing boat, caught up in the excitement of the catch. Grierson's speech in *On the Fishing Banks of Skye* contains more broad Scottish elements than we hear in filmed records of him speaking in other more formal contexts. This emphasis, combined with the unscripted immediacy of the delivery, contributes to an overall impression of 'intimacy and authenticity', the qualities Grierson advocated as the ideal aim of a good commentary.

By the mid-1930s, some progressive BBC producers were advocating a wider range of accents on the airwaves. Hilda Matheson, for example, wrote in 1933 that 'one would not ... choose a reader with Cockney vowels or a Northumbrian burr to read English lyrics. A voice of this kind might, however ... talk on new careers in engineering, or on fifty years of memories in shipbuilding.'[17] Matheson's comments highlight a similar pattern in GPO films. Slater's paralect is used in *Coal Face* partly because mining was strongly associated with regional identities. GPO films about more universal, abstract processes, such as *The Coming of the Dial* (1933, science and technology) and *Big Money* (1937, economics), link these 'higher' forms of knowledge to RP commentary. *Night Mail* (1936) incorporates a similar distinction between 'universal' and 'local' accents. Although Scott Anthony has argued that there may be a deliberate attempt in the film to represent national unity by mismatching the accents of the workers heard in the film and the locales in which they are seen, this does not apply to the commentary.[18] RP commentators are heard, irrespective of regional differences, as the overnight postal train passes through different parts of England, whereas Grierson's voice is only heard at the end of the film, after it has crossed the border into Scotland.

Politics, poetry and terminology

Grierson's comment on getting 'workmen on the job to do their own commentary' can also be understood in the looser sense of incorporating workers' 'idioms and accents' into the soundtrack by recording, as he put it, 'conversational scraps from a street, a factory, from any scene or situation'.[19] Wildtrack, non-sychronised snippets of dialogue or brief passages of synchronised speech were recorded, ideally on location, and subsequently woven into the soundtrack of GPO films alongside the commentary. As Table 3 shows, non-sychronised dialogue was more common in GPO films of the first part of the 1930s.

The use of non-synchronised dialogue clearly distinguished GPO documentaries from many other types of non-fiction film. This was particularly important during the earlier and middle part of the 1930s when theorists and polemicists such as Grierson and Rotha were establishing British documentary's identity and asserting its superiority to other types of non-fiction film. Synch dialogue predominated in GPO films later in the decade, particularly during Alberto Cavalcanti's tenure as head of the Unit.

One factor that cuts across the entire period of GPO film production is that workers' voices are almost always embodied or semi-embodied. Even if their voices are heard in wildtrack and are not linked to particular individuals, they are still closely associated with the atmosphere of a particular workplace. A typical example would be the extensive use of non-synch dialogue in *Six Thirty Collection* (1934). An intermediate technique is used in films such as *Cable Ship* (1933) and *The Horsey Mail* (1938). In the former, a foreman and a jointer speak on the commentary track about their areas of expertise, while also appearing onscreen (below). In the latter, postman Bob O'Brian is a protagonist within the film as well as one of the commentators. The repeated emphasis upon workers as embodied participants in the films, even when they also contribute to commentary,

GPO film	Non-synch speech	Synch speech
The Coming of the Dial (1933)	✗	✔
Six Thirty Collection (1934)	✔	✗
Weather Forecast (1934)	✔	✗
Coal Face (1935)	✔	✔
Calendar of the Year (1936)	✔	✔
Night Mail (1936)	✔	✔ predominates
Big Money (1937)	✗	✔
Roadways (1937)	✔	✔ predominates
What's on Today? (1938)	✗	✔
The Islanders (1939)	✗	✔ some Gaelic

Table 3 Non-synch and synch speech

(Jointer) *That's me on the left,*

sets boundaries to their expertise: they primarily explain technical processes relating to the workplace, rather than speaking about wider social or political issues or contexts that extend beyond it.

The recourse to embodiment also relates to a metaphor Ian Aitken uses when he argues that workers' voices and images are typically employed to add 'flesh' to the social and political values promoted by GPO films' RP voiceovers. According to Aitken, workers' voices and images lend a patina of authenticity to voiceover articulations of reformist values which could otherwise 'only be delivered at an abstract, didactic level'.[20] Andrew Higson, arguing along similar lines, describes British documentary movement films as addressing 'the spectator as a citizen of the nation, not as a subject of one or another antagonistic class'.[21] Voiceover, carefully integrated with synch and non-synch workers' dialogue, plays an important role in this argument.[22] There are no GPO films where class-inflected voices are set against each other as fundamentally antagonistic. Nevertheless, Aitken's and Higson's retrospective ideological analyses need to be qualified by disentangling the two keywords, 'voiceover' and 'commentary', that provide the title of this chapter.

The term 'voiceover' carries hierarchical connotations through a spatial metaphor that also implies an external imposition onto a film.[23] The term reinforces the assumption that information conveyed by unseen commentators speaks over the images, thereby subordinating visual to verbal elements, and fixing the meanings of documentary films. Yet 'voiceover' is a retrospective description when it is used to discuss GPO films. A keyword search of the digitised versions of British journals of record *Sight &*

Sound, *Monthly Film Bulletin* and *The Times*, revealed no instances of the term being used in relation to documentaries before the 1970s. From a historical perspective, the application of the term 'voiceover' to GPO documentaries is relatively recent, arising partly from suspicions about the supposedly unrealistic, didactic, or authoritarian nature of this technique in the wake of 1960s direct cinema, and partly from post-1970s theoretical concepts of reflexive documentary. The term is not invalid, and neither are Aitken's and Higson's arguments, but its historical provenance needs to be factored into discussions of the technique to which it refers.

British documentary and other non-fiction film-makers in the 1930s used the term 'commentary' to describe the speech of unseen commentators. 'Commentary' is a more neutral, open-ended term that does not carry the same hierarchical connotations as 'voiceover'. British theoreticians and non-fiction film-makers of the 1930s expressed a correspondingly flexible range of attitudes towards it. Rotha, in his influential book *The Film Till Now*, articulated a purist rejection of synchronised dialogue in feature films, but left open the question of whether commentary had a role to play in 'the great sound and visual cinema of the future'.[24] Andrew Buchanan, producer of *Ideal Cinemagazine* (1926–33), shared some of Rotha's reservations about synchronised dialogue in feature films but was confident that post-synchronised commentary, sound effects and music in documentary was entirely consistent with 'the fundamental basis of film construction ... movement', defined in terms of 'free' shooting and 'unhampered' editing.[25]

The primary focus of public discussions by British documentary theorists and practitioners of non-fiction commentary in the early 1930s, shortly after the coming of sound, was aesthetic rather than ideological.[26] Grierson and his colleagues wanted, for the sake of cultural prestige, to identify British documentary films with the most sophisticated uses of this technique. Grierson evaluated different types of documentary film speech in a 1934 *Sight & Sound* essay, 'Introduction to a New Art'. He was particularly interested in how different types of speech could be orchestrated within documentary soundtracks to create choral effects. A 'thousand and one vernacular elements' recorded on location could 'all be used to give atmosphere, to give drama, to give poetic reference'.[27] The 'very crudest form' of recorded speech was 'the commentary ... ordinarily attached to interest films'.[28] This highlights the historical shift in discussion of commentary and voiceover. In Aitken's and Higson's ideological analyses of GPO films, voiceover subordinates other vernacular elements such as workers' synch and non-synch dialogue. In Grierson's aesthetic schema this order of priority is reversed.

Discussing the GPO film *Six Thirty Collection*, where the commentary is mostly prosaic, Grierson ruminated on how easy it would have been to make letters on a sorting belt 'read themselves out in snatches, or for that matter we could have hired a poet to make *vers libre* of their contents'. He concluded that in this instance, however, such techniques 'would probably have overloaded the occasion'.[29] This is a tacit admission that, although this issue did not feature prominently in Grierson's theorising on sound, commentary in GPO films was designed with sponsors' requirements and multiple audiences in mind. For example, in a school a GPO film commentary might be reiterated and elaborated upon by a teacher after the screening. In this context commentary comes to the fore in its role as an effective technique for conveying certain kinds of technical and process-related information.[30] Simultaneously, at the burgeoning film societies of the 1930s, the same film might be screened before audiences inclined to look and listen for film art. Such audiences might be familiar with documentary theorists' ideas on sound published in *Cinema Quarterly*, *Sight & Sound*, or in Rotha's book *Documentary Film*. Consequently, a different reception context might prevail in these circumstances.

For Grierson, Rotha and other British documentary theorists and polemicists, the soundtrack should be constructed and listened to, by model audiences, as an integrated whole. Within this approach, commentary would be one of a range of elements within the sound design, alongside synch and non-synch dialogue, sound effects and music.[31] This may partly explain why there is a lower proportion of commentary in GPO films compared to some other types of non-fiction film in the 1930s. It is also one of the reasons why it is sometimes difficult to isolate commentary in GPO films for analytical purposes. In *Coal Face*, for example, the chorus that runs alongside Slater's commentary could be considered either as additional commentary or as part of the music.[32]

Grierson and Rotha argued in favour of the use of poetry in voiceover commentary. This tendency can be heard not only in canonised GPO films such as *The Song of Ceylon*, *Coal Face* and *Night Mail*, but also to some extent in less famous ones such as *Air Post* (1934) and *Six Thirty Collection*.[33] Compared to some other styles of non-fiction commentary, the forms of poetry used in GPO films could be more easily integrated with choral and musical effects. The use of poetry also further supported the claims made by Grierson, Rotha and others about documentary's aesthetic distinction, compared to other types of non-fiction and feature film.[34] Contemporary documentary theorists such as Stella Bruzzi validate ironic and reflexive uses of voiceover, mainly on ideological grounds. In the 1930s Grierson and Rotha, on the other hand, emphasised the aesthetic significance and the affective dimensions of the soundtrack, within which commentary would not necessarily predominate.

Notes

1. Ian Aitken, *Film and Reform* (London: Routledge, 1990), p. 145.
2. Martin Stollery, *Alternative Empires* (Exeter: University of Exeter Press, 2000), pp. 192–3.
3. John Grierson, 'First Principles of Documentary', in Forsyth Hardy (ed.), *Grierson on Documentary* (London: Faber, 1979), p. 36.
4. Mary Field and Percy Smith, *Secrets of Nature* (London: Faber, 1934), p. 213. I am grateful to Tim Boon for drawing this reference to my attention.
5. Paul Rotha, *Documentary Film* (London: Faber, 1936), p. 209.
6. Paul Rotha, *Documentary Film* [rev. and enlarged edn] (London: Faber, 1939), p. 248.
7. Harry Watt, *Don't Look at the Camera* (London: Elek, 1974), p. 75.
8. Edgar Anstey, 'Some Origins of Cinéma Vérité and the Soundtrack in British Documentary', paper for the UNESCO Round Table Meeting on the Soundtrack in Cinema and Television, 1966, p. 9.
9. The only deliberate exclusions from the sample of GPO films discussed here are narrative documentaries such as *North Sea* (Harry Watt, 1938) which predominantly employ synch dialogue and would therefore skew the results.
10. John Grierson, 'The GPO Gets Sound', *Cinema Quarterly* vol. 2 (1934), p. 216.
11. Rotha, *Documentary Film*, p. 208.

12. My discussion here focuses solely on celebrity voiceover commentaries. A particular strand of 1930s British documentary film, which could be described as the illustrated celebrity lecture, emerged during the latter part of the 1930s. In these films, rather than providing commentary, the source of which is never seen, an intellectual celebrity addresses the camera directly. *We Live in Two Worlds* (1937), featuring J. B. Priestley, was the first GPO film of this type, following the independent British documentary *Enough to Eat?* (1936), featuring Julian Huxley. The celebrities featured in these films connote expertise and cultural prestige rather than entertainment value. This development anticipates the increased use of celebrity commentators and lecturers in British wartime documentaries.

13. Forsyth Hardy, *John Grierson: A Documentary Biography* (London: Faber, 1979), p. 65.

14. Grierson, 'The GPO Gets Sound', p. 216.

15. Paul Rotha, *Documentary Diary* (London: Secker & Warburg, 1973), p. 105.

16. Mark Pegg, *Broadcasting and Society 1918–1939* (London: Croom Helm, 1983), pp. 160–1.

17. Hilda Matheson, *Broadcasting* (London: Butterworth, 1933), p. 68.

18. Scott Anthony, *Night Mail* (London: BFI, 2007), p. 27.

19. John Grierson, 'Introduction to a New Art', *Sight & Sound* vol. 3 (1934), p. 103.

20. Ian Aitken, 'The Documentary Film Movement: The Post Office Touches all Branches of Life', in John Hassard an Ruth Holliday (eds), *Organization-Representation: Work and Organization in Popular Culture* (London: Sage, 1998), p. 31.

21. Andrew Higson, ' "Britain's Outstanding Contribution to the Film": The Documentary-Realist Tradition', in Charles Barr (ed.), *All Our Yesterdays* (London: BFI, 1986), p. 77.

22. Higson (ibid., p. 79), for example, discusses how 'poetic ambiguity' is 'often contained by the imposition of a voice-over' in *Industrial Britain* (1931), and attributes considerable power to the 'voice of authority' in *Housing Problems* (1935).

23. Stella Bruzzi, *New Documentary*, 2nd edn (London: Routledge, 2006), p. 47, discusses some of the metaphors involved, as does Charles Wolfe, 'Historicising the "Voice of God": The Place of Vocal Narration in Classical Documentary', *Film History* vol. 9 (1997), p. 150.

24. Paul Rotha (with an additional section by Richard Griffith), *The Film Till Now* (London: Spring Books, 1967), p. 412. Bruzzi, *New Documentary*, pp. 47–8, selectively quotes Rotha from the same source as part of her general argument that a deep-rooted antipathy to sound, among theorists who assume film is an essentially visual medium, was the basis for long-standing negative attitudes to voiceover. However, Rotha's primary concern in *The Film Till Now* was that a specific use of sound, synchronised dialogue, would have a negative impact upon filmmaking. Rotha positively encouraged other 'creative' uses of sound in film.

25. Andrew Buchanan, 'Making the Documentary Film', *Sight & Sound* vol. 1 (1932), p. 48. *Ideal Cinemagazine* became *Ideal Sound Cinemagazine* in the early 1930s.

26. There has been extensive debate among cultural theorists about the relationship between ideology and aesthetics. My intention here is not to suggest a categorical separation between the two, but simply to consider GPO film commentary in relation to historical reception contexts in the 1930s, in some of which the particular aesthetic elements valued by Grierson would have been emphasised. In sketching these reception contexts, I am not proposing the more overtly 'aesthetic' ones have greater value. As Raymond Williams, *Marxism and Literature* (Oxford: Oxford University Press, 1977), p. 156, puts it in his discussion of 'aesthetic and other situations': 'Any concentration on language or form, in sustained or temporary priority over other elements and other ways of realizing meaning or value, is specific: at times an intense and irreplaceable experience, in which these fundamental elements of human process

are directly stimulated, reinforced, or extended; at times, at a different extreme, an evasion of other immediate connections, an evacuation of immediate situation, or a privileged indifference to the human process as a whole.'

27. Grierson, 'Introduction to a New Art', pp. 101 and 102.
28. Ibid., p. 103.
29. Ibid.
30. The schools context is reflected in the occasional use of children as commentators in Empire Marketing Board and GPO films, for example in *Spring on the Farm* (1933), and briefly in *The Song of Ceylon*.
31. Other documentary theorists and polemicists apart from Grierson and Rotha advocated this approach. The British documentary director Geoffrey Clark, 'Films to Music', *Cinema Quarterly* vol. 2 (1934), for example, similarly argued in favour of an integrated approach to the documentary soundtrack, where different elements become interchangeable.
32. I am grateful to Amy Sargeant for highlighting this issue. When calculating the percentage of voiceover commentary for *Coal Face* in Table 1, I only took Slater's commentary and not the chorus into account.
33. I discuss poetic elements in *Air Post*'s commentary on the *Screenonline* website: <www.screenonline.org.uk/film/id/1342214/> (accessed 2 April 2010). *Six Thirty Collection* uses some memorable lines of pseudo-surrealist vernacular poetry to describe a piece of machinery used by sorting office workers: 'Stockings and pants/Spectacles and circulars/Photographs and samples/They all pour up this conveyor belt/Which is known as the alligator'.
34. Grierson expressed his enthusiasm for *The March of Time*, and at the same time bracketed it as an archaic contrast to the modernism of British documentary films, by comparing elements of its style to ancient Greek drama. John Grierson, 'The Documentary Idea' (1943), quoted in Raymond Fielding, *The March of Time, 1935–51* (New York: Oxford University Press, 1978, p. 240.

14 / NATIONAL IDENTITY, THE GPO FILM UNIT AND THEIR MUSIC

E. Anna Claydon

The GPO films, seminal as they were in helping to construct the British social realist movement, are as much remembered for their sound worlds as their visual properties. Whether it is the crackling audio of the ensembles who played, or the (to our ears) richly evocative accents of the narrators, or the adventurous musical soundtracks, the sound worlds of the Empire Marketing Board, GPO and Crown Film Unit are utterly textural and utterly of their time and place. This timbre is largely the effect of Alberto Calvancanti's aesthetic, but it is also a reflection of the range of composers and film-makers employed by the Unit. In this chapter, I shall focus upon the way in which Benjamin Britten and W. H. Auden's sonic collage in *Night Mail* (1936) created and rein-forced concepts of national identity and place and how the use of sound in Humphrey Jennings's *Spare Time* (1939) established a semiotic musical sense of British identity by engaging with popular forms, a mode which he would later develop in *Listen to Britain* (1942). These are films which are much discussed and much loved, but for that same reason, it is worthwhile to step back, to distance ourselves somewhat and to re-examine the elements we can take for granted: what we hear that we know *too* well. Consequently, this chapter situates the development of a documentary 'national soundtrack' within its specific cultural and artistic contexts.

Benjamin Britten was the musical director for the Unit from September 1935 until late 1936. He had previously been part of the BBC team which shaped the soundscapes of the pioneering radio 'features' in 1934 and 1935.[1] Britten's earlier work and collabora-tion with the mass media echoes Jennings's work outside of the medium of film. Britten's experience of working in radio was indeed one of the reasons behind his appointment to the Unit. He was the key composer for the important *Coal Face* (1935), which Basil Wright described as 'part of a series of experiments with sound on which our group has been for some time engaged: and it was in a sense the test-tube form which the formula for *Night Mail* was created'.[2]

Coal Face can be placed securely within a tradition of British moving picture docu-ments, from *actualités* such as *A Day in the Life of a Coal Miner* (1910) to the Mitchell and Kenyon coal pit films. To represent the miner was already part of the iconography of British working-class national identity and had a place within British cinema innovation, revealing the humanity of Britain's most dangerous job outside the military. To place the mining story within a contemporary aesthetic prevented it from becoming nostalgic and gave it cultural currency within modernism. At the time, analysing the new documentary movement, Kurt London wrote that in *Coal Face*:

> Britten formed a unity of music, words spoken in chorus, and stylised noises. It is astonishing to observe how, with the most scanty material, using only a piano and a speaking chorus, he can make us dispense gladly with realistic sounds ... The rhythms of life are hard: hard likewise is the music and its interweaving with the speaking choruses. The general atmosphere of the film is dark, and its music neither makes it brighter nor does it underline the shadows superfluously. In a word, the power-ratio between picture and music is always most ideally balanced.[3]

The majority of *Night Mail*, in contrast to *Coal Face* (with its use of inter-titles and overt narrative structuring) is in a more observational mode, with three narrators shaping the journey of the overnight postal special from Euston to Glasgow. Its many sounds are emphasised and reinforced through editing and through images which contain a specific movement (for example, a switch being moved) which are synchronised with an overlaid sound (opposite). The presence of music, however, is limited to the opening titles and the final part of the film, accompanying Auden's poem. Considering that most audiences remember *Night Mail* because of the music and the rhythm of the poem, it is interesting that the film is, in fact, largely made up of diegetic sounds (sounds heard on the soundtrack which are linked to objects or actions

Coal Face

seen onscreen, in contrast to superimposed music) which many have forgotten, emphasising the power Britten and Auden had on the reputation of the film. Mitchell records
that, for the film, Britten was given his largest recording orchestra to date: a flute,
oboe, bassoon, trumpet, harp, violin, viola, cello and double bass. His 'percussion' were
compressed air in a canister, sandpaper on slate, a small trolley on a short piece of rail-
ing, booms for clanking sounds, a hand-cranked camera for metallic mechanical motion
sounds, a hammer on a boom or conduit, a siren and a bag of coal for throwing down a
shaft.[4] This meant that the soundscape Britten was creating was performing two tasks:
a musical one and a sonic imitation of the sounds of industry. The sound world of
industry entered the musical score and led Britten to radically rethink the meaning of
programmatic scoring.

The ensemble performing in *Night Mail* represents all the basic aspects of a large
orchestra. This meant that Britten could use the instruments in a short-hand form that
the audience would recognise as coherent with classical music and the film music they
heard in fictional films. Thus, the trumpet functions as herald and horn, while the
strings, with their flexibility of sound, work traditionally, playing chords and melody and
also using extended techniques alongside the atypical percussion section. The orchestration was clearly designed to work in partnership with the poem written by Auden and
viewers of the film should think of the music and voice working together as a complete
composition, with the spoken voice as a recitative. The most significant problem for
Britten, however, seems to have been layering the two together in post-production, and
Britten's diary for 15 January 1936 notes:

There is too much to be spoken in a single breath by one voice (and it is essential to keep the same voice & to have no breaks) so we have to record separately – me, having to conduct from an improvised visual metronome – flashes on the screen – a very difficult job! Legg speaks the stuff splendidly tho'.[5]

As such, the poem was thought of by Britten entirely in musical terms, substantiating a musical approach to Legg's narration as recitative. What recitative means musically is a carefully pitched but mainly unsung solo which is, typically, rhythmically in line with conversational speech. In opera, the recitative creates the link between dramatic action and full song or aria. In terms of national identity, the even voice Legg presents is symbolically very important because it signifies unity and an even-temperedness to the audience. Yes, it is a middle-class voice, but it is also a voice designed to make the work performed in the film something which crosses the landscape without accent: it reinforces the national identity at the same time as the film shows the regions as united by the rail (and the mail). As Dai Vaughan noted in 1983: the film 'articulates a meaning of "work" … *Night Mail* does, if nothing else, give form to a myth oppositional to that of the Great Artist.'[6] The content of the poem also reiterates this through reference to all kinds of people, and as such the film both develops some of the methods used by the Empire Marketing Board and predicts some of the methods for communicating national pride used by Cavalcanti in *Went the Day Well?* (1942) and David Lean in *This Happy Breed* (1944).

That *Night Mail* sought to present the nation, and to show audiences parts of the country they would not have seen, can be witnessed in the GPO morality tale of 'address your letter correctly' and the pride in the letters posted in Bletchley only thirty minutes before the train collects them, but there are errors which also belie the south-centric understanding of the line above Crewe by placing Warrington and Wigan in the wrong order. Nevertheless, this surprising error in the film ultimately adds to the film's charm, emphasising the poetry of the narration above the documentary reality. In conjunction with the performance styles of the musical ensemble and the 'acting' railway men, this geographical mistake lends *Night Mail* an amateurism (in both the sense of something not perfectly polished and in the sense of something coming from love of the subject) which is an important aspect of a number of the GPO and Crown Film unit films because it makes the art form and its subject matter more accessible and 'of the people'. This is a spirit which is also fundamental to Humphrey Jennings's films and which helps to take the work of the GPO Film Unit from being the output of an artistic elite to something more in tune with national identity/ies and with people. *Spare Time*, however, the first of Jennings's films in which this comparable spirit is particularly notable, is a film about the country beyond London and, thus, has a completely different tone in its expression of region: one of the people within industry, not the industry within people.

The aural filmic predecessor to 'This is the night mail, crossing the border' can be heard in the train sequences of Cavalcanti's *Pett and Pott: A Fairy Tale of the Suburbs* (1934). Helping to demonstrate that Cavalcanti's concept was later developed in *Night Mail*, Pat Jackson, writing in 1999, also saw signs of the film's best-known rhythmic content in Basil Wright's early draft script for *Pett and Pott*:

Basil's equivalent [of Auden's poem to come], scribbled in one of those large Post Office notebooks, read roughly as follows: 'Over close shots of the locomotive funnel belching smoke as its struggles up the Beattock gradient, the puffs gets slower and greyer and maybe we could lay over a voice saying, "I think I can, I think I can".'[7]

Added to this, *Pett and Pott* was reputedly an 'evolution' of an idea from Jennings, and elements of George Orwell's critique of suburban life in *Keep the Aspidistra Flying* (published two years later, in 1936). This confirms that *Pett and Pott* and *Night Mail* are linked in ways which emphasise that Jennings, Auden, Britten, Wright and Cavalcanti's approaches to sound design were always framed with the wit of the 1930s social journalist and not just the eye of the social realist. These elements, these connections among the writers, composers and film-makers of the 1930s, should accurately be seen as part of the way in which a debate about national identity was taking place: what was the *modern*, the technological British national identity, what did it look like, sound like and feel like? These were modernist questions which would be placed in a kind of stasis during World War II.

The presence of modernist answers in GPO films shows that a route was being carved out to a concrete understanding of what contemporary British identity was. This was done by representing Britain as a series of spaces. Space to live (modern housing), space to work (in the office, on the trains, at the post office – all in the service of something larger), space to identify with (regional identities coming through in the 1930s cinema), space to aspire to and, importantly, spaces in which to hear and be heard. It is all too easy for the post-World War II generation to forget that Britain was an aural media nation in the 1930s and 40s. It is all too easy to forget that the sonic spaces of the radio mapped onto and into the daily lives of people and helped to contribute to the mid-century national identity. That is why, when Jennings later made *Listen to Britain* in 1942, *hearing* the sounds of Britain was far more important than seeing the stars of the day for constructing national pride. The sounds of Britain make it more concrete, more real than its imagery alone.

In his later music, the creation of sonic spaces is something with which Benjamin Britten became particularly associated (consider, for example, the opening of *Billy Budd* (1951) with its evocation of the Suffolk coast), but these elements are evident in his music for the GPO Film Unit too and establish Britten as an explorer of *musique concrète* and avant-garde concepts of musical noise. *Musique concrète* means a form of electro-accoustic music in which sounds produced accoustically are processed electronically to produce a semiotically interesting and complex musical sound (in the sense of John Cage's 'organised noise'). Britten's experiments in *Night Mail* and Walter Leigh's in *The Song of Ceylon* (1934) further demonstrate the cutting-edge work in the Unit. They precede the accepted innovators of *musique concrète* (such as Pierre Schaffer who worked with the director Jean Rouch) in the 1950s.

The use of objects as instruments (the boom, the hammer, etc.) also link Britten and Cage more explicitly in terms of expressionism in the contemporary music of the 1930s and 40s. However, the pre-existing train rhythm provided Britten and Auden with something conventional to work with. This enabled the avant-garde to be couched within the familiar and made Britten's music almost folksy, using a set of rhythms and simple methods of composition which audiences recognised from nursery rhymes and programmatic music of the nineteenth century. A certain folksiness is absolutely central to Humphrey Jennings's *Spare Time*, which, as I noted earlier, utilised the spirit of the amateur, although here more literally through its celebration of what the working people of 1930s Britain do outside work. As Ian Aitken wrote in 1997:

> His *Spare Time* and *Listen to Britain* remain impressive, marked by a lyrical humanism and a sensitivity to the ordinary which stands out from the often stereotyped representation of working-class people found in some of the films made by the documentary movement.[8]

Lyrical humanism means, for *Spare Time*, the difference between people as cogs in a machine and people as sensual beings, and, as the narration, provided by Laurie Lee, says: 'Spare Time is a time when we have a chance to do what we like, a chance to be most ourselves.' Significantly, the audience is presented with people that are being signalled as 'ourselves': they are the everymen and -women of four urban British peoples. For the steel industry, the Steel, Peech and Tozer Pheonix Works Band (Sheffield) represents the working men; for the largely female and young cotton workers, the Manchester Victorians Carnival Band, dressed in satins and playing the kazoo (opposite), represents those new to the workforce but with history behind them; for the miners of Britain, the Handel Male Voice Choir of Pontypridd sings out; and for the workers of Bolton communities – crossing over between the cotton and coal industries – people are seen walking dogs, playing sports and enjoying a pint of beer in the pub. Basil Wright, however, had reservations about the way in which the people were represented, believing that it had a 'patronising, sometimes almost sneering attitude towards the efforts of low-income groups'.[9] This, I would argue, is an unfair judgment, because Jennings presents each group as people 'we' could know through small gestures such as helping the pianist at the Handel Male Voice Choir to take off her coat while still playing. The humour is not to be laughed *at* but to be laughed *with*.

Constructed from a combination of diegetic and non-diegetic sound but with the diegetic prioritised, the sound of the film provides an immediacy which echoes the theme of the film. This immediacy arises in part from the kind of diegetic sounds that the audience hears: we do not *just* hear a piano, we hear an out-of-tune piano; we do not *just* hear a band, we hear a band of hand-made kazoos played like trumpets by a troupe in hand-made costumes; we do not *just* hear and see a family preparing for tea, we hear the banter between a family which has its own language. These sounds are discovered by the film, they are observed in the spirit of the Mass Observation movement of which Jennings was a co-founder. These sounds are found within the film and encountered within the spaces between the narration.

In all of his musical films, Jennings was interested in *found musical objects* (of sorts) – that is, music found in the environment rather than music imposed upon the film. Where *Spare Time* is a little different is that Handel's 'Firework Music' is used to herald and close the film. The function of this is twofold: first, using music written for the state means that Jennings signalled that the music within the film is of equal status; and, second, using a recording of music associated with royalty identifies the people with their rulers and democratises the conceptualisation of nation. Given that the film was reportedly commissioned for the New York World Trade Fair, this democratisation is important. The presentation of everyday music-making as informal and dynamic indicates Jennings's identification with informal popular culture (even regarding the classical genres) rather than formal concert culture (which he later represented in *Listen to Britain*).

Spare Time

It is also important in examining the sound world which Jennings is presenting to consider the role of Laurie Lee's narration as part of the way in which the film seeks to present contemporary Britain to an external (American) audience. Lee (best known for his novel *Cider with Rosie*, published twenty years later in 1959 but set in the 1920s) is a conventional received pronunciation English-accented man who initially sounds like he is presenting the leisure hours of the British worker as a travelogue with a distinct detachment: that is precisely his function. *Spare Time* is not just a travelogue for American audiences, it is a travelogue for British audiences too. When George Orwell published *The Road to Wigan Pier*, in 1937, he was demonstrating an interest in industry from within the southern middle classes and performing a role which was both journalistic and performative: giving the working classes an authentic, albeit mediated, voice. At around the same time, Edgar Anstey, in *Housing Problems* (1935), was presenting the first *vox populi* interviews of Londoners in the slums and a little later, in *The Stars Look Down* (Carol Reed, 1939) and *Love on the Dole* (John Baxter, 1941), audiences were being faced with the social realities of the poor majority. Laurie Lee, therefore, aurally ushers the audience into the spare times of Britain and his voiceover becomes sparse and eventually so insignificant by the time we get to the Coal section of the film that, instead of introducing the working patterns (as with steel and cotton), he merely says, 'Finally, coal ...'. The introduction is not necessary any longer. The relationship between text, subjects and audience has shifted and the tempo has altered, as epitomised by one of the most interesting aspects of the presentation of music in *Spare Time*: the way in which tempo is manipulated, especially with the classical pieces present ('Rule Britannia', performed by the Manchester Victorians Carnival Band, 'Ombra mai fu' from Handel's *Xerxes* and 'Never was There a Shadow', from the Handel Male Voice Choir in Pontypridd). The impact of this shift in time signatures is both metaphorical and significant because the lengthening of phrases and the addition of notes, the slowing and speeding up of sections become a metaphor for *spare* time (as in the time within bars, the time signature), for the people finding the time within the framework to make these pieces their own. The manipulation of time is significant for another reason too, because within the context of a film which is trying to communicate something about a modern Britain which is proud of but not tied to its imperial past, the swung rendition of 'Rule Britannia', more than anything else in the film, evokes a modern Britain, a modern British identity and a modern British pride for the 1930s.

The music used in both *Night Mail* and *Spare Time*, then, signifies a democratising of 'high' culture and a raising of status of music and forms previously designated 'low' culture (to use the terms of the period). The music and sound also reinforce and develop a sense of place for different audiences, despite errors contained within each which lead to a homogenisation of region in both films. This means that both films reveal something about British national identity for audiences who are new to the films' content (for instance, the train as mechanics of empire and popular culture during leisure time as the soul of nation). Both films signal a sense of the moment. *Night Mail* draws on the structure of films Grierson admired (the temporally continuous narrative) while *Spare Time* privileges narratives that have long been used to represent Britishness – ultimately presenting a state of the nations narrative in which the brass band, choir and kazoo band evoke a present which is proud of its past.

This national soundtrack, then, is one which sits well alongside the intellectual efforts of the period and establishes a set of concepts which film soundtracks have used in documentary ever since. Sound and music *need not* simply reinforce action or be 'atmospheric'; they can be part of a commentary and make one not just *see* again, as the Mass Observation movement aimed to do, but also to *listen* again.

Notes

1. D. Mitchell, *Britten and Auden in the Thirties: The Year 1936* (London: Faber & Faber, 1981), p. 80.
2. Basil Wright, 'Britten and Documentary', *The Musical Times* vol. 104 (1963), pp. 779–80.
3. Kurt London, *Film Music* (London: Faber & Faber, 1936), quoted in John Huntley, *British Film Music* (London: S. Robinson, 1947) in Charles Wiffen, *Postal Music Research Project* (BCS Unit, Royal College of Music, 2003), p. 22; available at <http://postalheritage.org.uk/collections/music/downloads/Postal%20Music%20Research%Report%20_web%20version_.pdf>.
4. Mitchell, *Britten and Auden in the Thirties*, pp. 82 and 84.
5. Ibid., p. 84.
6. Dai Vaughan, '*Night Mail*', in Kevin MacDonald and Mark Cousins (eds), *Imagining Reality: The Faber Book of Documentary* (London: Faber & Faber, 1997), p. 121.
7. P. A. Jackson, *A Retake Please!* Night Mail *to* Western Approaches (Liverpool: Liverpool University Press, 1999), p. 23.
8. Ian Aitken, 'The British Documentary Film Movement', in Robert Murphy (ed.), *The British Cinema Book* (London: BFI, 1997), p. 63.
9. Basil Wright, cited at <www.screenonline.org.uk/film/id/443890/>

15 / TECHNOLOGY AND THE GPO FILM UNIT

Leo Enticknap

The GPO Film Unit came into existence towards the conclusion of a defining cycle of innovation followed by standardisation in the technologies used by western film industries. The conversion to sound, a process that took place roughly between 1926 and 1932 in mainstream cinema in the USA and Europe, established both the form of the technologies in commercial production and widespread use, and the cultural conventions surrounding the use of synchronous audio alongside the moving image. Also during the late 1920s, panchromatic film replaced orthochromatic as the industry standard and a range of speed and grain combinations established themselves in various sectors of the market. The Hollywood studios developed a collaborative, standardised methodology for studio lighting designed for use in conjunction with panchromatic film.[1] While a range of colour technologies were marketed and successfully demonstrated as proof of the concept, all of them carried at least one significant shortcoming that precluded their use within the production context and business models of mainstream western cinema. Colour, therefore, was only used in niche and experimental applications (including by the GPO) at this point and did not develop into a mainstream imaging technology until the mid-1950s.

The GPO Film Unit arrived on the scene of a technological *fait accompli*, and one that did not suit its purpose. The dust was settling from the technical standardisation of the late 1920s and early 30s, a process that had been driven almost entirely by the requirements of commercial entertainment film production in the Hollywood studios. It was consequently exported to those countries that represented Hollywood's principal export markets, of which the UK was the largest. As Barry Salt points out, the technology used in British film production throughout the 1930s was 'mostly American', with a two- to three-year time lag.[2] As his extensive theoretical and ideological writing reveals, John Grierson and the followers of his 'movement' did not want to make films in studios based on fictional narratives, deploying total control over the aesthetic properties of the image through the use of lighting, set and costume design and audio rerecording in post-production. On the contrary, they sought to, as Grierson put it, 'photograph the living scene and the living story',[3] a task to which the formats and infrastructure enshrined by the Hollywood behemoth were as ill-suited as, Grierson frequently alleged, its ideology.

The EMB's and GPO Film Unit's camera of choice, used for the principal photography on almost all their live action productions, was the Newman-Sinclair 'Autokine'. Its designer, Arthur Newman (1861–1943) had been active in the manufacture of cameras, post-production and projection equipment since 1896. The Autokine had several major drawbacks as far as a studio environment was concerned, most notably the maximum film capacity of 200 feet (just over two minutes at twenty-four frames per second [fps]) and the fact that it was relatively noisy in operation, making synchronous recording difficult. At least five variants of the Autokine were produced between its launch in 1927 and it being superseded by the Model 'D' at some point during World War II. Its initial customer base was the newsreel sector, within which it had achieved widespread sales before being adopted as the camera of choice for the EMB, and subsequently the GPO Film Unit. A significant part of the reason for the Newman-Sinclair becoming the documentary movement's camera of choice may well be Robert Flaherty's enthusiasm for the machine. As Elizabeth Sussex put it, Flaherty's period in Britain 'cast a halo around' the then-nascent British documentary movement, and his work provided the inspiration for much of Grierson's and Paul Rotha's theoretical approach to the portrayal of realism.[4] Flaherty's three major British projects (*Industrial Britain*, 1931, *Man of Aran*, 1933 and *Elephant Boy*, 1936) all made extensive use of the Autokine, which was judged by the author of what many regard as the standard history of motion picture camera technology to have 'contributed to British documentary film-making' during more than two decades.[5]

Advertisement for the Newman-Sinclair Autokine. £275 in 1938 adjusted for inflation is equivalent to £13,752 in 2009. The basic model, without lenses or turret, cost £125 (£6,251)

While it would seem reasonable to conclude that the Autokine provided the GPO's film-makers with an unprecedented level of flexibility and creativity in locations and environments that would have prevented the use of bulky studio cameras such as the Bell and Howell 2709 or the Mitchell, the imaging technology of the 1930s – and in particular the lenses, artificial lighting and film stocks available – did impose significant limitations.

Besides the bulk, weight, support and power requirements of the camera, the essential restricting factors for cinematography in natural light were the characteristics of the film stock and lenses in use at the time. Hollywood studio practice in the 1920s and 30s evolved to exercise a high level of control over the depth of field in each shot, primarily by adjusting the lighting to enable the use of an aperture setting that achieved the desired depth of field. Therefore, because a studio setting enables the use of almost limitless artificial light, film manufacturers during the classical period did not prioritise the development of high-speed stocks suitable for newsreel and documentary use, because the market for them was relatively small.

In a documentary setting with little or no artificial light available, compromises often had to be made as to the depth of field. Furthermore, the longer the focal distance of the lens, the smaller the minimum aperture size available tended to be. The

advertisement above states that the 2in (approximately 50mm) lens supplied in the Autokine outfit has a minimum aperture of f1.9 (the lower the f-stop number, the wider the aperture). Exposing a typical film-stock available in the mid-1930s, this would enable a medium close-up taken from a distance of 2–3 metres in bright sunlight with the subject in focus, or in overcast light with the subject's face in focus but the rest of the image somewhat soft. Significant artificial light would be needed to expose the same subject indoors or under overcast daylight. The 9in (approximately 230mm) lens, however, has a minimum aperture of f5.5, meaning that the same shot could be taken from a far greater distance, but either with a much higher level of ambient light required or accepting a significantly lower depth of field.

A description of the shooting constraints imposed by the imaging technology of the time can be found in Pat Jackson's account of the interior shots of the mobile sorting office in *Night Mail* (1936): he refers to the limited (by space and power supply) artificial lighting that was able to be used and the need for more restrictive shot set-ups than would have been required in a studio setting, not to mention a significant degree of improvisation required in order to shoot the footage mute and record the audio 'wild' (i.e., not in synchronisation with the camera at the moment of photography) for post-synchronisation afterwards.[6] Here it is important to remember that Grierson himself constantly stressed his view of technology as a democratising influence, and as the documentary movement's use of the Autokine (and the fact that most of the GPO's cinematographers had no previous knowledge or experience of camerawork before joining the unit) shows, strove to achieve a position whereby, as Grierson put it, 'the silly mystery with which the professional cameramen once surrounded their very simple box of tricks is over and done with'.[7]

The use of 16mm as a distribution and exhibition medium by the GPO Film Unit followed the launch of the first Bell and Howell 'Filmosound' projector in 1932. This technology removed three barriers to non-theatrical (i.e., in venues other than purpose-built cinemas) exhibition: 16mm stock was acetate-based, thereby eliminating the need for the safety precautions associated with nitrate; the new generation of projectors were truly portable, being no larger or heavier than a typical suitcase; and their operators required only minimal training. Along with the projectors themselves, Bell and Howell also produced the laboratory equipment needed to make 16mm reduction prints of productions originated on 35mm, and the service was offered by all the major commercial laboratories in London by the mid-1930s.

The documentary movement wasn't the only body that became interested in 16mm in 1930s

Britain. The Workers' Film and Photo League, among other leftist groups, used it in order to operate under the radar of political censorship.[8] At the other end of the political spectrum, the Conservative Party produced an in-house monthly newsreel, *Conservative and Unionist Film Review*, which was distributed on 16mm to constituency associations. The British Film Institute (BFI), founded in 1933, promoted the use of films in education, with 16mm being the principal distribution vehicle; a contemporary commentator envisaged its role as, 'a kind of cinema BBC'.[9] The unifying thread in the pre-war uses of 16mm in Britain is that it enabled an audience to be reached that 35mm could not, either because political and economic factors prevented that audience from being found in the commercial cinema, or because the film-makers involved did not intend their productions to be consumed as a paid-for leisure activity. Grierson's prophecy, quoted *ad nauseam*, that 'the future of the cinema might not be in the cinema at all',[10] indicates the importance the documentary movement placed on establishing an alternative distribution and exhibition infrastructure, partly in response to this opposition from the industry. Their first sustained attempt at non-theatrical distribution took place under the auspices of the EMB Film Unit, a precedent that was embedded and enlarged after its transformation into the GPO Film Unit. Its Central Film Library claimed that its films had been seen by a total of 4½ million people by the outbreak of the World War II,[11] and that 1,700 schools were equipped with 16mm projectors, including 400 with sound.[12]

However, the significance in the GPO's use of 16mm exhibition as far as the Unit's and the technology's long-term cultural impact is concerned does not lie in quantifying the number of bums on seats that Grierson did or did not manage to attract. The significance is that he used it at all, and that in doing so the documentary movement played a pivotal role in the technology's transformation from an amateur to a professional medium. The GPO and subsequently Crown Film Unit sound recordist, Ken Cameron, opined in 1947 that 'the whole system [16mm] has the atmosphere of a toy. Nevertheless, it is not a toy. It is the only means many people have of seeing films at all, and its potentialities for educational work are vast.'[13] As with portable camera technology and shooting techniques adapted for use in naturally lit locations, the GPO Film Unit had taken a technology that the commercial sector had ignored and developed it into a sustained alternative to mainstream practice, one that would integrate itself into that mainstream over the subsequent decades.

The final significant aspect of the GPO's use of imaging technology is that of colour. During the period of the unit's existence, its film-makers used three photographic colour systems, two of them almost completely rejected by the mainstream film industry and the third used in a radically different way. The 'three-strip' Technicolor process, so-called because three separate rolls of black-and-white film, each recording the subtractive negative of one of the primary colours, were exposed in synchronisation through a beam-splitting prism, that dominated the era was used once by the GPO (in Len Lye's *Trade Tattoo*, 1937) but not in the way the system had been intended. Instead of capturing

Location shooting on a tube train in *The City* (Ralph Elton, 1938), using daylight from the windows and the carriage's tungsten lighting. The compact, lightweight Newman-Sinclair enabled this shot to be obtained in a crowded setting, but at a cost to depth of field: the wide aperture needed to make do with the available light resulted in only the two standing passengers in the centre of the frame being in sharp focus

The super-imposition of live action and animation to form the Technicolor matrices in *Trade Tattoo* (1935)

live-action footage using the beam-splitting camera, Lye used the black-and-white negatives of out-takes from other GPO productions as one colour record, and animated patterns painted onto raw celluloid as another. The combination gives the impression of toned black-and-white photography in one shade with superimposed animations of a different colour when the constituent elements were combined in what Lye's biographer described as 'one of the most intricate exercises in multiple printing ever attempted'.[14]

The usual explanation given for their sparing use of Technicolor is that the documentary movement simply could not afford to use industry standard technologies, and this is certainly a major part of the reason. The fact that they did use the mainstream technologies as soon as they had the opportunity – RCA sound equipment from 1939 and three-strip Technicolor for a number of 1940s productions, most notably the feature-length *Western Approaches* (Pat Jackson, 1944) – simultaneously validates the 'invention borne of necessity' approach to understanding their earlier work and begins to reveal a hitherto dismissed aspect of why so much of the GPO Film Unit's output is still considered a cultural landmark, almost three-quarters of a century after its production. By looking closely at the systems and processes they *did* use in the early and mid-1930s, and in particular how their technical characteristics were exploited in the resulting films, we can begin to shed light both on the broader cultural legacy of the GPO Film Unit and on the relationship between main-stream and niche audiovisual technologies.

Dufaycolor, used by Len Lye in his other 1935 production, *A Colour Box*, was additive and initially also a reversal stock. It involved the use of a geometric pattern of translu-cent particles dyed in the primary colours, known as the 'réseau' (network), applied to the base side of the film, and a conventional panchromatic emulsion on the other side. The film was exposed with the réseau side facing the lens, which filtered the light reach-ing the emulsion behind it according to the intensity of the primary colour being filtered. In projection the process was reversed, with the réseau side facing the projector's light source and the emulsion facing the lens.[15] As the photosensitive emulsion was a normal black-and-white one, Dufaycolor required no special developing process: in fact, it was probably the only colour film realistically capable of being processed in the home until the launch of the E6 process in 1976. It is hardly surprising, therefore, that, like Kodachrome, its principal customer base was amateur photographers (both still and moving image), or that Dufaycolor was the main competitor to Kodachrome in this market in Europe throughout most of the late 1930s and 40s.

The major drawbacks with Dufaycolor in professional use were the duplication issues inherent in reversal film and that the density of the réseau had the effect of reducing the film's speed by about half in shooting, and yielding a much dimmer image in projection. A negative–positive variant of the process was developed in 1937, and to launch it Dufay-Chromex commissioned none other than Humphrey Jennings to direct three 'interest' shorts, *Farewell, Topsails!* (1937), *English Harvest* and *The Farm* (both 1938). The system was used on a small but sustained scale for newsreel items, advertisements and short films of other descriptions, but only one fictional feature film was ever shot on Dufaycolor. *Sons of the Sea* (Maurice Elvey, 1939) consisted largely of exteriors in bright sunlight, thereby mitigating the speed limitation. The curators of Britain's regional film archives, most of whom are the custodians of extensive collections of amateur Dufaycolor footage, and students of experimental film-making might think twice before writing the system's legacy off as little more than a minor footnote in the history of moving-image technology. I am trying to argue that its appropriation by Lye and the GPO Film Unit was significant in that it illustrates the tendency of critics and historians to shape their value judgments in the mould of mainstream industry expectations, and consequently that it is problematic to arrive at subjective 'good-' or 'poor'-type verdicts based on those judgments.

In one respect it could be argued that the choice of colour reproduction system for *A Colour Box* is irrelevant, because none of the images in the film were originated photographically. That was Lye's whole point – that the association of photographic imaging with the illusion of continuous movement created by the process of recording and reproducing discrete images in rapid succession is a dominant but not an inevitable one. To demonstrate this, he drew and painted shapes and motifs directly onto raw (i.e., uncoated with a photosensitive emulsion) cellulose nitrate film base, and created effects of visual movement by exploiting the fact that, in perceived effect, the projector cuts the film up into four-perforation sections and shows them to the viewer individually; the frame line created by the camera's aperture and the projector's intermittent mechanism

A frame grab from *The H.P.O.* (Lotte Reiniger, 1938), a GPO animation distributed in Dufaycolor. If you look closely, the réseau pattern is visible against the sky and the reddish area behind the fox's front legs.

is not necessarily created by an artist painting directly onto the film's surface, thereby inviting the viewer to recognise the importance of the phenomenon that is widely, but in strict physiological terms incorrectly, referred to as persistence of vision.[16]

The final process used by Len Lye at the GPO, Gasparcolor, represents the same story. It 'worked' in the sense that it enabled reproduction of the entire visible colour spectrum. But, once again, we are dealing with a technology that had one or more crucial attributes (though in this case, only one) which prevented it from going mainstream and forced it into the arms of the avant-garde; and, once again, we are dealing with this having been written off in the history books as simply a flaw when compared with the mainstream standards. Like Dufaycolor, it was originally a European technology, the promoter of whom eventually sought investment and business development opportunities during the British production boom of the mid-1930s. While Dufaycolor had its essential origins in amateur/consumer photography, Gasparcolor arrived in Britain with an established pedigree in experimental film-making.

Invented by a German chemist of Hungarian origin, Bela Gaspar, it was, like Kodachrome, a subtractive, three-colour reversal film. The processing was a lot simpler and cheaper, however, because the emulsion was substantive: in other words, the photosensitive emulsions were converted into dyes in developing, and did not need to be introduced in a separate processing stage, as they did in Kodachrome.[17] Emulsion was coated on both sides of the film: cyan and yellow on one side, and magenta on the other.

Rainbow Dance (1936), made by Len Lye in Gasparcolor

This was essentially what ruled Gasparcolor out of mainstream production use. Coating the film on both sides meant that it could not be used in a conventional camera (because the opaque emulsion layer on one side would prevent light from reaching the one on the other), and therefore exposure of the Gasparcolor stock in a camera would have required a beam-splitting arrangement similar to that used by Technicolor. Gaspar never invented a camera, and therefore the stock had to be struck by printing successive exposures. The only way of reproducing live action was to print from separation negatives.[18] Another issue was that the Gasparcolor system did not enable the use of a silver-only optical soundtrack: the optical soundtrack was exposed on the cyan and yellow side, and the magenta dye in that area flashed away. The result was a lower-contrast track and, thus, a worse signal-to-noise ratio than black and white could offer (Dufaycolor also suffered from a similar problem due to the presence of the réseau in the soundtrack area); even after a certain amount of digital noise reduction, this is still clearly audible in the Gasparcolor titles published in the BFI's three-volume DVD set of the GPO Film Unit's output in 2008–9. But these were not significant barriers to using Gasparcolor for animation. Before relocating to Britain, Gaspar had worked closely with the artist and animator Oskar Fischinger in Berlin in the early 1930s. Some of his early work, in particular *Kreise* (*Circles*, 1932), had established Gasparcolor as the medium of choice in this market sector.[19] It is not surprising, therefore, that the leading European figures in this area eventually made use of the process: besides Lye, they included Lotte Reiniger, George Pal, Alexandre Alexieff and Claire Parker.

In respect of the GPO's use of colour, Simon Brown argues that 'Grierson was happy to promote colour, or rather use colour to promote the GPO, in abstract form, but his cordiality did not extend to the live action subject. In Grierson's world, colour was art, but not the art of the documentary.'[20] This position ignores the technological and economic barriers to live-action colour photography in a documentary context during the period of the GPO's existence. Even if the GPO's film-makers could have afforded to use the Technicolor camera, it was so bulky and the film it used was so slow that it would have been physically impossible to shoot any of the productions on which their reputation now rests using the system. It was impossible to mass-duplicate live-action footage originated on Dufaycolor until the launch of the negative–positive variant in 1937, whereupon Jennings promptly took it up. And for Gasparcolor there wasn't even a camera: the system did not enable live-action footage to be originated, full stop. Rather, the significance of all three of these processes having been used under the GPO's roof at one time or another is to illustrate both the maverick nature of Grierson's operation and the need to evaluate the legacy of short-lived and/or small-scale media technologies in terms of how they were used, not how they couldn't be. Len Lye, Lotte Reiniger and Norman McLaren were all important cultural figures in their own right, producing work that asks profound questions about the physics and culture of moving-image capture and reproduction. In the 1930s they turned to a range of niche technologies in order to express those experiments. Just because these technologies did not sit within the mainstream technical standards framework the GPO Film Unit found itself fighting against throughout the six years of its life does not warrant writing them off as irrelevances or minor footnotes.[21]

The final, major area of technology used by the GPO and which illustrates the danger of this tendency is sound. The EMB Film Unit came into existence in 1929, just as the conversion to sound was reaching a critical mass; therefore, once again the documentary movement was having to respond to an establishing industry standard and did not have the opportunity to pre-empt it. The EMB was not, however, equipped for sound recording and post-production itself and, as a result, the first documentary movement films with synchronised audio were effectively co-productions with Gaumont-British Instructional. The movement's leading lights stressed time and time and again in their writing that they were not interested in using sound as a mere extension of the classical continuity system, or 'sound film glued to stage example', as Grierson put it.[22] As with colour and inspired heavily by Soviet cinema, Grierson and his close associates emphasised the desire to record and mix audio in order to communicate with the viewer independently and authentically ('we must make our sound help the mute, not reproduce it'[23]), expressing enthusiasm at the creative possibilities that optical sound-on-film appeared to offer.

The optical sound cameras and mixing equipment eventually purchased by the GPO in 1934 has been almost universally dismissed as an inferior cousin of its industry standard counterparts. According to Rachael Low, the Visatone-Marconi system has its origins in a forerunner of the SONAR ultrasound detection systems used in submarines, developed by the Royal Navy during the last years of World War I.[24] It was one of a number of systems developed to compete with the 'big two' imported from Hollywood and a third German system: the Radio Corporation of America's (RCA) 'Photophone' variable area system, the sound-on-disc and subsequently variable-density optical systems marketed by Western Electric under its subsidiary Electrical Research Products, Inc. (ERPI) and the German Tri-Ergon system. Surviving recollections from the documentary movement's principal activists agree almost universally that the GPO Film Unit chose Visatone-Marconi because it was cheap and because it could be purchased outright, without the need to pay ongoing licensing fees. Apart from the GPO, the 'quota quickie' impresarios Joe Rock and Julius Hagen appear to have been the system's only other major customers.

It is difficult to make much of an objective evaluation of the system, because to my knowledge no Visatone-Marconi equipment survives in any major museum collection and information about it in the technical and trade press is largely confined to advertisements, with little in the way of detailed technical specifications. The surviving Visatone-Marconi negatives and original release prints held by the BFI have a unilateral, unshuttered variable area soundtrack: the absence of shuttered ground-noise reduction (Watt calls it an 'open track'[25]), combined with the absence of orthochromatic stocks intended specifically for optical sound mastering until the late 1930s would certainly account for the poor signal-to-noise ratio remembered by Watt, and would support the contention that light-valve technology based on first-generation RCA Photophone (i.e., pirated) may well have been involved. Watt further recalls that the GPO's equipment enabled the mixing of up to two channels in post-production (many commercial features released by British studios at the time mix down five or six in more complex scenes involving multiple dialogue channels, music and effects).[26]

The reportedly inferior signal-to-noise characteristics and the practical limitations imposed on mixing in post-production by the Visatone-Marconi system have, as with the GPO's use of 35mm film and non-mainstream colour processes, gone down in the history books as being an obstacle the GPO's film-makers had to overcome rather than a technological framework that helped to shape their cultural approach. Arguably the two most widely celebrated GPO films for their creative use of audio, *Coal Face* and *Night Mail*, both worked within the limitations of Visatone-Marconi, and are remembered today precisely because their directors and music composer did not attempt to emulate the recording and mixing styles that had evolved and been enshrined in mainstream professional practice. As Ken Cameron rightly concludes, 'considering the limited technical resources of the old GPO Film Unit in the earlier days of sound, he [Alberto Cavalcanti] did some remarkable things'.[27]

In his book *100 British Documentaries*, Patrick Russell asks: 'How strongly does the technology involved in making documentaries affect their meanings? Films made with new tools often make interesting test cases.'[28] I would argue that the same observation applies to films made using unusual or unorthodox tools, and that the GPO Film Unit's working methods and output can all, to varying degrees, be considered test cases. The GPO's film-makers were both unable and unwilling to conform to the infrastructure of technical standards and conventions into which their workplace was born. It is for precisely this reason, among many others, that their legacy has achieved far more cultural significance and inspired far more film-makers that followed them than that of any other small-scale production company making sponsored films, certainly in Britain and arguably in the western world. It is to be hoped that the resurgence of interest in, scholarship related to and availability of the GPO Film Unit's output will help to enable greater understanding and appreciation of minority and alternative audiovisual technologies and their broader place in our cultural history.

Notes

1. David Bordwell, Janet Staiger and Kristin Thompson, *The Classical Hollywood Cinema: Film Style and Mode of Production to 1960*, London, Routledge (1985), pp. 294–7.
2. Barry Salt, *Film Style and Technology: History and Analysis*, 2nd edn (London: Starword, 1992), pp. 205, 213.
3. John Grierson, 'First Principles of Documentary', in H. Forsyth Hardy (ed.), *Grierson on Documentary* (London: Faber & Faber, 1946), p. 80.
4. Elizabeth Sussex, *The Rise and Fall of British Documentary* (Berkeley, CA: University of California Press, 1976), p. 23.
5. H. Mario Raimondo Souto, *Motion Picture Photography: A History, 1891–1960* (Jefferson, NC: McFarland, 2006), pp. 156–8.
6. Pat Jackson, *A Retake Please!* Night Mail *to* Western Approaches (Liverpool: Liverpool University Press, 1999), p. 27.
7. Originally published in *Cinema Quarterly*, Summer 1934; quoted in Sussex, *The Rise and Fall of British Documentary*, p. 44.
8. Bert Hogenkamp, *Deadly Parallels: Film and the Left in Britain, 1929–39* (London: Lawrence and Wishart, 1986), pp. 105–35.
9. Walter Ashley, *The Cinema and The Public* (London: Ivor Nicholson and Watson, 1934), pp. 13–16; Ivan Butler, *To Encourage the Art of the Film: The Story of the British Film Institute* (London: Robert Hale, 1971), pp. 83–96.
10. John Grierson, 'Summary and Survey: 1935', in Hardy, *Grierson on Documentary*, p. 119.

11. The Arts Council, *The Factual Film* (London: Political and Economic Planning, 1947), p. 15.

12. Ibid., p. 22.

13. Ken Cameron, *Sound and the Documentary Film* (London: Issac Pitman, 1947), p. 104.

14. Roger Horrocks, *Len Lye: A Biography* (Auckland: Auckland University Press, 2002), p. 151. For an account of Lye's work at the GPO, see also *Sight & Sound* vol. 18 no. 29 (1939), pp. 65–70.

15. For the full technical details of Dufaycolor, see Adrian Cornwell-Clyne, *Colour Cinematography* (London: Chapman and Hall, 1951), pp. 283–316.

16. For an explanation of the misuse of the term 'persistence of vision', see Leo Enticknap, *Moving Image Technology: From Zeotrope to Digital* (London: Wallflower, 2005), pp. 6–7. I proposed the phrase 'illusion of continuous movement' to replace it, but it doesn't seem to have gained many takers!

17. For a full technical account of the Gasparcolor process, see Cornwell-Clyne, *Colour Cinematography*, pp. 419–27.

18. Brian Coe, *The History of Movie Photography* (London: Ash and Grant, 1981), pp. 133, 136.

19. William Moritz, 'Gasparcolor: Perfect Hues for Animation', lecture at the Musée du Louvre, Paris, 6 October 1995; transcribed and translated at <www.oskarfischinger.org/GasparColor.htm> (accessed 27 May 2010).

20. Simon Brown, 'Dufaycolor: The Spectacle of Reality and British National Cinema', undated essay <www.bftv.ac.uk/projects/dufaycolor.htm> (accessed 27 May 2010).

21. Duncan Petrie, *The British Cinematographer* (London: BFI, 1996); Brian Winston, *Technologies of Seeing: Photography, Cinematography and Television* (London: BFI, 1995).

22. John Grierson, 'Creative Use of Sound', in Hardy, *Grierson on Documentary*, p. 96.

23. Ibid., p. 92.

24. Rachael Low, *The History of the British Film, vol. 7: Film Making in 1930s Britain*, 2nd edn (London: Routledge, 1997), originally published 1985, p. 78.

25. Quoted in Sussex, *The Rise and Fall of British Documentary*, p. 46.

26. Ibid., p. 48.

27. Cameron, *Sound and the Documentary Film*, p. 10.

28. Patrick Russell, *100 British Documentaries* (London: BFI, 2007), p. 227.

16 / MODERN ART AND DESIGN IN 1930S BRITAIN

Contexts and Legacies of the Documentary Film

Paul Rennie

In 1979 the Arts Council of England and the Hayward Gallery, London, organised a wide-ranging exhibition of British art and design from the 1930s. The exhibition was entitled The Thirties, and was remarkable for a number of reasons. The objects displayed spoke of a period of accelerated modernisation across every sphere of British society. Art and engineering were strikingly presented alongside each other as simultaneous expression of modernity.

The modernisation of the GPO was an important part of this process as mechanisation and the introduction of airmail services, as well as the massive extension of telephone and telegraphy, forged a new infrastructure designed to prepare the nation for a new global age. Notwithstanding these technological innovations, the systems of the Post Office were not yet automated. The precision of the Post Office system required strict discipline on the part of its people.[1]

Eventually, the Post Office began to communicate this modernisation through a variety of means. The GPO Film Unit was obviously part of this exercise, but so too were the

The GPO's publicity was part of a wider culture aggressively promoting aesthetic and technological innovation

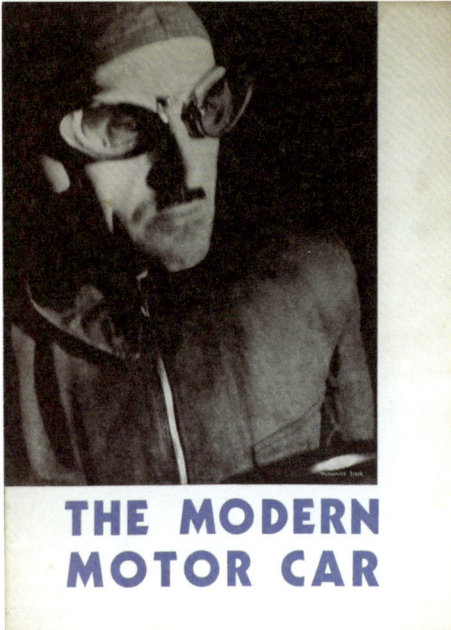

THE MODERN MOTOR CAR

poster communications of the Post Office along with the visible extremities of its great machinery. In design terms, the organisation made a number of important contributions. These ranged beyond the work of the GPO Film Unit and included Gilbert Scott's K6 telephone kiosk, posters and pamphlets, and very substantial advances in telephone and communication engineering. The post-World War II development of radar and computers was based, for example, on work carried out at the GPO's Dollis Hill Research Station.

The GPO Film Unit existed within a dynamic experience of modernity defined by the visual technologies of photography and cinema, the three-dimensional volumes of modernist space and the obvious acceleration associated with the mechanisation of modern life during the 1930s. The visual expression of these characteristics connects the GPO project to various experiments in fine art and design. These contexts allow us to position the GPO Film Unit within a tradition of visual culture in Britain that was experimental, expansive and emancipatory. The new visual economy was distinguished through its decisive and irreversible impact on ways of seeing that in turn reflected and nurtured a new psychological reality.[2] What follows is an attempt to briefly describe the various contexts that supported these efforts and promoted this new vision of the world. Accordingly, this chapter is focused on the ocular alignments across art, design, photography and film-making in 1930s Britain.

Modernity, society and the GPO

The development of the modern Post Office, suggested by Rowland Hill in 1837, roughly coincided with the Representation of the People Act (1832).[3] The Reform Act, as it became known, extended the franchise demographically and geographically and impacted heavily on the administrative and practical organisation of Britain's industrial economy.[4] The development of the modern Post Office also became an important part of civic assimilation. The system of postal collection, mail sorting, letter delivery and accounting constituted a series of verifiable processes managed through systems of observational control and were thus accountable to both the public and to the national administrative apparatus. Patrick Joyce has argued that the new democratic and panoptic sociology of industrial society, of which the Post Office was a part, began to define and express itself through new forms of civic architecture and organisation.[5] The conjunction of maps and numbers, within the context of rapid urban expansion, created a matrix of socialisation configured so as to promote economic discipline and civic responsibility.[6]

The aftermath of World War I prompted a massive reconfiguration of the social and political norms of industrial society as well as aggressive technological and administrative expansion. Integrating motorised transport into the postal service, for example, was largely prompted by the demands of military logistics during the Great War. As well as increasing capacity, mass transport and the development of telecommunications made it possible to coordinate men, machines and post within the GPO's enormous system.

Design, efficiency and visual culture

Modernity was expressed, in its early twentieth-century form, through a cybernetic integration of mechanical apparatus with the human form. Man and machine became integrated, beyond the factory floor and through a variety of powerful engines, into something bigger, more dynamic and with much greater physical potential. In these circumstances, the bicycle, car, aeroplane and tank were all manifestations of this ever-closer integration. It is not surprising that, after the bitter experiences of World War I, these cybernetic extensions were thought of ambivalently. Jacob Epstein famously gave this integration physical form in his 1913–14 sculpture *Rock Drill*.[7]

In Britain, however, there existed a group of people who believed that they could both harness the socially beneficial aspects of this transformation and manage its worst excesses. Indeed, post-war developments in administration, the economy and wider society created new opportunities for visual communication and a number of remarkable patrons emerged at this time who were interested in engaging and shaping the new common culture of mass democracy. Frank Pick at London Transport, Jack Beddington at Shell and Sir Stephen Tallents at the GPO were the leading proponents of this new design culture.[8]

At the GPO, Tallents utilised ideas, artists and architects that he had first employed at the Empire Marketing Board. The EMB was an organisation tasked with promoting trading links across the British Empire. The work of the GPO was about plugging the individual into a national and international network of communications. Both tasks impressed upon Tallents the need to use new methods of visual communication to promote the sensible use of new technologies.[9] Tallents worked with Pick, Beddington and the museum curator Kenneth Clarke to build up a cadre of native modernist talent.

Tallents' patronage of John Grierson was to prove crucial. Grierson had worked as a researcher in the new field of popular opinion in the USA and returned to Britain eager to apply the lessons he had learned. His enthusiasm for cinema, especially documentary cinema, was rooted in the belief that the camera was a technology able to enthral, encourage and emancipate. Under Tallents' direction, Grierson set about filming the complex workings of what was

Under Tallents' direction the GPO put modernist art to social, imaginative and bureaucratic ends, © Royal Mail Group Ltd 2011. Courtesy of The British Postal Museum & Archive

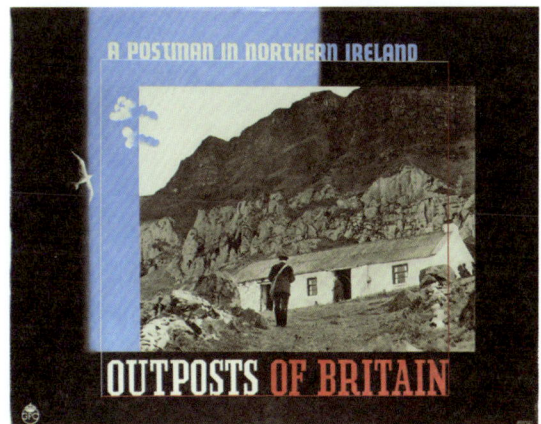

A POSTMAN IN NORTHERN IRELAND

OUTPOSTS OF BRITAIN

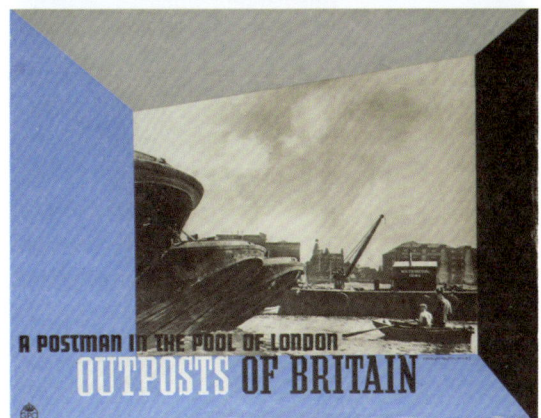

A POSTMAN IN THE POOL OF LONDON
OUTPOSTS OF BRITAIN

POSTING BOX AT LANDS END

OUTPOSTS OF BRITAIN

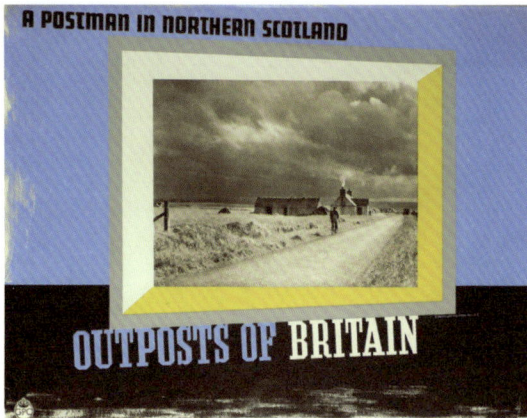

A POSTMAN IN NORTHERN SCOTLAND

OUTPOSTS OF BRITAIN

then both Britain's biggest employer, and the conduit by which the public were put in touch with the latest technologies.

Another important source of inspiration for the GPO Film Unit was the writing of the Soviet film-maker Dziga Vertov. Artists had interpreted the widespread mechanisation of society in a number of ways. The visual experience of cinema, especially the changing point-of-view and tracking shot, inspired the layered perspectives of cubism. Fragmentation and speed were expressed through a more complex visual plane. Implicit in each of these developments was a belief that the *intelligent eye*, directed by mechanical devices, could see further, more clearly and more truthfully than the unassisted 'naked' human eye.[10] Vertov expanded these ideas. According to Vertov, the political potential of this cybernetic integration of ocular engineering and new vision was expressed through an increasingly close identification with the technology of image-making. The association of film fragments, through abrupt editing and to the rhythms of the machine, created a new kind of film reality based on the complex geometries of this fragmentation.[11] Such thinking inspired the GPO Film Unit's attempt to extol a new form of citizenship.

The artistic legacy of the GPO Film Unit

The film experiments of the documentary movement had a much wider cultural impact than is generally assumed. This was because the Film Unit was connected, by virtue of its personalities and its themes, into a powerful cultural stream in part expressed through the proliferation of film clubs during the 1920s and 30s. These cine clubs, in turn, bridged a number of cultural spheres including modern art, surrealism and, as the decade progressed, a more urgent interest in the politics of mass participation.[12]

The GPO Film Unit also became a place where international ideas could arrive in Britain. Both Alberto Cavalcanti and Humphrey Jennings, for example, were a conduit between the GPO Film Unit and international avant-garde movements. Jennings, of course, was also one of the founders of Mass Observation, a movement that attempted to both straightforwardly record the views of the wider population and delve into what Carl Jung called the collective unconscious.

Such a catholic array of influences enabled the GPO Film Unit to become a far-sighted patron of filmic experimentation. Two remarkable efforts especially need to be mentioned. The first is a sequence by László Moholy-Nagy included in Stuart Legg's film *The Coming of the Dial* (1933).

László Moholy-Nagy had arrived in Britain from the Bauhaus, where he had played a crucial role in reconceptualising the art school as a place of technical training and industrial integration.[13] His sequence is born of a modernist understanding that light, whether artificial or sunlight, had powerful semiotic potential. Used in Legg's film about the laboratories that power the development of telecommunications, Moholy-Nagy's abstract sequence becomes pregnant with a series of meanings associated with progress, technology and democracy.[14]

The second particularly noteworthy film was Len Lye's *A Colour Box* (1935). Lye was an artist from New Zealand who moved to London in 1926. There he joined the Seven and Five Society (a circle of modernist artists) and exhibited in the 1936 International Surrealist Exhibition. He also began to make experimental films. *A Colour Box* may have been an advertisement for 'Cheaper Parcel Post' but it was the result of Lye's eccentric decision to paint vibrant abstract patterns directly on the celluloid itself and synchronise them to a popular dance tune.[15]

The work of Moholy-Nagy and Lye illustrates the richness of documentary film culture in Britain and influenced the role of documentary in the post-war period. For example, Jack Beddington created a documentary film unit at Shell. When Beddington

László Moholy-Nagy brought a Bauhaus influence to the GPO Film Unit

was placed in charge of film propaganda at the Ministry of Information, it was relatively easy for him to bring together the various personalities from both the GPO and Shell branches of the documentary scene. The work of the Ministry of Information is, nowadays, recognised as one of the most significant cultural manifestations of World War II.[16] The integrated communications environment of the Ministry became, after the war, the Central Office of Information (COI). The COI continued to make public information films until the 1970s. Peter Greenaway began his film career as an editor at the COI. Greenaway's early films, sponsored by the BFI, were structuralist projects that attempted to exploit the documentary form (and its associated way of seeing – Kino-eye) in other film genres.

The cultural and technical legacies of the GPO Film Unit also made substantial contributions to the development of television in Britain and at the BBC in particular. The BBC began, after World War II, to consider the development of television and to look for creative people to work with the new technology and within the new systems of televisual mass media. Peculiarly, they found that surrealist artists had just the right skills of technical DIY and in the visual potential of kinetic structures. The beginnings of children's television at the BBC for example, gave opportunity to a number of artists and surrealists. Later, Len Lye's specific legacy, of combining image and sound through a new kind of synchronisation, became evident in the 1980s with the development of the pop music video.

Thus, the cultural significance of the GPO Film Unit extends beyond documentary cinema. The Unit was part of the technical and cultural modernisation in Britain that later helped to express the groundswell of social democracy, post-war reconstruction, kitchen sinks and swinging London. The visual expression of these phenomena helped create the circumstances in which ordinary people began to see the world differently and to position themselves differently within it. The social progress Britain has made in the late twentieth century should be understood as a visual phenomenon that drew on art and design, and built upon visual technologies, to create a new world of possibilities. The GPO Film Unit played a key role in establishing the template for these quiet rebellions.

Notes

1. Issues of normalisation are usually presented as associated with social discipline. The work of Michel Foucault has been crucial in understanding the historical formation of the social body and the role of the systems and structures of power that assist this process. Antonio Gramsci, writing in his *Prison Notebooks*, conjectured that the experience of military discipline during World War I would transform the political potential of the working class.
2. The cognitive potential of visual intelligence was not widely understood before World War II. Walter Benjamin was the first writer to examine the political and sociological implications of the multiplication of images made possible by mechanical reproduction. The increasingly visual technologies of mechanised warfare (and the home front) transformed the general awareness of image culture. John Berger described these technologically enabled fields of perception and James Flynn (in *What is Intelligence? Beyond the Flynn Effect* [Cambridge: Cambridge University Press, 2007]) has substantiated these ideas through observation and measurement.
3. The process of democratic extension has always been a source of anxiety for the political and economic elites. During the 1840s, early Victorian Britain assimilated the extended franchise by imposing a series of standardisations across cultural, social and economic environments.
4. The link between observation and scientific methodology is well established. Scientific revolution and philosophical enlightenment devolve from the methodologies of observation, measurement and classification. It is rather surprising, in these circumstances, that the significance of observation in art and design is generally underestimated.
5. See P. Joyce, *The Rule of Freedom* (London: Verso, 2003).
6. The term 'panoptic' derives from the correctional structure of the panopticon theorised by Jeremy Bentham. Bentham was a Utilitarian philosopher concerned with developing the systems and structures of modern society. The panoptic society, nowadays evident in CCTV, is a secular version of the age-old myths attached to all-seeing deities. In terms of civic planning, the modernisation of Paris conceptualised by Haussmann during the 1860s is probably the most widely recognised example of reconfigured civil space. Interestingly, the new visual technology of photography was appropriated by the administration, at precisely this time, so as to provide evidential support for the new regimen of social order. J. Tagg (*The Burden of Representation* [London: Palgrave Macmillan, 1988]) describes the use of photography in relation to the growth of the state and as evidence in law.
7. The cybernetic integration of man and machine was exemplified by the creation of the robot by the science-fiction writer Karel Capek in 1921. Notwithstanding the labour-saving potential

and artificial intelligence of the machine, the robot is generally understood as a dystopian manifestation of industrialisation.

8. The patrons of design in the 1930s were each members of the Design and Industries Association. The Design and Industries Association (DIA) was formed in 1915 by a group of industrialists, business people and designers committed to the promotion and application of design to industrial manufacturing. This project sought to apply the benefits of good design to the largest number of people through the embrace of the scaling effects of industrial organisation. The DIA made the conceptual triangulation of education, design and social progress a practical reality.

9. The provision of a consistent level of service across very large organisations provided the immediate context of communication for both Frank Pick at London Transport and Stephen Tallents at the GPO. The general efficiency of each organisation was greatly improved through the education of the public in relation to spikes in demand. Accordingly, there were campaigns about travelling during the day and posting earlier.

10. Berger's seminal *Ways of Seeing* (London: Penguin, 1972) was presented associated with the cultural formation of ocular intelligence. The pictorial developments of fine art in the early twentieth century were, accordingly, understood as contributing to the development of the intelligent eye. For the first time, it became apparent that the world could be viewed from different perspectives and that critical tools could reveal the ideological geometry of these views.

11. It is impossible to understand the development of cubism and of abstraction generally without acknowledging the technological basis of these new representations of space. The various machineries of transport combined with the visual apparatus of the cinema to create powerful new illusions of speed and movement.

12. Both Benjamin and Gramsci theorised about the possible political potential of mass media in relation to the popular-front politics of the 1930s. In Britain, the conditions for the wide use of visual propaganda only came about as a consequence of World War II.

13. The Bauhaus pioneered a form of art and design education that positioned these practices within the context of an industrial specialisation of labour.

14. The rhetoric of modernism is usually about materials, functionality and economy and expresses itself through *fitness for purpose*. There is an equally important set of visual signifiers attached to the idea of light and transparency in modernism. The modernist International Style that developed in the 1930s was based on new building methods made possible by the engineering of steel-frame structures. These allowed the large spans and wide apertures of contemporary architecture to develop. These characteristics were promoted, variously and depending on context, as physically healthy and democratically sound. A number of buildings exemplify these themes, notably the Finsbury Health Centre, 1938, by Tecton Architects. The film *Housing Problems* (1935) provides a summary of these issues.

15. The combination of image and popular music provided for a powerful adjunct to the advertising, television and music industries of the late twentieth century. The 1980s witnessed the creation of a new form of promotional video for popular music. This was made possible by the development of new technology and by the creation of a more liberalised broadcast environment.

16. Calder's *The Myth of the Blitz* (London: Jonathan Cape, 1991) described the process by which the popular experience of World War II was transformed into a coherent story of national stoicism, comic light-heartedness and productive enterprise. The cultural mythologies of World War II persist within the stereotypes of national character.

PART FIVE

The GPO Film Unit and

Telecommunications Culture

THE GPO FILM UNIT AND TELECOMMUNICATIONS CULTURE

David Hay

Although the decade which preceded World War II was in many ways a golden period in the fortunes of the Post Office, before the arrival of Sir Stephen Tallents in 1933 the GPO's reputation was at a low ebb. Tallents' influence on the Post Office, on how the public perceived it in addressing them and how it saw itself, was profound.

Tallents, of course, had a particular regard for the value of films in his publicity strategy. He ensured that the Film Unit of the Empire Marketing Board joined him at the Post Office in 1933. However, the look and ethos of the films need to be understood against a wider programme of GPO publicity. His whole approach to publicity is detailed in the thoughtful Green Paper on the subject of 1935, one of a series of information papers issued primarily for Post Office staff.

The Green Paper argued that there were three purposes for Post Office publicity: the selling of its services (though he limited this to services with clear social and economic utility); informing customers about the Post Office and ensuring that its services were correctly used; and the creation of goodwill. In today's marketing language, this last area would be regarded as 'brand management', the requirement to project a positive image of the Post Office to its customers. To this end he considered that a strategy should also be concerned with internal publicity, to inform Post Office employees about the whole range of its activities so that they could understand their own contribution better, take greater pride in the organisation and act as ambassadors for the Post Office to their wider communities. The Green Papers themselves were part of this strategy.

There is no doubt that Tallents was a pioneer in what today are standard marketing and public relations techniques. What made him yet more distinctive in his day was his passionate belief that it was the duty of modern government to employ the arts for the interpretation of its actions and policies, and in particular the 'new' arts of broadcasting and cinema. He also made sure as far as possible that the artistic production of GPO 'publicity' (which included everything from the design of notepaper to exhibition stands to educational material for schools) was conducted in a spirit of creative experimentation.

The result was that by the end of the inter-war era many of the GPO's products and services – such as the Jubilee red telephone kiosk designed by Giles Gilbert Scott, the Speaking Clock and the 999 Emergency Service – had become iconic parts of the nation's cultural fabric.

Selling communications

Between 1925 and 1928 the Post Office had invested almost £1 million a month in the telephone network as it began the roll-out of automatic telephone exchanges which would enable subscribers to make local calls directly without involving a telephone operator. The result of this new technology, together with the introduction of new mass-produced telephone instruments using early plastics, was that the cost of having a telephone gradually began to fall. The Post Office also introduced new services during this period, such as the first transatlantic radio telephone service in 1926, direct telephone communications with countries in Europe and the expansion of the public telephone kiosk network. Much of this investment went unnoticed by the public. Indeed, despite the enormous investment in new technology, there was widespread concern by 1931 that Britain was lagging behind other countries in Europe in the take-up of the telephone. Up to 25 per cent of the capacity of the telephone network was lying idle.

The GPO Film Unit's work was part of a wider publicity effort to address this problem. The sales advertising of its products and services, which today would be considered the main purpose of a publicity campaign, was ironically the most contentious aspect of Tallents' new policy in the eyes of many in the Post Office's senior management. Despite criticism from the press, politicians and even from workers' associations and unions, until the change of policy inaugurated by Clement Attlee (who briefly served as Post Master General in 1931) and Tallents, the official position was that as a public service the Post Office should not market the telephone and other services commercially.

One way of understanding the work of the GPO Film Unit is as part of a broader effort to create a new advertising idiom that balanced the need for sales against the need for a government service to act responsibly. The visual material held in the BT Heritage Archive reveals the aesthetic quality of the work directed by Tallents. Its material success was such that by the end of 1939 the number of telephones in the UK had risen by over 50 per cent to over 3.25 million. Only New York and Chicago now had more telephones than London.

(left) The first Post Office press advertisement, January 1932. Only shortly after Tallents joined the Telephone Publicity Committee, it is very staid and Civil Service in style

(right) A press advertisement from 1934, showing a greater degree of imagination, in design, including a couple in passionate embrace!

Trade press advertisements from 1937 and 1938, the former a design by Norman Howard. They show a high degree of artistic design, including the use of photographic imagery to striking effect

Two leaflets from 1930 and 1939 advertising the picture telegraph service, an early form of facsimile transmission. The former is an example of what Tallents called ' a solemn injunction in the shape of a dismal looking notice', and contrasts with the highly visual style by the end of the decade

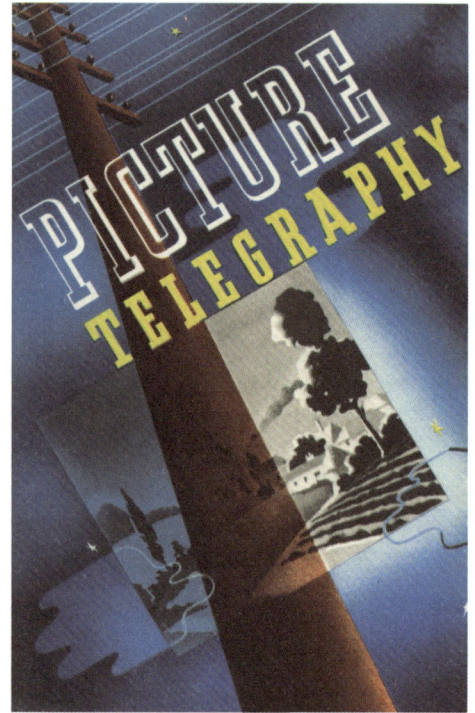

(left) Leaflet from 1934 advertising the Telephone 162, the first with a handset combining the transmitter and receiver. A dramatic view, it also includes an early version of the famous MacDonald Gill GPO monogram

(right) Publicity poster designed by Austin Cooper, 1935. An example of the artistic design favoured by Tallents

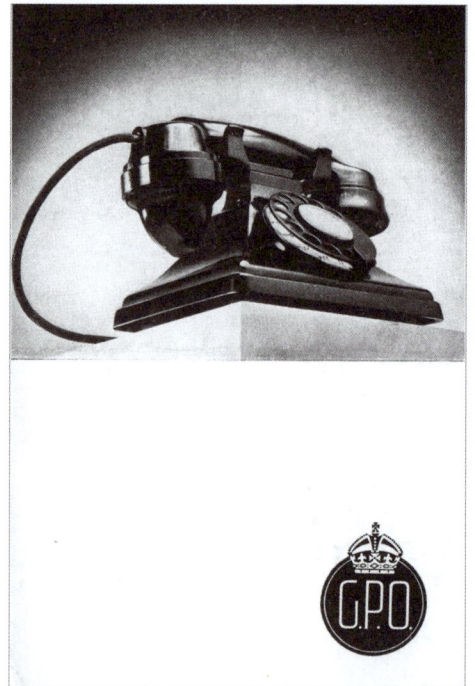

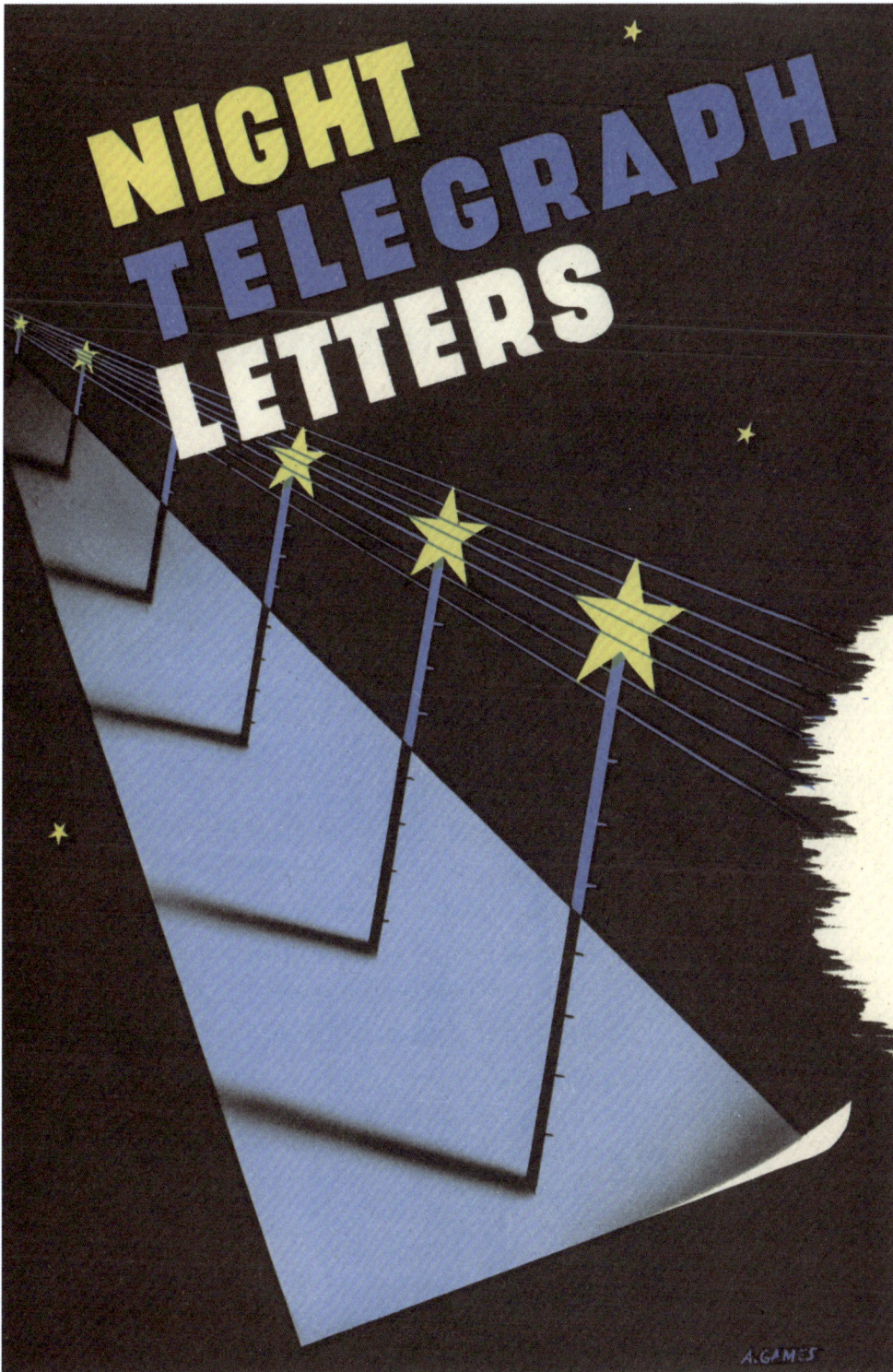

Leaflet from 1939 advertising night telegraph letters, an overnight service at cheaper rates. Tallents cited this service as one that was unknown to Publicity Committee members until it was advertised. Designed by Abraham Games

Publicity poster designed by Pat Keely, 1931. This was the first poster design commissioned by the Post Office

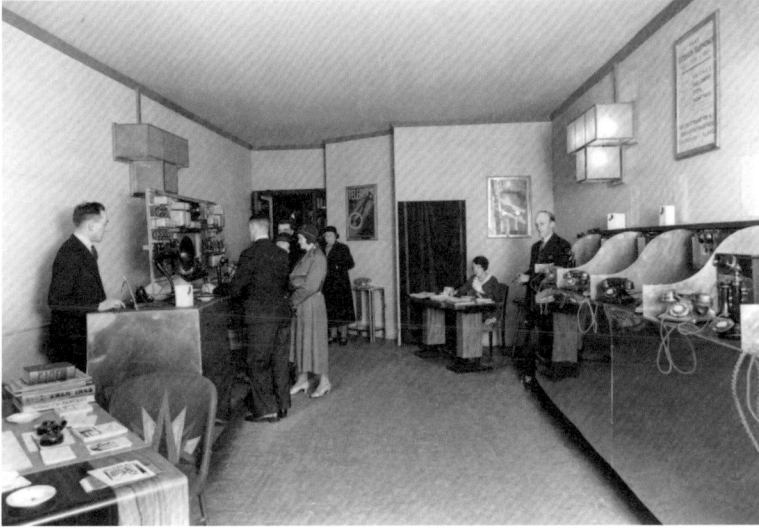

Post Office telephone publicity display, Brighton, 1933. Displays such as these soon included screenings of the films of the GPO Film Unit

Post Office sales office, 167 Euston Road, London, 1934. The Post Office until the 1930s had traditionally relied on a sales force of several hundred 'canvassers'. They signed up new subscribers in person and, until the change in publicity policy, were regarded as the best way of growing customer numbers

Informing customers

Although the Post Office did not originally approve of marketing the telephone and other services, it did recognise that as a public service it had a responsibility to actively inform its customers about its services. However, it did this rather passively with very dull and uninspiring notices or literature that could be picked up in sales offices or at local post offices.

Tallents emphasised the educational value of this activity, developing a more assertive 'public service' ethos of publicity. Engaging cinematic evidence of this strategy can be seen in films such as *N or NW* (1937).

Press advertisements from 1934 promoting new technology in use in the telephone network and Post Office investment in research. Communicating technical information was a challenge, but the Post Office solution was imaginative and in language a largely lay audience could understand. The same approach was used in GPO films, such as *The Coming of the Dial* (1933) in which the Galloping Gus telephone testing apparatus also features

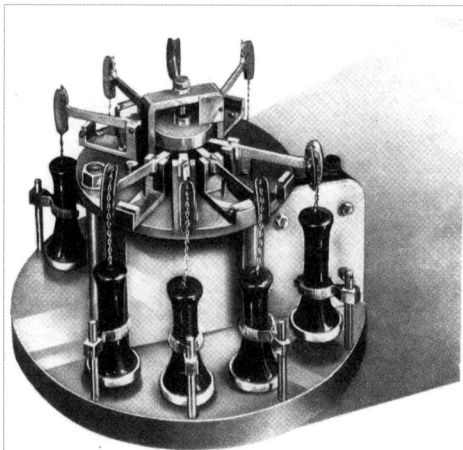

GALLOPING GUS

is the amusing nickname of one of the testing machines used by the Post Office Telephone Research Department. As the telephone earpieces are moved round and round they are automatically lifted and suddenly dropped — to test the durability of the magnets inside. The colossal task of handling over sixteen hundred million calls a year cannot be left to chance—there is the same exhaustive testing of every component detail throughout the Telephone Service.

TELEPHONE

An advertisement of the Post Office Telephone Service

YOUR ROBOT

Your robot is a friend you may never understand but whose pleasant duty it is to understand you. He responds to your signals, selects the best available route for your message, and then summons the number you want, without human aid or intervention. You can see him at work, and marvel. You can see thousands of similar robots working hard for other telephone subscribers, and marvel again. But when you are told that in one automatic telephone exchange unit there are 10,000,000 soldered joints you cease to marvel — your capacity for wonder is exhausted. You can therefore be content merely to accept your robot as your faithful, obedient and intelligent servant.

TELEPHONE

An advertisement of the Post Office Telephone Service

Engineers hauling cable near Sandringham, Norfolk, 1936. Use of photography featured a great deal in Post Office publicity, and there were in-house photographers as well as the Film Unit that produced images specifically for publicity use, in displays or literature. This view anticipates *A Midsummer Day's Work* of 1939 in portraying the work of a Post Office cable gang

Underground Cable, 1935. Original artwork by John Farleigh of the design that was produced as a GPO poster (PRD 121). A striking portrayal of the work of engineers working with underground cables, a subject covered by films such as *Under the City* (1934)

(left) Information booklet on the Post Office transatlantic radio telephone service, a design by Norman Howard, 1937. The technology was described in *Conquering Space* (1934) as 'the last conquest of space and time'

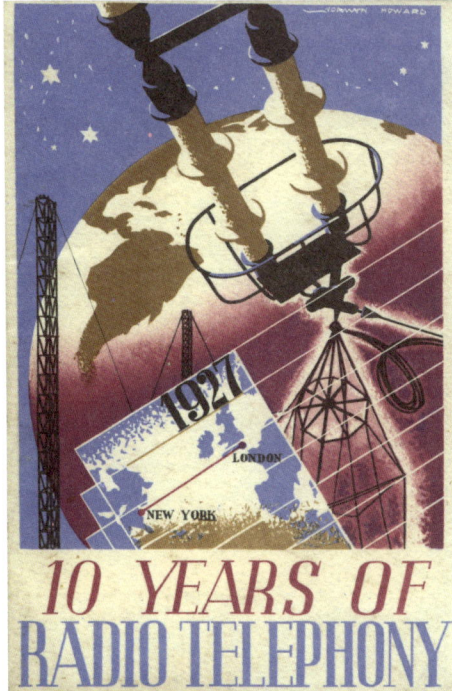

10 YEARS OF RADIO TELEPHONY

(right) Information leaflet on extension telephones, 1935. An example of the type of leaflet that Tallents believed should be 'simply written in good English and well laid out with good designs and good type'

EXTENSION TELEPHONES

THE POST OFFICE IS HAPPY TO ANNOUNCE a reduction in the charges for extension telephones installed in the same premises as the main telephone. From January 1st, 1936, the additional charge for the simplest form of internal extension has been reduced to 3s. 6d. a quarter—less than a halfpenny a day—in private residences, and to 4s. 0d. a quarter in business premises. The charges for other forms of internal extension have also been reduced.

IN THE HOME

WITH ONE TELEPHONE IN THE HOME, THE natural tendency is to place it in the position of most general usefulness at some sacrifice of privacy and comfort.

An extension telephone in the sitting-room, study or bedroom gives you greater comfort and privacy ; in the bedroom also it is at hand in emergency or sickness.

IN BUSINESS

AN EXTENSION TELEPHONE PLACED within easy reach of every member of your staff will save their time and save you money. The ease with which callers can be put into touch with the right person will enhance your reputation for business efficiency. Certain kinds of extensions also afford quick and efficient intercommunication between departments.

DISCUSS YOUR REQUIREMENTS WITH YOUR LOCAL SALES REPRESENTATIVE. HE WILL CALL AND ADVISE YOU IF YOU WILL FILL UP AND POST THE ENCLOSED CARD

(left) Information booklet, 1936, issued to subscribers at newly automated exchanges. *Introducing the Dial* (1935) similarly explained how the new system worked

AUTOMATIC EXCHANGE

(right) Information leaflet on telephone rental rates, 1934. Even routine literature could feature a high degree of artistic design

TELEPHONE RATES

Post Office
Exhibition, The
Strand, London
1933. The Post
Office took short
leases on a number
of street-front
properties around
the country to
mount exhibitions
on its work and
services. These also
typically showed
GPO films, and by
the end of 1934 over
77,000 people had
seen Film Unit films
at the Strand
Exhibition alone,
which received over
400,000 visitors
overall

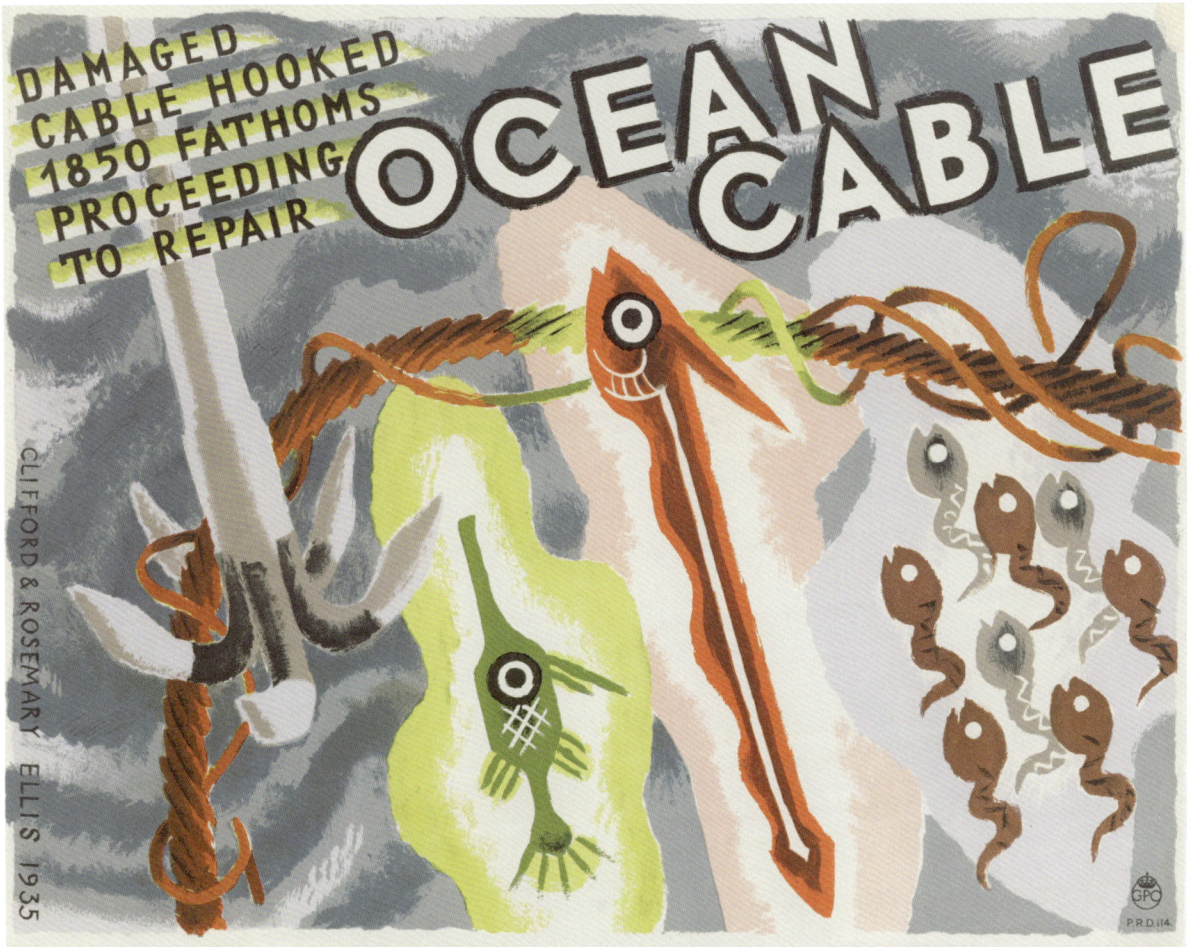

Ocean Cable, 1935,
designed by Clifford
and Rosemary Ellis.
The work of the Post
Office in repairing
submarine cables
was covered by the
GPO Film Unit's
Cable Ship (1933)

Creating goodwill

Until Tallents joined the Post Office in 1933 official policy had been to ignore attacks in the media but to respond only through the Post Master General in Parliament. Tallents understood that such an approach was damaging the reputation of the Post Office and demoralising its workforce. Goodwill and understanding between the Post Office and its customers, he argued, would encourage more use of its services, and motivate its employees to be more efficient. Films like *Night Mail* (1936), along with public exhibitions and displays, were designed to build a friendly relationship between the Post Office and its customers and build general awareness of its efforts to modernise.

Invitation to subscribers to visit their local telephone exchange, c. 1934. Tallents inaugurated a programme of special behind-the-scenes events to enable people to get a better appreciation of Post Office work

Poster Exhibition, Union House, St Martin Le Grand, London, 1938. Regular local displays during the 1930s were another feature of the Post Office strategy to create goodwill. This area of the poster exhibition displays posters publicising the work of the GPO Film Unit

Tallents also inaugurated a public programme of scripted talks on various aspects of Post Office work by local Post Office staff, supported by sets of slides. This image is a still from *The Coming of the Dial* (1933) which has then been hand coloured

Monochrome photograph of poster by Tom Eckersley & Eric Lombers, 1939 (PRD 122). Both films and posters were a critical part of Tallents' strategy of applying the arts to publicity

GRAHAM BELL'S TELEPHONE 1876

ERIC FRASER

One of a set of four posters for use in schools, designed by Eric Fraser, 1937. The educational programme of the Post Office included lesson notes for teachers and telephone demonstration sets for use in the classroom

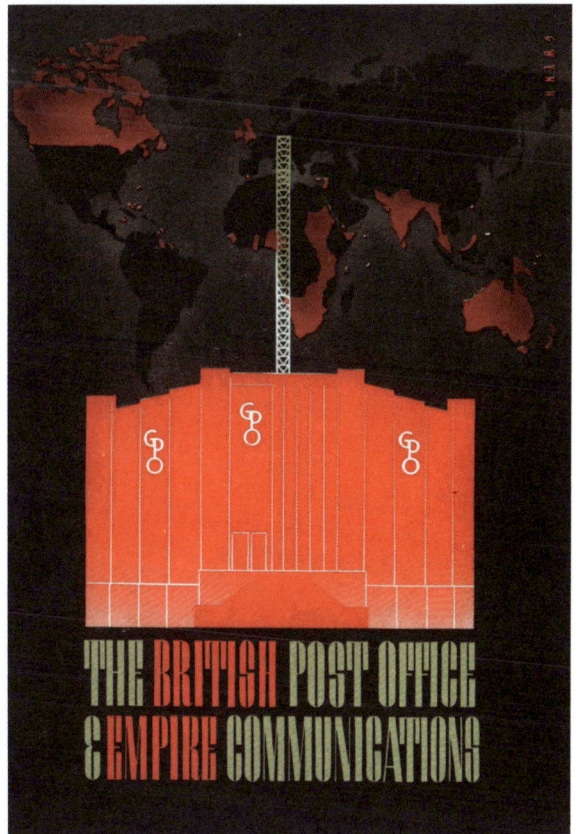

As well as smaller local displays, the Post Office was also a major presence at larger exhibitions. These two booklets accompanied the Post Office exhibition at Charing Cross underground station in 1936, and at the Empire Exhibition at Glasgow in 1938

Lecture slide promoting *The Post Office Magazine*, 1934. This Tallents-inspired review of the Post Office announced that 'It is the declared policy of the Post Office of 1934 to take the public into its confidence and enlist the cooperation of its customers'

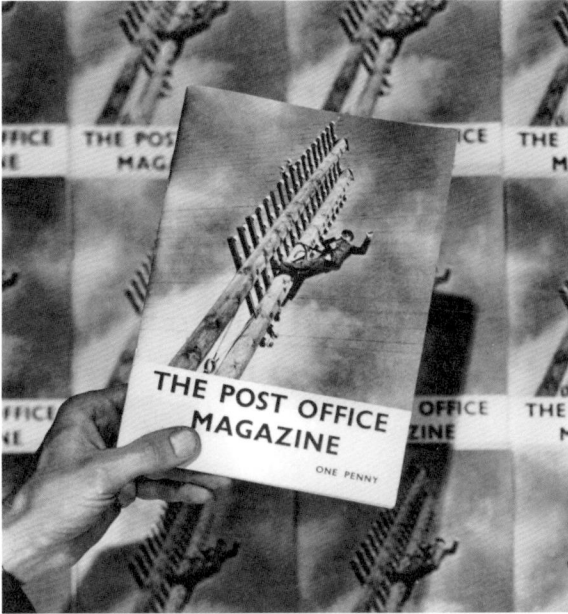

Lecture slide promoting *The Post Office Magazine*, 1934. An internal circular announced that this new in-house magazine, introduced in January 1934 , would 'keep the staff more fully informed of the main activities of the Post Office, and ... maintain and further encourage esprit de corps'

Post Office exhibit at the Glasgow Radio Exhibition, September 1934. Between 1932 and 1934 the Post Office had staged over 70 displays at general exhibitions or in shops taken on short lease, many of which also screened GPO Film Unit films

Communication in society

The GPO Film Unit's films, along with new GPO services like greeting telegrams, the Speaking Clock and the 999 Emergency Service, were important to shaping the look and feel of an emerging mass-participation media society. The GPO's publicity work in this area was not just an institutional attempt to explain its actions and market its services, but to build pride in a modern national infrastructure and even create new forums for civic activity.

Press advertising and publicity leaflet for the Speaking Clock, introduced in London in July 1936, and later made available throughout the country. The press advertisement is perhaps a little startling by today's standards, but like so much of the archive material is a window into society's mores of the day and what was and wasn't considered acceptable. The Speaking Clock was the subject of the GPO Unit's film of the same name, *At the Third Stroke* (1939)

London Telephone Directory L–Z, May 1937. This was the directory that features in the GPO Film Unit film *Book Bargain* (1937). The film describes some of the surprising statistics behind the making of the directory, such as that 5,000 miles of paper and 56 tons of ink were required to produce it. Two issues each of the two parts to the London Directory were produced each year, requiring paper that would be enough to circle the globe

Poster publicising the number of telephone operators working in the telephone network by Duncan Grant (1939). In the 1930s the Post Office was one of the country's largest employers, and had traditionally been a large employer of women. Almost 25 per cent of the quarter of a million workforce were women, the majority as telephonists or telegraphists. Despite increasing automation, most people would encounter a telephonist when making a call, and their work was featured in films such as *The Fairy of the Phone* (1936) and *The New Operator* (1932)

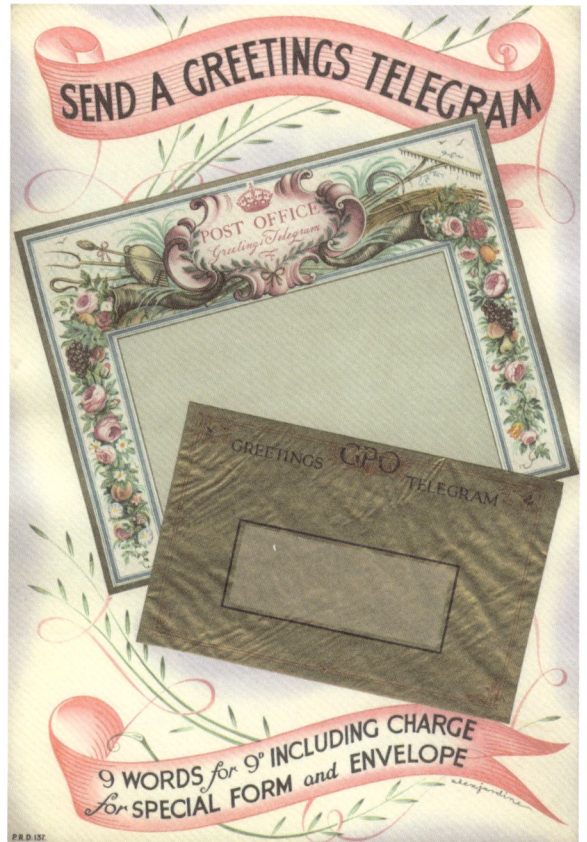

Poster publicising the telegraph service, 1936. The service was in general decline from the early part of the twentieth century. Although publicity including films such as *Nine for Six* (1939) temporarily reversed the decline during the 1930s, it lost money throughout this period

Publicity poster for greetings telegrams by Alex Jardine, 1936. They were introduced the previous year to counter the public perception of the telegram as a bad-news message. The greetings telegram was largely responsible for the temporary halt in the decline of the telegraph, helped by films such as *The Heavenly Post Office* (1938)

Telegrams were delivered by messenger boys, a popular job among 14–16-year-olds straight from school, many of whom went on to senior positions in the Post Office. A common sight on Britain's streets, their work was portrayed in the GPO Film Unit's *A Job in a Million* (1937)

Publicity poster by Andrew Johnson from 1936 for the famous Jubilee K6 red telephone kiosk, designed by Giles Gilbert Scott and introduced the same year to commemorate the silver jubilee of George V in 1935. Now a national icon, it was initially disliked in some parts of the country because of its colour

Press information advertisement from 1936 on police telephone and signal systems provided by the Post Office. Police kiosks and telephone pillars were also once common street furniture. A few remain as listed buildings (and, of course, as the TARDIS in the BBC's *Doctor Who*), but they have long been superceded by mobile police communications

HOW TO DIAL

Before commencing to dial lift receiver and wait for dialling tone (a purring sound)

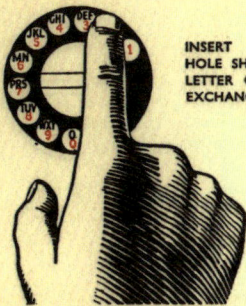

1 INSERT FINGER IN HOLE SHOWING FIRST LETTER OF NAME OF EXCHANGE REQUIRED

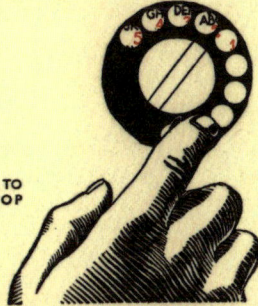

2 TURN DIAL TO FINGER-STOP

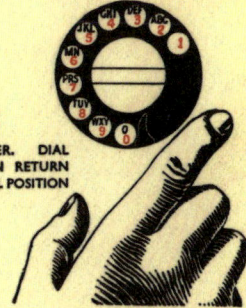

3 LIFT FINGER. DIAL WILL THEN RETURN TO NORMAL POSITION

REPEAT FOR 2ND AND 3RD LETTERS OF EXCHANGE NAME AND FOR FOUR FIGURES

FREE EMERGENCY CALLS
DO NOT INSERT COINS. LIFT RECEIVER,
DIAL 999 AND ASK EXCHANGE FOR
FIRE, POLICE, AMBULANCE

CO 152

Instructions on using the dial and the recently introduced 999 Emergency Service, 1937. Now increasingly a memory, the dial at the time was the latest technology that enabled people to make calls automatically with less need for an operator. The GPO Film Unit described the technology in *The Coming of the Dial* (1933)

Images within this chapter courtesy of BT Heritage

PART SIX

Films

17 / 'GO THE WAY THE MATERIAL CALLS YOU'

Basil Wright and *The Song of Ceylon*

Jon Hoare

Basil Wright completed *The Song of Ceylon* at the GPO Studio in Blackheath in late 1934. The project carried over from the EMB Film Unit after the demise of the Empire Marketing Board in 1933. However, instead of the four educational travelogues initially commissioned by the Ceylon Tea Propaganda Board, Wright produced a highly experimental, poetic and impressionistic single film combining montage editing with a complex multilayered soundtrack to striking effect. Although its 'official' roots lay in the promotion of Empire tea and the resources of the Post Office, Wright deliberately set about creating a work of art that captured his own response to the island of Ceylon (Sri Lanka). *The Song of Ceylon*'s bold visual style and inventive use of the GPO's newly acquired Visatone sound recording technology place it at the heart of the documentary movement's creative approach to non-fiction film-making.

With the exception of a few references to modern technology spanning the globe, *The Song of Ceylon* is clearly unrelated to the day-to-day workings of the Post Office. In its early years the GPO Film Unit acted at times like an independent mini studio. Alongside Wright's film, it completed projects such as *Coal Face* (1935) and *BBC – The Voice of Britain* (1935) that had nothing to do with promoting postal services. Pushing the limits of its enlightened sponsorship by official (and corporate) bodies linked to the British state, the documentary movement continued to develop as an innovative and 'alternative' school of film-making. John Grierson and Stephen Tallents – acting independently of their paymasters – vigorously encouraged such creative freedom. Contributions from artists, film-makers, musicians and poets – including W. H. Auden, Benjamin Britten, Alberto Cavalcanti, Walter Leigh, László Moholy-Nagy, Len Lye and Lotte Reiniger, reveal connections to a wide range of avant-garde influences.[1] Responding to such sources of inspiration, *The Song of Ceylon* was Basil Wright's outstanding contribution to inter-war Britain's 'alternative' film culture.

Basil Wright

The London Film Society's monthly film screenings were the catalyst for 'alternative' film culture in Britain. From 1925 to 1939 the society championed the emerging idea that film was a new art in its own right. They screened the latest international, experimental and independent films, introducing work by the likes of Clair, Eisenstein, Dreyer, Dovzhenko, Vertov and Vigo.[2] These modern classics were screened alongside a choice selection of early cinema.

Basil Wright joined the Film Society while a student at Cambridge (1926–9). He later credited the screenings for his filmic education – it was his 'oasis in a cinematic desert'. For his twenty-first birthday, in 1928, Wright persuaded his family to buy him a 16mm cine camera. Responding to symphonic films such as Cavalcanti's *Rien ques les heures* (1926) and Ruttmann's *Berlin: Symphony of a City* (1927), he began creating elaborately edited amateur films. Meanwhile, his student articles echoed the shift of interest within art cinema from the theatricality of German expressionism to the outdoor, metropolitan and rural realism of Soviet and European films. Intrigued by the work of Eisenstein and Pudovkin, Wright contemplated the expressive use of sound in counterpoint for psychological effect.[3] In the soundtrack for *The Song of Ceylon* he would put Soviet ideas into practice.

The Film Society's fifth season started explosively on the 10 November 1929 with the joint premiere of Grierson's EMB production *Drifters* (1929) and Eisenstein's *Battleship*

Sergei Eisenstein dressed as a policeman (centre) and Basil Wright bespectacled and smoking (back right) at the London Film Society in 1929. Courtesy of BFI Stills, Posters and Designs

Potemkin (1925). Describing the impact of Grierson's film, Wright later wrote: 'it told me all at once what I wanted to do – the poetry of reality expressed in moving images'. In the audience sat the future of documentary in Britain: Arthur Elton, Edgar Anstey, Paul Rotha and Basil Wright.

When, later that November, the Society offered a practical film-making course with director Hans Richter and a series of lectures by Sergei Eisenstein, Wright had the money to sign up for both.[4] Richter's course proved chaotic but Eisenstein's lectures were formative and Wright made detailed notes: 'Go the way the material calls you … the scenario changes on location and the location shots change in the montage.'[5] This was liberating – allowing a film to fluidly be finessed into an idea – rather than working to a predetermined shooting script. It gave Wright the confidence to adopt an instinctive approach to shooting on location and editing in the cutting room.

Wright contemplated Eisenstein's theories and sought an introduction to Grierson; meanwhile Grierson had watched his amateur films and was impressed by their cutting. Early in 1930 Wright joined the newly established EMB Film Unit.[6] The legendary director of *Nanook of the North* (1922), Robert Flaherty, accompanied him on the shooting of his first film, *The Country Comes to Town* (1933). More films followed, including the delicate pastoral *O'er Hill and Dale* (1932). Alone in the West Indies, his experience of British imperial exploitation was captured in *Cargo from Jamaica* (1933). As the EMB came to an end, Grierson wrote: 'Wright is now I believe the best lyrical documentary director in the country.'[7]

'Go the way the material calls you'

In December 1933, as the EMB Film Unit transferred to the GPO, Grierson despatched Wright to Ceylon to fulfil the Ceylon Tea Propaganda Board's commission. Although expected to cover the island's life and industry, the Tea Board gave Wright a free hand – no scenario was written. Accompanied by John Taylor – recently returned from work on Flaherty's *Man of Aran* (1934) – Wright set out by steamer, arriving in Colombo on New Year's Day 1934.[8] After the EMB's budgetary constraints, the Tea Board's generosity was striking: plush rooms at the Grand Oriental Hotel, offices at the Chamber of Commerce, a large convertible Minerva touring car and a crew of porters in a furnished truck. For Wright, being put in contact with Lionel Wendt was their most valuable contribution. Ethnically a Burgher – the name the Islanders used to describe the intermarried descendents of Sinhalese and Europeans – Wendt had studied law at Cambridge and music in London.[9] Acting as Wright's guide, he sensitively explained Wright's intentions, creating a sympathetic understanding between the film-makers and the islanders.

Immersed in a month-long search for inspiration, Wright toured the length of Ceylon. With no means of recording sound on the island, the whole film was shot silent.[10] Principal filming took place in villages surrounded by rice fields, in fisheries operated by sail-propelled catamarans and among the buried cities of Anurajapura and Polonnaruwa. After filming the great annual pilgrimage to the summit of the island's highest mountain Sri Pada (Adam's Peak), Wright told his mother it was the most impressive thing he had ever seen.

Briefly alone in the stillness by the four granite sculptures of Buddha at Gal Vihara in Polonnaruwa, Wright glimpsed a man laying an offering – a scene recreated in the film's final sequences. Free to work according to the feelings Ceylon aroused in him, Wright sought to understand the ways in which civilisations of the past, present and future had been touched by the island and its people. The daily work and character of Ceylon's people and the stupendous remains of its past civilisations began to add up to a total conception, an idea of the island that dominated his filming. Wright said he was led by inner impulses; key sequences demonstrate his instinctive approach. Graham Greene responded to the sensitive conclusion of the film's first section:

> Here, as a priest strikes a bell, Mr Wright uses one of the loveliest visual metaphors I have ever seen on any screen. The sounding of the bell startles a small bird from its branch, and the camera follows the bird's flight and the notes of the bell across the island, down from the mountain-side, over forest and plain and sea, the vibration of the tiny wings, the fading sound.[11]

Wright was compelled to film the birds without a clear sense of how they might fit together or relate to the final film(s). Later, during the editing, he found such material created exactly the atmosphere he sought. Through these transformative moments he offers us a fleeting connection to the island's private, spiritual life. Robert Gardner has reflected on the power of Wright's instinctive cinematic vision:

> I am reminded in this connection of the almost literally transporting spirituality he evoked … in the beginning of *Song of Ceylon,* where stone, birds, air and water are joined to create an overwhelming atmosphere of holiness … the tintinnabulations of those relentless bells guiding the senses into novel excitations, the effect is transfiguring. We are in his grip and we are changed forever.[12]

Early in May 1934, after seven weeks of almost continual shooting, Wright sailed for London with more than 20,000ft of film. However, before he could edit the Ceylon footage Wright served a short stint as studio manager at the newly formed GPO Film Unit.[13] As part of Wright's contribution to the Unit's collaborative film *Pett and Pott* (1934) – devised by Cavalcanti as a lesson in the expressive use of sound – he persuaded Walter Leigh to compose the score.[14]

Following a detailed analysis of all the material shot in Ceylon, Wright decided the film required a complex soundtrack of five elements: genuine Sinhalese sounds, an orchestral score by Leigh, natural sounds, synthetic sounds and a narration.[15] With no technology available to make recordings in Ceylon, in the studio Leigh produced layers of synthetic sounds (elephants, ships, trains), haunting atmospheric music, voices and narration synchronised to Wright's skilfully edited images. Glissandos on chromatic tubular bells provided unearthly sounds and metal strips struck with hammers created gong-like clanging. Distortion and short-wave signals were recorded from a wireless in the studio. The local Blackheath church choir were taught the chant 'De gita, de dum' by two Sinhalese – Ukkuwa, the chief dancer from the film, and Suramba, the virtuoso drummer.[16] Chaperoned by Wendt, they came to London to add authenticity and rhythm to the soundtrack. The German, French and English voices included Cavalcanti, Grierson, Leigh and Wright. A further group of Sinhalese recruited from the East End of London contributed snatches of dialogue and pianissimo religious chanting.

Basil Wright (facing camera) with his Newman Sinclair camera, on location in Ceylon, 1934 (*The Song of Ceylon*). Courtesy of BFI Stills, Posters and Designs

Leigh and Wright treated film sound as an art with unexplored frontiers.[17] Leigh described how the sound score was not only an accompaniment to the visuals, but added an element they did not contain, while the commentary was calculated as an effect and not as a 'necessary nuisance'.[18] Wright adapted the narration from Robert Knox's *An Historical Relation of the Island Ceylon* published in 1681. He discovered the book by chance in an antiquarian London bookstore.[19] Finding the right voice to speak the narration proved challenging, but after a procession of actors and broadcasters were tested, Wendt stepped in. In contrast to the received pronunciation (RP) voiceovers associated with British documentary – and the authority over the visuals such voices implied – Wendt's intonation (itself an aural blend of Ceylon's imperial history) added exactly the right 'out-of-time' atmosphere sought by Wright.

Synopsis

The Song of Ceylon is a complex film constructed in a circular form and divided into four titled sections – Wright hastily added them before the premiere at the Film Society.[20] Peering in through the jungle foliage, the first, 'The Buddha', introduces the spiritual life of the island, culminating in the pilgrimage to the summit of Sri Pada amid chiming bells. The second, 'The Virgin Island', reveals aspects of traditional village life and work: rice fields, fishermen and dancing children. The third sequence, 'The Voices of Commerce', introduces the booming, buzzing sounds of the modern imperial marketplace. New technology: radio interference, Morse code, stock prices, international voices and ships horns juxtapose with the natives' manual labour and Ceylon's industries. Commerce explicitly links the lives of the islanders to the tea-drinking audiences of 1930s Britain. Finally, 'The Apparel of a God' returns to spiritual contemplation: first, quiet individual Buddhist devotion, then the swirling rhythmical ecstasy of the dancing group. Coming to rest on the serene seated Buddha, the camera withdraws – as it had entered at the start – through the great revolving fans of palm. Setting its exquisite imagery, air of mysticism and historical narration against the disruption of modernity, *The Song of Ceylon* encourages us to reflect on the West's representation (and exploitation) of the East.

'Outside with the bills of lading and the loudspeakers'

Wright offers an intricate portrait of Ceylon, its people and their place in the modern world. Revealing what he saw as the 'timeless' qualities of life on the island – traditions seemingly unchanged for generations – he sought to demonstrate how such continuity coexisted with modernity. Tea, coconuts and copra worked by hand were transported and sold into a global marketplace with new technology. Telegraph and telephone wires, train tracks and radio signals, stock prices and shipping manifests were the links connecting the ancient and the modern, the East and West, the coloniser and the colonised. Offering criticism of this imperial relationship, the film makes it clear that the long-term presence of Empire and global trade were still (in 1934) dependant on traditional working practices. The tea industry might be factory-based in later processes but the lines of tea pickers, like the men husking coconuts, were engaged in unmechanised physical labour.

Wright's representation of Ceylon distanced him from Robert Flaherty's documentary film-making – which too often deliberately removed evidence of the modern world. *The Song of Ceylon*'s montage editing of sound and image, visually and aurally demonstrated Grierson's belief that documentary films should represent the present day in both their subject matter and method of construction. For Grierson, documentary could reveal to audiences the 'matrix of interconnections' that underlay society.[21] This, he hoped, would bring people closer together in their understanding and their involvement in the interdependent workings of the modern world. Wright's film uses movement to express these international interconnections. Shifting between the traditional and the modern, the global and the local, religion and commerce, he celebrated the rhythms of twentieth-century Ceylon's spiritual and material life. Critics who have misread the use of Knox's seventeenth-century text as a straightforward description of what appears onscreen have missed Wright's intentional irony.

At times the soundtrack and the visual track are juxtaposed for critical effect. For example, the narration in the opening section as the camera looks out across the island from the summit of Sri Pada appears innocent and descriptive, evoking the beauty of Ceylon. Repeated at the end of the film's third section, the same words take on a critical dimension. Wendt describes 'a virgin island … rich in mines of all kinds of special stones like a maid decked with jewels', over an image of a young woman (a tea picker) with a large basket on her back. The metaphor is clear, the island, covered with plantations is literally picked of its wealth. Writing in 1936, Paul Rotha elaborated on Wright's critical use of sound:

> Extensions of this imagistic use of sound are found in Wright's *Song of Ceylon*. The rhythmic noise of a mountain train is continued over an elephant pushing down a tree, an association of power and at the same time a comment. The market prices of tea, spoken by radio-announcer and dictated in letter form by business executives are overlaid on scenes of natives picking in the tea gardens, the 'Yours truly' and 'Your obedient servant' of the dictation being ironically synchronised over the natives at their respective tasks.[22]

Although Wright and Rotha saw *The Song of Ceylon* as critical of imperial economics, these elements of the film are subtle and not obvious to everyone. However, Wright did make Ceylon's connections to Britain and the global marketplace explicit – the islanders are actively involved in the twentieth century. By the standards of the 1930s, *The Song of Ceylon* provided a progressive view of a non-western culture. Nonetheless, in Wright's personal vision, the history, multicultural complexity and contemporary politics of Ceylon's relationship within the British Empire is unexplored. While Sinhalese Buddhist culture is a dominant theme, the islands' other communities – including its Burgher, Muslim and Tamil people – are not clearly revealed. Knox's words, although at times used ironically, are still the commentary of a fellow westerner. The film does not give any of the contemporary Ceylonese a voice. Although Wright's film touches on industry and metropolitan life, his focus is on the rural, agricultural and evidently traditional aspects of the island. But then *The Song of Ceylon* is not presented as an authoritative lecture. Instead, Wright attempted to immerse us in sensory impressions, in feelings that bring to the viewer something of his personal response to Ceylon. Rather than bombarding viewers with empirical facts, he offers us a poetic encounter, the island remains beyond our grasp. Graham Greene explained how Wright's vision did not claim authority over Ceylon or its people:

> Mr Basil Wright was content to accept the limitations of ignorance, of a European mind, to be 'on the outside, looking in'; the film is a visual record of the effect on a sensitive Western brain of old, communal, religious appearances, not of a life which Mr Wright pretends to *know*'.[23]

Greene saw the film as a life Wright observed, we look in – most poignantly at the man who leaves his offering to Buddha – but are left outside with the bills of lading and the loudspeakers.[24]

Legacy

An agreement with the Ceylon Tea Board gave the GPO £250 to allow the film's completion. The project no doubt fed the animosity Whitehall bureaucrats felt towards Grierson and Tallents and their free-spirited approach to the Unit's productions. Some historians attempt to compartmentalise the so-called 'Griersonian' documentary as a dry informational, didactic form of non-fiction film-making. *The Song of Ceylon* reveals the truly inventive film culture Grierson created at the GPO. Wright acknowledged: 'It was Grierson who built a protective wall around me, and stood sentry at the gates, so that I could finish *Song of Ceylon* in peace.'[25] Grierson saw the 'courage of poetry' in *The Song of Ceylon* and *Night Mail*'s (1936) use of montage. He traced this to Eisenstein's *Old and New* (1929) and *Romance Sentimentale* (1930) rather than the violent montage of *Battleship Potemkin*.[26]

Keen-eyed viewers might note that *The Song of Ceylon*'s credits make no reference to either the GPO or its tea-industry sponsors. Produced by Grierson with direction by Wright, the film is presented as the production of a company called Cinema Contact.[27] Wright and Grierson were GPO staff, but Cinema Contact was their own business, formed to bail out Edinburgh-based film journal *Cinema Quarterly* – relaunched as *World Film News* in 1936.[28] Indicating the freedom they enjoyed while simultaneously working within the British state, this was an early example of the documentary movement's growing independence from the GPO's control and beyond the Treasury's purse strings.[29]

At the 1935 International Film Festival in Brussels, *The Song of Ceylon* won first place in the documentary class and the 'Prix du Gouvernment' for the best film in all classes. Roger Manvell's later claim that *The Song of Ceylon* was: 'possibly the greatest British-produced film in any category up to 1935', demonstrates its significance as a canonical art film.[30] Meanwhile, its role in empire marketing was downplayed. On its release, *The Song of Ceylon* received praise for its experimental, artistic merits, but it was not at all what the Tea Board wanted. Although Wright had enjoyed free reign, they held Grierson to the contract for four travelogues.

Made from *The Song of Ceylon*'s cut-outs and shown non-theatrically across Britain to schools and societies, these educational shorts included maps, illustrations and historical information about the island's industries and cultural diversity.[31] Lacking *The Song of Ceylon*'s intentionally contested relationship between sound and image, they featured straightforward instructional narrations. Rotha estimated the total cost of the Ceylon project at £3,000; for this sum the Tea Board got an international award-winning film for nothing and four short travelogues for their own use.[32]

While the travelogues were forgotten about, *The Song of Ceylon*'s international standing grew. In 1946 inclusion in a documentary programme at the Museum of Modern Art New York prompted a write-up in *Time* magazine:

> Basil Wright's extraordinarily beautiful *The Song of Ceylon* ... bears about the same relation to ordinary travelogues that Keats's Ode on a Grecian Urn bears to a cheap pottery catalogue.[33]

The Song of Ceylon has developed and maintained the status of a classic art film. Initially widely circulated in Britain's film society circuit, in recent years it was included in Tate Britain's rolling screenings of 'artists' films'. Internationally, the film helped inspire the ethnographic film movement in the social sciences and, since 1986, the Royal Anthropological Institute has awarded a film prize in Wright's name:

> For a film in the ethnographic tradition, in the interest of furthering a concern for humanity – in order to acknowledge the evocative faculty of film – as a way of communicating their concern to others.[34]

Attaching particular value to innovative forms of film-making, the prize is a fitting tribute to Wright's inventive, poetic and humanist contribution to the art of documentary.

Throughout his life Wright remained fascinated by his experiences making *The Song of Ceylon*. Interviewed in 1969, shortly after revisiting Sri Lanka, he described its creation:

> *Song of Ceylon* was an experiment ... It's the only film I've made that I really loved, and it was in fact a religious experience ... this film grew like a tree growing out of one's navel. Each morning there would be another branch there; you'd have to sort of cut it off, or prune it or keep it as it was, and gradually the film emerged. I still cannot understand. I walked into an unconscious process, shot the material and turned it into the film it is, which has the curious validity of being loved and admired and delighted in by the Ceylonese of today, the young people there today, which surprised me last month when I was there. I was terribly pleased at that ... Well, this was a magical film, you see. I can't think of the rules of that.[35]

Notes

1. The first two years at the GPO Unit were a rather playful period with comic and experimental films like *Pett and Pott* (1934), *The Glorious 6th of June* (1934) and *The Fairy of the Phone* (1936) offering a different sense of the documentary movement than is traditionally associated with Grierson's project.
2. In response, film societies sprang up across Britain in the late 1920s and early 30s, while 'art-house' programming in cinemas like the Everyman and the Academy reflected a growing audience for films previously deemed commercially unsuitable.
3. See Sergei Eisenstein, Vsevolod Pudovkin and Grigori Alexandrov, 'The Sound Film: A Statement', *Close Up* vol. 3 no. 4, October 1928, pp. 10–13, and Jamie Sexton, 'The Audio-

Visual Rhythms of Modernity: *Song of Ceylon*, Sound and Documentary Filmmaking', *Scope: An Online Journal of Film Studies*, May 2004.

4. It was the considerable sum of 5 guineas for the lectures and 20 for the workshop. Len Lye also attended the workshop. A disgruntled Paul Rotha lacked the money to participate, although he spent some time with Eisenstein, visiting the Wellcome Collection where his father was curator and drinking coffee in a Lyon's Corner House. This episode is recounted in Rotha's book *Documentary Diary* (London: Secker & Warburg, 1973).

5. Richter's resulting film, *Everyday* (1929), was actually completed at a much later date and appears as an extra on the BFI DVD *Dreams that Money Can Buy*. If you look closely a bespectacled Basil Wright appears as an office clerk.

6. His initial job was to turn footage from the Gold Coast into a short advertising film on cocoa. Further short advertising films followed.

7. John Grierson, 'The EMB Film Unit', *Cinema Quarterly* vol. 1 no. 4, Summer 1933, pp. 203–8.

8. John Taylor joined the EMB Film Unit in 1930 after leaving school. On Aran, Taylor was Flaherty's production assistant, cameraman and film developer. Although a highly adept technician and later an accomplished director in his own right, Taylor's contributions to *Man of Aran* (1934) and *The Song of Ceylon* have largely gone unrecognised.

9. Wendt had studied music at the Royal Academy of Music in London. He was a practising lawyer and well-known musician but is now renowned as a photographer, a career he began in the 1930s. His photography was exhibited in London in 1938 and his book *Lionel Wendt's Ceylon* was published in 1950 (London: Lincolns-Prager). The Lionel Wendt Art Centre is in Colombo, Sri Lanka.

10. In Ceylon there were no facilities for processing 35mm film, the reels of exposed negative were returned by ship to Britain, a process that took many weeks. With no rushes to check their progress, Taylor instead shot 35mm movie film stock in his Leica stills camera (a gift from Flaherty), mirroring the movie cameras' aperture settings etc. Taylor processed these shots on location in a developing tank cooled by rapidly melting blocks of ice despatched from Colombo wrapped in towels. He photographed over 1,000 stills.

11. Graham Greene, 'Song of Ceylon', *The Spectator*, 4 October 1935, in John Russell Taylor (ed.), *The Pleasure Dome: Graham Green The Collected Film Criticism 1930–40* (Oxford: Oxford University Press, 1980), pp. 25–6.

12. Robert Gardner, 'Obituary: Basil Wright', *Anthropology Today* vol. 4 no. 1, February 1988, pp. 23–5.

13. The Arts and Crafts-style building that housed the GPO Film Unit's studio was known as the Blackheath Art Club and can be found at 43 Bennett Park, Blackheath, London. Formerly artists' studios, the building has been converted into flats.

14. Wright met Leigh at Cambridge. Leigh had been a student of the German composer Paul Hindemith before working at the avant-garde Festival Theatre with Humphrey Jennings. Leigh wrote musicals with fellow GPO collaborator V. C. Clinton-Baddeley. Leigh's sister Charlotte is the lead character in the GPO's *The Fairy of the Phone*.

15. For Wright's account of making the film see: Basil Wright, 'Filming in Ceylon', *Cinema Quarterly* vol. 2 no. 4, Summer 1934, pp. 231–2.

16. Wright referred to him as Suramba, although some accounts give his name as Gunaya.

17. Alberto Cavalcanti played a part in the soundtrack but later acknowledged it was Leigh and Wright's creation. A young Pat Jackson assisted in the film's editing. See Elizabeth Sussex, *The Rise and Fall of British Documentary* (Berkeley, CA: University of California Press, 1975).

18. Walter Leigh, 'The Musician and the Film', *Cinema Quarterly* vol. 3 no. 2, 1935, pp. 70–4.

19. Knox, an English sailor and adventurer, spent twenty years living on the island and observing its people.

20. The film was premiered at the Film Society on 16 December 1934. Wright later explained the titles broke up the film's true circular form or 'Mandala'.

21. Ian Aitken provides the most thorough understanding of Grierson's theoretical approach to documentary film. See, for example, Ian Aitken, *Film and Reform: John Grierson and the Documentary Film Movement* (London: Routledge, 1990).

22. Paul Rotha, *Documentary Film* (London: Faber & Faber, 1936), p. 222.

23. Graham Greene, 'Kilou the Tiger', *The Spectator*, 24 April 1936, in Taylor, *The Pleasure Dome*, p. 66.

24. For more recent critical analysis of *The Song of Ceylon* see William Guynn 'The Art of National Projection: Basil Wright's *Song of Ceylon*', in Barry Keith Grant and Jeanette Sloniowski (eds), *Documenting the Documentary: Close Readings of Documentary Film and Video* (Detroit: Wayne State University Press, 1998), pp. 83–98, and Martin Stollery, *Alternative Empires: European Modernist Cinemas and Cultures of Imperialism* (Exeter: University of Exeter Press, 2000).

25. Basil Wright, *The Long View* (London: Secker & Warburg, 1974), pp. 112–13.

26. Grierson made this suggestion in an episode of the BBC TV programme *Omnibus*, titled *The Name Grierson – The Word Documentary* (1973).

27. In Britain, the most widely seen print of *The Song of Ceylon* is the version the BFI include on the GPO compilation DVD *Addressing the Nation*. Internationally, the titles may appear slightly differently.

28. *World Film News* promoted the documentary movement and its work, but also celebrated a diverse international range of commercial and independently produced films – including Hollywood productions. Less highbrow than *Close Up* or *Cinema Quarterly*, it was also advertising work by the GPO unit and emerging independent units – like Strand and Realist.

29. Wright left the GPO in 1937, setting up his own independent production unit the Realist Film Unit. Grierson left the same year and founded the documentary advisory and research organisation Film Centre.

30. Roger Manvell, *Film* (Harmandsworth, London: Pelican, 1946), p. 99.

31. Wright and Taylor were involved in the creation of these four travelogues. They are titled *Dance of the Harvest*, *Monsoon Island*, *Negombo Coast* and *Villages in Lanka*. The BFI dates the production of all four travelogues as 1934.

32. Rotha, *Documentary Diary*, p. 128.

33. This quotation appears in an article titled 'Cinema: Eye for Fact', in *Time* magazine, Monday, 28 January 1946. It has also been accredited to Stephen Tallents: see Stephen Tallents, 'The Documentary Film', *The Journal of the Royal Society of Arts* vol. 45 no. 4733, 20 December 1946, p. 80.

34. The American ethnographic film-maker Robert Gardner organised the film prize in Wright's name. The prize is given biennially at the Royal Anthropological Institute's film festival. Between 1957 and 1997 Robert Gardner was the Founding Director of the Film Study Center at Harvard University. He is the director of *Forest of Bliss* (1986).

35. Basil Wright, interviewed by G. Roy Levin: see G. Roy Levin, *Documentary Explorations: 15 Interviews with Film-Makers* (Garden City, NY: Doubleday, 1971), p. 54. Wright saw the film as the product of inner compulsions; it came from the subconscious and from the guts.

18 / *THE HORSEY MAIL*

Documentary as Landscape

David Matless

Flood event

On the night of 12 February 1938, during a north-westerly gale, high waves were driven against the sand-hills of the east Norfolk coast with such force that they demolished 517 yards of the dunes at Horsey. Salt water poured through this breach and flooded 7500 acres of low-lying hinterland.[1]

This description of the 1938 Norfolk sea floods opens 'The Horsey Flood, 1938: An Example of Storm Effect on a Low Coast', a paper presented by J. E. G. Mosby to the Royal Geographical Society on 13 February 1939. Mosby was a Norfolk schoolmaster and county director of the Land Utilisation Survey; he outlined the flood event and its aftermath, with photographic overviews of the scene. The sea breach was filled by the end of March, but the sea broke through again on 3 April 1938 and covered much of the previously flooded area, the water lying on some areas for up to four months. Mosby's map of 'Flooded area, Horsey and district, 1938' marks the village of Horsey, left high and dry, and the sites of drainage mills. Mosby provides a surveying understanding of a flood landscape.

One item escaping Mosby's attention is the arrival of the GPO Film Unit, with director Pat Jackson making from this 'example of storm effect' a 1938 documentary film about the postal service. Jackson worked with cameraman Fred Gamage, music for the film was by Victor Yates, and also credited on the titles were 'postmen' Bob O'Brian and Claude Simmonds.[2] Jackson's *The Horsey Mail* (1938) shares some of the sense of survey animating Mosby's account, but also, in keeping with the conventions of documentary film, homes in on a human story, and in doing so provides an intriguing example of documentary as landscape.

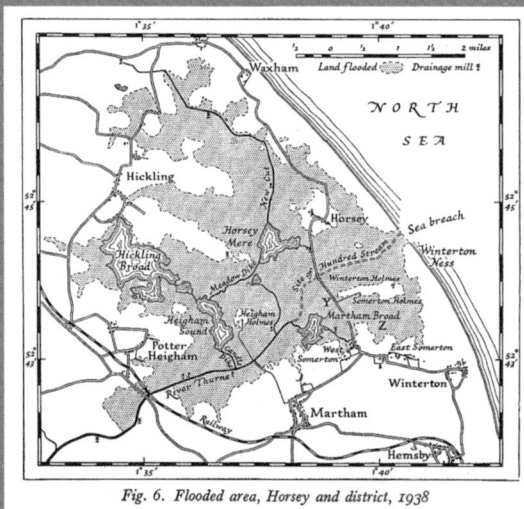

Fig. 6. *Flooded area, Horsey and district, 1938*

Flood documentary

The Horsey Mail's nine minutes is made up of 1 minute 15 seconds of newsreel-style beginning, a newsreel-style end from 7 minutes 30 seconds, with 6 minutes 15 seconds of postal story in the middle. The titles roll over an image of mill sails turning against a flood background, most likely Somerton Mill shot from the higher ground to the south. The opening received pronunciation (RP) narration and a mixture of aerial and ground views situates the event: a flood tide, a north-westerly gale, a '700 yard' breach in the wall of dunes, '10,000 acres underwater', Horsey and outlying farms now islands. An aerial view east shows an unnamed Horsey Mill turning in the flood. The land may be unworkable for four or five years and, if the gap is not closed, worse flooding may come. Roads are 5 feet under water, but the telephone still works, the telephone lines shown running above the flood.

A different RP narrator takes over as the film moves to road level with the postmen. Claude Simmonds cycles his lengthened round past an RAC sign stating 'Road Flooded Impassable', his daily delivery to Horsey extended from two to fifteen miles. The Yarmouth Head Postmaster has decided to give Claude motorised help, with a van from Yarmouth depot driven by Bob O'Brian (he and Claude are from then on always referred to by their first names). Here a different voice enters, that of Norfolk-accented Bob, preparing to

leave the depot; as the narrator mentions his name he interjects: 'Yes, that's me there. They've put off my winter leave so I could take Claude by van to Waxham. I got my thigh boots from the boy Herbert at the office.' A pair for Claude is added, and Bob is away. Catching Claude on his bicycle, pleased to see him (they hadn't met since the last darts match at the Cock Inn – Claude is 'the local champ round our way'), the bike goes into the van, the boots go on and they drive past refugees heading in the opposite direction, possessions on carts, flooded houses left behind. Bob and Claude travel to Waxham for the boat approach to Horsey from the north. The narrator wonders if Bob will sink his van, and Bob counters: 'This is where the Post Office takes to the boats. Old Claude used to be a fisherman, so if there's a bit of boating to be done, he's the boy.' Dismounting the van, meeting men with a rowing boat, a gentle pastoral string and piano music takes over from the previously hurried piano drive as the boat sets out; effectively setting up an ironic contrast of leisured sound and the labour of rowing in a bleak February. Bob tells of a woman waking up to find ducks around her upstairs bedroom, and the main road is followed into Horsey to avoid underwater field obstacles. Abandoned vehicles, parts of ploughs, protrude above the surface. Dry land achieved, the music slows to resolution, and the first half closes with a brief blank screen.

Claude and Bob emerge, round a building, into 'Horsey High Street', where they divide to cover different parts of the round, Claude heading to isolated dwellings. In the second half scenes of chill and bleakness are counterposed with smiles as the postmen get through. Bob and Claude meet Charlie Kerrison with his boat to row to the isolated Ford's Farm, a mile towards the breach in the dunes. Claude takes Ford the post, and a woman, Milly, brings some tea out – she was at school with Claude. The boat leaves and waves an oar as Ford and Milly wave back. The final section leaves the postmen behind, the opening narrator voice returns, and we see workers labouring to fill the remaining 100 yard gap in the dunes, with three days before the next high tide. Sandbags are laid, a wall of wooden piles behind, and a bank of earth and rubble; hand labour, crane work. This is temporary labour for those out of work from the floods; the film includes worker close-ups as well as panoramic shots. Mills turn to pump water from the fields into the river, and the final sequence is from the top of Horsey Mill, panning across the flood, and with shots upward into the sails and wheel. The narration ends: 'Until the road appears again Claude must row six miles every day to deliver the Horsey mail.'

Pat Jackson had begun work at the GPO Film Unit as a messenger boy in March 1933, aged seventeen, and became assistant to Harry Watt on *Night Mail* (1936), providing the narrative commentary for the non-verse sequences. Jackson later wrote, directed, cast and edited *Western Approaches* (1944) on the Battle of the Atlantic, nominated for an Oscar. Jackson emphasised story documentary with non-professional actors, and in this presented himself and Watt, in contrast to the approach of Basil Wright and other followers of Grierson, 'imprisoned in the expositional mould'.[3] Jackson recalled *The Horsey Mail* in his 1999 memoir, *A Retake Please!*. This was his first directorial credit, aged twenty-two, coming after an unmade project on the Postal School:

> Licking my wounds at the wasted time spent on the Postal School, the sea conveniently decided
> to break through on the Norfolk coast at a place called Horsey. I was sent off to film the incident.
> Whether there was a film to be made of it was questionable, but mine was not to reason why! ...
> We were on safe ground filming the sea breaking through the sea wall of sand dunes and sand-
> bagging the gap, and postmen rowing across flooded fields with farm equipment poking through
> the flood water. But invention on my part was sadly lacking. I should have been much more
> imaginative, thought up all sorts of little incidents to have brought the subject fully alive.[4]

Jez Stewart connects Jackson's comment to a contrast between the 'warmth and life' of the central story, and the 'formulaic, newsreel style' of the opening and closing sections, implying lack of imagination in the newsreel confinement of a story documentary.[5] One might also suggest, though, that an imaginative treatment could have interwoven those two modes further, moving between detached overview and intimate human story; between, as it were, J. E. G. Mosby and Claude Simmonds, with each perspective telling in the understanding of the flood landscape.

The GPO, the regional and the rural

Jackson's phrase that 'the sea conveniently decided to break through ... at a place called Horsey', could be taken as indicating a process whereby a film-maker happens to travel to an unknown out-of-the-way place before retreating to finalise a film at a metropolitan base. The geography of documentary, however, entailed more than a fleeting exploitative visit, and documentary set itself as going beyond a visitor perspective. Both *The Horsey Mail* and the 1936 *The Saving of Bill Blewitt*, directed by Watt with Jackson as assistant, and set in Mousehole in Cornwall using local people as actors (including Blewitt as himself), alighted on places already heavily scripted through tourist narrative, and affected to sidestep a holiday visitor vision (Blewitt's rivals in purchasing a working fishing boat are tellingly a visiting couple intent on buying for pleasure). *The Horsey Mail* in part achieves this sidestep simply by being set in bleak winter, but, like *The Saving of Bill Blewitt*, sets out a social landscape of everyday life and work which might cut across a viewer's leisure associations with Cornwall or the Norfolk Broads; Horsey is at the upper end of the Broads river system, and Horsey Mill was then, as now, a classic Broadland tourist icon. A complication here is, of course, that leisure associations might themselves include images of local people and their labour, whether through personal encounter or artistic and touristic imagery. Documentary as a way of seeing based on geographical movement thus finds itself representing places already represented, and making a choice as to how to present itself; whether to follow touristic conventions, directly challenge them in the name of realism, or attempt to work productively with the tensions arising from a group of people arriving at a place already represented, seeking to represent it anew.

The 'country' for the GPO Film Unit, and indeed the GPO in general, could mean both the rural and the regional; things beyond the town, regions beyond London. Such movement could be a trip into past tradition to escape the modern world, but it could also involve the recording and appreciation of a contemporary life where tradition thrived alongside modern development. Viewing the country through frames at once rural and regional helped foster the latter outlook, and the GPO Film Unit, and Jackson's work within this, follows this trajectory in the late 1930s, as indeed does the GPO as an institution. The GPO went through a process of regionalisation after the Bridgeman Report of 1932 in an attempt to modernise its internal structure, with regional directors in place for the whole country by 1940.[6] The postal landscape is thus one in which regionalisation and modernisation could be synonymous, in keeping with a powerful discourse of the region informing planning philosophy at the time.[7] This organisational alignment of the regional and the modern could match a cultural impulse to uphold and foster modern regional life in the GPO's wider presentation of itself, including via the work of the Film Unit, and in the image of the modern postal worker.[8] Region could here be signalled by representations of Northern urban industrial life, as in Jennings's films, by the cross-country interconnections of *Night Mail*, and by the rural regions tracked in films such as Cavalcanti's *A Midsummer Day's Work* (1939), following underground cable-laying through the Chilterns, and a classic expression of a culture of landscape aligning the modern and traditional in representing a newly ordered progressive rural England.[9] In the latter connection it is interesting to note that, after the war, Sir Stephen Tallents, key figure in the GPO's restyling of itself in the 1930s and in the shaping of the Film Unit, would provide the preface to Cecil Stewart's 1948 *The Village Surveyed*, a study of Tallents' home village of Sutton-at-Hone in Kent, the record of a survey and plan produced by academics, planners, students and local residents, and styled as a drama with 'cast' and 'scene'.[10] *The Village Surveyed* effectively extended a documentary ethos to post-war rural planning.

Local voice

As with *The Saving of Bill Blewitt*, *The Horsey Mail* is geographically embedded not only through visual images but in voice, though here *The Horsey Mail* stands out in involving a local voice in commentary rather than filmed dialogue. Accent registers differing connections in the narration of place, in a manner relatively unusual in documentary film. The mixture of RP narration and Norfolk Bob, and their different geographical grains of voice, gives the film a distinctive inflection. Bob never speaks direct to camera, his words sometimes accompanying his screen presence but more often working in dialogue with the narrator. This sharing of descriptive work makes for a form of narrative equality, different in effect to if Bob had been presented as a local respondent, interviewed speaking to camera in the field, a testifying object for a framing commentary.

Narrator and Bob generally speak separately, but as Claude trudges off through the water in the second half of the film Bob begins to sing 'I Do Like to be Beside the Seaside' over the narrator, and banter ensues, with the narrator eventually joining in. Local voice here provides comic effect, plucky stoicism, amusement alongside the narrator's serious authority, but there is more to Bob (and by implication the silent Claude) than local rustic comedy. As well as sketching in elements of his own and Claude's life and character – Bob has pigs and chickens, Claude throws 'a very pretty dart, they tell me' – Bob also offers commentary on agriculture, land use and flooding: 'They used to tell me as a youngster that the sea always found its own level. Well, she's found it this time – about ten mile inland.' The narrator states that Mr Ford had spent money treating the land with salt; Bob comments: 'Well, he's got enough to go on with now.' *The Horsey Mail* works a distinction between an authoritative outside narrator and Bob's local knowledge inflected with sayings, lore and stoic wit, but this is not a distinction between informed outsiders and insiders living through relative ignorance. The voices are equally if differently articulate, and the audience is given the aural prospect of a rural accent carefully enunciating an at times analytical script, as when the boat is steered along the main road to Horsey Mill to avoid underwater obstructions: 'The idea is, if we go gliding over some of those meadows, we are liable to hit our bottom on a plough.' With a Norfolk-accented voice joining the description of events, the film achieves a unique register.

Landscape iconography and social geography

It is instructive to set GPO films within the landscape iconography and social geography of their settings. *The Horsey Mail* works with the landscape iconography of Broadland, with symbolic features such as mills and boats also offering camera view-

points. The flood event indeed heightens the usual topographic conventions; this is flat landscape with limited viewpoints, notably mill towers, and the flood makes for an even flatter landscape than usual. The film's closing image from Horsey Mill has sun reflected in the waters, a final moment holding out classic pictorial beauty against the preceding counter-pastoral bleakness. Broadland was, by this time, a heavily filmed and photographed landscape, following the region's late-nineteenth-century touristic discovery, and there are occasional flickers of a Norfolk Broadland pastoral of boats rowing past pollarded willows; but, in general, any conventional picturesque visual language is put to one side, and the parallels are only with the bleaker elements of P. H. Emerson's late-nineteenth-century photography of Broads life and landscape.[11] This stretch of invasive water is far from any reed-fringed or tree-lined broad or river. And Bob and Claude's Broadland boating, whatever the occasional mood-lightening comedy of pushing off and clambering in, is hard work.

Setting *The Horsey Mail* within its local social geography, however, indicates a notable absence. The narrator comments that displaced residents have moved into Horsey Hall. One such person, shown loading possessions and people onto a cart while receiving post from Bob, is 'Arthur Dove the millman. He's moving into Horsey Hall. There are a good many of the villagers living there temporarily.' Dove is a regular character in other contemporary Horsey stories, including in the writings of his employer Anthony Buxton, owner of the Horsey estate and resident at Horsey Hall, and a self-consciously socially and ecologically active landowner. Buxton is a striking absence in the film, never mentioned. Horsey Hall is never shown, nor indeed the village church; the only buildings filmed are ordinary houses, farms and the mill. Jackson shoots the ordinary person, the GPO democratically serving a place without evident social hierarchy. One can contrast here P. V. Daley's account of 'The Norfolk Floods' in the April 1938 *East Anglian Magazine*:

> Superhuman efforts by Major A. Buxton, of Horsey Hall, Inspector Brehamy of the RSPCA Mr Dove of Horsey, the local police and other inhabitants of the Horsey district saved a good deal of animal life. Chickens, pigeons, dogs and cats all clamoured together under one roof out of the way of the rising waters, natural enmity being forgotten in the fear of death.[12]

Daley presents animal and human hierarchies crossed in the face of danger. Buxton would later detail the natural history of the floods in the *Transactions of the Norfolk and Norwich Naturalists' Society*, and become the event's chief local narrator, his position at Horsey giving requisite authority as naturalist and landowner.[13] *The Horsey Mail* and Buxton document different social landscapes.

The Horsey Mail in circulation

Postman
of the
Flood

The Horsey Mail was a response to an unexpected
event, not planned in advance, but both film and
associated material in *The Post Office Magazine*
(founded in 1934 and with a circulation of around
180,000 by 1938) drew on an existing iconography of the post getting through against
exceptional weather; indeed, similar images recur in *Post Office Magazine* coverage of the
January 1939 East Anglian floods.[14] There was also an established postal iconography of
picturesque boat delivery, ironically strong in a *Post Office Magazine* story on 'The Post in
Broadland' issued in the month *after* the flood, March 1938, telling of busy holiday
summers and relaxed local winters, though with no mention of the Horsey breach.[15]

In May 1938 *The Post Office Magazine* carried a one-page feature on Claude
Simmonds as 'Postman of the Flood', stressing heroic effort and novel, waterborne delivery: 'On a sunny morning last February Postman Claude Simmons strode determinedly
along the picturesque village street of Horsey – and made history!'[16] In keeping with
other *Post Office Magazine* articles sharing a subject with a GPO film, no mention is made
of *The Horsey Mail*, and there is also no mention of Bob O'Brian. Rather, Simmonds is a
lone operator, though the surviving telephone allows Mrs Goose and her daughter Freda
at Horsey post office to stay open, handling trunk calls for the four journalists who have
reached the village. Simmonds finds himself in peril as the repaired sea defences are
breached again:

> The little boat was caught half-way along the road by a terrific current, and came within an ace of
> being capsized. The wind dashed foam-laden water over its sides, and, with Horsey in sight, the
> postman was compelled to turn back. Wet through, he was still undefeated.

Simmonds keeps going, changes clothes, cycles to Winterton, then three miles along the
sandhills, across the sea breach at low tide, inland to the flood, and a final push of the
bike through the water to deliver the Horsey mail.

As with any GPO documentary, it is worth attending to the geographical circulation
of the finished film. The Post Office Publicity Committee meeting on 19 May 1938
noted:

> *Horsey Mail.* This one reel film was shot in Norfolk during the recent floods and shows the
> adventures of two postmen whilst engaged on the delivery of mails to farms and villages isolated by
> flood water./The film has been completed and will be shown in the Exhibition cinema in Glasgow.[17]

The film would, thus, appear to have had its first public showing in the GPO pavilion at
the Empire Exhibition in Glasgow, within a programme of documentaries. A story of two
Norfolk postmen finds itself part of one of the last great formal British imperial displays.
GPO films were also distributed via evening film displays in public buildings, organised
by local head postmasters.[18] *The Horsey Mail* thus featured in south-east regional
displays in autumn 1938, possibly in Norwich, Cambridge and Colchester, but certainly
in Great Yarmouth from 7–11 November, exhibiting a recent local disaster/spectacle to a
local audience. The display was opened by the mayor; a week earlier, on 31 October,

Simmonds and O'Brian had been presented with cheques for £5 in, as *The Post Office Magazine* reported:

> A pleasing ceremony ... in the Great Yarmouth Sorting Office ... a token of the Department's appreciation of the devotion to duty shown by these officers during the Horsey Floods. ... These postmen also figured prominently in the Post Office film displays which opened at Great Yarmouth on November 7, for they were the principal actors in the film 'Horsey Mail,' which showed how they took a boat to deliver letters and parcels to villages isolated by the inroads of the sea.[19]

Bob and Claude achieved a form of local stardom.

The documentary landscape

The Horsey Mail, and the GPO Film Unit's productions in general, stand as fascinating workings of the language of landscape in terms of representations of land and sea, in the deploying of filmic perspective, whether distant, panoramic, close-up or intimate and in the styling of people in their places. The way in which the documentary mode moves across such categories belies any crude distinction between an outside overview and an inside human story; rather documentary at its most successful could be argued to productively work the tensions of perspective and inhabitation, outside overview and everyday practice, which constitute landscape.[20] Documentary film can be regarded in this sense as a notable landscape genre. RP narrators and Bob, aerial views and Claude on foot, work together to produce the documentary landscape.

The Horsey Mail may finally be set within the wider depiction of landscapes of emergency. The film anticipates coverage of the 1953 North Sea floods, in England and Holland, but also might be regarded as, in effect, a practice run for the wartime documentary, with images of the post continuing to be delivered whatever the circumstances and perils. Several GPO figures played a role in the wartime Ministry of Information. For Horsey in 1938 read the East End in 1940–1, as lauded in the Ministry of Information's 1942 *Front Line*, with its photographs of services ongoing over bomb sites, a pillar-box being emptied in the rubble: 'The Milk Comes ... And The Post Goes'.[21] The GPO becomes an icon of ongoing everyday life within a landscape of emergency. There is resilience in the face of catastrophe, but the landscape of emergency also attains a curious calm after disaster, a paradoxical temporary stability. After the dunes have been breached, or the bombs have fallen, after the land has been deluged, or the buildings flattened, the surface of things lays still; rubble piled up, flood waters rippling over fields. The postman comes and goes across the face of the waters, the Horsey mail always gets through.

Notes

1. J. E. G. Mosby, 'The Horsey Flood, 1938: An Example of Storm Effect on a Low Coast', *Geographical Journal* vol 93, 1939, pp. 413–18 (quotation p. 413).
2. *The Post Office Magazine* coverage of the flood, discussed later in this chapter, gives a different spelling of both names, as R. J. O'Brien and Claude Simmons; I have followed the spelling on

the film credits here, though it is unclear which is correct. A website describing the building of military defences at Winterton in World War II, however, includes a photograph of the local Home Guard c. 1943, listing Claude Simmons, with his home village as Somerton; <www.pillbox-study-group.org.uk/johngreenwinterton.htm> (accessed April 2010).

3. Pat Jackson, *A Retake Please! Night Mail to Western Approaches* (Liverpool: Liverpool University Press, 1999), p. 33. Scott Anthony, *Night Mail* (London: BFI, 2007).

4. Jackson, *A Retake Please!*, p. 57.

5. Jez Stewart, Notes for *The Horsey Mail* in booklet for DVD collection *We Live in Two Worlds*, GPO Film Unit Collection Volume Two, BFI, 2009.

6. M. J. Daunton, *Royal Mail: The Post Office Since 1840* (London: Athlone, 1985).

7. David Matless, *Landscape and Englishness* (London: Reaktion, 1998).

8. Alan Clinton, *Post Office Workers: A Trade Union and Social History* (London: George Allen and Unwin, 1984)

9. Matless, *Landscape and Englishness*.

10. Cecil Stewart, *The Village Surveyed* (London: Edward Arnold, 1948). On Tallents, see Anthony, *Night Mail*, chapter 1.

11. John Taylor, *A Dream of England: Landscape, Photography and the Tourist's Imagination* (Manchester: Manchester University Press, 1994), chapter 3; John Taylor, *The Old Order and the New: P. H. Emerson and Photography, 1885–1895* (London: Prestel, 2006); David Matless, 'Action and Noise Over a Hundred Years: The Making of a Nature Region', in P. Macnaghten and J. Urry (eds), *Bodies of Nature* (London: Sage, 2001), pp. 141–65.

12. P. V. Daley, 'The Norfolk Floods', *East Anglian Magazine*, April 1938, pp. 268–72, quotation p. 268.

13. Anthony Buxton, *Fisherman Naturalist* (London: Collins, 1946), pp. 104–16; Anthony Buxton, 'General Effects of the Flood', *Transactions of the Norfolk and Norwich Naturalists' Society* vol. 14 no. 4, 1938, pp. 349–73. The latter is within a series of contributions on 'The Norfolk Floods', pp. 334–90, including J. E. G. Mosby on 'Mapping the Flooded Area', pp. 346–8.

14. *The Post Office Magazine*, 'Floods of Anglia', April 1939, pp. 150–1.

15. Martin Grand, 'The Post in Broadland', *The Post Office Magazine*, March 1938, pp. 108–9.

16. *The Post Office Magazine*, 'Postman of the Flood', May 1938, p. 204.

17. Post Office Publicity Committee minutes, 19 May 1938, 'General Progress Report', item 9, page 5; Royal Mail Archive, POST 108/11.

18. Post Office Publicity Committee minutes, 3 February 1938, 'General Progress Report', item 10; Royal Mail Archive, POST 108/11.

19. *The Post Office Magazine*, January 1939, 'Midlands, East and Wales' section, p. 37.

20. John Wylie, *Landscape* (London: Routledge, 2007); Matless, *Landscape and Englishness*.

21. Ministry of Information, *Front Line 1940–1941* (London: Ministry of Information, 1942), p. 57.

19 / THE GPO AT PLAY

What's On Today and *Spare Time*

Richard Haynes

This chapter analyses the place of sport in two GPO films from the late 1930s. In *What's On Today* (1938) the passion for sport is revealed through the mass appeal of mediated sport, as consumed through sporting news and commentaries. The film places emphasis on the modernity of sport, electronically communicated through the ingenuity of the Post Office engineers, sports journalists and broadcasters. In contrast, *Spare Time* (1939), as the title suggests, presents a lyrical look at recreational pastimes where the focus is on participation and spectatorship, and what its director Humphrey Jennings called 'the natural gaiety of working people' in a range of industrialised, urban communities. Both, in different ways, provide a way in to understanding the social and cultural history of sport and its mediation. They are both important visual documents of sporting life in the late 1930s, made all the more poignant given the restriction on such practices shortly after the films were made with the outbreak of war in September 1939.

Academic interest in sports documentary has largely concentrated on selective texts, such as Leni Riefenstahl's *Olympia* (1938) or more recent hit film documentaries such as *Hoop Dreams* (1994), *When We Were Kings* (1996) and *Touching The Void* (2003). While these films are important, and are arguably canonical, they represent a small proportion of documentary work on sport. Much of non-fiction film on sport is pretty mundane: biopics of long-forgotten sporting heroes; official film documentaries that fall short of Riefenstahl's visionary style; or instructional films that are dry and lack narrative appeal. But one question that arises from such films is their merit to the sports historian. This centres on the meaning of sport in society, and how and why sporting practices were caught on film. In this vein the BFI's 'Mitchell and Kenyon' archives have proven a boon to film and sports historians alike, and are highly suggestive of the rich sporting cultures that existed in Edwardian Britain.[1] The historical value of the Edwardian actuality films also applies to the early documentary films on sport made by the GPO. But before discussing the value of GPO films to sport historians, I want to briefly sketch out the place of sport in British society during the 1930s.

British sport between the wars

Sport, like cinema, enjoyed a huge boom during the 1930s. As social historians of sport have noted, sport in the inter-war period began to gain wider approbation as a key element of British public life.[2] In the Edwardian era and the immediate years after World War I, sport as a recreational pursuit had prospered through the leadership and organisation of both the public schools and the Church, which conferred on activities like athletics, cricket and rugby union a sense of morality heavily wedded to wider Christian ethics and social purpose.[3] Sport was also strongly influenced by perpetuating Victorian middle-class attitudes, which manifested themselves in notions of 'amateurism', 'sportsmanship' and 'team spirit'. Many of these wider cultural associations of sport were also carried forward into conceptions of, and pride in, nationalism, with major sporting events frequently receiving royal patronage, giving them approval and prestige.

Spectator sport, which focused on both amateur and professional sports, generally grew in the 1920s and 30s, although fluctuations caused by economic crisis and changing tastes did mean some sports struggled to remain financially viable. At the height of the depression in the early 1930s, horseracing, county cricket and association football all suffered economically in some shape or form. However, some sports, such as greyhound racing and motor sport, developed rapidly during the 1930s; both were commercially driven, the former by gambling, the latter by the interests of the burgeoning motor industry.

The media's focus on sport, in newspapers, cinema newsreels and through radio 'eye-witness' reports and live outside broadcast commentaries, increased the public visibility and knowledge of sport and sporting stars. Major sporting occasions such as Wimbledon, Test Cricket, the FA Cup Final, the Derby and the Oxford and Cambridge Boat Race formed part of an increasingly ritualised national sporting calendar. Sport also created a new era of popular heroes: Fred Perry in tennis and Jack Hobbs in cricket, who stood out as the 'best of British' sport, although the idea of sporting celebrity – heavily associated with the commercial excesses of professionalism – remained vulgar to the upper-middle-class guardians of sport. It is also notable, as it is today, that the sport stars receiving most attention were male. Many women were socially and institutionally excluded from particular sports, although in some sports such as football, women enjoyed a popular following with mass-media attention from cinema newsreels.[4]

The mediation of sporting events solidified the position of watching sport as a key characteristic of British popular entertainment and, while its impact on actual participation in sport is very difficult to gauge, there is plenty of evidence to suggest that people's passion for sport ran deep and wide. There were wider opportunities for leisure and recreation during the period, but also a more concerted effort by central and municipal authorities to provide amenities and opportunities for physical activity to improve health and general wellbeing.[5] The establishment of voluntary sports and leisure organisations such as the National Playing Fields

The GPO films tapped into the increasing importance of spectator sports. Courtesy of BFI

Association, the Youth Hostels Association, the Ramblers Association and the National Cyclists' Union, to name but a few, did much to promote outdoor recreation. Almost all of these organisations were middle-class institutions that attracted a cross-section of society. But some sports and recreations were firmly based in working-class culture and organisations, and much of this activity centred upon the Working Men's Club and Institute Union, an affiliation of working men's clubs.[6]

It is in this context that the documentary films relating to sport within the GPO archive have significant value to the sports and media historian. They reveal both the broad passion for sport in Britain during the mid- to late 1930s and the role sport played in the everyday lives of various communities across the country, invariably communicated through the mass media.

A nation of sports lovers

What's On Today, directed by Richard McNaughton, begins with the opening titles cut out of a newspaper which peels away as the documentary starts. The visual metaphor is simple and effective: we are looking behind the headlines of the daily sporting news. We are shown people playing various sports, from horse riding and golf to children playing cricket in the street, in order to emphasise that Britain is a nation of sports lovers. We are then located in Pudsey, West Yorkshire, in August 1938 and introduced to Mrs Hutton and other working-class folk in a range of settings, from backyards to a building site. We hear in the background the sound of a radio commentary, and we are told that this is the BBC's Howard Marshall commentating on the Ashes Test match. The commentary and the attentive audience in Pudsey were focused on the momentous achievement of a young English batsman, Len Hutton. The familial and regional ties of the Yorkshire cricketer are significant. Through a recording of Marshall's commentary, phlegmatic and mellifluous, we hear the moment in which he announces Hutton's world record-breaking Test innings in the fifth and final 'timeless' Test at the Oval, as he passed Wally Hammond's previous record of 336. Hutton went on the score 364, still a record innings by an English batsman.

Hutton later noted that he had been made aware of the record by the morning papers, which gave him the desire to go on to score the record innings. Once in his sights, his resolve to score one of the highest Test innings in history led former England cricketer Colin Cowdrey to lionise, 'It was not so much a beautiful innings as a quite remarkable achievement.'[7] In the same article on his hero, Cowdrey suggests: 'Hutton was born into a family circle of cricket, where all those around him lived for the game and talked little else.'[8] McNaughton's film captures some of this feeling that Hutton's ties to Pudsey and the Yorkshire people mattered. It also mattered that it could be shared, in a quite public sense, through radio.

In his commentary for the BBC, Marshall went on to say, 'We're pretty sure that in Pudsey they are listening, and that they are extraordinarily proud of this young man who has come to such great things.'[9] Indeed they were; and the Mayor of Pudsey sent a telegram to Hutton with the message, 'The Joy Bells are ringing in Pudsey!'[10]

The BBC had begun regular outside broadcasts from sport in 1927 and throughout the 1930s the commentaries from sport rapidly gained a popular audience. By the late

1930s, the BBC had become a familiar point of access to
live sports commentaries, as well as news, eye-witness
reports and features. Running commentary had been gradually improved and techniques standardised, with many,
like Marshall, becoming distinctive household names
alongside those of the sporting heroes they covered.[11]
Ashes Test matches at Lords and the Oval had also been
the first to be televised by the fledgling BBC television
service, albeit limited to a thirty-mile radius from
Alexandra Palace.[12]

Like most sports of the era, the Ashes Series received
much attention from the newsreels covering Hutton's
momentous innings. But, unlike radio, neither newsreels
nor the sporting press could deliver the immediacy effect of
live radio commentary, reconstructed in McNaughton's
film. This shared audience experience around key sporting
occasions, and the role the GPO played in connecting the
BBC coverage to the nation through its miles and miles of
cabling, was clearly the trigger for the GPO Film Unit to
commission McNaughton to direct a film on the sporting

In the 1930s the
GPO and the BBC
were critical to the
delivery of national
sporting events
such as the Derby,
© Royal Mail Group
Ltd. Courtesy of The
British Postal
Museum & Archive

passions of the British. The cricket commentary becomes a lead example of the British
public's appetite for national sporting events delivered from the press box and commentary booth, consumed with relish by its audience.

From the re-enacted communal listening experience of Mrs Hutton, we are invited to
follow the GPO as it sets up the telecommunications infrastructure for the coverage of
the 1938 Isle of Man Tourist Trophy. For historians of motor sport, the 1920s and 30s
are viewed as the 'heyday' or 'golden age' of the Motor-Cycling Tourist Trophy (TT) on
the Isle of Man inaugurated in 1907 by *The Motor Cycle* magazine.[13]

Like many major British sporting occasions of the period, the event received royal
patronage, HRH Prince George attending the Senior race for the first time in 1932.[14]
During this period the event became more popularised in the national press and cinema
newsreels, and as a consequence attracted more crowds, advertising and commercial
interest. McNaughton's film estimates that 50,000 spectators lined the course, and
shows many arriving by sea at Douglas from Liverpool, Belfast and Dublin. Adverts were
strategically placed at the key bends and areas where spectators congregated or film
cameras were positioned. Some of these ads, for brands such as Dunlop and the *News
Chronicle*, are captured in *What's On Today*, and were also prominent in newsreel footage
from the period. The footage provides strong evidence of the commercialisation of sport.

The BBC first broadcast from the TT in 1933. According to Dick Booth, motorcycling
had an increasingly important place in the BBC's outside broadcasts from the early
1930s.[15] Sport brought a ready-made audience to its service and in return its exposure of
sport helped promote and foster a wider national interest. The BBC's principal motor-
cycling commentator, Graham Walker, had been a former champion motorcyclist and
also worked for a number of the leading British manufacturers – Norton, Sunbeam and
Rudge-Whitworth (whose bikes are featured in the film). Walker, who can be heard on
McNaughton's film, argued that the TT helped sustain the British motorcycling industry,

carrying serious benefits for sales. He began commentating for the BBC in 1933 and, as a leading rider of his generation, was knowledgeable and informed of the machines and their riders. More crucially, he had a 'natural and distinctive microphone presence'.[16] As his son, and former BBC motor sports commentator Murray Walker, noted in his autobiography, his father 'made you feel as though you were there, with an infectious enthusiasm overlaid by total knowledge of his subject, and he was the BBC's top man on the sport for 31 years'.[17] It is this sense of actuality, of being there through the commentators' narrative, that the film tries to re-enact. The filmed highlights provide evidence of the accuracy and true sense of excitement Walker conveyed in his commentaries, assisted, as ever, by the dedication of GPO and BBC engineers.

The BBC's senior technician for outside broadcasts was Robert Wood and it was his responsibility to organise the logistics of microphone positions, and liaison with the Post Office for the laying of coaxial cables to sporting venues. This is graphically represented in McNaughton's film as the route of the telecommunications is mapped out to illustrate where the main broadcasting links occur and how a link-up to the Isle of Man was achieved. 'Often the start was delayed by mist and other programmes were disrupted,' recalled former commentator Robert Hudson, 'consequently, it became unpopular with the planners.'[18]

Another concern was the sheer scale of the event. The film reveals some of the contours and terrain of the mountain race, which sprawled and weaved its way across the Manx countryside. As another BBC commentator, John Arlott, notes in the *Oxford Companion to World Sports and Games*:

> Starting at the town of Douglas on the south-east coast, the course takes a wide sweep to the west and north to enter the town of Ramsey on the north-east coast and thence return to the starting point, each lap measuring 37³/4 miles (60.7km) and taking in over 200 bends while climbing from sea level to an altitude of over 1,300ft (396m). This circuit is the epitome of the natural road course, all the roads used being ordinary public highways closed for the racing and practice sessions.[19]

The rough terrain made the technical achievement of coverage all the more astounding, and the dangers involved in laying the lines across the island are captured by McNaughton in a short dramatic episode in which GPO engineers are seen scaling the wall of a quarry with near-tragic consequences. The film captures the way in which the race runs through small villages on the island, past thatched-roof cottages and the thousands that flanked the circuit, a distinguishing feature of this classic race.

The film uses quick edits and fast panning shots to emphasise the speed of the bikes as they pass. The impression of speed reflects the record-breaking speeds of the 1938 race, with Harold Daniell breaking the lap record at 91mph, an achievement that stood for a further twelve years.

The film ends by reflecting on the many great British sporting events and occasions that the collaboration between the GPO and the BBC provides. The film tries to capture the meaning of spectator sport to the British public, which by 1938, was a deeply ingrained aspect of popular cultural life. Although not a remarkable film, McNaughton's story of the Ashes and the Isle of Man TT gives a sense of the joy and shared national experience broadcasting had begun to bring to its audience during this period. Not until television superseded radio as a dominant form of broadcasting in the 1950s would that sense of excitement generated by live coverage be taken to a new level of sound and vision.

'A chance to be most ourselves'

Of all the GPO film-makers, Humphrey Jennings did more than any other director to capture and transform the ways in which the British saw themselves and understood their common values and cultures. As an artist, he had been actively involved with the British surrealists of the early 1930s, and in 1936 was a co-creator of the Mass Observation movement with his friend and journalist Charles Madge. Jennings was fascinated by the impact of industrialisation on the British population. The GPO had initially envisaged a project called *British Workers*, comprised of two films to reflect the working and recreational lives of working-class people, and to be presented at New York's World's Fair. Jennings, a recent employee, set off to the North of England and Wales to film in Manchester, Salford, Bolton, Sheffield and Pontypridd.[20] The intention of the film, eventually titled *Spare Time*, was 'to show the natural gaiety of working people, and the varied expression which it finds'.[21] The film shows the influence of large-scale industry on the leisure pursuits of three centres of industrial Britain – steel, cotton and coal – that provide the backdrop for brief, but perceptive cameos of working-class people indulging in selective popular cultural pastimes and entertainments. The film begins with the narration of poet and film-maker Laurie Lee asking: 'Between work and sleep comes the time we call our own. What do we do with it?'

Although the film does not solely concentrate on sport – it includes the Steel, Peech and Tozer works band, gardening, theatre, dancing, a fairground, a male voice choir and, most famously, a Mancunian 'jazz' marching band – a significant proportion of the film is dedicated to sporting pastimes in the three regions concerned. Around the mills of Sheffield and the Don Valley, where the livelihoods of thousands of families relied on the manufacture of steel at the Phoenix Works, the film shows lurchers being taken for a run on waste ground, racing pigeons being tended to, men playing darts in a working men's club, a professional football match (most likely Sheffield Wednesday at Hillsborough), which is then linked to an advert for a pools coupon that reads, 'All these winners each received £5,129 for 1 penny on the world's largest penny points pool.' We then see men submitting bets or pools coupons.[22]

The leisure lifestyles of the inter-war period are captured in *Spare Time*. Courtesy of BFI

The snippets of sport, combined with images of steel mills and a family enjoying a luxurious-looking pie for their evening meal, help to form a picture of a community of people who share common working practices and leisure lifestyles, all in the shadow of the heavy industry that sustains them. Many sports clubs emerged and blossomed in the inter-war period. A good proportion of them were organised, and indeed sponsored, by local employers, with works teams and sporting facilities springing up all over the country. As well as the

brass band featured in the film, employees of Steel, Peech and Tozer also established a minor football league team, a tennis club and, more unusually, the Phoenix Golf Club, built on an area of scrubland near to the factory in 1932. The Phoenix club provides evidence that working-class men with ingenuity and motivation could transcend established social class barriers associated with middle-class sports. In this context, the Sheffield Phoenix Cycling Club, formed in 1922, is most likely the one featured in Jennings's film. Cycling provided access to the surrounding countryside of urban conurbations and, in newly formed cycling clubs, offered an opportunity for the mixing of different classes and sexes. The film shows two young men in the backyard of a working-class Victorian terrace fixing a wheel to a bike, before cutting to shots of a group of cyclists, both men and women, primly dressed, cycling through the countryside and taking refreshment.

The second industrial area Jennings visited was that of the cotton mills of North West England, around Manchester and Bolton. The documentary focuses on broader leisure and entertainment practices familiar to an emerging concept of the 'weekend', where mill workers had Saturday afternoon and Sunday off. The only sport shown from the region is wrestling. Historically, Lancashire towns like Bolton and Wigan were hotbeds of wrestling culture in Britain and the style of wrestling that emerged became the originator of 'catch as catch can wrestling' that would later influence the style of amateur wrestling now seen at the Olympic Games. In the main, wrestlers came from the coal mines and not the mills as the film intimates, but this particular style of wrestling became very popular across the region, with many miners making an additional income. Of interest in Jennings's film are the shots of the crowd sat at ringside: all well suited and groomed, predominantly but not exclusively male and quite reserved for sports spectators.

The third and final sequence in the film takes us to Wales and the mining region around Pontypridd. Again, Jennings shows us a range of leisure activities, including a fairground, a male voice choir assembling for rehearsal, shopping on the high street and people relaxing with a cup of tea. Martin Johnes points out that the depression in Wales impacted on the more formalised sports clubs during the inter-war period, but the unemployed often turned to indoor games of billiards, snooker and table tennis to pass the time of their 'enforced leisure'.[23] Facilities for sport were therefore crucial and the documentary features sport in two social environments: one formal, the other informal. Sport often took place in working-men's clubs or pubs and the film reveals some of this activity focusing on a group of men crowding around a three-quarter-size snooker table in front of a bar. More formal sports clubs were often channelled through organisations like the YMCA, where community and church halls doubled up as recreational spaces. Jennings's film shows teenage boys playing basketball, a sport that was popularised both before and after the war. Most surprising, perhaps, is the absence of any footage of rugby union in the film, a sport heavily associated with the mining towns of south Wales. We can only assume that Jennings ran out of time or could not get access to rugby during his visit, but given the work–leisure

Jennings's film captures something of Lancashire's wrestling heyday. Courtesy of BFI

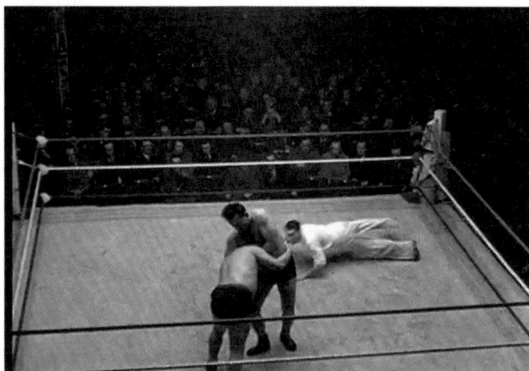

axis of the film, the close ties of the mining community with rugby union is an unexpected omission. Nevertheless, the film provides an excellent example of Jennings's emerging approach to film, less concerned with the narrative realism of Grierson, instead providing an impressionistic and gently moving collage of sport and leisure activities representative of the people and communities he came across on his travels through Britain's industrial heartlands.

Conclusion: the power of sport's visual culture

Sport in film has become an increasingly productive area for sports historians to explore representations of sport and the cultural history of two important features of twentieth-century popular culture. This visual turn in sport history has largely concentrated on fictional film and therefore, quite detrimentally, avoided a whole field of non-fictional film dedicated to sport. There are notable exceptions. Work on early boxing films by Streible emphasises the importance of sport in the promotion of film, but also the usefulness of surviving archives to understand the meaning and practices of boxing in the early part of the twentieth century.[24] The need for early cinema to appropriate sport to boost its appeal is an important indicator of the popularity of spectator sports like boxing, football, rugby and cricket during this period. Most crucially, as Russell has noted, a significant proportion of the early footage of sport in the 'Mitchell and Kenyon' films placed as much emphasis on the crowd as the action on the field of play.[25] Early film represents a broader image of the people and reveals far more of popular pastimes than we see in contemporary coverage of televised sport. This observation is arguably relevant to *What's On Today* and *Spare Time*: both help us to understand the place of sport in late-1930s Britain. In their own ways, both films captured the emotional attachment many people had for sport, as fans and communities – an achievement worthy of acknowledgment and celebration.

Notes

1. V. Toulmin, *Electric Edwardians: The Story of the Mitchell and Kenyon Collection* (London: BFI, 2006).
2. M. Huggins and J. Williams, *Sport and the English, 1918–1939* (London: Routledge, 2005).
3. Ibid., p. 4.
4. M. Huggins, 'And Now, Something for the Ladies: Representations of Women's Sports in Cinema Newsreel, 1918–1939', *Women's History Review* vol. 16 no. 5 (2007), pp. 681–700.
5. S. G. Jones, *Workers At Play: Social and Economic History of Leisure, 1918–1939* (London: Routledge, 1986), pp. 90–1.
6. Ibid., p. 71.
7. C. Cowdrey (1967) 'Len Hutton', in John Arlott (ed.), *Cricket: The Great Ones* (London: Pelham, 1967). p. 144.
8. Ibid.
9. BBC Sport website, 'The Great Innings – Hutton's 364' <news.bbc.co.uk/sport1/hi/cricket/8083859.stm> (accessed 20 March 2010).

10. D. Mosey, *Best Job in the World* (London: Pelham, 1985).

11. R. Haynes, ' "Lobby" and the Formative Years of Radio Sports Commentary, 1932–52', *Sport in History* vol. 29 no. 11 (2009), pp. 25–48.

12. R. Haynes, 'The Early Courtship of Television and Sport: The Case of Cricket, 1938–56', *Journal of Sport History* vol. 36 no. 3 (2009), pp. 415–31.

13. J. Stroud, *Little Book of TT* (London: Green Umbrella, 2007).

14. Ibid., p. 52

15. D. Booth, *Talking of Sport: The Story of Radio Commentary* (London: Sports, 2008).

16. Ibid., p. 84.

17. M. Walker, *Murray Walker: Unless I'm Very Much Mistaken* (Edinburgh: HarperCollins, 2002), p. 6.

18. R. Hudson, *Inside Outside Broadcasts* (Newmarket: R & W, 1993), p. 136.

19. J. Arlott, *Oxford Companion to Sports and Games* (Oxford: Oxford University Press, 1975).

20. K. Jackson, *Humphrey Jennings* (London: Picador, 2004), p. 212.

21. From a GPO paper cited in ibid., p. 211.

22. Jackson (ibid.) suggests they are handling postal orders, but a closer inspection suggests they are betting slips, a boom activity during the 1930s.

23. M. Johnes, *A History of Sport in Wales* (Cardiff: University of Wales Press, 2005).

24. D. Streible, *Fight Pictures: A History of Boxing and Early Cinema* (Los Angeles: University of California Press, 2008).

25. D. Russell, 'The Football Films', in V. Toulmin, S. Popple and P. Russell (eds), *The Lost World of Mitchell and Kenyon: Edwardian Britain on Film* (London: BFI, 2004).

20 / *THE SILENT VILLAGE*
The GPO Film Unit Goes to War

Wendy Webster

In a 1954 essay, Lindsay Anderson wrote: 'It might reasonably be contended that Humphrey Jennings is the only real poet the British cinema has yet produced.'[1] Many subsequent writers have endorsed Anderson's view that a hallmark of Jennings's work was its 'poetic style'. His verdict that Jennings's best work was produced during World War II is also widely shared, with considerable agreement on which wartime films were his finest – *Listen to Britain* (1942) and *Fires Were Started* (1943) feature in most lists, including Anderson's. Within this literature *The Silent Village* (1943) is rarely discussed at any length. Those who offer brief mentions of the film reach different views. Anderson himself was not a fan: 'For all the fond simplicity with which he sets the scene, the necessary sense of conflict and suffering is missed in his over-refined, under-dramatised treatment of the essential situation.'[2] Angus Calder, on the other hand, calls the film 'a neglected masterpiece'.[3]

The first inter-title in *The Silent Village* informs the audience: 'The village of Lidice in Czechoslovakia was a village of miners. This film in their honour was made in a similar Welsh mining community – the village of Cwmgiedd.' One reason for neglect of the film may be the doubleness involved in transposing Lidice onto Cwmgiedd and casting Welsh villagers, in Jennings's formulation, to 'play themselves and themselves as the people of Lidice'.[4] This doubleness means that *The Silent Village* is not usually included in discussions of the 'people's war': an image and narrative which has attracted a great deal of attention. It also means that the film does not fit readily into discussions of the GPO Film Unit (renamed the Crown Film Unit [CFU] in 1940) or Jennings's work. Other film units made the bulk of documentaries about wartime Allies, including those from occupied Europe, while CFU wartime documentaries focused on the British war effort, both armed services and home front. A film depicting events in a Czechoslovakian village was, therefore, something of a departure from normal CFU fare. For Jennings, the film's geographical and national references to Wales as well as Czechoslovakia were a particular departure. Jennings made a range of home-front films which paid tribute to civilians, including those working in the fire and ambulance services, and in factories, mines, transport and on farms. But despite considerable effort in wartime propaganda to show unity across the differences of British national identity by incorporating Scotland and

Wales (though rarely Northern Ireland), Jennings's films characteristically celebrated Englishness.

This chapter takes the doubleness of *The Silent Village* as its focus. What did it mean for the treatment of place, language and sound? What was the significance of its transnational themes within what I call here a wartime 'culture of tribute'? In addressing these questions, the chapter argues that through a merger of a 'people's war' in Britain and 'people's resistance' in continental Europe, *The Silent Village* goes beyond the national, linguistic and political references of most wartime documentaries and deserves more attention in literatures on the British documentary film movement, Humphrey Jennings's films and the history of British wartime propaganda.

The Silent Village was inspired by Viktor Fischl, a Jewish Czechoslovakian exile in Britain who worked for the Czechoslovakian government in exile. Fischl wrote to the CFU, sending a synopsis for a film about events in the Czechoslovakian village of Lidice in June 1942. The village had been destroyed because its population stood accused of involvement in the assassination of Reinhard Heydrich – second-in-command of the SS. All the men of the village had been shot, the women and children deported and the village razed. Fischl's synopsis began: 'This is the small village of Lidice somewhere in Czechoslovakia. And this is the village of X in Wales. It is not so long ago since these two villages were exactly like one another.' At the CFU, Jennings thought this 'one of the most brilliant ideas for a film that we'd ever come across'.[5]

'Crown' was a renaming of the GPO Film Unit: in 1940 Ian Dalrymple, who managed it, considered this more appropriate for a Unit that had been transferred to the Films

Division of the Ministry of Information and was engaged in making official wartime propaganda.[6] The Ministry of Information had presided over the development of an image of a 'people's war' and sanctioned the making of *The Silent Village* almost immediately as it was proposed. The proposal fitted a 'culture of tribute' in wartime Britain that was increasingly developed from 1941: one that honoured every conceivable anti-Nazi activity, group and nation. Radio programmes were a significant part of this culture in series like *They Shall Rise Again* and *Salute To*, both broadcast in 1942. Sometimes doubts were raised about the appropriateness of a particular tribute: the BBC reported that the Foreign Office was not keen on saluting Mexico – 'their point is that Mexico is doing nothing much in the war' – but the programme went out all the same.[7] Tributes to resistance in occupied Europe featured prominently in this culture. But they characteristically portrayed a conservative continent with emphasis on history, heritage and freedoms enjoyed before Nazi occupation and the awaited liberation was an event that would restore past freedoms rather than producing any new order.

Occupied Europe was also a concern of exile and émigré film-makers in Britain. Jiri Weiss who, like Fischl, was a Jewish Czechoslovakian exile in Britain, addressed the documentary movement in late 1941 in *Documentary Newsletter*, advocating propaganda that showed not only the face of Britain but also 'the face of Poland, of Holland, of Czechoslovakia'. Specifically, he advocated an image that did not focus on 'notables' like Queen Wilhelmina of the Netherlands and King George of Greece, but on ordinary people 'over there, at home, facing the terror of the enemy'.[8] The GPO Film Unit's interest in showing ordinary people on film had been extended in imagery of the British war effort as a 'people's war'. Weiss argued for British production of a similar image of occupied Europe. He does not call it a 'people's resistance', but this is an appropriate term, suggesting its close correspondence to the 'people's war'.[9]

By 1942, what Weiss had advocated was becoming prominent on British screens in a prolific cycle of feature films, often popular at box offices, which showed resistance across a wide range of European countries – Belgium, Czechoslovakia, Denmark, France, the Netherlands, Norway, Yugoslavia – focusing on ordinary people. In addition, a substantial number of documentaries paid tribute to exiled armed forces continuing the fight, including Belgians, Czechoslovakians, French and Poles.[10] In 1945 Weiss directed a documentary on this theme, *Night and Day*, which showed one of the crews of a Czech squadron working for Coastal Command – a different angle on the picture painted by the CFU's earlier *Coastal Command* (1942).

In showing ordinary people in *The Silent Village*, Jennings adopts techniques developed by the GPO Film Unit before the war and familiar from some of Jennings's previous films. There is no use of professional actors and no use of a voiceover to anchor the meaning of images and distract attention from Welsh working-class sound. But Jennings departs significantly from Fischl's synopsis for a film that would contrast a Welsh mining village with Lidice and its terrible fate as well as from Weiss's advocacy of showing the people of occupied Europe 'over there'. When Weiss directed *Before the Raid* (1943) – a film of the same length as *The Silent Village* and the only other substantial CFU film about European resistance – he could not film it on location and established a Norwegian fishing village through images of nets, wharves and fishing boats. For obvious reasons, location shooting was impossible for all films set in occupied Europe. *The Silent Village* is unique among these in acknowledging and naming its British location.

The Silent Village begins by establishing the close and harmonious life of Cwmgiedd/Lidice before Nazi invasion and occupation. Imagery of miners and mine work was familiar from pre-war GPO documentaries – notably *Coal Face* (1935), which celebrated their heroic labour – as well as from Jennings's GPO and CFU wartime films, which incorporated imagery of mines and miners alongside other home-front workers.[11] But *Coal Face* had focused on the coal industry and was not concerned with the community or domestic life of miners, only with their work. The nearest it gets to interest in the life of pit villages is a shot of a miner walking past a washing line. *The Silent Village* shows the life of miners as one of community: showering together at the end of a shift, discussing increasing rates of silicosis at a trade union meeting. From the outset, the mine and its work are also part of a wider community encompassed by shots of chapel, shop, school, cinema, pub and domestic interiors.

This close and harmonious life finds different expression with the arrival of Nazis: unity against them by all villagers, regardless of occupation, age or gender. Working-class men are the main organisers of resistance: the trade union takes strike action, miners take to the hills and organise guerrilla resistance from a ruined castle, their blackened faces serve as camouflage as they lay explosives in the mine. The role of women is limited, but the female schoolteacher's involvement in producing an underground newspaper which calls for sabotage is shown. Alberto Cavalcanti, formerly a colleague of Jennings at the GPO Film Unit, had imagined the invasion of an English village by Germans masquerading as British soldiers in *Went the Day Well?* (1942), but his portrayal of the resistance of English villagers was obviously fictional. Through its Cwmgiedd/Lidice setting, *The Silent Village* not only shows the fate of Lidice, but also imagines the invasion of a Welsh village and, through its elision of Welsh and Czechoslovakian, credits Welsh villagers with the courage shown by those in Lidice.

In a BBC broadcast, Jennings told listeners that *The Silent Village* portrayed 'the clash of two types of culture', what he called 'this new-fangled, loudspeaker, blaring culture invented by Dr Goebbels' against 'the ancient, Welsh, liberty-loving culture which has been going on in those valleys way, way back into the days of King Arthur'.[12] The comment suggests the extent to which 'Welsh', not 'Czechoslovakian', takes a central place in the portrayal of resistance. Attention to Wales was also characteristic of publicity for the film which, like Jennings's BBC broadcast, told the story of its production, so focusing on Wales. A three-page spread in *Picture Post* featured stills from the film alongside 'real-life' photographs of 'village children' and 'an ordinary village crowd', and included several photographs of villagers setting out to see themselves in the film which was premiered at Cwmgiedd Welfare Hall. The article approved of this location rather than a 'magnificent London cinema': 'it was right that they should be the first to see it. It was their film.'[13] Through such publicity, *The Silent Village* became a story about Wales as much as Czechoslovakia.

Sound is particularly important to the film's celebration of Welshness. In contrast to German 'blaring', the village and its resistance resonates with the harmonies of traditional community, patriotism and Christianity. The portrait of close community in the first section of the film is conveyed as much by sound as imagery: hymn-singing in the chapel in Welsh, male voice choirs on the soundtrack also singing in Welsh, school children reciting lessons in Welsh, laughter in the cinema. In the second section sound and image come together against a common enemy. Music with a Welsh harp plays over

images of guerrilla fighters meeting at the castle. A male voice choir sings the traditional Welsh folk song 'All Through the Night' over images of men setting explosives in the mine. There is prolonged silence on the soundtrack after the radio pronouncement of a death sentence on the villagers over images of their vigil through the night. As the camera shows dawn breaking, the silence is broken by the sound of men singing the Welsh national anthem in a final act of defiance as they await execution in front of the chapel and its cemetery. They continue to sing as they watch the women and children of the village being marched away and the commands for execution are given. Their singing ceases only with the sound of German gun fire.

GPO documentaries had made experimental use of sound, and Jennings's own interest in sound-portraits of everyday life was particularly apparent in *Listen to Britain*, his home-front film. It includes snatches of foreign languages over shots of radio equipment that show the work of the BBC Overseas Service, but otherwise its 'people's war' is an English-speaking enterprise. *The Silent Village* is exceptional in introducing linguistic diversity into a sound-portrait of Britain. Wartime awareness of the need to show unity across differences of national identity within Britishness meant that Scottish and Welsh

The use of school children's voices is just one example of the film's evocative use of sound (*The Silent Village*). Courtesy of BFI Stills, Posters and Designs

characters were often heard in wartime films, but they speak English, albeit with accents that indicate their non-Englishness. Britishness is presented as a monolingual culture. Resistance in continental Europe was also characteristically heard as English-speaking, its languages recast as English. In *The Adventures of Tartu* (1943), a feature film set in occupied Czechoslovakia which came out in the same year as *The Silent Village*, Glynis Johns provides a Welsh accent for her role as a Czech resister, but she speaks in English, while other Czech resisters speak English in received pronunciation (RP).

The *Monthly Film Bulletin* review of *The Silent Village* spoke of the Welsh language as 'relatively unknown' but judged that its use enhanced the strength of the pictures.[14] Jennings did not expect the audience to understand it, and thought that recording so much of the film in Welsh might even 'to a certain extent ... suggest that it is Czech'.[15] His use of Welsh nevertheless disrupted the dominance of English in a 'people's war' and 'people's resistance', celebrating Welsh as the language of community and resistance. Welsh speaking is also made a significant issue within the film when the first words the schoolteacher speaks in English announce a German order banning Welsh speaking in schools. This offers a veiled reference to English attempts to suppress Welsh and one of the schoolteacher's lessons is on 'the conquest of Wales'. But the film focuses on the clash between German and Welsh/Czechoslovakian culture, not the clash between English and Welsh. Since Lidice is transposed onto Cwmgiedd, the suppression of Welsh language and culture equally stands for the German suppression of Czechoslovakian.

Against Welsh sound as traditional, melodious, Christian and patriotic, German sound is rasping and oppressive. The 'coming of fascism', first announced in an inter-title, is registered in the film by jarring sound – martial music blaring from a loud-speaker van followed by a German order: 'Achtung! Achtung!' Jennings explained in his broadcast: 'We proposed not to show any Germans ... the main feeling of oppression, the existence of the invisible Germans is carried in the film by a German speaker, sometimes he's speaking on a loudspeaker, sometimes on radio sets, and so on – one voice.'[16] Michael Powell and Emeric Pressburger treated German sound similarly in their feature film on downed British airmen in Holland – *One of Our Aircraft is Missing* (1942). Powell later attributed to Pressburger the decision to 'hear Germans everywhere, but only to see them in the distance, if at all'.[17] In *One of Our Aircraft*, the unseen enemy means that the source of German sound is rarely identified visually, but in *The Silent Village* a recurrent image shows loudspeakers and radios as its source, contrasting with the visual imagery of those listening: the community of villagers united in resistance.

In *Listen to Britain*, shots of radio equipment in the sequence on the BBC Overseas Service evoked the role of modern sound technology in the British war effort. In contrast, in *The Silent Village*, disembodied speech by Germans that emerges from sound technology suggests a barbarism of modernity. For much of the time, this speech is in English inter-spersed with occasional German words and phrases, its Germanness established mainly by a guttural German accent. It remains disembodied in the sequences that show the final fate of Lidice but is in German. During production, a request went out for translation to establish the correct German terms for the words of command for a military execution – 'Halt! Attention! Present arms! Lower arms! Load! Take aim! Fire!' It explained that: 'our actual intention in the film is to have the orders spoken in German and accompanied by the sound, only, of what each order would involve'.[18] Following these commands and then the sound of gun fire, the radio announcement of the destruction of the village is also in

German, accompanied by Wagner, over shots of the ruins of the village, still burning. Translation is then provided through an inter-title which is in gothic script, emphasising the Germanness of such action. But if the film involved translation, it also presented a repertoire of brutal and oppressive sound, so tainted that it has no English or Welsh equivalent; so foreign that it is, in effect, untranslatable.

In his BBC broadcast, Jennings noted that what had been done in *The Silent Village* was 'through the help of anti-Nazi refugees in this country who know the mentality of the Nazis and the mentality of Nazi propaganda'. *Cinegram*, a wartime film magazine, produced an edition on the film with a foreword by Jan Masaryk, the Foreign Minister of the Czechoslovakian government in London, which noted that not all of the men of Lidice had died: two were serving in the Czechoslovakian forces in exile, and one of these was married to a Welsh woman.[19] Such transnational themes were not extended to the dissemination of the film which had overseas distribution but could not be shown in occupied Europe. Favourable reviews of *The Silent Village* demonstrate how far Jennings's use of government-sponsored propoganda to make a film celebrating international working-class solidarity was uncontentious. *The Times* commented that 'this imaginative record is one of the most powerful exercises in intelligent propaganda yet witnessed on the screen'.[20] *Monthly Film Bulletin* said: 'By reconstituting in simple and homely fashion the known in terms of the unknown it conveys more clearly than film has done before the full tragedy of Nazi occupation.'[21] *Documentary Newsletter* struck a sour note, commenting that its 'strangely oblique approach robs the film of any direct impact', but this was characteristic of its reviews of Jennings's wartime films.[22]

Cinegram told the history of Cwmgiedd strikes in 1911, 1922 and 1926, and of the miners' 'bitter blazing hatred for the owning companies', commenting that all the miners of Cwmgiedd 'know more about the Soviets than they know about Surrey'.[23] But the film stops short of mentioning that many miners in the area were communist. After the Soviet Union entered the war in 1941, the Ministry of Information orchestrated British propaganda that offered praise for the virtues of the Russian people, while managing to avoid references to communism. Despite the prominence of communists in resistance movements, resistance films followed the same model.[24] *The Silent Village* is no exception. Strikes and sabotage were scarcely activities that would have earned wartime tributes for British miners, but the strike in the film is directed against German fascism and there is no mention of communism or action against domestic capitalism. Even so, *The Silent Village* ends with a celebration of international working-class solidarity when the villagers of Cwmgiedd who have been playing the villagers of Lidice begin to play themselves and pay tribute to the courage of the villagers of Lidice. The final section of the film is dominated by the voice of D. D. Evans, speaking in English to fellow trade unionists at a meeting. He tells them: 'The Nazis were wrong. The name of Lidice has not been obliterated. The name of Lidice has been immortalised. It will live in the hearts of miners the world over.'

Reviews demonstrate how far Jennings's use of government-sponsored propaganda to make a film celebrating international working-class solidarity was uncontentious. D. D. Evans's speech at the end of the film nevertheless departs significantly from the vision of nation offered by the 'people's war' which emphasised the British war effort and unity between British people across differences of class, gender, age and region. It also offers a different 'people's resistance' from the common celebration of the continent as a place of heritage and tradition. The 'we' he invokes unites the working classes everywhere. In its

The Silent Village speaks to international working-class solidarity as well as national unity. Courtesy of BFI Stills, Posters and Designs

focus on working-class unity that crosses national boundaries and on tribute and counter-tribute between working-class communities, the film shows the international solidarity of the industrial working classes standing for decency, humanity and civilisation in opposition to Nazism. In celebrating a predominantly Welsh-speaking and working-class community and its solidarity with working-class communities the world over, it attributes to them, in D. D. Evans's words, 'the power, knowledge and understanding to hasten the coming of victory – to liberate oppressed humanity, to make sure there are no more Lidices. And then the men of Lidice will not have died in vain.'

Notes

I would like to thank the Humanities Research Centre, RSHA at Australian National University, for the award of a Visiting Fellowship in 2010. I researched and wrote this chapter there. Thanks are also due to the Leverhulme Trust for the award of a Fellowship in 2007–9 for my project on Englishness and Europe. The research I did on the resistance narrative during this Fellowship provides the context for this chapter.

1. 'Only Connect: Some Aspects of the Work of Humphrey Jennings', in Kevin MacDonald and Mark Cousins (eds), *Imaging Reality: The Faber Book of the Documentary* (London: Faber & Faber, 1996), p. 153. The essay was originally published in 1954.

2. Ibid., p. 159.

3. Angus Calder, *The Myth of the Blitz* (London: Jonathan Cape, 1991), p. 260.

4. Humphrey Jennings, 'The Silent Village', BBC radio broadcast, Home Service, 26 May 1943, in Kevin Jackson (ed.), *The Humphrey Jennings Film Reader* (Manchester: Carcanet Press, 1993), p. 72.

5. Ibid., p. 67.

6. Ian Dalrymple, 'The Crown Film Unit, 1940–43', in Nicholas Pronay and D. W. Spring (eds), *Propaganda, Politics and Film, 1918–45* (Basingstoke: Macmillan, 1982), p. 213.

7. Memorandum from Assistant Director, Features, 21 July 1942, BBC, Written Archives Centre, R/19/1076/1. Salute to Mexico was broadcast on 26 July 1942.

8. Jiri Weiss, 'An Allied Film Unit', *Documentary Newsletter* vol. 2 no. 1 (December 1941), p. 233.

9. Wendy Webster, '"Europe Against the Germans" : The British Resistance Narrative, 1940–50', *Journal of British Studies* vol. 48 (October 2009), pp. 958–82.

10. For a listing of these films see Frances Thorpe and Nicholas Pronay, with Clive Coultass, *British Official Films in the Second World War: A Descriptive Catalogue* (Oxford: Clio Press, 1980).

11. See, for example, *Listen to Britain* (1942) and *Diary for Timothy* (1945).

12. Jennings, 'The Silent Village', p. 75.

13. 'A Welsh Village Makes a Film in Honour of Czech Lidice', *Picture Post*, 3 July 1943.

14. *Monthly Film Bulletin* vol. 10 no. 114, June 1943, p. 61.

15. Jennings, 'The Silent Village', p. 73.

16. Ibid., pp. 72–4.

17. Quoted in Robert Murphy, *British Cinema and the Second World War* (London: Continuum, 2000), p. 143.

18. National Archives, INF 5/90

19. Noel Joseph, '*The Silent Village*: A Story of Wales and Lidice', *Cinegram Review* no. 14 (London: Pilot Press, 1943), p. 3.

20. *The Times*, 10 June 1943.

21. *Monthly Film Bulletin* vol. 10 no. 114, June 1943, p. 61.

22. *Documentary Newsletter* vol. 14 no. 5 (1943), p. 216.

23. Joseph, '*The Silent Village*', p. 16.

24. For propaganda about the Soviet Union, see Ian McLaine, *Ministry of Morale: Home Front Morale and the Ministry of Information in World War II* (London: George Allen and Unwin, 1979), pp. 197–208.

21 / VISUALISING THE WORLD

The British Documentary at UNESCO[1]

Zoë Druick

On 23 August 1953, American film writer Arthur Knight, currently serving as a programmer for the Ford-sponsored TV show *Omnibus*, penned an enthusiastic personal letter to Paul Rotha and Basil Wright commending their recently released film, *World Without End*. 'Unquestionably,' he wrote, 'it is the most important, most exciting documentary of all the postwar era. Never before has the work of the United Nations and its agencies been made to seem so urgent and important.'[2] The most significant production of the United Nations Film Board, *World Without End*, a fifty-three-minute black-and-white film with a score by Elizabeth Lutyens and script by Rex Warner, explores the role of international aid in Mexico and Thailand and promotes the United Nations and its agencies as disinterested purveyors of modernisation and social change. The film's non-theatrical objectives were ambitious. It was made to screen in high schools, but was also shown internationally at film festivals such as Edinburgh, Heidelberg and Auckland and broadcast internationally, as Knight's letter implies, on the BBC and ABC. If Paul Rotha's own reports are to be believed, the film had the largest distribution of any documentary in the decade after 1945 and was seen by 'many, many millions' in eight different language versions.[3]

The provenance and production of *World Without End*, as well as its distribution and reception, have much to relate about the trajectory of western state-funded documentary in the 1950s. In hindsight we can infer that *World Without End* marks the end of a quarter-century British experiment with film for public information that began at the Empire Marketing Board, matured at the GPO Film Unit and then expanded onto a global canvas. Not only was it to be one of Paul Rotha's last films before he traded his director's chair for new challenges (and one of Wright's last) but it represented the application – and possibly the watering down – of ideas about internationalism formulated in the 1930s and 40s.[4] In what follows, I consider the making of *World Without End* as a pivotal moment for a set of ideas about film and politics embodied by the film-makers Basil Wright and Paul Rotha.

Without doubt, UNESCO owed a debt to the British vision of film-making. John Grierson himself was the first director of the Mass Communication division at UNESCO (4 February 1947 to 30 April 1948). In his wake, film-makers Arthur Elton, Paul Rotha and Basil Wright were involved on an ongoing basis with UNESCO until the late 1960s. Rotha and Wright's film production company, International Realist, was formed in order to field contracts from the UN when Grierson first took up the post.[5] Rotha and Wright also sat on a number of UNESCO committees and made conference presentations on UNESCO's film work at the Edinburgh Film Festival, among other places.[6] As late as 1967, Wright penned a UNESCO mission report on the development of a Ugandan film unit.

For the film-makers, this film was part of a trajectory of sponsored work about global issues. From the melancholic Orientalism and sophisticated contrapuntal sound of his best-known film, *The Song of Ceylon* (1934), Wright was a strong supporter of what he called development media.[7] Rotha, one of the documentary film movement's most energetic chroniclers, made a series of 'world'-themed films, first for the British Ministry of Information during the war with *World of Plenty* (1943), followed afterwards by *The World is Rich* (1947) and ending with the production of the BBC television series *The World is Ours* (1954).[8] *World Without End* clearly fits into the trajectory traced by Rotha from wartime British documentaries to international development. As Jack Ellis has put it, '*World Without End* … was the last big brave representation of internationalism from the old Griersonians.'[9] But how similar were the earlier films with this UNESCO film? I begin by examining the film's connection to Rotha's work for the British state. In the sections that follow I examine the conflicting messages about development and the global village encapsulated by *World Without End*. I conclude with some reflections on the influence of the emergence of television on the technological internationalism of the global film genre, of which *World Without End* is a particularly good example.

World Without End marked a watershed in the British documentary movement's thinking. Courtesy of BFI

World of Plenty and The World is Rich

World Without End merits comparison with two earlier films by Rotha, *World of Plenty* and *The World is Rich*, an exercise that highlights both continuity and difference in the transition from national to international sponsorship. Both *World of Plenty* and *The World is Rich* utilise a combination of maps of the world, stock footage of current events, project-specific re-enactments and footage of speeches by world leaders to situate a crisis in food as a failure of distribution and planning. Using elegantly designed Isotype charts, the films show that food production and consumption could be organised in a far more fair and equitable way. Both films highlight the uneven distribution of resources that prevail in times of crisis, depression and war, and the inevitabilities of the black market and other forms of criminality that such inequities produce. While *World of Plenty* focuses on abuses of the food market during the depression and calls for a new 'world strategy' of food, *The World is Rich* takes this idea one step further, connecting the goal of equitable distribution with UN agencies such as the Food and Agriculture

John Boyd Orr, Scottish nutritional scientist and inaugural director-general of the UN Food and Agricultural organisation. Courtesy of BFI

Organisation (FAO) and the United Nations Relief and Rehabilitation Administration (UNRRA). While *World of Plenty* focuses on the devastation of the natural disasters of flood and drought during the depression era, the dominant disaster in *The World is Rich* is the inhuman violence wrought by war. The dropping of the atomic bomb at Hiroshima is given particular attention and the famine in India that follows, both chronologically and in the film, is represented almost as a cosmic retribution for such an unthinkably violent act.

John Orr, whose inter-war research had been heavily backed by the Empire Marketing Board, provides a commanding presence in both films. In *World of Plenty* he appears as a concerned scientist and public official, often shot directly addressing the camera in close-up with ideas about the new science of nutrition (vitamins!) and the eugenic improvement of the British population even on wartime rations. He appears again in *The World is Rich*, this time as the knighted inaugural director-general of FAO. Orr plays a particularly significant role when, after the end credits have been displayed, he interrupts the film to say that, although it may be the end of the film, it is just the beginning of a great world plan for food.

World of Plenty uses two dominant narrators, one English, one American, to express differences in international attitude towards plans for world food organisation. While the English narrator presents the situation of world food production and distribution, the American constantly interrupts and asks for plainer speech. 'Can't you stop using fancy words?' he implores. 'I'm all confused now.' The two voices, and the relationship between them, which travels over the course of the film from tentative to strongly committed, uses irony to connect the viewer to the film's message. As in *London Can Take It!* (Humphrey Jennings and Harry Watt, 1940), made for the GPO three years before, the American narrator is deployed to foster credibility for the film's message with an American audience. The film ends with a speech by American vice-president Henry Wallace in which he delivers a message about the century of the common man in which 'there can be no privileged people'.

World of Plenty is formally innovative in the multiplicity of narrators that it uses; indeed the multi-vocal aspect of the film becomes a distinctive structuring device.[10] Beyond the two main voices, there is also an Englishwoman's voiceover heard when maternal and child health is being discussed. This strategy was to be repeated and expanded in *The World is Rich* which uses no less than seven voices, one of the most notable of which is a man with a Caribbean accent who adds an ironic tone to the discussion of the modernisation and mechanisation of farm work in the name of efficiency. Who will find jobs for all those displaced workers, he wonders. Where the earlier film ended with a speech by Wallace, this post-war film features excerpts from a speech by Fiorello Enrico La Guardia, the long-serving mayor of New York, now director-general of UNRRA, before giving the last word to Sir Orr.

Both films hold the unfettered marketplace to account for the ills and injustices of the world and, through cross-cutting and voiceover, draw direct connections between plenty in one location and want in another. In one hard-hitting sequence in *The World is Rich*, for instance, an image of a plump hog is shown before one of a starving person. The narrator makes the link explicit, asserting that it is not too much to say that because a hog was fed in one country, in another someone died.

In both films there is direct reference to their compilation of shots from around the world. In *The World is Rich*, the plain-speaking American narrator invites the American viewer on a 'free trip to London' thanks to the 'synthetic time and space' of the movie in order to investigate conditions there. Similarly, close to the end of *The World is Rich* an American narrator somewhat sarcastically invites the viewer to hop aboard the 'magic carpet' and let the 'genie of the motion picture camera' transport you to an 'earthly paradise' where 'time stands still'. This sequence is used to ridicule those who would not support the modernisation of farming techniques. The accompanying shots highlight the backbreaking and inefficient labour of 'primitive' farming methods. The self-reflexive irony and multiplicity of voices in both films creates an offscreen drama of conflicting viewpoints and compellingly invites the viewer to take a position and judge for him- or herself. There are multiple entry points to the debate; experts take their turn alongside ordinary people. The overriding message is one of the need for rationality in the face of the irrational market and compassion for the needs of ordinary people in a system that is structured to favour the wealthy. The United Nations and its agencies are represented as progressive forces for global justice.[11]

The World is a Village

Made five years after *The World is Rich* and ten after *World of Plenty*, *World Without End* also crafts an international storyline, self-reflexively mediated by the camera in notable ways. As in the earlier films, *World Without End* utilises montages of stock shots to visualise geopolitical issues, such as war and poverty. However, unlike the earlier films, the UNESCO-sponsored film has only one narrator, an Englishman, thereby losing the international multi-vocality characteristic of the earlier work. There is no synchronised discourse in the film, rendering everyone mute; nothing is heard directly from either ordinary people or experts. This places even greater significance on the words written by Rex Warner, a classicist with a penchant for universal platitudes, in place of the political discussion found in the earlier films. The new narrative form manifested in *World Without End* parallels the Cold War emphasis on positive propaganda for peace without the mess of politics, something that might be seen in relation to the folksy image of the global village emerging at the time.

World of Plenty attempted to speak over the national and ideological differences of the age. Courtesy of BFI

The global village concept that came to prominence in the 1950s provided a metaphor for a new experience of time–space compression wrought by emergent technologies of transportation and communication, not to mention warfare. Although the concept is now closely associated with Marshall McLuhan, it was coined by Wyndam Lewis in his

1949 essay, 'A New Kind of Country', published in his collection, *America and Cosmic Man*. Lewis writes, 'now ... the earth has become one big village, with telephones laid on from one end to the other, and air transport, both speedy and safe'.[12] As directed by their producers at UNESCO, in *World Without End* Wright and Rotha took this small world concept and the universal humanist sensibility associated with it and welded it to the work of the UN.

The story of the film's production highlights the important role UNESCO played in combining Wright and Rotha's prior experience and perspectives with this new frame-work. In February 1951, a UN film board meeting with representatives from all the UN agencies determined that a film should be made to reflect the work being done by their constituents. Immediately afterwards, Ross McLean, the head of UNESCO's Films and Visual Information Division, not to mention former Chair of the National Film Board of Canada and another of John Grierson's lieutenants, visited the site of a new fundamen-tal education centre in Patzcuaro, Mexico, sponsored by the Mexican government and the Organisation of American States. The work being done there reflected the agenda of UNESCO to increase literacy and improve techniques pertaining to agriculture and health. Plans were immediately made for film footage to be taken of the centre and its work but no finished film was completed. In the United Nations General Conference of 1951 a resolution was taken to produce a film provisionally titled *The World is a Village*. A year later, McLean was in talks with one of the best-known documentary film-makers in the world, Basil Wright of International Realist, to create a storyline for a film on the topic of 'Living in a World Community' that would use Patzcuaro as one of its locations, as well as another one yet to be determined in South East Asia. As McLean wrote to his superior, 'The film is thus an enlargement of the earlier work done at Patzcuaro, and will supplement it by providing a picture on a larger canvas for a wider audience.'[13]

After much consultation, a storyline was accepted. Along the way, many non-film-makers were involved in the process, including Willard Beatty of the Division of Fundamental and Workers' Education who suggested that the film use a narrator rather than synchronous sound for practical reasons. 'Any good film can have a hundred sound tracks in as many vernaculars and thereby double its usefulness,' he observed. Maurice Liu, secretary of the United Nations Film Board, pressed for the film to deal only with one community, but the film-makers resisted. The film project pushed forward with a budget of £11,000. Wright requested a list of stock shots from the UN library, including close-ups of 'men, women and children of many different nations, colours etc. They should not be doing anything which distracts the audience's eye from their faces. We are interested in what they stand for and not in what they are doing.' Despite an original plan to film in Burma, the plan was changed to Thailand when it was established that the UN agencies had had far more of an impact there. Ross McLean encouraged Rotha to remember that 'warm human touches and a dash of humour always help. We have in all our work at the UN the habit of being too damned ponderous and of forgetting that in spite of the difficulties people have to face up to they still manage to draw a good deal of fun from their lives.'[14]

The working title for the film, until the very final edits, was *The World is a Village* (despite McLean's suggestion to change it to *Neighbourhood*[15]) and an early draft of the script in the UNESCO archives proposes the links between the global village and the UN directly: 'The World Village idea which we call the United Nations is the greatest idea

Man has ever evolved. It is an idea embracing all people everywhere, you and me and these Russians and Chinese and Indians and Africans. Everyone, everywhere.' The point is made exceedingly clear: 'Unless we see the whole world as a kind of village, and try to solve its problems as villagers try to solve their problems between themselves, mankind may well perish.'

Back and forth from Mexico to Thailand

The film utilises a structure suited to its global village theme. Filmed by the two directors simultaneously in the different countries – Wright in Thailand and Rotha in Mexico – it visually links people in developing nations together through the inter-cutting of the two national contexts, but, more to the point of the film, the regional contexts of Latin America and South East Asia, while the narration retains an omniscient (and first-world) point of view.[16] The film opens from the perspective of outer space as we see a spinning globe wreathed in what appears to be cigarette smoke. (An original script idea went further to include a finger stopping the spinning globe at random spots, which the film would then display.) The narrator makes a number of stentorian assertions, 'I am a man myself' and 'we are looking at human beings', which immediately distinguishes the film from Rotha's earlier, more political and playful films (the French title for the film was *Je suis un homme*).

The film's overriding tone is one of ahistorical universalism: problems of health and infrastructure are much the same everywhere, with regional inflections. As Cecile Starr aptly put it in a review published in *Saturday Review*, 'the film leaps like a wild animal from Mexico to Thailand, and back and forth, giving the bewildering impression that people and problems are somewhat alike all round the globe'.[17] There is nothing like the connections between plenty and want made in the 1940s films, largely because the developed world is almost completely absent. Over the course of the film a number of problems relating to health, agriculture and education are exposed and then solved by UN agencies (often with the help of DDT and other herbicidal chemicals). The film ends in a crescendo of positive images. A mobile library bringing 'new ideas and the latest information' to a rural community in Thailand; people in a visual literacy class in Mexico; children learning traditional performance practice in Thailand; shots of temples and statues of Buddha; an elaborately costumed Mexican dance. The children are healed of a disfiguring disease called 'yaws' in Thailand, students trained in fundamental education graduate in Patzcuaro. And suddenly the United Nations headquarters in New York appears for the first time in the film and the village metaphor re-emerges. The narrator says that: 'Now, as the world shrinks, the neighbours are closer together.' Over a montage of children carefully selected to represent different races, the narrator affirms, 'we all live in the same world'. A distressed child's face fades to the globe as ominous music sounds.

Children play an important part in establishing the film's global village tone. Courtesy of BFI

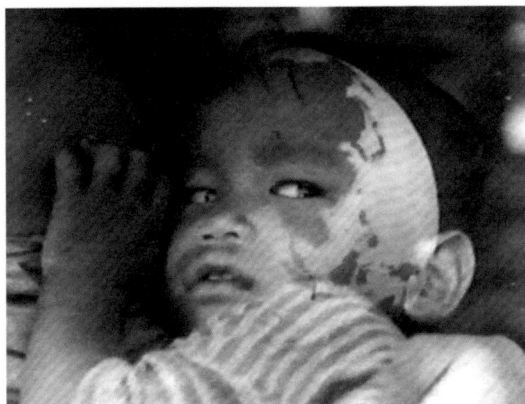

As this brief description shows, the film combines a certain amount of decontextu-alised particularity with vague universalisms. This sense of disconnection to historical time is partly due to issues that emerged during the film's production. During pre-production the Secretary-General of the UN, Trygve Lie, who, it was intended, would be included giving a speech about the United Nations, tendered his resignation. Ensuing negotiation about the value of keeping the film from dating too quickly resulted in the decision not to include any speeches by UN officials or other politicians. In *World of Plenty* and *The World is Rich*, films made before the widespread appearance of television, the sequences depicting world leaders might be said to contribute to the films' value. In its step away from current events, *World Without End* reflects its provenance in a world where leaders could be seen on TV any night of the week.

Technological internationalism

Nevertheless, television is the hidden subtext of this film. Rotha was himself poised to take on the position of Head of Documentaries at BBC Television (1953–5), where he commissioned *The World is Ours*, a series made in collaboration with the UN. In a book he edited in the mid-1950s, *Television in the Making*, he included a chapter by Henry Cassirer, inaugural head of UNESCO's television service. Not only does Cassirer empha-sise that film is the best format on which to transport shows internationally; he also highlights that the offscreen narrator is the 'most feasible and economical way for the adaptation of filmed programmes, provided these do not contain any important lip synch dialogue sequences'.[18] In his view, films made in this style have the greatest poten-tial to take television beyond narrow national frameworks towards international under-standing. Thus, despite being shot on film, the form and content of *World Without End* both indicate that it was made with an eye towards television, where, in the event, it did secure distribution.

World Without End reflects its production by an agency attempting to bring about precisely the kind of technologically mediated internationalism that television in its formative years symbolised. While it purports to show connections between things, in this case the plight of villagers in Thailand and Mexico, the very arbitrariness of the examples' connection (their almost random choice and the original idea of a finger point-ing to a spinning globe) and the invisibility of the western powers except through the UN edifice, and the very prominent use of both narration and music, makes the story tellingly obscure. *World Without End* is very much embedded in the development discourse that characterised post-war western internationalism and represents an encounter between a new global world order and the perspectives – and contradictions – of the British documentary film movement.

In sum, in *World Without End* we see the internationalism of films made by Wright and Rotha and their compatriots in the context of earlier production at the EMB, GPO and MOI connecting to a highly capitalised and technologised form of modernisation, one attempting to substitute progress for politics. Certainly, the modernisation seen in *World Without End* is presented without the distinctive commentaries suffused with complex layers of melancholy and irony found in some of the earlier British-made films. Indeed, it conveys its ideas with an excessive earnestness at times, despite McLean's warning. In part this reflects the shift to secondary students as the imagined audience for non-theatrical cinema in the 1950s and the need for translated voiceover narrations demanded by television. Nevertheless, in its residual commitment to depicting the 'common man' and to making connections between conditions in a world made small by the power of weapons of mass destruction and television alike, *World Without End* is an important document of the twilight of the British documentary film movement.

Notes

1. This research was made possible by a grant from the Social Sciences and Humanities Research Council of Canada. I gratefully acknowledge the assistance of Mahmoud Ghander and Jens Boel of the UNESCO Archives, Paris. My thanks to Cassandra Savage and Laurynas Navidauskas for research assistance.
2. Letter from Arthur Knight to Paul Rotha and Basil Wright, 23 August 1953. Unless otherwise noted, all archival documents referenced in this chapter are from the *World Without End* production file housed at the UNESCO Archives, Paris (ref. #: 341.134.073.533.450.1)
3. Paul Rotha, *Rotha on the Film* (London: Faber & Faber, 1958), p. 98.
4. Elizabeth Sussex gives this account of the fate of International Realist: 'Shortly after [making *World Without End*], Wright was advised by his accountants that International Realist was making so much profit that "the most convenient thing to do would be to go into liquidation before we went into the upper company tax bracket." So International Realist went into voluntary liquidation. "It suited me," says Wright, "because I didn't particularly want to run a company. I was getting tired of running companies."' Elizabeth Sussex, *The Rise and Fall of British Documentary* (Berkeley, CA: University of California Press, 1975), p. 183.
5. Ibid., p. 182.
6. 'New Directions in Documentary', Edinburgh Film Festival International Conference (1951). Wright participated on the panel 'New Horizons', discussing UNESCO's work on using film to raise standards of living and education in underdeveloped countries. Wright and Rotha both participated on the panel 'The Sponsor and the Creative Artist'.
7. Basil Wright, *The Long View* (London: Secker & Warburg, 1974).
8. Jay Leyda, *Films Beget Films* (London: Hill and Wang, 1964), p. 77.
9. Jack C. Ellis, *John Grierson: Life, Contributions, Influence* (Carbondale: Southern Illinois University Press, 2000), p. 286.
10. Timothy Boon, *Films of Fact* (London: Wallflower Press, 2008), p. 129.
11. Perhaps this radical message was what inspired pressure from 'high places' in the United States and the United Kingdom to prevent either film from reaching public screens. Paul Rotha, *Documentary Diary* (London: Secker & Warburg, 1973), p. 284.
12. Wyndham Lewis, *America and Cosmic Man* (Garden City, NY: Doubleday, 1949), p. 21. McLuhan, a friend and admirer of Lewis, later utilised the term in *The Gutenberg Galaxy*, published in 1962 (Toronto: University of Toronto Press). Released a decade earlier, in 1953, *World Without End* is much closer to Edward Steichen's famous *Family of Man* exhibit at MoMA in 1955 than to McLuhan. But all of these sentiments were perhaps most memorably condensed and commodified by the Sherman Brothers in their song 'It's a Small World', written to accompany Disney's exhibit of the same name, which debuted at New York's 1964 World's Fair, later opening permanently at Disneyland in 1966.

13. Ross McLean to William Beatty, 7 August 1952. *World Without End* file, Paul Rotha Papers, University of California, Los Angeles, Department of Special Collections.
14. Ross McLean to Paul Rotha, 18 November 1952. *World Without End* file, Paul Rotha Papers.
15. Ross McLean to Basil Wright, 25 November 1952. *World Without End* file, Paul Rotha Papers. 'I react violently against Ross's idea about "neighbourhood",' wrote Rotha to Wright 15 December 1952. *World Without End* file, Paul Rotha Papers.
16. It is interesting to note that Rotha ordered a copy of his film *The World is Rich* to show to the students and staff at CREFAL (Centro Regional de Educacion Fondamental para la America Latina), the school in Patzcuaro where he was filming. Thomas Baird to Paul Rotha, 13 November 1952. *World Without End* file, Paul Rotha Papers.
17. Cecile Starr, 'One World', *Saturday Review* vol. 13 no. 2 (1954), n.p.; transcription in *World Without End* file, Paul Rotha Papers.
18. Henry Cassirer, 'Will TV Link the World?', in Paul Rotha (ed.), *Television in the Making* (London: Focal Press, 1956), p. 158.

22 / COUNTERPOINTS AND COUNTERPARTS

Film at the Post-war GPO

Patrick Russell

Seven decades after the GPO Film Unit's seven years of film-making were brought to an end, their appeal endures. Few, if any, historians, either of the documentary form or of cinema in Britain, have since felt able to ignore them. Even those intent on demolishing their reputation take them seriously enough to judge the demolition worthwhile.

Equally few ever mention that, following a hiatus during World War II, the GPO resumed its engagement with film – on different terms, it is true, but on a larger scale and over a longer period. To take a contemporary example, the film *Let's Do Business*, made by Take 3 Productions for Post Office Ltd, won Gold in the 'Motivational Training' category of the 2010 awards of the International Visual Communications Association. This is a form of film-making at least as economically vibrant as contemporary 'documentary' and a mode that perhaps more obviously derives from the 1930s GPO Film Unit. But while the forms and functions of today's 'audio and visual communications' ('corporate video' in common parlance) resemble the celebrated work of the Unit, they have inherited nothing of its cultural reputation.[1]

It is a matter of curiosity that the most reflexively despised of today's moving-image forms should be so closely related to 'Britain's greatest contribution to world cinema' of the past, and that the connection is so rarely remarked upon. What bridges the two, in time, is the long period of British documentary production commencing at the end of World War II and declining only with the post-war consensus itself. To this long-overlooked period the post-war film work of the GPO offers fruitful introduction – not least because the iconic status of its pre-war counterpart renders it an automatically interesting point of comparison. What follows is a short account of post-war GPO film-making, a closer look at one of those forgotten films and a few thoughts on their meanings.

A swift survey

At the end of World War II, the Crown Film Unit – formerly the GPO Film Unit – remained in place, but peacetime quickly wrought two key changes upon it. First, Crown's wartime overseer, the Ministry of Information, was replaced in 1946 by the

Central Office of Information (COI). Second, the swathe of independent film units that had grown up to supply the MoI's additional needs now competed against Crown for the COI's business.

Thus, in the post-war period, the GPO's film commissioning was now to be routed through the COI. In these early post-war years the GPO, showing scant interest in its recent past, proved to be one of the more modest official spenders on film. Major reforming departments like the Ministries of Health and Education and the Home Office saw greater call for ambitious film projects. Among state industries and services, the appointment of films officers at the National Coal Board (NCB) and British Transport Commission (BTC), both newly nationalised bodies, were more significant developments for documentary film-making culture.[2]

GPO public relations officers at first concentrated on two areas. Short-form 'fillers' for cinemas, on subjects such as the importance of correct addressing, and the promotion of the greetings telegram service, had clear precedents. Their pre-war counterparts were items like Lotte Reiniger's *The H.P.O.* (1938) or the Len Lye films. Reiniger herself was behind a couple of the post-war examples (*Not Without License* [1949], on the novel topic of TV licences, and *Christmas is Coming* [1951], on the classic subject of posting early for Christmas). These films resembled wartime fillers, not least because of their occasional reliance on celebrity: see *Postman's Nightmare* (1948), another post-early-for-Christmas exhortation, in the form of one of Cyril Fletcher's 'odd odes', or *Pack It Up* (1953), featuring Tommy Cooper. The second strand of GPO film-making was internal films such as *Telephone Cable Plumbing* (1948) and *Safety Precautions at Power Crossings* (1953). This training programme was modest compared to those of the NCB and BTC, though they share an underlying theme: the progressive shift towards mechanisation and automation.

At the end of the 1950s a cautious rethinking of the place of film at the GPO is evident – probably attributable to Toby O'Brien, a forward-thinking public relations officer. While the GPO continued to use films for training, a number of other production programmes opened up. One was a sequence of educational films for secondary schools, often produced in collaboration with the Educational Foundation for Visual Aids. These included titles such as *The Story of the Letter Post* (1961) and a pair of films on the circuitry principles of *Long Distance Telephony* (1965). This initiative constituted both the GPO's own return to the classroom (a site for 16mm projection that had served the 1930s GPO well) and its belated recognition of the educational successes that film sponsors like ICI, Unilever and, to a lesser extent, British Petroleum and the NCB, had been having for several years.

Partly aimed at the same viewership was the targeted recruitment attempted by films like *Two of a Kind* (1964). Another new area was business-to-business communication, as in *Business Connections* (1963) and the bang-up-to-date *Be Telexpert* (1963). Most encouraging to creative film-makers was the GPO's new willingness to embrace – or to re-embrace – the 'prestige' film-making of classy documentaries for general audiences. The most lavish of these was the Oscar-nominated Technicolor featurette *Thirty Million Letters* (1963), produced by British Transport Films, which was clearly conscious of its status as a modern counterpart to *Night Mail* (1936) (BTF, of course, being headed by Edgar Anstey, formerly of Grierson-era EMB and GPO). At least as many were focused on the more *zeitgeist*-y telecommunications side of GPO business, as indicated by prestige titles including *A Sound of Living* (1964) and *Ship to Shore* (1965), directed respectively by Eric Marquis and Sarah Erulkar, two talented members of the overlooked generation of post-war documentarists. An indication of increased GPO spend on film was the quality of the units it was contracting with. Both before and immediately after Crown's 1952 demise, the GPO had worked with stolid, lower-budget production companies like Kinocrat Films, Films of Great Britain, Huntley-Ward Films and Stanley Schofield Productions. By this time, its suppliers were major producers such as World Wide Pictures, the Realist Film Unit, Rayant Pictures and the two most prolific members of the Film Producers Guild: Verity Films and Technical and Scientific Films.[3]

In 1966, O'Brien formalised the GPO's burgeoning screen ambitions by appointing a films officer, bringing it in line with British Transport and the NCB, and cutting out the COI middleman. This position was first occupied by Aubrey Jones, then for many years by Gerry Boarer (an unsuccessful applicant when Jones got the job, Boarer in the meantime made waves in O'Brien's department by commissioning a successful series of TV commercials). Style and wit were evident in communication films of this period, such as Rayant's *Liz and Sally* (1967), aimed at girls of school-leaving age (the eponymous recruits were played by Judy Stevens and Susan George, respectively) and Verity's *What Is Giro?* (1967), selling the advantages of the soon-to-open Girobank to the small-business community. Boarer's most stunning successes, however, were products of his fruitful negotiations first with the Rank Organisation and then with MGM's theatrical distribution arm that created opportunities for cinema release. The key film here is *Picture to Post* (1969), a twenty-three-minute documentary on stamp design made by Erulkar at Rayant, which in terms of commercial cinema distribution is among the most successful British shorts in history. It is also a fascinating post-war complement to pre-war GPO screencraft. Erulkar's imaginative use of photographic and editing effects and her discreet experimentation with Eastmancolor's range of colours and shades feels like a genteel, yet more expansive, counterpart to the youthful vibrancy of Lye. Alongside its sporadic successes with cinema release, the GPO also ran a 16mm library supplying non-theatrical audiences both with these newer films and 'classics' – such still-popular GPO Film Unit titles as *Night Mail* and *North Sea* (1938).

The GPO, to whose earlier history post-war documentary owed so much, thus became its most spectacular late developer. It did so at the point at which sponsored documentary was at its greatest, but most illusory, heights. Audience figures and production standards were arguably at their most impressive at the end of the 1960s, but both began declining in the early 1970s, and fell away increasingly sharply as each year of that gloomy decade wore on.

In 1970, the GPO name was consigned to history, as was its status as a government department. It was now – like the NCB, British Rail and the recently renationalised British Steel – a state corporation. Further, a sharp division was created between its postal and telecommunications arms. The latter became British Telecom, the former was renamed the Post Office. British Telecom now ran its own films programme, which was not particularly

The success of Sarah Erulkar's *Picture to Post* demonstrated the enduring critical and commercial appeal of GPO films. Courtesy of BFI Stills, Posters and Designs

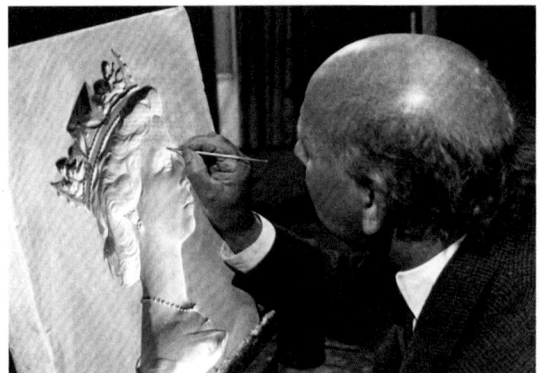

acclaimed. Continuing as the Post Office's films officer, Boarer at first sustained his run of success with hits such as *The Rainbow Verdict* (1971). Soon, however, the scope of the films he was able to produce became ever narrower. Boarer's retirement in 1985 coincided with the increasing prevalence of corporate video production at Royal Mail, BT and elsewhere, as 16mm projectors and the entire school of documentary film-making that had served them since the 1930s were consigned to history.

A brief case study

The film *Counterpoint* (1959), directed by John Krish at Basic Films, sits about halfway through the period just sketched. Its content and context further illuminate the GPO's post-war work – and post-war British documentary in general. The film's internal reception at the GPO placed Toby O'Brien in an uncomfortably conflicted position: personally invested in its success as its direct sponsor but pressurised by office politics to restrict public access to it.[4]

    Counterpoint had originated with O'Brien's 1957 commitment to undertake publicity making better known to the public the sheer complexities of counter work, and more specifically to deepen their understanding of why clerks were often to be found balancing the day's accounts while at the counter (most older post offices had no alternative office space in which they could do so), and why positions were often to be found closed, causing long queues at adjacent counters. O'Brien proposed both a poster and, at the heart of the campaign, a film. Via the COI he contracted Basic Films, then run by Sam Napier-Bell and his business partner Leon Clore, one of the most underrated figures in post-war film culture.[5] Clore was a wealthy but modest Svengali remembered (if at all) for his patronage of Free Cinema and the exiled Joseph Losey. John Krish, among the most gifted of the generation that included talents such as Marquis and Erulkar, was a recent recruit to Basic who, immediately prior to taking on *Counterpoint*, had won great acclaim with *I Want to Go to School* (1959), an absorbing study of a primary school.[6]

    Krish delivered a script which, just like the school film, deployed the timeless 'day-in-the-life' format but which took the form of lightly comic fiction rather than observational documentary. *Counterpoint*'s protagonist, the amiable, slightly wistful, Reg Hooper, begins the film on his way to work, and ends it on his way home. In between he is shown selling stamps and dealing with telegrams, money orders, pensions and various licences, answering customer queries and doing his book-balancing. The members of the public that he encounters represent a cross-section of amusingly exaggerated types (including a businessman in a hurry, an elderly dodderer and a flirtatious young lady). The film is, thus, a sort of jaunty morality play – holding up a mirror to the public while also shining a light for them upon lesser-known parts of other people's work in the interests of mutual understanding. All of which places it squarely in the lineage of the British documentary movement.[7]

    On the big screen 'sponsored film' and 'documentary' were still near-interchangeable terms regardless of whether dramatisation was involved. In 1959, even the budding television documentary had only in recent years moved firmly away (in favour of journalistic or observational forms) from the BBC's early post-war practice of running live, factually based acted drama as a form of 'documentary'. *Counterpoint* is

not merely an entirely scripted film, it is also entirely professionally acted and even includes a dream sequence in which, over his sandwiches, put-upon Reg imagines what it would be like if his customers really appreciated his work. Krish himself had begun his career as a Crown junior and is acutely conscious to this day of having been closer to the Jackson–Watt–Holmes school of GPO/Crown thinking, whereby dramatisation was an acceptable and often a preferable means of working up a 'factual' subject, than to that of Grierson (a figure for whom, in common with much of his generation, Krish had little time).[8] While most wartime subjects had called for serious, even noble treatment, *Counterpoint* typifies what was a frequent post-war tendency to invert the heroic story documentary of the past into a slightly sourer comic idiom. (Richard Massingham, for whom Krish had also briefly worked at the end of the 1940s, is worth citing as an influence here.)

 'Documentary' veracity was built into the production process. Before writing the script, Krish spent a day in a working post office, closely observing everything going on at and behind the counter. GPO officers were seconded to him as advisers on counter procedure and shooting took place over approximately a fortnight at a vacated head post office on the High Street of Crawley, Sussex. The director opined at the time that:

> In spite of the difficulties of shooting on location and the obvious restrictions we all believe that it is best to come here rather than make the film in the artificial atmosphere of the studio. The actors respond to the atmosphere and I hope it will be a realistic picture which makes people think. It is a picture with a message.[9]

Krish recalls phoning the COI some time in 1960, months after completing production, to enquire how the film was doing and being told it was doing nothing. It was sitting on the shelf and there it would stay. This, he was told, was because the Post Master General Reginald Bevins had 'banned' the film, having objected to what he took to be its satirical jibe at himself – that the name of the daydreaming protagonist was Reg. According to Krish, this was a coincidence – shooting had already been completed by the time Bevins was appointed.

Surviving documentation seems neither to confirm, nor to disprove, the explanation of Bevins' motive volunteered by Krish's COI contact. Information in the surviving files is consistent both with Bevins having indeed been affronted by the name (but having probably used other grounds to justify his hostility to the film) and with him having had more objective concerns. What is clear is that Bevins' lack of enthusiasm for *Counterpoint* severely restricted its distribution.

O'Brien arranged a press screening at the COI's theatre for 15 March 1960, during that year's 'Postal Week'. Krish's film premiered alongside another new release, *Machines for Moving Mails* (1959), an internal mechanisation-training film produced by the little-known Marcus Cooper Productions. Bevins introduced the screening; his script, probably written for him by O'Brien, states that

> One job a good film can do perhaps better than any other publicity medium is to help towards better understanding between a commercial organisation and its customers ... We are sending copies of these films to our regions so that Head Postmasters can show them to members of our Local Advisory Committees, to Rotary clubs, Women's Institutes and so on. We will show them to our staffs wherever possible. We shall offer them for television and within a few weeks the Central Film Library will have copies that people can borrow for showing.

This was not to be. Apparently, Bevins himself saw the films for the first time simultaneously with the pressmen to whom he had just introduced them. A hand-written memo of two days later records: 'The PMG has made some criticisms of *Counterpoint* and for the moment at least the film is not being offered for possible showing on TV. The PRO informed Mr Dand, COI, of the situation this morning.' What the criticisms *were* isn't specified, but they put O'Brien in a tricky spot. At every stage (script, rough cut, show copy), he'd wrung *Counterpoint* through the appropriate bureaucracy: approval by the Postal Services Department, by the Taylor Committee (remit: industrial relations) and by the Union of Post Office Workers. The latter were particularly enthusiastic (their long-standing complaints that counter work should be better understood were the principal prompt for the whole campaign). If *Counterpoint* were to be withdrawn even before release, awkward questions would be triggered.

Meanwhile, journalists duly published their reviews. Though confined to the usual specialised periodicals and columns devoted to sponsored film production, they were notably positive.[10] Momentary panic was caused when a quarterly supplement to the Central Film Library's 1960–1 catalogue mistakenly included the still-embargoed film in its listings. The COI, not normally famed for proactive enthusiasms, secured O'Brien's permission for *Counterpoint*'s submission to the International Labour Film Festival in Stockholm, but O'Brien subsequently felt obliged to refuse COI requests for release to the Edinburgh and Florence film festivals. The BBC even chased transmission rights:

under normal circumstances, the summit of any films officer's ambition for a film's distribution.

In an attempt to break the impasse, O'Brien introduced screenings for the Post Office Advisory Council and subsequently the Post Office Joint Production Council. A few reservations were raised, that perhaps echoed the unspecified criticisms earlier made by Bevins. Some judged the film a little undignified, others felt it placed insufficient emphasis on such reforms as counter mechanisation, set to reduce the scale of the problems depicted. (Concern was also expressed that the film could have a counterproductive effect on recruitment: Reg's working day starts at 8.15am and ends at 6.45pm!) Throughout, the revealing counter-argument was that *Counterpoint* was an honest, human *documentary*: a picture (albeit comic) of how things really were, not of how they should ideally be. The balance of the debate was twice in *Counterpoint*'s favour.

Finally, in January 1961, ten months after *Counterpoint* was trade press reviewed, the Post Master General formally agreed the compromise O'Brien had long reconciled himself to: that it could be made available on request, but only if introduced by a GPO official, who would need to emphasise that it was a 'straightforward documentary' in which 'no attempt has been made to idealise the circumstances or the characters' and also that steps were being taken to improve matters. Prints were kept out of the Central Film Library, who were asked to direct all enquiries to the GPO. Distribution must, then, have been extremely limited: possibly only one print was ever made, the one premiered at the COI, which no longer exists. Its negative remained at Humphries Film Laboratories, the industry mainstay at which many millions of feet of film were processed over the post-war decades. Humphries was closed in 1985 and subsequently some 20,000 cans of unclaimed negative and preprint acetate film made their way to the BFI's Berkhamsted vaults: among them, the original mute and sound negs of *Counterpoint*. In 2004, a retrospective of John Krish's documentary work was staged at the National Film Theatre, in preparation for which a new polyester-stock 35mm print was made.

Counterpoint might easily not have survived at all: having done so, its negs, untouched by man or machinery since at least 1961, yielded a new print of exceptional technical quality.

Rainbow verdicts

Several salient facts about British documentary's post-war state can be inferred from the preceding account of 'Carry on *Counterpoint*'[11] and the fate of the GPO's 'late' output in general. These include documentary's continuing relevance as a social tool, the continuing creativity of its practitioners, the adaptation of pre-war and wartime aesthetic forms to post-war conditions, and the fascinating, sometimes uncomfortable, role played by officials directly responsible for a film's sponsorship in mediating filmic imaginations and edgy internal politics.

It is easy enough to see how such facts might be invoked to justify the exclusion of such films from the avant-garde canons of aesthetic appreciation, but they do not justify their long-standing exclusion from the *history* of documentary as an industrial and cultural practice. Even had it received the distribution originally hoped for it,

Counterpoint is unlikely to have been registered by cultural history. Films like *Thirty Million Letters* evidently had wider contemporary reach than many 1930s classics had had in their day, but it could not rescue them from a critical fate justified more by subjective assumption than by objective reasoning. The post-war film intelligentsia having married nineteenth-century romanticism to late twentieth-century cynicism, films as short and sweet as *Counterpoint* were rubbished as an irrelevance. Today, the suspicion with which the motives of institutions acting as patrons of culture or media are regarded is all but universal. We assume their motives are cynical, and thus the cynicism is ours as much as theirs.

Notes

1. The International Visual Communications Association (IVCA), <www.ivca.org>, currently headed by Marco Forgione originated in North America but is today a London-based organisation. It developed a UK base in the 1980s, eventually absorbing and overtaking the functions of the British Industrial and Scientific Films Association whose links to the documentary movement, particularly through such figures as Anstey and Elton, were entrenched. The IVCA's promotional showreel, at the time of writing, includes brief clips from some GPO Film Unit productions, indicating that the sector's awareness of its heritage is as least as sophisticated as that of the TV and independent documentary communities.

2. An important related fact is that these two newly nationalised bodies became two of Europe's largest employers overnight. The GPO had headed the list of large-scale UK employers of the inter-war period.

3. The GPO engaged Realist's services for *The Importance of Being ERNIE* (1964), about the famous Premium Bond selection method. Realist was, at the time, overseen by J. B. Holmes, who, back in the day, had briefly been in charge of the GPO Film Unit. *ERNIE* was not the only pre-war connection to be found in the GPO's output of the period. Another is the deployment of Fred Gamage as photographer of several pictures made for the GPO by Verity Films.

4. The present account of *Counterpoint*'s history is derived from the recollections of John Krish; from trade press; and from paper records contained in the Postal Museum and Archive files POST 122/448 and POST 122/996, from which all unattributed quotations in this chapter are taken.

5. The GPO would twice re-engage Basic on significant projects. *In Touch With the World* (1964) exemplifies the 'general survey' documentary to which almost all 'major' sponsors sporadically turned. This nationwide snapshot of GPO work (from night-shift letter sorting and morning deliveries, through telephone operating and troubleshooting) was directed, in largely televisual style, by John Fletcher, best known for his fine sound recording on many of the Free Cinema films produced by Clore. *Over the Counter* (1968) is an exercise in futurology, alternatively titled *The Post Office in 1997*; it was directed by Napier-Bell, who by now had broken away from Clore to run Basic Films solo (and less successfully).

6. *A Day in the Life* is, incidentally, the title of a 2010 theatrical and DVD release of an anthology of Krish's best short films, many of which deployed the 'day-in-the-life' structure. This release (along with releases such as the DVD boxed-set *Shadows of Progress*) saw Krish's previously neglected career secure belated acclaim, including the *Evening Standard* Award for Best Documentary release for 2010. These immensely satisfying developments occurred between

the drafting of the present chapter and its printing, and make for a fascinating case study of how, in the twenty-first century, many canons of twentieth-century film-making are sure to expand.

7. In the 1930s, encouraging the public to use postal services efficiently was a publicity goal, as indicated, for instance, by Stephen Tallents' 1934 invitation to one artist to design a satirical poster: 'Instead of merely commanding them to post early, we will show how ridiculous they look, and what inconveniences they suffer, when they post late … From time to time our Post Office walls shall be a mirror of the public's folly. This should amuse the public and delight our staff, who cannot individually answer back our more tiresome customers.'

   My thanks to Scott Anthony for drawing my attention to this quotation, strongly resonant with the aims and methods of *Counterpoint*. Scott informs me that, though the poster was never officially issued, the artist's design, like many of the compositions in *Counterpoint*, makes great play of the contrast between the spaces on either side of the great divide between clerk and customer.

8. Introducing the film in 2004, Krish advised his National Film Theatre audience: 'Aircrew, Merchant Seamen, Firemen, brave people who were acting scripted scenes, often looked ill at ease with dialogue. I was 17 then, earning a pound a week. I asked Jack Lee why nobody used actors and was instantly trodden underfoot. I didn't ask anyone else. These were purists – and "actor" was a dirty word. There were others working in documentary who, because they never used actors, believed they were the only ones making real films and that people in features were just playing at it. It was snobbery and ludicrous and it's still around.'

9. Undated and unidentified local newspaper cutting, contained in POST 122/448 (almost certainly from *The Crawley Observer*).

10. The *Financial Times*' Industrial Films column surmised: 'Now it appears that the GPO has returned to its earlier [1930s] policy of producing films for prestige reasons to form part of a public relations programme employing various media … *Counterpoint* follows the tradition established by *Night Mail* in that it portrays the everyday work of the post office staff – this time the counter clerk. But whereas the pre-war documentary was a social commentary packed with dramatic visual and sound affects, *Counterpoint* is a glimpse of the public seen through the eyes of the post office clerk. He himself is seen to be the man next door, long suffering, hard worked, but still retaining his sense of humour … Films with this form of documentary treatment may not have the solemn grandeur of pre-war sponsored films but there is no reason why, like them, they should not still be enjoyed by audiences 25 years after they are made. Anon. (probably P. Robinson Rigg), 'To See Ourselves …', *Financial Times*, 22 March 1960, p. 25.

11. Thanks to John Krish himself for this apt three-word summation of his banned film's troubled history. As he comments today: 'Is there anything funnier than a civil servant being serious?'

PART SEVEN

The GPO Film Unit and the

Modern Post Office

THE GPO FILM UNIT AND THE MODERN POST OFFICE

The GPO Film Unit's work was but the most visible aspect of a radical transformation in the operation of the Post Office in the 1930s. *The Post Office Magazine*, which launched alongside the *Weather Forecast* series of films in 1934, gave GPO film-makers a popular forum for trying out story ideas and getting feedback on its work from postal workers. In its enthusiasm, scientism, paternalism and occasionally lame humour, *The Post Office Magazine* – with a circulation that quickly climbed above 150,000 – provides a fascinating lens through which we can begin to reconsider the relationship between the film-makers and the wider workforce of the GPO that provided the bedrock of their audience.

G.P.O. Films

Display at Manchester

Audience of 15,000

WHOEVER selected Manchester as the first provincial centre for a three months' display of films made by the G.P.O. Film Unit under Mr. John Grierson chose well. Before the doors opened on the first day applications for over 15,000 seats had been received from 400 societies, banks, political organisations, and firms representing every phase of life in and around the city. Attractive notices prepared for exhibition at the counter could not be put up as all seats up to January 10th, 1936, had been filled.

The Lord Mayor of Manchester, Alderman S. Woollam, and members of the City Council attended the first display on September 30th. Strenuous work by the Office of Works had converted a dusty lumber room into a handsome up-to-date cinema capable of holding three hundred people, and the Parks Committee of the Corporation were good enough to supply palms and plants. The films were shown by members of our engineering staff, who had received special training in the technique of projection.

The object of the display is to give the staff and public an insight into the many and varied activities of the department, and among the films on the opening day were those dealing with the Air Mail, the Central Telegraph Office and the Savings Bank Department. Industrial Britain, one of the films produced by the Unit in the days of its connection with the Empire Marketing Board, was appropriately included as it had many associations with the Midlands.

Finally there was Colour Box, an extraordinary innovation. It is a film made without a camera, the colour patterns having been painted directly on to clear celluloid. It is a stream of tints synchronised with music, and, just as the audience is wondering just what it is all about, into the pattern creeps a Post Office advertisement.

At other displays the programme will include "Telephone Workers," a film showing the part played by the telephone in the development of a district: "The Coming of the Dial," illustrating the change over from manual to automatic and having as a background the work of our Research Department at Dollis Hill; and "Under the City," a film dealing with engineering work deep down beneath the streets of London.

383

August 1935, p. 271
© Royal Mail Group
Ltd 2011. Courtesy
of The British Postal
Museum & Archive

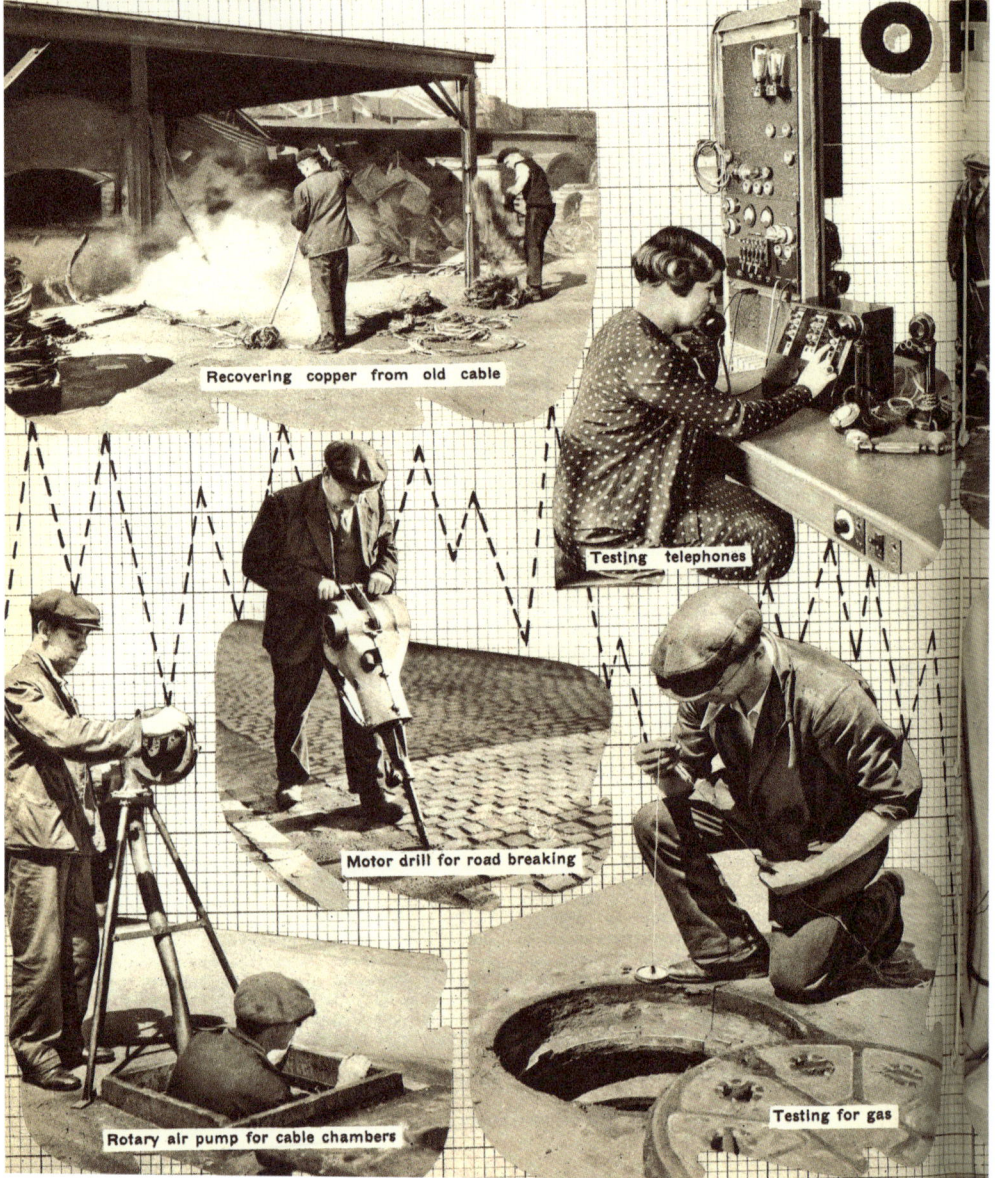

ODD JOBS of the
OF

Recovering copper from old cable

Testing telephones

Motor drill for road breaking

Rotary air pump for cable chambers

Testing for gas

September 1936, pp. 306–7 © Royal Mail Group Ltd 2011. Courtesy of The British Postal Museum & Archive

POST OFFICE

Pumping water from manhole

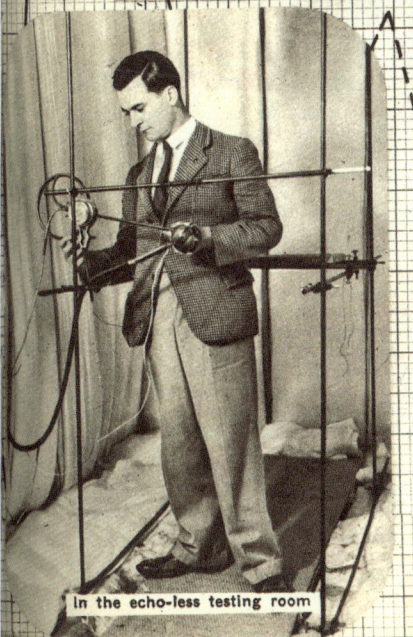

Rocking table test for ships' auto-alarm apparatus

Stripping cable recovered from English Channel

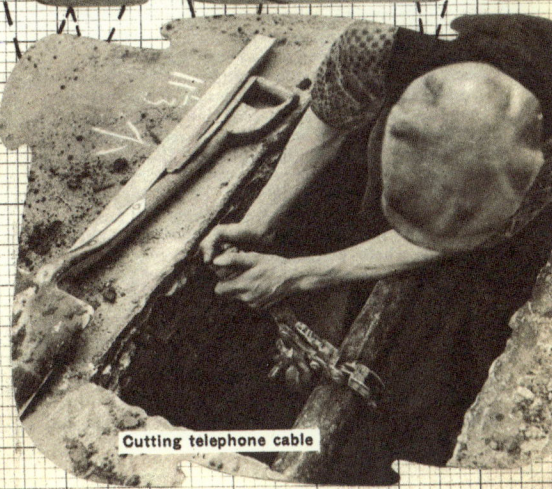

In the echo-less testing room

Cutting telephone cable

HEALTH and DIET

by THE CHIEF MEDICAL OFFICER to the POST OFFICE

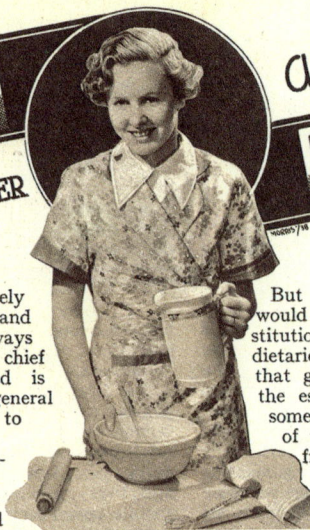

HEALTH is so largely dependent on food and drink that it is always well to bear in mind the chief functions of both. Food is necessary to maintain the general structure of the body; to keep up bodily heat; to provide the energy required for action; and, in young people, to secure adequate growth and development. Drink is necessary to maintain the proper amount and basis of the different circulating fluids of the body, and to keep the various tissues of the body, in popular phraseology, sweet and clean, and the excretory organs well flushed out.

The principal heat-producing foods are the fats, bacon and meat fat, fish oils, butter and cream; and more of these are therefore wanted in cold weather and cold climates—hence the predominatingly fatty diet of the Esquimaux, for instance. The principal body-building and muscle-maintaining foods are the proteins. These are obtained most easily and in greater concentration from meat-stuffs. But probably enough can be obtained—at any rate for some people, as certain vegetarians have shown—from such vegetables as peas and beans, and from some of the nuts, with the addition of cheese and eggs. But a relatively greater bulk of food has generally to be eaten (and digested) in order to secure this. The principal energy-producing foods are the carbohydrates, bread-stuffs, starches and sugars.

Recent researches have also shown that, for the proper maintenance of health, for the avoidance of what are known as deficiency diseases, such as rickets and scurvy, and for adequate resistance to some bacterial infections, substances known as vitamins are essential. In the ordinary mixed diet of the average household in this country, assuming that fresh fruit and green vegetables are included, all the necessary vitamins will usually be found.

But a loaf or two of whole-meal bread would be a helpful addition, or substitution, in most weekly household dietaries; and it is useful to remember that good pasteurised milk contains all the essential vitamins, though it may sometimes be a little deficient in one of them that can be easily supplied from the juice of an orange.

As regards the quantity of food eaten, it can be said, roughly speaking, that it is very difficult for normal, active and growing young people to eat too much; and good sweets and chocolate, in a reasonable amount, are excellent for the rapid replacement of expended energy. This is also true for adults after hard exercises. But for grown-up people there should be a proper relationship between the amount and kind of food eaten and the physical work that their jobs in life involve. Probably it would be true to say, in terms of the Post Office, that postmen as a group require more food than administrators as a group.

As regards drink, many middle-aged and elderly people, and women in particular, tend to drink too little, and various minor maladies could be overcome merely by the drinking of an extra two or three glasses of fluid during the twenty-four hours.

Lastly, though with some trepidation, a word might perhaps be said about alcoholic drinks. Strictly and scientifically speaking these are seldom necessary; and as regards actual food-value, an equivalent amount of money spent, say, on milk, butter or cheese, would be a much better investment. But as a great bulk of ordinary human, as well as of medical, experience has shown, these drinks have another value. They may help worried and tired people to enjoy and digest a meal better. Taken in reason, they have a specific action in many people in helping to break down certain inhibitions, awkwardnesses and shynesses. They do in fact—and it is no small matter——help to make glad the heart of man.

110

Rocket Mails

By — Leslie Dare

WHEN the centenary of the Penny Postage Act of 1839 is celebrated we shall be reminded of the wonders of the Postal Services in all parts of the world. But one of the most interesting aspects of the subject is likely to receive little notice, that is, the story of rocket posts.

Mail-carrying rockets are still in their experimental stage, but there is little doubt that their possibilities are great. Colonel Lindbergh has told us that " the rocket is now in that most interesting period of discovery where the shorelines are unplotted and the future limited only by imagination."

Now the rocket has an ancient origin. The Chinese discovered them seven centuries ago, but apparently made little headway in putting them to any practical use. It was 1826 even before rockets were brought into play for saving life at sea. So far as the mail rockets are concerned we do not go back more than a dozen years, but in that time things of vital interest have been performed.

Beginning in July, 1928, an Austrian scientist, Ing. F. Schmiedl, began a series of experiments to test the practical use of rockets as message carriers. Scientific data was obtained by registering instruments carried in the rockets, but one mishap marred the complete success of this venture. The sixth rocket exploded, wrecking all the instruments it carried.

Nevertheless, to this scientist goes the credit of arranging the first rocket mail flight in the world. It took place over Austrian territories in February, 1931.

In this country considerable interest was aroused a few years ago when mail-carrying rockets were undergoing their " trials." This time it was a German named Herr Gerhard Zucker who was responsible for the arrangements. His apparatus was an aluminium cartridge propelled by a rocket. This was fired from a launching rack, and when the rocket had exhausted its energy a parachute floated the mail-bag down to earth.

The first experiment took place in the small hours of June 6, 1934, on the Sussex Downs. It was a success and aroused the interest of official circles. Upwards of 3,000 letters were carried and delivered through the medium of the Brighton post office.

The second attempt with the mail rocket brought excitement and danger to its sponsors. In July, 1934, Herr Zucker planned to shoot a mail consisting of 4,800 letters (4 of which were addressed to the King) from Harris to the island of Scarp in the Outer Hebrides. The first firing resulted in a terrific explosion in which the German nearly lost his life. A second attempt was made but again misfortune came. This second rocket also exploded, scattering the mail far and wide.

In spite of these setbacks Herr Zucker firmly believed in the eventual success of mail-carrying rockets. He went so far as to express the opinion that rockets held the key to postal services of the future, and to back up his convictions promptly proceeded to stage yet another attempt. He went down to the Isle of Wight intending to span the Solent with his novel form of air transport. Just prior to the attempt, however, he received official instructions that the rocket must be made to fall into the sea. Which meant reducing the quantity of explosives in the rocket. It is assumed that this was the cause of yet another failure in this persistent man's fight to prove his faith. At any rate, wind blew the rocket off its course and the mail dropped in Pennington Marshes, from which point it was recovered and conveyed to Leamington for delivery through the usual channels.

It would appear that from this point interest in the project has been somewhat lulled—at least in this country.

In the U.S.A., they have experimented with rockets propelled by motors which give more power than explosives. They have also demonstrated the possibilities of despatching mail-carrying aeroplanes by this means, and the results have been sufficiently encouraging to justify the belief that the future holds much of interest in this unusual sphere of activity.

57

February 1939, p. 57 © Royal Mail Group Ltd 2011. Courtesy of The British Postal Museum & Archive

London's Further Education Scheme

'ADULT education is a force making for peace in the world through the understanding of other people's problems; individually it affords us a ready means of escape from the parish pump." This was the theme of Sir William Beveridge's address at the meeting held in King George V Hall on September 23 to inaugurate the 1936–37 session of the Post Office further education classes. Major G. C. Tryon, the Postmaster General, in introducing Sir William, expressed his satisfaction at the increasing popularity of the movement which now claimed the adherence of 2,000 students. Moreover, each of these had that genuine eagerness to learn and that desire for education for its own sake which would encourage the teachers to give of their best. He cordially thanked Mr. Gilbert and his colleagues of the Whitley Committee for the splendid and varied programme that they had prepared.

Sir William Beveridge, who is Director of the London School of Economics and an ex-civil servant, said that education has no time limit. Some of his best students comprised civil servants and other professional workers engaged in part-time studies. He compared the advantages of the selective and purposeful scheme of further education in the Post Office with the acquisition of " useless " knowledge and the aimless study of facts having no bearing on life. He was particularly glad to see so much attention being paid to the study of the political and social sciences. These did not lend themselves to experiment as did the natural sciences, but nevertheless we could profit from the observation of the experiments being forced on other nations, whose social problems were, after all, essentially the same as our own, and learn to understand more fully the relationship between man and man. He also appreciated the vocational courses; however proficient we might be on our own particular job, there was always room for the little extra which means so much.

Mr. E. M. Rich, Education Officer for London, expressed his appreciation of the ready manner in which the Post Office co-operated with the L.C.C. in furthering this education scheme. Classes in almost any conceivable subject could be arranged provided that 15 to 20 prospective students made the demand.

Mr. T. H. Boyd, Assistant Director General, Sir William Beveridge and the Postmaster General at the opening ceremony

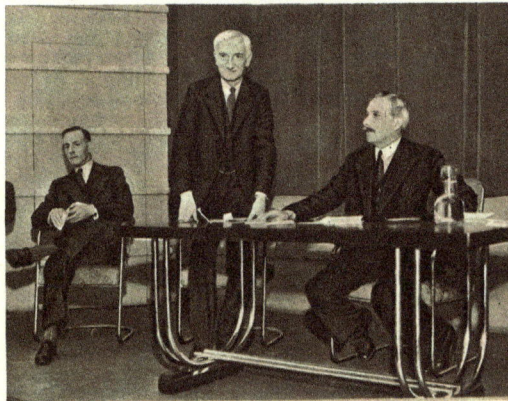

Mr. Gilbert, Deputy Comptroller and Accountant General, stressed the point that the success of the scheme depended entirely on staff co-operation. The programme had never before covered such a wide range of cultural activity. Even the study of straight thinking was provided for—a subject with great possibilities. Special six-week literary and cultural classes had been arranged for those whose leisure is limited, and there would also be a series of film lectures.

Further particulars can be obtained from Mr. H. J. C. Flower, Accountant General's Department, Room 24, Ground Floor, Headquarters Building, E.C.1.

376

November 1936, p. 376 © Royal Mail Group Ltd 2011. Courtesy of The British Postal Museum & Archive

Building a New World

by H. Herdman

By courtesy " Wellington Journal"

Model Farm designed and constructed by Oakengates Fellowship

FOR the past two years the Post Office has entered into the social life of the men and women who have had the misfortune to be unemployed in the mining town of Oakengates, in Salop. During 1936 two more centres of social activity have been maintained—at Dawley and Iron Bridge—the latter centre being in the capable hands of Mr. E. L. Westell as Chairman. At each place an experienced Warden has been engaged and real social work is being carried out by a local committee.

It is now over two years since the G.P.O. (Headquarters) Social Service Association took over the maintenance of the Oakengates centre from the National Council of Social Service, renaming it "The Fellowship." The buildings were redecorated and the necessary equipment for the varied programme of social activity was installed to meet the anticipated increase of membership. From a dozen members attending the "Good Companions" when the change-over took place, to 200 members now being catered for is a splendid record of the first centre which proves to the subscriber the usefulness of the scheme.

All phases of social work are carried out under the guidance of fully qualified instructors and lecturers. In addition the physical culture and keep-fit classes recently organised have reached a high standard. The football team, to show its fitness, secured the Runners-up Cup and miniatures of the Wellington League. Tennis and folk-dancing have been in evidence during the summer and the Jazz Band has given performances at local carnivals. The musical side has been developed under the conductorship of Mr. W. V. Horton, Postmaster of Oakengates. Gardening has been undertaken, and special prizes for best kept gardens awarded.

The Fellowship is a busy centre of industry and some really fine specimens of furniture have been made and exhibited by the members. Recently, at the invitation of the Economic Department of Harper-Adams Agricultural College, Newport, Salop, the Fellowship constructed a model of a typical Staffordshire farm, built to a scale of ⅜in. to a foot, the model covering an area of 42 square feet. The building of the farm took eight weeks to complete. Twelve members of the Club, under the supervision of Mr. G. E. Bocock, handwork instructor of the Shropshire Association of Mutual Service Clubs, and the Warden—Mr. J. H. Grainger—undertook the work. The model was made of wood and metal, coloured and painted to match the Staffordshire landscape. In conjunction with the model, which was exhibited in the Hall of Agriculture at the Royal Show, Wolverhampton, economic data was displayed giving particulars of the cost of managing such a farm. The work of construction provided healthy discussion, and keen interest was evinced in the undertaking by all the members. The model was inspected locally by tradespeople and visitors who expressed appreciation of the value of the social service undertaken by the local committee, under the chairmanship of Mr. H. Herdman, Head Postmaster of Wellington.

Recently, one of the unemployed men, in passing a vote of thanks at a function held at the Club, stated that since the G.P.O. Social Service Association had taken an interest in Oakengates "it had created a new world for many of its inhabitants," and in the writer's opinion those few words summarise the value of the work and offer tangible recompense to the workers and subscribers of the three Shropshire centres.

395

September 1937, p. 395. Text © Royal Mail Group Ltd 2011. Courtesy of The British Postal Museum & Archive

Mr. J. Davis

A Link with Dickens

JOHN DAVIS, born 1849 and appointed postman in 1867, delivered letters to Charles Dickens at 26, Wellington Street, Strand. He was a member of the force of Special Constables formed for the protection of the City and also served for 28 years in "D" Company of the Post Office Rifles, which was recruited from the staff of the Western Central Office. Mr. Davis was superannuated with the rank of Overseer as long ago as 1898. The reason for his premature retirement was ill-health, a condition which, judging from his photograph, he is thoroughly "enjoying" at 88. Perhaps this is the result of his retiring on Primrose Day.

Plymouth Bowls Again

THE newly formed bowls club is full of enthusiasm, and although Dame Fortune has not yet smiled on them in the nature of a win, some very close games have been played, the latest "achievement" being to lose to the strong Civil Service club by only 3 shots. With this form the first win cannot be long delayed. Four rinks have been entered for the Surveyors' trophy.

A Brave Messenger

A BOLTING horse is an unusual occurrence these days, and such a contingency could scarcely be included in the curriculum of a boy messenger's training; but Boy Messenger R. C. Astbury, of Portsmouth, handled the situation in a manner worthy of the trick riders of Bertram Mills or the Royal Corps of Signals. He was returning to the office when a horse drawing a baker's van dashed from a side street, narrowly missing two women with perambulators. He gave chase on his cycle, rode up beside the horse, but found it impossible to hold the reins. He jumped from his cycle to the shafts, lost his footing, hung on to the side of the van, and finally climbed to the seat and brought the horse to a standstill.

Western District Outing

THE District Managers' Staff (Western District, Exeter) held their annual outing on Saturday, June 26, at Salcombe, the famous Devonshire beauty spot which Tennyson so frequently calls to mind in his "Moaning at the Bar." Over 80 members of the staff attended

South of

and for the eighth successive outing we were privileged to have King Sol in all his glory. The afternoon was given over to bathing and non-strenuous competitions on Millbay Sands. Much amusement and interest was created by the bathing beauty contest, ankle contest, the men's comedy race (all scratch) and the musical balloon race. The staff band made its debut on this occasion, and although not up to B.B.C. standards, practices are continuing with more hope for next year.

Portsmouth

THE Head Postmasters' Golfing Society Challenge Cup, presented by the Rt. Hon. A. H. Illingworth, M.P., Postmaster General 1916–1921, has been brought to Portsmouth for the first time by Mr. W. H. Smith, Head Postmaster. It is by no means the first time that it has been brought to the South of England, having been won four times by Mr. F. H. Gibson, Head Postmaster of Southampton, and four times by Mr. A. T. Warren, Head Postmaster of Swindon. As Mr. Smith was runner-up in last year's contest there is more than a hope that the cup will find a resting place in Portsmouth for some years to come.

Mr. Smith has been elected President of the Portsmouth Civil Service Sports Association, in succession to Rear Admiral R. Ross Turner, Admiral Superintendent of Portsmouth Dockyard.

In Memoriam

THE Eastbourne postal district staff heard with deep sorrow on Monday, June 14, of the sudden passing of Major A. W. A. Headley, Head Postmaster. The fact that he would have retired in January next made the unexpected news the more poignant.

After service in the Saving Bank Department and as

St. Ives, Cornwall

372

August 1937, pp. 372–3 © Royal Mail Group Ltd 2011. Courtesy of The British Postal Museum & Archive

England

an Assistant Surveyor in the South Midland Surveying District Major Headley was appointed Head Postmaster of Eastbourne in 1925, and in the ensuing period made many friends. His genial manner, kindly disposition and unfailing courtesy were esteemed both by the members of the public with whom he came into contact and by his staff, over whom he exercised a wise and beneficent control. Major Headley was for many years Chairman of the South Eastern District branch of the Head Postmasters' Association and was held in high regard by his brother Head Postmasters and his colleagues on the Surveying Staff. The Civic Authorities and leading business men of Eastbourne combined with past and present members of the Eastbourne Office, Surveyor's Staffs and Head Postmasters to pay tribute to his memory.

Remarkable Family Record

DOCUMENTARY proof of an inter-family connection with the Post Office service, aggregating 236 years, is in the possession of Mr. E. F. H. Manley, of Bristol. Continuously from 1811 to 1915, members of the families of Strode and Manley were either Postmasters or Postmistresses of Warminster. The last member of the latter family to occupy the position was Mr. George Strode Manley. His wife was a daughter of Mr. William Toomer, Postmaster of Salisbury (1854–1886), and herself served for nine years as first clerk at that office. Her brother, Mr. W. H. A. Toomer, became Postmaster of Barnstaple and of Tonbridge, Kent. In 1650 a John Manley was Postmaster General, and it would seem probable that he was an ancestor of the Warminster family.

The Trout Fishing Broadcast

MR. HARRY PRICE, Sub-Postmaster of Drewsteignton, Exeter, who took part in a broadcast talk on trout fishing in the Regional programme on June 30, has spent thirty out of his sixty years in the old-world village of Drewsteignton, close to the River Teign. He has been Sub-Postmaster since 1919 and

Flushing, Cornwall

Telephone Belles of the Sunny South

Auxiliary Postman since 1923. His record salmon weighed 26 lb. Mr. Price served in the Royal Navy and was awarded the D.S.M. for War services. He was a member of the crew of the "Ophir" at the time when she conveyed King George V and Queen Mary (then Duke and Duchess of York) on a cruise round the world. Mr. Price, who is an artist as well as a fisherman, kept a log in which he interpolated many water-colour sketches of scenes and ships, people and places.

Contributory Scholarships

THE Central Council of the University Scholarship Association has received information from the academic secretary of the University College of the South West that the senate has awarded the P.O. Scholarship to Miss K. M. Hunter, of Liskeard Grammar School, who is the daughter of Mr. C. H. Hunter, Overseer, Liskeard. The successful student last year was from the same school. This year candidates were put forward from Liskeard, Plymouth, Exeter and Barnstaple, and it is interesting to note that awards which are at the disposal of the college have been given to each of our entrants, one of them, Mr. G. E. Bryant, of Devonport High School, having been offered an open scholarship of £80 per annum. It is confidently hoped that this expression of appreciation of our work by the college will lead to increased support from those whom we are trying to serve.

373

THE POST OFFICE MAGAZINE

Volume One, Number Eleven   **November, 1934**

1934—2034

WHAT will the Post Office of a hundred years hence think about the Post Office of 1934? In August last we celebrated the 150th anniversary of the first journey of a mail coach. The Post Office of 2034 may well be recalling the hundredth anniversary of the first introduction of an inland air mail into the country. This Magazine, we feel sure, will be celebrating its first centenary.

Everything which we now regard as particularly modern is sure then to seem quaint and old-fashioned. The photographs of Post Office functions in our pages will look as antiquated as the groups of our bearded and crinolined ancestors and ancestresses look to-day. Many of our operations will probably seem as slow as the 10 mile an hour mail coach has long appeared to us. The men and women of 2034 may well find the up-to-date telegraph and telephone equipment, of which our engineers are so justly proud, as cumbrous as the old models which we already stare at in our museums. Of the 6,000 million letters, which we now handle each year so busily, a few packets, tied up as curios, at most are likely to remain.

It is amusing to wonder what changes will have taken place in the world of communication meantime. Our grandchildren, perhaps, will be carrying in their pockets some simple apparatus, enabling them to speak by wireless to anyone in the world. Our telephone kiosks may have become television boxes, where for a trifling fee the passer-by may exchange smiles or scowls, greetings or criticisms, with his friends and his enemies at a distance.

If only we could see our successors of 2034, we should no doubt make fun of their clothes and their coiffures. Our ways and fashions are sure to seem comical to them. Let us hope only that any of them who turn in 2034 the pages of this November Magazine will think as kindly of us as we have thought this year of the old mail coach guards and drivers. Let us hope, too, that they will recognize their inheritance of a fine tradition of service from the Post Office of 1934.

487

POSTSCRIPT

Roy Mayall

In the November 1934 edition of *The Post Office Magazine* the editor finds himself speculating about the future of the Post Office. What will it be like in a hundred years' time, he asks? And he makes a number of interesting predictions. 'Everything which we now regard as particularly modern is sure then to seem quaint and old fashioned,' he says. 'Of the 6,000 million letters, which we now handle each year so busily, a few packets, tied up as curios, at most are likely to remain.' He would probably be surprised to learn that the Royal Mail, not quite a hundred years on, now handles in the region of 24,000 million letters a year – that's four times 1934 levels – while packets, which he imagines as curios, are currently the biggest growth area in the delivery market.

This has come about because of a strange alliance between old and new technologies, between the letter-box and the computer. These days people don't send so many personal letters, preferring to use email and text. But they do order things online, from Amazon and eBay, most of which is delivered by the Royal Mail.

The editor of the magazine continues to speculate about the future: 'Our grandchildren, perhaps, will be carrying in their pockets some simple apparatus, enabling them to speak by wireless to anyone in the world,' he says. This line seems particularly prescient. The next, by contrast, is both prescient and quaint at the same time. 'Our telephone kiosks may have become television boxes, where for a trifling fee the passer-by may exchange smiles or scowls, greetings or criticisms, with his friends and enemies at a distance,' he says. We would recognise the 'television boxes' as computers, of course, but to the 1930s mind such a technology would necessarily have to be publicly owned and publicly accessed. This is the limitation of his vision, that he places the technology in kiosks rather than in people's living rooms.

And therein lies the difference.

Back then the GPO was a public institution. The Post Master General of 1934 had responsibility not only for the post, but for telecommunications and broadcasting. It would have been inconceivable to anyone living in that era to picture such innovations taking place outside of the public domain.

What would our erstwhile editor think of the changes that have taken place within the Post Office over the last eighty years? Probably he would be disappointed. Not only has telecommunications and broadcasting been taken out of its hands, but even the post itself is about to be privatised. The Post Office and the Royal Mail have been separated. The GPO no longer exists. It stopped making films many years ago.

However, looking back over these old films, one is struck by how familiar a lot of it is. For instance, in the film *Air Post* (1934) we see the workers sorting the letters into countries and then into towns. This would be done by machine these days, but the wooden sorting frames they use to separate the letters are still in use in every office, for dividing up the mail into individual rounds. In the film the letters are then tied up into bundles and dropped into sacks. They are tied up with string, whereas today they would be sealed with plastic or bundled up with elastic bands. But the drop bags in their metal frames into which the bundles are loaded would be familiar to any postal worker today. These frames still exist within every office and are used for sorting packets. The sacks are made of plastic rather than hessian, but the basic configuration of the frame is the same: a criss-cross lattice of squares from which the sacks hang, open at the top, ready to receive their contents.

Another similarity with today's postal service lies in the nature of the skills. 'These men have memories like geography books,' says the narrator, as we watch them flicking the letters into their individual slots. 'They know the names of little villages in every country in the world.' It's probably been a few years since the Royal Mail employed workers with dedicated memory skills about the small villages of the world (there are large-scale sorting machines to perform this operation these days), but even today the average postal worker is expected to know the names of all the streets on every single round in his district and to be able to sort the mail into the frames accordingly: a skill which it can take several years to master.

What this film shows, along with several others, is the importance of the network to the postal business. The rickety-looking bi-plane seems particularly old-fashioned, but the network of airports and drop-off points which the GPO established in the 1930s is still in existence. This also applies to the delivery offices and sorting offices throughout the UK, whose lineage is even more ancient. We get the feeling of an evolved system of communication embracing the nation, and linking it to the rest of the world.

The most powerful sense you get from these films is their inclusiveness. The Post Office is seen as a unitary force, drawing people in from all parts of the country, from all backgrounds, welcoming them in to the same all-embracing community.

One of the most intriguing films for a modern-day postal worker is the one called *Six Thirty Collection* (1934), as this shows a typical office in action during a peak period. The uniforms are different, but the atmosphere is very similar. Postal workers don't wear peaked caps any more, but the energy and the sense of urgency link us clearly back to those times. We recognise the air of bustling efficiency and, even though some of the procedures appear different, the basic structure of the job is fundamentally unchanged.

The post-box is emptied. The postman brings in his sack, drops the keys off at the office, and hangs up his hat and coat while exchanging a few jovial words with his colleagues. After this he pours the contents of his sack onto the facing table. It's called the 'facing table' because the letters are turned face-up, ready to be franked. This part of the job is done by machine in the big metropolitan sorting offices these days, but the facing table as a piece of equipment was still in use in delivery offices until recently, and most older workers would recognise it.

We would probably also recognise some of the conversations if we could hear them. The film is a bit clumsy at capturing the day-to-day interactions of the men, who seem wooden and awkward in front of the camera. Every so often someone shoots a self-conscious glance towards the lens, to show how uncomfortable he is with its presence.

The noisy chaos of the office drowns out most individual conversations, but some snippets do remain. So we have 'mind your back, Henry', and 'hold tight', and 'gangway please', all of which are to do with alerting fellow workers to your presence within an enclosed space. At one point someone is whistling 'Lazy Bones' by Hoagy Carmichael, obviously a popular song that year. The lyrics are peculiarly inapt given the amount of frenetic activity going on all around, but perhaps it reflects the worker's fantasy of what he'd like to get up to later in the day, once the work is finished. Later someone else is talking above the rattle of the machinery. 'How's the old allotment, Bert?' he asks, though we don't get to hear the answer.

There would obviously be a lot of banter in the office, just as there is today, but *Six Thirty Collection* fails to capture most of it. A later film, the justifiably celebrated *Night Mail* (1936) does manage to do a much better job of picking up on the verbal sparring of the workers. The scene isn't an office, but the Postal Special on its way from London to Glasgow, but the nature of workplace banter in both locations would be instantly recognisable.

There are several interesting exchanges. Two in particular stand out. One involves two postmen standing by the track, bundling up the mail ready to be netted and captured by the speeding train as it rushes by.

'There's something in these bags all right, Bert,' says the one.

'Must be old Fred's coupon night,' says the other.

It's obvious that the lines are rehearsed by the way the men say them, but there's also something authentic in them. They sound like a genuine exchange between two blokes at work. You get the feeling that they must have been based on a conversation overheard by the film-makers earlier on, repeated for the benefit of the camera.

A later conversation also suggests a similar origin. The workers on the train are preparing to drop off the mail bags. One of them, in overalls, is picking up the last of the mail.

'Any more for Carnforth?' he says.

There's a brief exchange about whether all the letters have been cleared, but once it is established that they have been, the sorter turns back to the man in overalls. 'Best of luck,' he says. 'Take it away, Sonny Boy.'

'Righto, Handsome,' comes the reply.

It's those ironic titles, 'Sonny Boy' and 'Handsome', which make it clear that these are genuine exchanges, based on real conversations, and it's reassuring to know that this kind of affectionate insult was in vogue in the 1930s, just as it is today.

Some things never change.

THE PROJECTION OF BRITAIN

THE END

The GPO Film Unit in 1983: at least once a year the documentarists visited Paul Rotha in his retirement home near Oxford. (l to r) Michael Orram, Edgar Anstey, Stanley Hawes, John Taylor, Basil Wright, Paul Rotha (courtesy of Wolf Suschitzky)

Arthur Elton, Basil Wright, Harry Watt, Edgar Anstey (courtesy of Wolf Suschitzky)

FILMOGRAPHY

The following is an alphabetical list of GPO Film Unit titles held within the BFI National Archive compiled by Steve Foxon. This list does not include post-war titles commissioned by either the General Post Office or latterly the Post Office. It does, however, include titles produced by the GPO Film Unit for the Trade and Industries Development Association (TIDA).

AIR POST (1934)
The airmail service at
Croydon aerodrome.
Prod. Arthur Elton
Dir. Geoffrey Clark
Cam. A. Jeakin and J. Taylor
B/W
Sound
1,058ft
12 minutes

ARP BIRMINGHAM.
GLOUCESTER STREET
EXPERIMENT (1939)
Experimental demolition of
a house in order to assess
types of emergency exits.
Prod. co. GPO Film Unit

ARP LIVERPOOL. SOUTH
CHESTER STREET
EXPERIMENT (1939)
Experimental demolition of
a house in order to assess
types of emergency exits.
Prod. co. GPO Film Unit

ARP NORTHAMPTON.
SHELTER TEST (1939)
Film showing reinforced
basements before and after
test explosions (20 March
1939)
Prod. co. GPO Film Unit

AT THE THIRD STROKE
(1939)
Comical advertisement for
the Post Office's Speaking
Clock service.
Prod. co. GPO Film Unit
Dir. Richard Massingham

BANKING FOR MILLIONS
(1934)
A tour of the various departments at the Post Office
Savings Bank HQ.
Prod. co. GPO Film Unit
Dir. Raymond Spottiswoode
B/W
Sound
1,816ft
25 minutes

BBC – DROITWICH (1935)
The building of the new
long-wave broadcasting
station at Droitwich,
Worcestershire.
Prod. co. GPO Film Unit
Dir. Harry Watt
Prod. John Grierson
B/W
Sound
1,323ft
14 minutes

BBC – THE VOICE OF BRITAIN (1935)
Impressionistic survey of the BBC.
Prod. co. GPO Film Unit and the BBC
Dir. Stuart Legg
B/W
Sound
5,507ft
59 minutes

BIG MONEY (1937)
The financial administration of the GPO.
Prod. co. GPO Film Unit
Dir. Harry Watt

BOOK BARGAIN (1937)
The printing of the London telephone directory.
Prod. co. GPO Film Unit
Dir. Norman McLaren
B/W
Sound
727ft
8 minutes

BRITAIN AT BAY (1940)
World War II propaganda designed to boost morale of British people after fall of France.

Nazi Germany had swallowed Czechoslovakia, invaded Poland and Norway, overrun Holland and Belgium. The French government had given in. Britain was alone, at bay ... 'The future of the whole civilised world rests on the defence of Britain.'

There are no credits listed on the film although it was probably edited by Stewart McAllister, and it is thought that Humphrey Jennings may have worked on it.
Prod. GPO Film Unit
Sponsor: MoI
Dir. Harry Watt
Compilation commentary written and spoken by J. B. Priestly
Music: Richard Addinsell
B/W
Sound
7.25 minutes

BRITAIN CAN TAKE IT! (1940)
How Londoners are facing up to the Blitz.
Shortened version of *London Can Take It!* made for release in Great Britain.

'The film was a collaboration by the whole unit. Everything else stopped for it,' Harry Watt has said. 'I think I wrote the script. At least I wrote it down, but let us say it was a communal script. It was one night of the blitz, from sunset to sunrise. The whole theme was how extraordinary it was was that London went back to normality so quickly. We worked literally night and day.'

The American journalist Quentin Reynolds, who presents it as a film dispatch from London, took it straight to the White House, where (under the title *London Can Take It!*) it gave Roosevelt the kind of material he needed to swing US popular opinion behind Britain in the war.
Dir. Harry Watt, Humphrey Jennings
Cam. H Fowle, Jonah Jones
Ed. Stewart McAllister, Jack Lee
Sound: Ken Cameron
Commentary written and spoken by Quentin Reynolds
B/W
Sound
8.5 minutes

BRITAIN'S COUNTRYSIDE (1934)
Every industrial area in Britain has its countryside: South London, the farmlands of Surrey and Sussex, the hills of Wales, West Lancashire, North of the Clyde, the Western Isles.
Dir. Marion Grierson
Sponsor: TIDA
B/W
Silent
373ft (16mm)
10 minutes

BRITISH GUIANA (1933)
Geographical conditions, agriculture and industries in British Guiana.
Prod. co. GPO Film Unit

CABLE SHIP (1933)
The repair of a submarine cable in the Channel.

The repair of a submarine cable is shown in detail. The men who are doing the work explain their particular jobs in the stages of mending the cable.
Prod. GPO Film Unit

Dir. Alexander Shaw and
Stuart Legg
Cam. A. Jeakins and
J. Taylor
B/W
Sound
1,116ft
12 minutes

CALENDAR OF THE YEAR
(1936)
Survey of activities of a year
and the part played by the
GPO in those activities.
Prod. co. GPO Film Unit
Dir. Evelyn Spice

also
CALENDAR OF THE YEAR
(1940 version)
B/W
Sound
1,454ft
16 minutes

CAUSE COMMUNE, LA
(1940)
A film illustrating Britain's
war effort to help her allies
in France.
Dir. Alberto Cavalcanti
Prod. co. GPO Film Unit

CHRISTMAS UNDER FIRE
(1941)
Quentin Reynolds' second
film dispatch from London
to America shows Christmas
1940, the year of the blitz.
By this time Ian Dalrymple
was head of the GPO Film
Unit, which had now been
renamed the Crown Film
Unit, and most appropriately
the names Crown and GPO
appear, for once, together on

the credits. It was the first
time that King's College
Chapel choir had ever been
filmed, and Dalrymple
remembers that they did it
because they thought it
might be their last chance.
Dir. Harry Watt
Commentary: Quentin
Reynolds
Carols sung by King's College
Chapel, Cambridge
35mm
B/W
Sound
10 minutes

CHILTERN COUNTRY, THE
(1939)
Country scenes in the
Chilterns.
Dir. Alberto Cavalcanti
Prod. co. GPO Film Unit
Sponsor: TIDA

CITY: A FILM TALK BY SIR
CHARLES BRESSEY, THE
(1939)
The Bressey Report and the
growth of London and its
transport.
Prod. co. GPO Film Unit
Dir. Ralph Elton

COAL FACE (1935)
The work of the British coal
miner.
    A prestigious experiment
in sound, which was directed
by Cavalcanti on the cutting-
room bench using coal-
mining shots made by
various members of the unit
over a long period, and
introduced the Auden/
Britten collaboration that

was to make the later *Night
Mail* such a hit. The theme of
the coal miner and the
importance of his work in
British industry is very characteristic of Grierson, but
the poignant lyricism stems
entirely from Cavalcanti's
handling of the Britten
music and the Auden lines ...

'O lurcher loving collier;
    black as night
Follow your love across
    the smokeless hill;
Your lamp is out and all
    the cages still;
Course for her heart and
    do not miss,
For Sunday soon is past
    and Kate, fly not so
    fast,
For Monday comes when
    none may kiss;
Be marble to his soot and
    to his black be white.'

Prod. John Grierson
Dir. Alberto Cavalcanti
Ed. William Coldstream
Music: B. Britten
Song: W. H. Auden
Sound: E. A. Pawley
B/W
Sound
1,042ft
11 minutes

COLOUR BOX, A (1935)
Abstract animated advertisement for cheaper postal
rates.
    Len Lye pioneered the
technique of painting
directly on to clear film
stock, and this is the first

film that he brought to Grierson. Grierson said it was marvellous and told him to go away and paint the new cheaper rates for parcel post on the last sequence so that the Post Office could buy it. As a consequence, Lye joined the GPO Film Unit.
Prod. GPO Film Unit
Dir. Len Lye
Multiple print and pre-print elements (including colour separations) and 35mm VCs
35mm
Colour (Dufaycolor)

COMING OF THE DIAL, THE (1933)
The introduction of the dial telephone system to Great Britain.
Dir. Stuart Legg
Prod. John Grierson

COMMUNITY CALLS (1937)
A new housing development is connected to the telephone network.
Prod. co. GPO Film Unit

CONQUERING SPACE: THE STORY OF MODERN COMMUNICATION (1934)
The benefits to mankind of new discoveries in the field of communication.
Prod. Stuart Legg
Ed. G. A. Shaw
B/W
Sound
1,005ft
11 minutes

COPPER WEB (1937)
GPO telegraph poles and cables.
Prod. co. GPO Film Unit
Dir. Maurice Harvey

CTO: THE STORY OF THE CENTRAL TELEGRAPH OFFICE (1935)
The development of the Central Telegraph Office.
Prod. co. GPO Film Unit
Prod. Stuart Legg
B/W
Sound
1,868ft
20 minutes

DAILY ROUND (1937)
A postman dreams of how his working life can be improved.
Prod. co. GPO Film Unit
Dir. Richard Massingham and Karl Urbahn

DISTRESS CALL (1938)
Shorter version of *North Sea*.
Dir. Harry Watt

DO IT NOW (1939)
Alternative title: *If War Should Come* (1939) (sponsored by Home Office). Shows what people must or must not do in wartime.
Prod. co. GPO Film Unit and ARP Film Propaganda
See also *If War Should Come*

EDINBURGH (1934)
The Forth Bridge and other approaches to Edinburgh lead up to some views of the castle and other historic buildings, with shots of present-day streets and the characteristic 'closes' of Edinburgh.
Prod. GPO Film Unit
Dir. Marion Grierson
Sponsor: TIDA
B/W
Silent
344ft (16mm)
10 minutes

FAIRY OF THE PHONE, THE (1936)
Comedy based on instructions given in the London telephone directory.

A fanciful comedy with musical sequences including a catchy opening number featuring a chorus of telephonists. The script was based on page 6 of the 1936 London directory – instructions to subscribers on how to use the telephone – and the very practical fairy of the title repeatedly materialises out of thin air to make sure users do this properly.
Prod. Basil Wright
Dir. William Coldstream
Cam. James E Rogers
Music: Walter Leigh
Sound: C. Sullivan, with Charlotte Leigh and members of the London telephone service.
B/W
Sound
1,135ft
12 minutes

FIRST DAYS, THE (1939)
London during the first days
of World War II: 3 September
1939 – Britain is at war with
Germany. The sirens sound
and Londoners prepare …

This unique record of the
first days of war shows many
actual and some recon-
structed scenes of air-raid
precautions (shelters,
barrage balloons, sandbags,
wardens), military training,
the evacuation of children,
the ill and aged, and paintings and art treasures to the
country. Without the GPO
Film Unit most of these
images of the lull before
hostilities broke out would
not exist.
Prod co. GPO Film Unit
Prod. Alberto Cavalcanti
Dir. Humphrey Jennings,
Harry Watt and Pat Jackson
Ed. R. Q. McNaughton
Commentary writer: Robert
Sinclair
23 minutes

FIVE SKILLED METAL
CRAFTSMEN (c. 1933)
Prod. co. GPO Film Unit

FORTY MILLION PEOPLE
(1939/40)
Changes in social services
since the Industrial
Revolution.
A shorter version of *Health
of the Nation* (1939)
Dir. John Monck
Prod. co. GPO Film Unit

FOUR BARRIERS (1937)
Switzerland's economic
history.
Prod. co. GPO Film Unit, in
collaboration with Pro
Telephon-Zurich.
Dir. Alberto Cavalcanti

FRENCH COMMUNIQUE
(1940)
The war as seen through the
eyes of the French.
Prod. co. GPO Film Unit
Prod. Alberto Cavalcanti

FRONT LINE, THE (1940)
Documentary about Dover
filmed during the Battle of
Britain.

Dover – 15 September
1940. For three months the
town has been a frontier
target for the Reich, but the
spirit of the people is
undaunted.

'There was only one
hotel left in existence in
Dover,' Harry Watt recalled
to Elizabeth Sussex, 'and
stationed at that hotel were
the volunteers of Europe –
the American correspon-
dents who had seen
Czechoslovakia fall, Poland
fall, Belgium fall, Holland
fall. And they were there to
see the fall of Britain …'
Dir. Harry Watt
Cam. Jonah Jones
6 minutes

GARDENS OF THE ORIENT
(1936)
The tea-gardens of India and
Ceylon.
Prod. co. GPO Film Unit.
Reconstructed and edited by
Gaumont-British Screen
Services

GLORIOUS SIXTH OF JUNE
(1934)
Tongue-in-cheek drama,
using Post Office staff, about
reductions in Post Office
charges.
Prod. GPO Film Unit
Dir. Alberto Cavalcanti
B/W
Sound
909ft
10 minutes

GOD'S CHILLUN (1938)
Account of the slave trade in
the West Indies and the
islands' development since
emancipation.
Prod. co. GPO Film Unit
Words by W. H. Auden

GPO FILM DISPLAY (1938)
A compilation of extracts
from GPO films, probably
intended for showing by
mobile cinemas.
Prod. co. GPO Film Unit

GRANTON TRAWLER
(1934)
The work of a trawler on the
Viking Bank in the North Sea.

'In the thirties we were
all in it together,' Grierson
said. 'We could all edit well.
We could all write well.
There was no part of it we

couldn't do, even camerawork. The one credit I was absolutely insistent on was putting my name as cameraman on *Granton Trawler*. I had to put my name on because there was nobody else on the picture except me. It was a solo effort. It's a sweet little film.'

'Although normally a very good sailor, Grierson had been terribly seasick on the trip,' Edgar Anstey recalls. 'What I found very exciting – it's still in the film – was that where, because of the rough seas, the camera had fallen over and Grierson was perhaps too sick to save it, you got absolutely wonderful shots for a storm sequence, whirling sky and sea.'

Although uncredited, Cavalcanti is known to have added the soundtrack of simple noises and snatches of Scots conversation.
Prod./Dir./Cam. John Grierson
Ed. Edgar Anstey
Sound: E. A. Pawley
B/W
Sound
11 minutes

HEALTH OF THE NATION (1939)
Changes in social services in Britain since the Industrial Revolution (see also shorter version, *Forty Million People*).
Prod. co. GPO Film Unit, in collaboration with the BBC
Dir. John Monck
Sponsor: Ministry of Health

HEALTH IN WAR (1940)
The organisation of medical services in Britain during the war.
Dir. Pat Jackson
Prod. co. GPO Film Unit
Sponsor: MoI and Ministry of Health

HEAVENLY POST OFFICE, THE (1938)
aka The H.P.O.
A colour silhouette animation by Lotte Reiniger promoting GPO.

The famous animator's silhouettes in this film illustrates the theme – 'It's heaven to receive a greetings telegram. Be an angel and send one!'
Dir. Lottie Reiniger
Music: Brian Easdale
Asst: R. M. Harris
Dufaycolor
Sound
4 minutes

HOP GARDENS OF KENT (1933)
Oast houses and hop picking in Kent.

Hop picking in the Kent countryside and the journey from the grain in the field to the pint glass in your local.
Prod. GPO Film Unit
Sponsor: TIDA
B/W
Silent
401ft
4 minutes

HORSEY MAIL, THE (1938)
Delivery of mail to Horsey village in Norfolk during a period of flooding.

When the sea wall at Winterton in East Norfolk gives way and Horsey village and many outlying farms become islands in the water, it is more difficult for postman Claude Simmonds to make his daily round. Van driver Bob O'Brian is sent out to give him a lift, but there still comes the point where the Post Office has to take to the boats. Until fifteen square miles of flooded land are drained and the road appears again, Claude will be rowing six miles every day to deliver the Horsey mail.

A charming early effort by the man who was to make the wartime feature documentary about the battle of the Atlantic, *Western Approaches*.
Dir. Pat Jackson
Cam. F. Gamage
Music: Victor Yates
8.5 minutes

HOW STAMPS ARE MADE (1936)
Stages in the production of King George V Jubilee stamps.
Silent version of *The King's Stamp*
Prod. co. GPO Film Unit

HOW THE DIAL WORKS (1937)

This film, with the help of diagrams, shows the essential principle of the automatic telephone system.
Prod. co. GPO Film Unit

HOW THE TELEPRINTER WORKS (1940)

Models are used to demonstrate the working of a teleprinter.
Dir. J. D. Chambers
Prod. co. GPO Film Unit
Dufaycolor

HOW TO TELL A PHONE (1936)

Humorous instructions on the correct way to use the telephone.
Dir. William Coldstream
Prod. co. GPO Film Unit
Short silent version of *The Fairy of the Phone*

IF WAR SHOULD COME (1939)

Instructions regarding home precautions and the general behaviour of civilians in the event of war, emphasising that Britain is prepared for any emergency.
Alternative title: *Do It Now*
Prod. co. GPO Film Unit
See also re-edit, *Do It Now*

INTRODUCING THE DIAL (1934)

How the automatic dialing system works.
Dir. Stuart Legg
B/W
Sound

732ft
8 minutes

ISLANDERS, THE (1939)

The importance of Post Office communication to remote islands.

Islands of Britain, mountain peaks of a drowned landscape, mysterious and inaccessible ... This beautifully photographed documentary shows life on Eriskay, Guernsey and Inner Farne, islands that are linked to Britain by means of the Post Office.
Prod. J. B. Holmes
Dir. Maurice Harvey
Asst dir. Stewart McAllister
Cam. H Rignold and Jonah Jones
Music: Darius Milhaud
Commentary: Jack Livesey
Sound: Ken Cameron
17 mins

ISLAND OF CONTRAST (1936)

Travelogue of Ceylon.
Prod. co. GPO Film Unit
Reconstructed and edited by GB Screen Services
Sponsor: TIDA

JOB IN A MILLION, A (1937)

Recruitment film for the GPO.

Not many employers in the 1930s offered a secure job with a pension at sixty, so there was always a queue of boys hoping to become messengers at the Post Office. Proud to be among

the successful applicants, John Truman reports for work on his first day ... He is under-height and will have to grow a lot before he is eighteen, but he is given special exercises and his mother will be able to buy more milk for him now that he is earning 12/6 a week ... The film shows John through the various stages of his two-year probationary training up to the final examination and prize day.

This little-known dramatised documentary, showing the Cockney lad at home with his mother as well as at his work, is a perfect example of the breakthrough effected by the GPO Film Unit at a time when working-class people were usually presented as merely comic characters in British feature films.
Dir. Evelyn Spice
Music: Brian Easdale
Ed. Norman McLaren
Cam. S. Onions
Sound: G. C. Diamond
Nitrate OSN and OMN, 35mm safety fine grains and Nitrate 35mm VC (cond 333). Donor largely PRO
B/W
Sound
17.5 mins

JOHN ATKINS SAVES UP (1934)

Romantic comedy about savings and the Post Office Savings Bank.

The clerk, John Atkins, puts five shillings into the

Post Office Savings Bank every week of his life. He is a very careful fellow who keeps his summer clothes in mothballs and never forgets to shut the gate behind him when he sets off for the city along his tree-lined street. But the cover girl on a holiday magazine at the tube station sets him dreaming about a place called Summersea and, by a curious combination of circumstances, none of the events that follow could ever have happened without the Post Office Savings Bank ...

Apart from its fascination as a record of particular kind of middle-class lifestyle of the period, this little-known fictional documentary is a surprisingly early example of the genre.
Dir. Arthur Elton
Cam. J. D. Davidson
Commentary: V. C. Clinton-Baddeley
Players: Leslie Higgins (the clerk)
Eileen Lee (the girl)
18 minutes

KING'S STAMP, THE (1935)
Production of the King George V silver jubilee stamp.

Sequences showing the designing, lithographing and printing of the King George V Silver Jubilee stamp are followed by a short history of postage stamps, with dramatised scenes about Rowland Hill and the

amusing reactions of the general public to these 'new government labels' (notably the Penny Black) in 1840.

Directed by the painter William Coldstream, in his twenties, the subject is photographed in both monochrome and colour, which is used for sequences showing the production of the Jubilee stamp, examples of early stamps, and items in the royal stamp collection.
Dir. William Coldstream
Designer of Jubille Stamp: Barnett Freedman
Music: Benjamin Britten
Cam. F. H. Jones and H. E. Fowle
Sound: E. A. Pawley
B/W and Dufaycolor
Sound
1,838ft
19.5 mins

LETTERS TO LINERS (1937)
A film of a Mediterranean cruise showing the special arrangements made for the delivery and despatch of the ship's mail.
Prod. co. GPO Film Unit

LINE TO THE TSCHIERVA HUT (1937)
Laying of a telephone line by Swiss telephone workers to Tschierva mountain hut.
Prod. co. GPO Film Unit, in collaboration with Pro Telephon-Zurich
Dir. Alberto Cavalcanti

LOCOMOTIVES (1934)
The development of the early steam locomotive, using scale models from the Science Museum.
Prod. co. GPO Film Unit
Dir. Humphrey Jennings

LONDON CAN TAKE IT! (1935)
How Londoners are facing up to the blitz (version released for overseas audiences)
Dir. Harry Watt and Humphrey Jennings
Sponsor: MoI
Commentary: Quentin Reynolds
(See also short version, *Britain Can Take It!*)

LOVE ON THE WING (1938)
The Empire Airmail service.

An early colour animation film by the internationally renowned Norman McLaren who joined the GPO Film Unit in 1937. The theme of the film is the airmail service; the music is Jacques Ibert's 'Divertissement'.
Prod. GPO Film Unit
Dir. Norman McLaren
Cam. Jonah Jones and Fred Gamage
Colour (Dufaycolor)
4 minutes

MAKING A SAND MOULD AND CASTING ALLUMINIUM ALLOY (1934)
Detailed technique of making a mould and casting alluminium alloy.
Prod. co. GPO Film Unit
Sponsor: TIDA

MARKET PLACE (1934)
A short description of the work of the Post Office in relation to the life of a typical market town.
Sponsor: GPO

MEN IN DANGER (1939)
Survey of working conditions in English mines and factories.
Dir. Pat Jackson

MEN OF THE ALPS (1937)
Swiss geography and history.
Prod. GPO Film Unit, in collaboration with Pro Telephon-Zurich
Dir. Alberto Cavalcanti

MEN OF THE LIGHTSHIP (1940)
A reconstruction of the German attack on the *East Dudgeon* lightship in January 1940.
    'Year in, year out, all round our coasts, the beam of the lightship shines through the night and its siren pierces the fog banks. Light and fog signals reach vessels of all nations equally, and for three centuries lightships and lighthouses were considered international ... until 29 January 1940.'

This reconstruction of the events surrounding the Nazi bombing of the *East Dudgeon* lightship and the fate of those who manned it, made more money in cinemas in its first few years than any other GPO/Crown production, with the sole exception of Harry Watt's *Target for Tonight*. The director, David Macdonald, came from the commercial industry and had worked with Cecil B. DeMille, but it was Cavalcanti who told him to throw out his entire cast of actors and 'use real people', and it was Stewart McAllister (later Humphrey Jennings's close collaborator) who edited the material to such effect.
Prod. GPO/Crown Film Unit
Prod. Alberto Cavalcanti
Dir. David Macdonald
2nd Unit Dir. Charles Hasse
Asst: C. Taylor
Cam. Jonah Jones
Sets: Edward Carrick
Ed. Stewart McAllister
Dialogue: David Evans
Script: Hugh Gray
Music: Richard Addinsell
Conducted by Muir Mathieson
Sound: Ken Cameron
With officers and men of the Royal Navy and Trinity House
B/W
Sound
25 minutes

MESSAGE FROM GENEVA (1936)
The land-line linking the BBC with Zurich. The importance of the League of Nations.
Prod. co. GPO Film Unit and Pro Telephon-Zurich
Dir. Alberto Cavalcanti
B/W
Sound
780ft
8 minutes

MESSENGER BOY (1937)
The recruitment and training of Post Office messenger boys.
Prod. co. GPO Film Unit
Sponsor: GPO/COI

METHODS OF COMMUNICATION (1934)
Primitive and modern, simple and complex means of communication in Britain today. The film shows how the barriers of distance are overcome by instantaneous telegraphic and telephonic communication.
Prod. co. GPO Film Unit
A more detailed silent version of *Conquering Space* (1934).
B/W
Silent
1,929ft
21 minutes

MIDSUMMER DAY'S WORK, A (1939)
Laying of underground telephone cables from Amersham to Aylesbury.
    During that ominously perfect summer that

preceded the outbreak of World War II, they are laying an underground telephone cable in the Chilterns from Amersham to Aylesbury, about eighteen miles. We track along the route and see the gangs at work, labouring with their shirts on in the sun, amid much rural splendour – not least the cottage where Milton finished 'Paradise Lost', and the eighteenth-century Adam residence of the descendents of Sir Francis Drake.

There is no director credited on the film, and there might have been none on location. James E. Rogers, who shot two of Cavalcanti's avant-garde films in France in the late 1920s and later introduced Cavalcanti to Grierson, was a very distinguished freelance cameraman at this time.
(Some footage reused from *Chiltern Country*)
Prod. GPO Film Unit
Ed. R. Q. McNaughton
Commentary: Robin Duff
Cam. Jonah Jones and James E. Rogers
35mm
B/W
Sound
1,110ft
12 minutes

MODERN POST OFFICE METHODS (1937)
The use of mechanical aids in the Post Office, including the Post Office underground railway and its driverless trains.
Prod. co. GPO Film Unit

MONY A PICKLE (1938)
A film advocating thrift by use of the Post Office Savings Bank.

A comedy on the theme of Scottish thrift with an introduction and five short episodes, the most ambitious of which shows a young couple conjuring up the 'wee hoose' of their dreams, where a gas cooker replaces the range and they have a kitchenette with lots of new fittings, including a brass sink with chromium taps, and they can wash the dishes in the kitchen and themselves in the bathroom and never have to wait their turn at one sink any more.

There are no technical credits on the film, which was made for the Scottish Post Office Savings Bank, but it is thought there may have been anything up to five directors (each writing his own episode) including Cavalcanti, Richard Massingham and Norman McLaren. Stewart McAllister is also known to have been involved.
Prod. Alberto Cavalcanti
B/W
Sound
948ft
10 minutes

NEGOMBO COAST (1934)
Everyday life in Ceylon; its people, their trades and their produce. With a special emphasis on their fishing industry.
Dir. Basil Wright
B/W
Sound
817ft
9 minutes

NEW OPERATOR, THE (1934)
Recruitment film for the Post Office, showing the importance of the telephone operator.
Dir. Stuart Legg,
Prod. John Grierson
B/W
Silent
759ft
8 minutes

NEWS FOR THE NAVY (1938)
The GPO mail sorting system illustrated by the progress of a package destined for one of HM ships.

Evelyn sends a newspaper to her fiancé Bert Higgins AB, who has gone to sea on HMS *Incredible*. On her mother's advice she risks a penny-halfpenny stamp and addresses the package to the ship c/o the GPO London. We follow the package in the care of the Post Office from letter-box to Mount Pleasant and along the GPO's own underground electric railway to the Foreign Section a mile away. It reaches Bert's ship in Bermuda, where he seems more than happy to pay the extra penny-halfpenny due.

This is one of the first films that Norman McLaren directed at the GPO before he specialised in animation.
Prod. GPO Film Unit, with the cooperation of the Admiralty and the London Postal Region.
Dir. Norman McLaren
Cam. H. Fowle and F. Gamage
Sound: G. Diamond
Players: Evelyn Corbett and J. F. Hoggard
B/W
Sound
953ft
10 minutes

NIGHT MAIL (1936)
The night journey of the Postal Special from London to Glasgow.

The most celebrated documentary of them all, *Night Mail* hardly needs an introduction. Showing the Postal Special's nightly run from London to Scotland, it has all the qualities that British documentary stands for, from its realism through its perfect structure to the inspirational character of its appeal. The first part of the film shows the train as it appears to those who change the signals for it and stand by as it rushes past, giving and receiving mail. After the halt at Crewe station, we join the postal workers inside the

train, and in the third and final section we pull out of the night towards the moment that all Scotland awaits. They are still asleep there, 'but shall wake soon and long for letters'. Grierson's voice tells us, 'and none will hear the post-man's knock without a quickening of the heart, for who can bear to feel himself forgotten'.
Prod. John Grierson
Dir. Harry Watt and Basil Wright
Sound dir. Cavalcanti
Verse: W. H. Auden
Spoken by Stuart Legg and John Grierson
Music: Benjamin Britten
Cam. H. Fowle and Jonah Jones
Ed. R. Q. McNaughton
Sound: E. A. Pawley and C. Sullivan
With workers of the Travelling Post Office and the LMS railway.
B/W
Sound
24 minutes

NINE FOR SIX (1939)
Dramatised ad for the Post Office telegram service.

The Meadowhead School football team lose their only ball immediately before their match with the Council School, Bromford. They get the Bromford team to bring a ball with them by sending a nine-word telegram for sixpence, which reaches its

destination within twenty minutes.

There are no credits on this film, which was probably edited by Stewart McAllister. The discovery at McAllister's family home in Wishaw of a sequence cut in 16mm (originally was 35mm) suggests he may have been preparing a version for distribution to schools.
Silent with titles
7 minutes

N OR NW (1937)
The importance of using the correct postal district address.

Len Lye's first non-abstract film, this is a dramatic piece of some sophistication, with a partic-ularly choice selection of background music. This story concerns a girl who is on the point of breaking off her engagement when the wrongly addressed letter of apology from her fiancé finally arrives.
Supervision: Alberto Cavalcanti
Dir. Len Lye
Sound: Jack Ellitt
Cam. Jonah Jones
Players: Evelyn Corbett and Dwight Godwin
7.25 minutes

NORTH OF THE BORDER (1937)
Dir. Maurice Harvey
Prod. Alberto Cavalcanti
Prod. co. GPO Film Unit

NORTH SEA (1938)
Reconstruction of event in 1937 when an Aberdeen trawler got into distress, and the role of the Wick Radio service in saving it.

The film dramatically reconstructs an actual incident in which the Aberdeen deep-sea fishing trawler *John Gillman* was assisted by Wick Radio station when it got into difficulties in a storm in the North Sea.

Harry Watt cast the entire crew from the unemployed at the local labour exchange, with the exception of skipper Mattie Mair and Bill Blewitt, the postmaster from Mousehole, Cornwall, who already had acting experience in Watt's *The Saving of Bill Blewitt* and had also been a fisherman all his life. The exteriors were shot off the coast of Aberdeen in winter. 'We wanted it stormy of course, so when all other fishing boats were running for harbour we would plough out,' Watt recalls. 'They were so beautifully built, those trawlers, that they couldn't take sea over the bows. We put many gallons of water in the bows to make her put her head into the water.' The interiors on the trawler were filmed at the GPO Film Unit's Blackheath studio on a set like a wooden saucer that could be rocked and moved about and was so advanced for its time that it fooled a Hollywood producer who saw the film.
Prod. Alberto Cavalcanti
Dir. Harry Watt
Ed. R. Q. McNaughton
Music: E. Meyer
Design: Edward Carrick
Sets: Jack Bryson
Asst dir. Brian Pickersgill
Cam. H. Fowle and Jonah Jones
Sound: G. Diamond
With the trawlermen and townspeople of Aberdeen and Post Office radio operators
B/W
Sound
32 minutes

OH WHISKERS (1939)
Live action and animated toys illustrate the importance of cleanliness and eating good food.
Prod. co. GPO Film Unit
Animator: Brian Pickersgill
Sponsor: Ministry of Health

ON THE FISHING BANKS OF SKYE (1938)
Experimental film linking great line fishing off the north-west coast of Scotland to a free commentary by John Grierson.
Prod. co. GPO Film Unit

PENNY JOURNEY (1938)
The story of a postcard from Manchester to Graffam, Sussex.
Dir. Humphrey Jennings
Prod. co. GPO Film Unit

PETT AND POTT (1934)
Subtitle: A Fairy Story of the Suburbs
Promotes the use of the telephone, using the story of two neighbouring families, the Petts (conventional and happy) and Potts (unconventional and quarrelsome).
Prod. co. GPO Film Unit
Dir. Alberto Cavalcanti
B/W
Sound
2,637ft
29 minutes

PINES AND POLES (c. 1935)
The use of pine logs in the production of telephone poles. Possibly intended to be shown with *Wires Go Underground*.
Prod. co. GPO Film Unit

POSTAL SPECIAL (1939)
Shortened classroom version of *Night Mail*.
Dir. Basil Wright
Prod. co. GPO Film Unit

POST HASTE (1934)
The history of the Post Office illustrated by documents and quotations.
Dir. Humphrey Jennings
Prod. co. GPO Film Unit

POSTMASTER GENERAL ON A POST OFFICE PROBLEM (1936)
Appeal from Post Master General to the public to stagger their mail throughout the day.
Prod. co. GPO Film Unit

RADIO INTERFERENCE
(1936)
A dramatised explanation of
how the Post Office traces
sources of radio interference.
Prod. co. GPO Film Unit
Dir. Harry Watt

RAINBOW DANCE (1936)
Experimental colour short
promoting the Post Office.

A wholly captivating
animation film in brilliant
colour involving an actual
dancer who leaps into action
at the sight of the rainbow
that comes out after rain.
The message is 'The Post
Office Savings Bank puts a
pot of gold at the end of the
rainbow for you.'
Prod. Basil Wright
Dir. Len Lye
Dance: Rupert Doone
Synchronisation: Jack Ellitt
Cam. Frank Jones
Gasparcolor
4 minutes

ROADWAYS (1937)
The development of roads
and road traffic since 1918
and its effects on industry.

The film traces the
history of transport with
particular emphasis on the
heavy growth of road traffic
from 1918 until 'the new
world' of the 1930s, when
jokes about lady drivers were
nonetheless still *de rigueur*.
There are some dramatised
scenes, notably of long-
distance lorry drivers. The
message is that, although
the GPO is training it's

drivers 'to a new road sense
and a new responsibility',
the troubles of the roads
have not been solved yet and
anxiety is echoed by E. H.
Meyer's disturbing score.
Prod. Cavalcanti
Dir. William Coldstream and
Stuart Legg
Asst dir. Ralph Elton
Ed. R. Stocks
Music: E. H. Meyer
Cam. Jonah Jones and H. E.
Fowle
Sound: George Diamond
14.5 minutes

ROAD TRANSPORT
(c. 1938)
The rapid development of
road transport and problems
of congestion. Silent film
made up using elements of
Roadways (1937).
Prod. co. GPO Film Unit
B/W
Silent
293ft (16mm)
8 minutes

RT HON SIR HOWARD
KINGSLEY WOOD, MP:
POSTMASTER GENERAL
(1935)
The services of the GPO
introduced by the Post
Master General.
Prod. co. GPO Film Unit

ST JAMES'S PARK (1934)
Documentary on facilities of
St James' Park, London.

Possibly edited from
material shot by Edgar
Anstey in 1932 before
embarking on HMS

Challenger to shoot
Uncharted Waters.
Dir. Marion Grierson

SAVING OF BILL BLEWITT,
THE (1936)
Cornish fishermen are able
to save up for a new boat.
Promotional film for Post
Office National Savings
bank.

This fictional film made
in the documentary style,
about two fishermen whose
boat is wrecked but who
manage to save up enough to
buy another, was a break-
through for its time.

Harry Watt described to
Elizabeth Sussex how he was
told to make a film about
saving, which was anathema
to him, and, being mad
about fishing, set off to find
an angle in some fishing
village. When he eventually
arrived in Mousehole,
Cornwall, it was pouring
with rain: 'I go into the pub,
and there's one man in the
pub at the bar. So I say,
"Have a drink" and he has a
drink. He asks me to have a
drink, and we're drinking
double rums. By lunchtime
I'm stewed, and he's stewed.
We're absolutely paralytic. I
stand up and say, "Well I
must find the postmaster."
He says. "I am the postmaster." And this was Bill
Blewitt. He became quite a
well-known character actor
in British films.'
Prod. Alberto Cavalcanti
Dir. Harry Watt

Asst. Pat Jackson
Cam. Jonah Jones and
S. Onions
Music: B. Britten
With villagers of Mousehole,
Cornwall
24.5 minutes

SAVINGS BANK, THE
(1934)
The operation of the Post
Office Savings Bank.
Dir. Stuart Legg
B/W
Sound
549ft
6 minutes

SIMPLE MAGNETISM AND
ELECTRICITY (1936)
The principles of magnetism
and electricity as applied to
the transmission of speech
by telephone.
Dir. Ralph Bond
Prod. co. GPO Film Unit
B/W
Sound
1,267ft
14 minutes

SIX PENNY TELEGRAM
(1935)
Cheerful animated advert
with the chorus 'Send a
Wire'; promoting the
telegram service – nine
words for sixpence.
Music by Benjamin Britten
Thought to be a lost film:
newly discovered (2007).

SIX THIRTY COLLECTION
(1934)
The work of the Western
District Sorting Office in
London.
Dir. Harry Watt and Edgar
Anstey

THE SONG OF CEYLON
(1934)
The life and people of
Ceylon.
Prod. co. GPO Film Unit
Dir. Basil Wright
Sponsor: Empire Tea
Marketing Bureau, Ceylon
Tea Propaganda Board
B/W
Sound
3,555ft
40 minutes

SPARE TIME (1939)
Showing how workers in
three industries (steel,
cotton and coal) spend their
spare time, this film is
famous as the first intima-
tion of Humphrey
Jennings's unique style.
Jennings had been involved
in Mass Observation, a
precursor to the social
sciences of today, and his
approach to working people
differed from that of earlier
British documentaries in
stressing their individuality
instead of presenting them
as symbols of the dignity of
labour. Jennings was also a
painter, and his interest in
surrealism is often evident
in the images he chooses. In
addition, his expressive use
of music as an integrating

device in this film antici-
pates the complex style of
his poet documentaries of
the war.
Prod. Alberto Cavalcanti
Dir. Humphrey Jennings
Asst dir. D. V. Knight
Cam. H. Fowle
Commentary: Laurie Lee
Sound: Y. Scarlett
With the Steel, Peech and
Tozer Phoenix Works Band;
the Manchester Victorian
Carnival Band; the Handel
Male Voice Choir; and the
people in Sheffield,
Manchester, Bolton and
Pontypridd.
B/W
Sound
14 minutes

SPEAKING FROM AMERICA
(1938)
Explanation of the radio
telephone link between the
UK and the USA
Dir. Humphrey Jennings

SPRING OFFENSIVE (1940)
aka *Unrecorded Victory, An*
(1940)
The reclamation of a derelict
farm in East Anglia.
Dir. Humphrey Jennings
Prod. co. GPO Film Unit
Sponsor: MoI

SQUADRON 992 (1940)
The training of recruits in the
barrage balloon unit and the
transfer of the unit northwards after the first German
raid on the Forth Bridge.

In response to a request
for a film that showed the

importance of the balloon barrage, Harry Watt made this compelling drama-documentary about the training of a balloon squadron and its first assignment to the Forth Bridge, which had just been unsuccessfully raided. For his reconstruction of the raid itself, Watt got the Air Force to put German markings on their planes, which caused considerable consternation. Watt also claims he was 'arrested twice as a spy, because film-making was absolutely unknown and anybody with a camera was a spy'.

Cavalcanti thought this film, along with *The First Days*, would be considered very important later. Such documentary records of history as it unfolded would ultimately matter more than the experimental work in his opinion.

Prod. Alberto Cavalcanti
Dir. Harry Watt
Asst dir. Julian Spiro
Cam. Jonah Jones
Ed. R. Q. McNaughton
Music: Walter Leigh
Conducted by Muir Mathieson
Sound: Ken Cameron
Commentary written by W. D. H. McCulloch and spoken by Lionel Gamlin
Sponsored by the MoI
26 minutes

SS *IONION* (1939)
Military and cargo vessels in the Mediterranean.

Dir. Humphrey Jennings
Prod. co. GPO Film Unit

STORY OF AN AIR COMMUNIQUÉ, THE (1940)
How figures of destroyed enemy aircraft are compiled and released to the press.

Made for the Ministry of Information to show how accurately the figures for destroyed enemy aircraft were compiled and checked, this film has no technical credits apart from that of the GPO Film Unit itself. Concentrating on a single communiqué (the one for 15 September 1940) and looking at the individuals concerned with it (from fighter pilots to intelligence officers through fighter command to the world's newspapermen assembled at the Ministry of Information), the film is a lesson in how to make a human story out of bald statistics.

Prod. GPO Film Unit
Dir. Ralph Elton
Sponsor: MoI
With officers and men of the Royal Air Force
B/W
Sound
6.5 minutes

STORY OF COTTON, THE (1940)
The spinning and weaving of cotton in a cotton mill.
Prod. co. GPO Film Unit

STORY OF THE WHEEL (1935)
The development of transport illustrated by models and diagrams from the British Museum, the London Museum and the Science Museum.

Prod. co. GPO Film Unit
Dir. Humphrey Jennings

TELEPHONE (1934)
Abstract advert for the telephone. A film poster.

TELEPHONE WORKERS (1933)
Shows how the telephone system is extended to new towns and suburbs.

London is growing outwards and the GPO is working to bring telephones to new areas and helping to bring communities out of isolation.

Prod. John Grierson
Dir. Stuart Legg
Cam. Gibbs
B/W
Sound
1,630ft
18 minutes

TOCHER, THE (1938)
Subtitle: A Film Ballet by Lotte Reiniger
Silhouette animation of a fairy tale.

A delicate silhouette film by the celebrated innovator of the technique. The fairy tale shows how Angus, with the help of the Wee Folk, wins his true love in the nick of time by presenting to her

father, in a casket, a Post
Office Savings Bank book.
A film ballet by Lotte
Reiniger
Rossini themes arranged by
Benjamin Britten
5 minutes

TRADE TATTOO (1937)
Abstract experimental film –
urging the public to post
early in the day.

It can only be because he
thought this such a brilliant
example of Len Lye's art as
animator that Grierson,
most unusually, put his own
name on the opening credits.
The theme is that to maintain the rhythm of workaday
Britain you must post early,
and those that know the
GPO Film Unit titles will
find added interest in identifying some of the workaday
images on which Lye has
imposed his gorgeous colour
and irresistible patterns.
Prod. John Grierson
Dir. Len Lye
Music ed. Jack Ellitt
Music by Lecuona Band
Technicolor
6 minutes

TRAVELLING POST OFFICE
(1936)
How the Post Office's night
mail train from London to
Aberdeen collects and
distributes mail en route.
Prod. co. GPO Film Unit

UNDER THE CITY (1934)
The technical problems
involved in diverting cables
round a new Tube escalator.
Prod. co. GPO Film Unit
Dir. Alexander Shaw
B/W
Sound
1,270ft
13 minutes

WAR AND ORDER (1940)
Police work during World
War II in Britain.
Dir. Charles Hasse
Prod. Harry Watt
Prod. co. GPO Film Unit
Sponsor: MoI

WAR LIBRARY ITEMS 1, 2, 3
(1939)
Three cinemagazine items:
Who are you? The work of
enumerators during the
national registration of
September 1939. Standing
by: Hospitals preparing to
receive any casualties that
may occur during air raids.
Where's the fire?
Prod. co. GPO Film Unit

WEATHER FORECAST
(1934)
Work of Meteorological
Office in preparation of the
weather forecast for farmers,
seamen, pilots, etc.
Prod. co. GPO Film Unit
Dir. Evelyn Spice

WELFARE OF THE
WORKERS (1940)
Designed to encourage
industrial workers with news
of what the Ministry of

Labour was doing to safe-
guard working conditions in
wartime.
Dir. Humphrey Jennings
Prod. co. GPO Film Unit
Sponsor: MoI

WE LIVE IN TWO WORLDS
(1937)
J. B. Priestley talks about the
worlds of nationalism and
internationalism as exemplified by Switzerland.
Dir. Alberto Cavalcanti
Prod. co. GPO Film Unit and
Pro Telephon-Zurich

WHAT'S ON TODAY (1938)
Preparations made by GPO
to help BBC with the outside
broadcast of a major sporting event.
Dir. Richard Q. McNaughton
Prod. co. GPO Film Unit

WIRES GO
UNDERGROUND, THE
(c. 1938)
The history and develop-
ment of inter-city under-
ground cable networks,
1899–1938.
Prod. co. GPO Film Unit

WORLD EXCHANGE (1936)
About the international telephone exchange in London,
focusing on the route taken
by a phone call from
Switzerland to Montreal.
Prod. co. GPO Film Unit

NOTES ON CONTRIBUTORS

Scott Anthony is a journalist and Leverhulme Fellow at Christ's College, Cambridge. He is the author of the BFI Film Classic *Nightmail* (2007) and *Public Relations and the Making of Modern Britain* (2011).

James G. Mansell is Lecturer in the Department of Culture, Film and Media at the University of Nottingham. He is the author of the forthcoming book *Sound and Selfhood in Early Twentieth-Century Britain*.

Timothy Boon is Chief Curator at the Science Museum; his exhibitions include Health Matters (1994) and Making the Modern World (2000). His first monograph, *Films of Fact: A History of Science in Documentary Films and Television* was published in 2008.

E. Anna Claydon is Lecturer in the Department of Media and Communication at the University of Leicester. Her key publications include *The Representation of Masculinity in British Films of the 1960s* (2005) and 'Masculinity and Deviance in '70s British Cinema', in the collection *Don't Look Now* (2010).

Charles Drazin lectures on the cinema at Queen Mary, University of London. His books include *The Finest Years: British Cinema of the 1940s* (1998), *Korda: Britain's Only Movie Mogul* (2002) and *In Search of the Third Man* (2000). He is also the editor of the journals of John Fowles.

Zoë Druick is Associate Professor in the School of Communication at Simon Fraser University, Canada. Her books include *Projecting Canada: Documentary Film and Government Policy at the National Film Board* (2007); *Programming Reality: Perspectives on English–Canadian Television* (2007); and *Allan King's* A Married Couple (2010). She is currently co-editing a collection on the international influence of John Grierson.

Leo Enticknap is Lecturer in Cinema in the Institute for Communications Studies, University of Leeds. He is the author of *Moving Image Technology: From Zoetrope to Digital* (2005).

Barbara Evans is Associate Professor in the Department of Film at York University in Toronto, Canada. A former department chair and graduate programme director, she specialises in documentary history and production.

Steven Foxon is a moving-image preservation consultant specialising in British non-fiction film. Originally with the British Film Institute, he has played a major role in the preservation of several prestigious British documentary collections including the Arts Council England Collection, British Transport Films, Crown and the GPO Film Unit.

Sir Christopher Frayling is an historian, critic and award-winning broadcaster. He was Rector of the Royal College of Art 1996–2009 and Chair of Arts Council England 2005–9.

David Hay is Head of BT Heritage and Corporate Memory. He has worked at BT for the past twenty-three years, developing the company's records collections into one of the UK's leading corporate archives (www.bt.com/archives). David is also responsible for Connected Earth, BT's ground-breaking heritage project and partnership with leading UK museums (www.connected-earth.com).

Richard Haynes is Senior Lecturer in the School of Arts and Humanities, University of Stirling and Director of the Stirling Media Research Institute. He is author of several books on media sport, including *Power Play: Sport, the Media and Popular Culture* with Raymond Boyle. His next book, *Played in Black and White: The First 30 Years of BBC Television Sport*, will be published in 2012.

Jon Hoare is a film historian and collector who is researching the life and work of Basil Wright.

Kevin Jackson's most recent publications include *Moose* (2008), *Bite* (2009) and *The Worlds of John Ruskin* (2009). He is completing a study of the year 1922.

David Matless is Professor of Cultural Geography at the University of Nottingham. He is the author of *Landscape and Englishness* (1998), and editor of *Geographies of British Modernity* (2003) and *The Place of Music* (1998). He is currently working on a book entitled *In the Nature of Landscape: Cultural Geography on the Norfolk Broads*.

Roy Mayall is a pseudonym for a postal worker who works in a delivery office somewhere in the south-east of England. He is the author of *Dear Granny Smith: A Letter from Your Postman* (2009) and blogs at roymayall.wordpress.com

Michael McCluskey is a PhD student in the Department of English, University College London. His thesis, 'Country, City, Cinema: Humphrey Jennings and the Landscapes of Modern Britain', considers Jennings's cinematic construction of cities, suburbs and countrysides.

Paul Rennie is Head of Context in Graphic Design at Central Saint Martins College of Art and Design, part of the University of the Arts, London. He is the author of *Design – GPO Posters*, published by the Antique Collectors' Club (2010).

Jeffrey Richards is Professor of Cultural History at Lancaster University. His books include *The Age of the Dream Palace* (1984), *Hollywood's Ancient Worlds* (2008) and *Britain Can Take It* (1994).

Patrick Russell is Senior Curator (Non-Fiction), BFI National Archive. He is author of *100 British Documentaries* (2007) and co-editor of *The Lost World of Mitchell and Kenyon* (2004) and *Shadows of Progress: Documentary Film in Post-War Britain* (2010).

Amy Sargeant is Reader in Film at the University of Warwick. She has written extensively on British silent and sound cinema, being author of *British Cinema: A Critical History* (2005) and co-editor, with Claire Monk, of *British Historical Cinema: History, Heritage and the Costume Film* (2002).

Martin Stollery is currently an associate lecturer with the Open University. His first book, *Alternative Empires* (2000), deals with the representation of empire in British documentary films of the 1930s, and his more recent work includes co-authoring *British Film Editors* (2004).

Yasuko Suga is Associate Professor of Design History at Tsuda College, Japan. Her published works in English include the co-edited volume *The Diary of Charles Holme's 1889 Visit to Japan and North America with Mrs Lasenby Liberty's Photographic Record* (2008) and articles on aspects of British design in *Design Issues*, *Journal of Design History* and the *Journal of William Morris Studies*.

Dai Vaughan is a documentary film editor and author of several books on documentary film, including *Portrait of an Invisible Man: The Working Life of Stewart McAllister, Film Editor* (1983) and *For Documentary: Twelve Essays* (1999).

Wendy Webster is Professor Emeritus of Contemporary British History at the University of Central Lancashire. She has published widely on questions of migration, ethnicity, gender, imperialism and national identity, including *Imagining Home: Gender, Race and National Identity* (1998), *Englishness and Empire, 1939–1965* (2005) and (with Louise Ryan) *Gendering Migration: Masculinity, Femininity and Ethnicity in Post-war Britain* (2008).

INDEX

Notes
Page numbers in **bold** denote extended/detailed treatment; those in *italic* refer to illustrations or extensively illustrated sections
In the Filmography, items of background information are indexed but not standard credits.
n = endnote. *t* = table/diagram.

List of Illustrations

Whilst considerable effort has been made to correctly identify the copyright holders, this has not been possible in all cases. We apologise for any apparent negligence and any omissions or corrections brought to our attention will be remedied in any future editions.

BBC – The Voice of Britain, GPO Film Unit; *We Live in Two Worlds*, GPO Film Unit; *N or NW*, GPO Film Unit; *Pett and Pott: A Fairy Story of the Suburbs*, GPO Film Unit; *6.30 Collection*, GPO Film Unit; *Night Mail*, GPO Film Unit; *The Saving of Bill Blewitt*, GPO Film Unit; *North Sea*, GPO Film Unit; *The First Days*, GPO Film Unit; *Spare Time*, GPO Film Unit; *Penny Journey*, GPO Film Unit; *Spring Offensive*, GPO Film Unit; *London Can Take It!*, GPO Film Unit; *Listen to Britain*, Crown Film Unit; *Fires Were Started*, Crown Film Unit; *A Diary for Timothy*, Crown Film Unit; *Words for Battle*, Crown Film Unit; *Family Portrait*, Wessex Film Productions; *The Men of the Lightship*, Crown Film Unit; *Weather Forecast*, GPO Film Unit; *Rainbow Dance*, GPO Film Unit; *Trade Tattoo*, GPO Film Unit; *Cable Ship*, GPO Film Unit/New Era Films; *Coal Face*, EMPO/GPO Film Unit; *The City*, GPO Film Unit; *The H.P.O.*, GPO Film Unit; *The Song of Ceylon*, GPO Film Unit/Denning Films/Cinema Contact Ltd; *The Silent Village*, Crown Film Unit; *World Without End*, International Realist; *Picture to Post*, Rayant Pictures; *Counterpoint*, Basic Films/Central Office of Information.

Images © Royal Mail Group Ltd 2011. Courtesy of The British Postal Museum & Archive

Advert in The Post Office Magazine
Night Mail poster [POST 109/377]
'Visit the Post Office Film Display' poster (Pat Keeley) [POST 118/506]
'Outposts of Britain: A Postman in the Pool of London' [POST 110/4143]
'Visit the Post Office Film Display' poster (Tom Eckersley & Eric Lombers) [POST 118/972]
Post Office Exhibition leaflet (G. R. Morris) [POST 110/6036]
'Address Your Letters Plainly' poster [POST 110/1179]
'His Needs Come First' poster [POST 100/3197]
'Think Ahead Write Instead, Telegraph and Telephone' poster [POST 109/191]
'My Day's Work at the Film Unit'
Grierson resignation letter
'Outposts of Britain: A Postman in Northern Ireland' [POST 110/3183]
'Outposts of Britain: Posting Box at Lands End' [POST 110/4144]
'Outposts of Britain: A Postman in Northern Scotland' [POST 110/2495]
'Postman of the Flood'
'Telegrams at the Derby'
'GPO Films'
'Proudest Men in Blackpool' cartoon
'Odd Jobs of the Post Office'
The Post Office Magazine article
'Rocket Mails'
'London's Further Education Scheme'
'Building a New World'
'South of England'
'Health and Diet'

'You Are Wanted on the Telephone ...' [TCE 361/ARC 1463]
'Keep in Touch – Telephone' [TCE 361/ARC 1464]
'Radio Telephony' (Norman Howard) [TCE 361/ARC 1465]
'The Whole World at Hand' [TCE 361/ARC 4]
'Post Office Telegraphs' [TCB 394/T 424G (1929)]
'Picture Telegraphy' [TCB 392/PG 213 (1939)]
'Always at your Service' poster (Austin Cooper) [TCB 319/PRD 77]
Telephone advertising leaflet [TCB 392/PG 2 (1939)]
'Night Telegraph Letters' [TCB 392/PG 2 (1939)]
'Make Life Easier' poster (Pat Keeley) [TCE 361/ARC 1467]
Post Office telephone publicity display [TCB 417/E 8270]
Post Office sales office, 167 Euston Road [TCB 417/E 8747]
'Galloping Gus' [TCE 361/ARC 1457]
'Your Robot' [TCE 361/ARC 1468]
Engineers hauling cable [TCB 473/P 1164]
'Underground Cable' poster (John Farleigh) [Post 109/385]
'10 Years of Radio Telephony' [TCB 318/PH 657]
'Extension Telephones' [TCB 318/PH 213]
'Automatic Exchange' [TCB 318/PH 637]
'Telephone Rates' [TCB 318/PH 9]
Post Office Exhibition, The Strand [TCB 417/E 8706]
'Ocean Cable' poster (Clifford & Rosemary Ellis) [TCB 319/PRD 114]
'You are cordially invited ...' [TCB 475/ZB 32]
Poster exhibition, Union House [TCB 417/E 10682]
The Coming of the Dial slide [TCB 439/48]
'Visit the Post Office Film Display' poster (Tom Eckersley & Eric Lombers) [TCB 473/P 2417]
'Graham Bell's Telephone 1876' [TCB 319/PRD 149]
'Post Office Exhibition', Charing Cross [TCB 325/EHA 136]
'The British Post Office & Empire Communications' [TCB 325/EHA 23)]
'The Post Office 1934' lecture slide [TCB 475/ZB 41]
'The Post Office Magazine' lecture slide [TCB 475/ZB 38]
Glasgow Radio Exhibition [TCB 417/E 9111]
'Phone Tim for the Right Time' [TCE 361/ARC 1458]
'The Correct Time by the Speaking Clock' [TCB 318/PH 202]
London L–Z Telephone Directory, May 1937 [TCB 655]
'20,011 Telephonists' poster (Duncan Grant) [TCB 319/PRD 225]
'Tell the glad news by telegraph!' [TCB 319/PRD 125]
'Send a greetings telegram' [TCB 319/PRD 137]
Telegraph messenger boys [TCB 263/6]
'Police Communications by G.P.O.' [TCB 361/ARC 1469]
Jubilee K6 Telephone kiosk publicity poster (Andrew Johnson) [TCB 319/PRD 135]
'How to Dial' [TCB 394/CO 152]